Love and Eugenics in the Late Nineteenth Century

Love and Eugenics in the Late Nineteenth Century

Rational Reproduction and the New Woman

ANGELIQUE RICHARDSON

OXFORD
UNIVERSITY PRESS

OXFORD
UNIVERSITY PRESS
Great Clarendon Street, Oxford OX2 6DP

Oxford University Press is a department of the University of Oxford.
It furthers the University's objective of excellence in research, scholarship,
and education by publishing worldwide in

Oxford New York

Auckland Bangkok Buenos Aires Cape Town Chennai
Dar es Salaam Delhi Hong Kong Istanbul Karachi Kolkata
Kuala Lumpur Madrid Melbourne Mexico City Mumbai Nairobi
São Paulo Shanghai Taipei Tokyo Toronto

Oxford is a registered trade mark of Oxford University Press
in the UK and in certain other countries

Published in the United States
by Oxford University Press Inc., New York

First published 2003

British Library Cataloguing in Publication Data
Data available

Library of Congress Cataloging in Publication Data
Data available

ISBN 0–19–818700–9

1 3 5 7 9 10 8 6 4 2

Typeset in Minion by
Cambrian Typesetters, Frimley, Surrey
Printed in Great Britain
on acid-free paper by
T.J. International Ltd,
Padstow, Cornwall

For my friends

with love

Acknowledgements

The warm generosity of friends and colleagues has been vital in the thinking about and writing of *Love and Eugenics in the Late Nineteenth Century*. I would also like to thank my extending family, in Britain and Sri Lanka. My greatest thanks are to Dorothy Porter, who saw the project through from its earliest stages, and whose generosity and scholarship are an inspiration. I am also most grateful to Peter Faulkner, Regenia Gagnier, Colin MacCabe, Rupert Mann, Laura Marcus, Richard Seaford, and Sally Shuttleworth for reading and commenting on earlier manuscript drafts. My especial thanks are to the late Chris Brooks, writer, unexampled scholar, and Professor of Victorian Culture at Exeter. Chris shared with us his vision of freedom and equality, seeing 'the unique gentleness with which the majority of people respond to each other and to the world in general'.

I would like to thank David Amigoni, Gillian Beer, David Bradshaw, Karen Edwards, David Feldman, Beryl Gray, Lee Grieveson, Ann Heilmann, Sanna Hurnaus, Robert Lawson-Peebles, Sally Ledger, George Levine, Teresa Mangum, Phillip Mallett, Peter New, Claire Noble, John Plunkett, Diane Purkiss, Andrew Richardson, Catherine Robson, Marion Shaw, Tony Simoes da Silva, Michael Slater, Paul Spencer, David Trotter, Chris Willis, Charmaine Wyre, and, at Oxford University Press, Sophie Goldsworthy and Frances Whistler. I would like to express my thanks to the late Roy Porter. I am also grateful to my postgraduate and undergraduate students at Exeter for stimulating and challenging discussions over the last five years.

I am grateful to many communities and institutions, including the British Association of Victorian Studies; the faculty members of the Dickens Project at the University of California at Santa Cruz; the Exeter Genomics Research Institute; the Science in the Nineteenth-Century Press Project (Leeds, Sheffield, and MIT); the English and History Departments at Birkbeck College, London; the School of English and the School of History, Politics, and Social Sciences at the University of Exeter; the Thomas Hardy Society, and the Wellcome Trust Centre for the History of Medicine, University College London.

Some of my research on late nineteenth-century eugenics has appeared in *Critical Quarterly*, the *Journal of Victorian Culture*, the *Thomas Hardy Journal*, *Victorian Studies*, and *Women: A Cultural Review*. I am grateful to these publications for providing me with critical forums and feedback. I am also most grateful for the opportunities I have had to present my research at conferences and seminars. I would like to thank the Centre for Medical History, University of Exeter; the Council for College and University English; the departments of English at the Universities of California at Santa Cruz, Hull, Leeds, Loughborough, Oxford, Sheffield, Southampton, the West of England, Manchester Metropolitan University, and University College, Worcester; the History and Philosophy of Science Department at the University of Cambridge; the Institute for English Studies, London; Leeds Centre for Victorian Studies, Trinity and All Saints College; and the Wellcome Trust Centre for the History of Medicine, University College London.

I gratefully acknowledge the Arts and Humanities Research Board and the School of English and the Research Committee of the University of Exeter for providing me with a year's research leave in 2000–1, during which time I was able to bring the project to completion. I would also like to thank the British Academy for funding my attendance of overseas conferences in 1999 and 2001. For financial support during the early stages of my research, I am grateful to the British Academy; to Birkbeck College, London; and to the British Federation of Women Graduates.

I am grateful to the librarians and archivists of Bath Central Library, the Bodleian Library, the British Library and Collindale Newspaper Library, the Fawcett Library, London Library, the National Library of Scotland, New York Public Library, the Manuscripts Room, University College London, the Library of Congress, Washington, and the Wellcome Library for the History and Understanding of Medicine, for their time and assistance. I would also like to thank Dorchester County Museum, for permission to quote from the letters of Thomas Hardy; University College London for permission to quote from the Galton archive; and the Trustees of the National Library of Scotland for permission to quote from the correspondence of Sarah Grand. For permission to reproduce the illustrations, I am grateful to the *Daily Mirror*, *Punch*, the British Library, the Centre for the Study of Cartoons and Caricature at the University of Kent at Canterbury, Exeter University Library, the John Bennett Shaw Collection at the University of Notre Dame, and the Museum of London.

Contents

List of Illustrations

How could you bear it yourself? What would you feel if you were poor against the system under which you live? I have always been uneasy when I had to ask myself that question, and of late years I have had to ask it so often, that I have seldom had it out of my mind: and the answer to it has more and more made me ashamed of my own position, and more and more made me feel that if I had not been born rich or well-to-do I should have found my position *un*endurable, and should have been a mere rebel against what would have seemed to me a system of robbery and injustice. Nothing can argue me out of this feeling . . . the contrasts of rich and poor are unendurable and ought not to be endured by either rich or poor.

William Morris, *Letters* (1 July 1883)

Man has already furthered his evolution very considerably, half consciously and for his own personal advantage, but he has not yet risen to the conviction that it is his religious duty to do so deliberately and systematically.

Francis Galton, *Inquiries into Human Faculty and its Development* (1883)

The rise of women—who form the majority of the race in most civilized countries—to supreme power in the near future, is certain . . . I find it an unfailing source of hope. One cannot help feeling that along the purely masculine line no striking social advance is likely to be made. Men are idealists, in search of wealth usually, sometimes of artistic visions; they have little capacity for social organization . . . When it is a question of stamping out a lower race—then is our time! It has to be done . . . on the whole we stamp them out as mercifully as may be, supplying our victims liberally with missionaries and blankets.

Havelock Ellis, *The New Spirit* (1890)

Each child born is a new citizen to assist the social common growth . . . Once maternity is considered essentially as citizen-making in the first place, and not as the accidental result of the private relation to an individual, then the similarity between the woman's movement and the labour movement will be again complete . . . the efficient regulation of the labour of married women during the child-bearing years . . . will come none too soon to stop the degeneration of physique which is going on in certain classes of the labouring population . . . Sexual rather than natural selection must inevitably be the means by which woman will seek to make her maternal activity of the highest social value. To the most careful sexual selection the woman advocates of woman's emancipation are incessantly urging their sisters. These are indeed the first signs that woman is beginning to realise that maternity is a social activity, which not only demands serious thought on her part but at the same time gives her special claims on the community at large. The unlimited reproduction of bad stock is not only an injury to the community at large; it is a peculiar injury to woman, in that it lessens the value of maternity, and throws her into competition with man without any claim to special protection or to special provision during the years of child-bearing. These are the new features of the woman's problem of the near future—the steps which are converting it from the cry of the unmarried for equality of opportunity to the cry of the married for the reconciliation of maternity with the power of self-determination.

Karl Pearson, 'Woman and Labour' (1894)

Nature decrees the survival of the fittest; you exercise your skill to preserve the unfittest, and stop there—at the beginning of your responsibilities, as it seems to me. Let the unfit who are with us live, and save them from suffering where you can, by all means; but take pains to prevent the appearance of any more of them. By the reproduction of the unfit, the strength, the beauty, the morality of the race is undermined, and with them its best chances of happiness.

Sarah Grand, *The Beth Book* (1897)

It belongs to our century, and to us, for the first time in human history to apply the principles of science and humanity to social problems . . . for the first time now we are trying deliberately to frame our collective ideals of social life on science and love . . . With the power to control the birth-rate, comes the ideal of quality rather than quantity.

Dora F. Kerr, 'The Conversion of Mrs Grundy', *The Adult* (May 1898)

They picked up stray bits of bread the size of peas, apple cores so black and dirty one would not take them to be apple cores, and these things these two men took into their mouths, and chewed them, and swallowed them; and this, between six and seven o'clock in the evening of August 20, year of our Lord 1902, in the heart of the greatest, wealthiest, and most powerful empire the world has ever seen.

Jack London, *People of the Abyss* (1903)

A progressive system of general reform has to embrace and combine rational breeding, rational training and a rational order of life . . . 'Indiscriminate survival' gives way before that 'rational selection and birth of the fit' which is a fundamental condition of social well-being—the master-spring to a rapid evolution of general happiness.

Jane Hume Clapperton, *Vision of the Future, Based on The Application of Ethical Principles* (1904)

It will be a higher and healthier love than ours now-a-days, equally distant from that of Don Juan and that of Werther. De-sentimentalization is out of the question. Once there was marriage by rape; Love was almost unknown. Marriage by purchase followed and conjugal affection was rare. Marriage by contract we have yet, and Love is still a fickle bird. One day marriage by selection, a Eugenic bond will come about. Then Love will be permanent. Then man may realize a threefold ideal: that physical beauty which the grand sculptors of Greece have shown us in their statues, that enthusiasm of the mind which the great scholars of the Renascence possessed, that spiritual love and hope which inspired the *Vita Nuova*. Man will unite within himself these partial excellences, these scattered units of that archetype—the Superman.

M.A. Mügge, 'Eugenics and the Superman: A Racial Science and A Racial Religion', *Eugenics Review* I (1909)

It is to the women of the country we must look in this great eugenic movement.

Mrs Alec Tweedie, 'Eugenics', *Eugenics Review*, 12 (1912)

It might still not be too late to rebuild the human house upon such an architectural plan that poverty might fly out of the window, with the reasonable prospect of love coming in at the door. In short [the capitalist] might have let the English poor, the mass of whom were not weak-minded, though more of them were growing weaker, a reasonable chance, in the form of more money, of achieving their eugenical resurrection themselves.

G. K. Chesterton, *Eugenics and Other Evils: An Argument Against the Scientifically Organized State* (1918)

It must be remembered that it is not only inanimate objects, but human beings also, which differ in regard to their capital values.

Leonard Darwin, *The Need for Eugenic Reform* (1926)

Prologue

The development of the idea of eugenics as rational reproduction in late Victorian Britain has been largely overlooked. For this, there are several reasons. One is the atrocities of Naziism, which have overshadowed early manifestations of eugenics and encouraged a perception of eugenics as a product and practice of the Third Reich. Another is the assumption that eugenics has primarily or exclusively to do with race. Eugenics was deeply inflected by different national concerns, so that while in Germany it centred on issues of mental health and in the United States it was a discourse on race, in Britain it was primarily a discourse on class. It was here part of the debates on class and poverty that intensified with the increasing unrest of the urban poor in the closing decades of the nineteenth century. A third factor is that the most virulent expression of eugenic ideas was not within legislative acts and public policy, but within popular and intellectual cultural discourses; early British eugenics was primarily a matter of rhetoric and representation.

Love and Eugenics in the Late Nineteenth Century: Rational Reproduction and the New Woman shows that the most sustained expressions of eugenic ideas were to be found in fiction and, in particular, in a body of late nineteenth-century feminist fiction which has for the most part only recently been rediscovered. Social purists such as Ellice Hopkins and New Woman writers such as Sarah Grand and George Egerton drew on Darwin's and Galton's ideas, arguing for the vital contribution of women in regenerating the British imperial race. Initially these groups of writers and activists were neglected as socially unimportant but, with the death of the Great Man theory of history, and the feminist expansion of the literary canon, their significance has been reassessed. However, the story of their role in the development of eugenic ideas remains obscured. This is partly due to the complicated nature of their relation to eugenics, engaged, as they were, with the fundamental questions of their time and committed to forms of social and political change. It is also due to the reluctance of feminist history and, in particular, feminist literary history, to accept the role played by women in the early history of eugenic thought. Acknowledging the intimate relations between early feminism and eugenics has proved uncomfortable, but is necessary to a fuller understanding of New Woman writers.

1 Introduction

> In his part of London it almost made his blood run cold to think of the many early marriages. Self-restraint was that which the Christian men and women of Bethnal Green must bring to bear upon their fellows.
>
> *East London Observer*[1]

> The streets were filled with a new and different race of people, short of stature, and of wretched or beer-sodden appearance.
>
> Jack London[2]

> The family is not only a domestic question, not only a social question . . . it is, finally, a racial question.
>
> Henry Havelock Ellis[3]

In 1882 'unemployed' became a noun,[4] Nietszche pronounced God dead, and British women were entitled to own their property after marriage.[5] Time-hallowed belief systems were in crisis, and traditional social, political, and gendered hierarchies were crumbling. With *The Origin of Species; or, The Preservation of Favoured Races in the Struggle for Life* (1859), and, twelve years later, *The Descent of Man, and Selection in Relation to Sex*, Darwin had dealt a body blow to anthropocentrism, calling into public question the idea of God, and consigning mid-Victorian confidence to the past: 'progress was no invariable rule'.[6] As Malthusian

[1] 'The Archbishop of Canterbury on the Evils of Bethnal Green', *East London Observer* (25 February 1888), quoted in William J. Fishman, *East End 1888* (1988; London: Hanbury, 2001), 37.

[2] *People of the Abyss* (1903; London: Pluto, 2001), 3.

[3] Henry Havelock Ellis, *More Essays of Love and Virtue* (London: Constable, 1931), 65.

[4] *OED.*

[5] Friedrich Nietzsche, *The Gay Science* [*Fröhliche Wissenschaft*], trans. by Josefine Nauckhoff (Cambridge: Cambridge University Press, 2001), 109. The 1870 Married Women's Property Act had enabled women to retain their earnings and inherit personal property and small amounts of money; all other possessions acquired before or during marriage became the property of their husbands. The 1882 Married Women's Property Act mandated that married women could keep all personal and real property acquired before and during marriage.

[6] Darwin, *The Descent of Man, and Selection in Relation to Sex*, 2 vols. (1871; Chichester: Princeton University Press, 1981), i. 177. The 1,250 print run was oversubscribed when the *Origin* went on sale to the trade on 22 November 1859 (Adrian Desmond and James Moore,

economies vied with the idea of a divine Creator, science was coming to be seen either as a system of ethics functioning as an alternative to religion, or as a new religion; a new way of regaining a sense of direction and design and of providing solutions to the pressing social questions of the day: the Woman Question; the question of the poor (were they really an eternal presence?); and the maintenance and expansion of empire in the wake of fierce international competition and an apparently degenerating British race. Enter eugenics and the New Woman.

In 1883 Francis Galton, Darwin's first cousin, coined the term eugenics. Taken from the Greek *eugenes*, eugenics means 'good in stock'.[7] Galton defined eugenics as

> the science of improving stock, which is by no means confined to questions of judicious mating, but which, especially in the case of man, takes cognisance of all influences that tend in however remote a degree to give to the more suitable races or strains of blood a better chance of prevailing speedily over the less suitable than they otherwise would have had. (*Inquiries into Human Faculty*, 25)

In 1908, in his autobiography, he defined it as 'the study of agencies under social control that may improve or impair the racial qualities of future generations, either physically or mentally'.[8] He recalled that the *Origin* had encouraged him to 'pursue many inquiries which had long interested me and which clustered round the central topic of Heredity and the possible Improvement of the Human Race,' declaring that it

> made a marked epoch in my own mental development, as it did in that of human thought generally . . . Its effect was to demolish a multitude of dogmatic barriers by a single stroke, and to arouse a spirit of rebellion against all ancient authorities

Darwin (Harmondsworth: Penguin, 1992), 477), and by December 1859 a further 3,000 had been printed. A second edition was called for within three weeks of the publication of the *Descent*, and by the end of March 1871 4,500 copies were in circulation (Desmond and Moore, *Darwin*, 579).

[7] Galton, *Inquiries into Human Faculty and its Development* (London: Macmillan, 1883), 24–5. Galton first outlined his ideas on racial improvement in 'Hereditary Talent and Character', *Macmillan's Magazine* 12 (1865), 157–66; 318–27, while preparing material for his book *Hereditary Genius: An Inquiry into its Laws and Consequences* (1869). On the writing of this paper, see Karl Pearson, *The Life, Letters, and Labours of Francis Galton*, 4 vols. (Cambridge: Cambridge University Press, 1914–30), ii. 77: 'in 1864—we suddenly find the whole doctrine of eugenics as the salvation of mankind developed half a century too early!' For Galton's discussion of the genesis of these ideas, see *Galton Papers*, 57: amended typescript of Galton's autobiography, 'Memories of My Life'. See *Galton Papers*, 120/5 for reviews of *Hereditary Genius* from newspapers, journals, and magazines.

[8] *Galton Papers*, 57: amended typescript of Galton's autobiography, 'Memories of My Life', 370.

whose positive and unauthenticated statements were contradicted by modern science.[9]

Darwin's evolutionary theory of descent through modification had laid the foundations for eugenics, replacing paradise with primordial slime. Man had not fallen from Grace, but risen from the swamps. And, as architect of his own destiny, he might rise still further. Embracing the idea of evolution, eugenists argued that through the judicious control of human reproduction, and the numerical increase of the middle class, paradise on earth might be gained, and Britain's supremacy in the world maintained. Born and bred among the competitive Victorian middle class, eugenics was a biologistic discourse on *class*: a class-based application of the evolutionary discourse which proliferated in the wake of Darwin. Aiming at 'racial improvement' by altering the balance of class in society, it was, Galton argued, 'practical Darwinism': 'I shall treat of man and see what the theory of heredity, of variations and the principle of natural selection mean when applied to Man.'[10] The idea that humans might breed selectively, that they might exercise conscious control over the biological quality of the race, was given precise formulation and a new, apparently scientific, authority.[11]

[9] *Memories of my Life* (London: Methuen, 1908), 298; see also MS, 339.

[10] Pearson, *The Life, Letters, and Labours of Francis Galton*, ii. 86.

[11] On the development of British eugenics in the nineteenth and twentieth centuries see Donald MacKenzie, *Statistics in Britain 1865–1930: The Social Construction of Scientific Knowledge* (Edinburgh: Edinburgh University Press, 1981). For studies on the development of eugenic thinking in Europe, see Gunnar Broberg and Nils Roll-Hansen (eds.), *Eugenics and the Welfare State: Sterilization in Denmark, Sweden, Norway and Finland* (East Lansing: Michigan State University, 1996); and, in America, see Diane B. Paul, *Controlling Heredity* (Atlantic Highlands: Humanities Press, 1995); Marouf Arif Hasian, *The Rhetoric of Eugenics in Anglo-American Thought* (Athens: University of Georgia Press, 1996); Edward J. Larson, *Sex, Race and Science: Eugenics in the Deep South* (Baltimore, Md.: Johns Hopkins University Press, 1995); see also Ian Robert Dowbiggin, *Keeping America Sane: Psychiatry and Eugenics in the United States and Canada*, 1880–1940 (Ithaca: Cornell University Press, 1997). On eugenics in Britain and America, see Daniel Kevles, *In the Name of Eugenics: Genetics and the Uses of Human Heredity* (1985; Cambridge, Mass.: Harvard University Press, 1995). Kevles considers eugenics from its inception in the late nineteenth century to the development of human genetics as a scientific and medical discipline. See also Donald J. Childs, *Modernism and Eugenics: Woolf, Eliot, Yeats and the Culture of Degeneration* (Cambridge: Cambridge University Press, 2001), and David Bradshaw, 'Eugenics: "They Should Certainly be Killed" ', in Bradshaw (ed.), *Modernism* (Oxford: Blackwell, 2002), 34–55. Bradshaw argues, persuasively, for Woolf's ultimate rejection of imperial ideologies.

THE RISE OF THE NEW WOMAN

1884

In the year that Galton coined the term eugenics, the first New Woman novel, Olive Schreiner's *The Story of An African Farm*, was published. According to the *Westminster Review* it 'first clearly sounded the note of this revolt, as it has been called, against the old and hitherto sanctioned ideas regarding the closest and most exacting tie between man and woman'.[12] *Love and Eugenics in the Late Nineteenth Century: Rational Reproduction and the New Woman* is concerned with the intersection of eugenics and the New Woman. The New Women who form the focus were, in different ways, as concerned with the questions of poverty, sickness, health, national efficiency, and labour capacity, as they were with the changing role of women, the issue for which they are currently generally known and celebrated. In the words of Karl Pearson, Professor of Applied Mathematics and Mechanics at University College London from 1884 and, from 1911, Britain's first National Professor of Eugenics, 'there has never been a Labour Question without a Woman's Question also'.[13]

Also in 1883 *Ideala*, by the popular writer and women's rights campaigner Sarah Grand, was doing the publishers' rounds. Completed when Grand was 26, it was, according to the novelist Margaret Oliphant, 'the expression of a great many thoughts of the moment, and of a desire which is stronger than it ever has been before, cultivated by many recent agitations and incidents, for a new development of feminine life, for an emancipation, which even those who wish for it most strongly could not define and scarcely understand.'[14] This was certainly true but, coexisting with this desire for emancipation, and always threatening to undercut it, was a eugenic subtext that persisted through Grand's work, as I shall show in Chapters 5 and 6. *Ideala* contained the blueprint of Grand's fiction: the sorry story of 'a highly bred' woman who married a 'man of loose morals',[15] which found its most sensational expression in her syphilitic bestseller of 1893, *The Heavenly Twins*.

In the closing decades of the century the New Woman—a term which

[12] Thomas Bradfield, 'A Dominant Note of some Recent Fiction', *Westminster Review*, 142 (1894), 541.

[13] 'Woman and Labour', *Fortnightly Review*, 61 (1894), 561–77 (563), repr. in Pearson, *The Chances of Death*, 2 vols. (London: Edward Arnold, 1897).

[14] Margaret Oliphant, 'The Old Saloon', *Blackwood's Edinburgh Magazine*, 146 (1889), 256–62.

[15] 'Sarah Grand and Mr Ruskin', *Woman's Signal* (25 January 1894), 57.

Grand claimed responsibility for introducing into common currency[16]—rapidly came to dominate fiction, both as theme and writer, becoming synonymous with modernity itself. As the American journal the *Humanitarian* reported in 1894:

> That very word 'new', strikes as it were the dominant note in the trend of present-day thought, present-day effort and aspiration. It sounds out from every quarter. The new art, the new literature, the new fiction, the new journalism, the new humour, the new criticism, the new hedonism, the new morality . . . Lastly, more discussed, debated, newspaper paragraphed, caricatured, howled down and denied, or acknowledged and approved, as the case may be, than any of them, we have the new woman.[17]

More than a hundred novels and a far greater number of short stories were published by and about the New Woman before the century was out, and magazines studied, celebrated, and satirized her without respite. The New Woman soon became equally visible in the United States, with *A Study in Bloomers; or, The Model New Woman*, a lavishly illustrated exploration of this female phenomenon, by the American novelist George F. Hall appearing in 1895.[18]

In spite of the iconic status of the New Woman in the closing years of the nineteenth century, the phenomenal success of New Woman fiction, and the social impact of the New Woman debates that raged in fiction and the press and at the dinner table, she was, for much of the twentieth century, silenced, excised from history and from the literary canon.[19] In

[16] See Athol Forbes, 'My Impressions of Sarah Grand', *Lady's World*, 21 (1900), 883. For further discussion of the genealogy of the term, see Ann Ardis, *New Women, New Novels: Feminism and Early Modernism* (New Brunswick: Rutgers University Press, 1990), 10–28; Ellen Jordan 'The Christening of the New Woman: May 1894', *Victorian Newsletter* 48 (1983); David Rubenstein, *Before the Suffragettes: Women's Emancipation in the 1890s* (Brighton: Harvester, 1986), 16–23; Talia Schaffer, ' "Nothing but Foolscap and Ink", Inventing the New Woman', in Angelique Richardson and Chris Willis (eds.), *The New Woman in Fiction and in Fact* (Basingstoke: Macmillan, 2001); Michelle Elizabeth Tusan, 'Inventing the New Woman: Print Culture and Identity Politics during the *Fin-de-siècle*', *Victorian Periodicals Review*, 31 (1998), 169–82.

[17] Mrs Morgan-Dockerell, 'Is the New Woman a Myth?', *Humanitarian*, 8 (1896), 339.

[18] For the centrality of the New Woman to American culture, see George Hall, *A Study in Bloomers; or, The Model New Woman* (Chicago, Philadelphia, and Stockton: American Bible House, 1895); A. Richardson (ed.), *Women Who Did: Stories by Men and Women 1890–1914* (Harmondsworth: Penguin, 2001); and Christine Stansell, *American Moderns: Bohemian New York and the Creation of a New Century* (New York: Henry Holt, 2000), esp. ch. 7.

[19] Except, that is, for Thomas Hardy's Sue Bridehead, an ambivalent candidate for a New Woman, 'a woman of the feminist movement', 'the intellectualized, emancipated bundle of nerves' produced by modern conditions. In 1911 Hardy thought about turning *Jude the Obscure* into a play called 'The New Woman': see Michael Millgate, *Thomas Hardy: His Career as a Novelist* (1971; Macmillan, 1994), 312.

recent decades, a century after she first appeared in print, she has made a comeback in academic literary circles and, now the subject of numerous critical works, she is being restored to her place in history. Sally Ledger has explored the variety of literary and social forms which New Woman writing took, considering the relation of the New Woman to other social and cultural movements of the period,[20] and Ann Heilmann has considered relations between a broad range of New Woman writing and second-wave feminism.[21] Thus, the diversity and pervasiveness of the New Woman in late Victorian culture is emerging.

However, the oppressive ideas that coexisted with the emancipatory theories of some New Women—ideas that were supremely class conscious—remain largely unexamined, as the focus remains on her more progressive aspects.[22] For example, in *Rebel Women: Feminism, Modernism and the Edwardian Novel* (1994), Jane Eldridge Miller emphasized the disruptive and subversive nature of New Woman

[20] Sally Ledger, *The New Woman: Fiction and Feminism at the Fin de Siècle* (Manchester: Manchester University Press, 1997). On New Women who took up socialist politics, see Ledger, *The New Woman*, ch. 2. See also Angela Ingram and Daphne Patai, (eds.), *Rediscovering Forgotten Radicals: British Women Writers, 1889–1939* (Chapel Hill: University of North Carolina Press, 1993), especially Chris Waters, 'New Women and Socialist-Feminist Fiction: The Novels of Isabella Ford and Katharine Bruce Glasier'; and Ann Ardis, 'The Journey from Fantasy to Politics': The Representation of Socialism and Feminism in Gloriana and *The Image-Breakers*'. On the New Woman and popular culture see Patricia Marks, *Bicycles, Bangs, and Bloomers: The New Woman in the Popular Press* (Kentucky: University Press of Kentucky, 1990). See also Sarah Wintle, 'Horses, Bikes and Automobiles: New Women on the Move', in Angelique Richardson and Chris Willis (eds.), *The New Woman in Fiction and in Fact: Fin de Siècle Feminisms* (Basingstoke: Palgrave, 2001); David Rubenstein, *Before the Suffragettes: Women's Emancipation in the 1890s* (Brighton: Harvester, 1986); and Rubenstein, 'Cycling in the 1890s', *Victorian Studies*, 21 (1978), 47–71. For an excellent study of changing attitudes towards motherhood and sexuality, see Claudia Nelson and Ann Sumner Holmes (eds.), *Maternal Instincts: Visions of Motherhood and Sexuality in Britain, 1875–1925* (Basingstoke: Macmillan, 1997).

[21] Heilmann, *New Woman Fiction: Women Writing First-Wave Feminism* (Basingstoke: Palgrave, 2000). For extensive primary materials on the New Woman, see Ann Heilmann, (ed.), *The Late Victorian Marriage Question: A Collection of Key New Woman Texts*; *Sex, Social Purity and Sarah Grand*, 5 vols. (London: Routledge (with Thoemmes Press, 1998)) and Ann Heilmann (ed.), *Sex, Social Purity and Sarah Grand*, 4 vols. (London: Routledge, 2000). See also Ann Heilmann, *New Woman Strategies: Sarah Grand, Olive Schreiner, and Mona Caird* (Manchester: Manchester University Press, 2004).

[22] A notable exception is Ledger, *The New Woman*, ch. 3. See also Lyn Pykett, who notes the repressive aspects of the social-purity feminists' version of the New Woman in her analysis of early modernism, *Engendering Fictions: The English Novel in the Early Twentieth Century* (London: Edward Arnold, 1995), 14. See Mary Poovey, *Uneven Developments: The Ideological Work of Gender in Mid-Victorian England* (London: Virago, 1989), esp. ch. 1, for an excellent discussion of the complexities and contradictions in Victorian attitudes towards womanhood.

fiction,[23] and in *New Women, New Novels: Feminism and Early Modernism* (1990) Ann Ardis, recovering concealed links between early New Woman feminism and modernism, argues that New Woman novelists replaced the pure woman, the Victorian angel in the house,[24] 'with a heroine who is either sexually active outside of marriage or abstains for political rather than moral reasons'.[25] She foregrounds New Woman novels which challenge essentialist thinking about class, genetics, maternal instinct, and sexual determinism, arguing for 'the New Woman novelists' sensitivity to the *social* construction of that "yoke of biological femininity" '.[26] Likewise, Patricia Murphy, while acknowledging a 'troubling essentialism' in Sarah Grand's work, goes on to argue that *The Heavenly Twins* 'emphasises the importance of nurture as opposed to nature, interrogating assumptions of biological determinism and stressing the significance of environmental influences'.[27] Evidence to the contrary is dismissed as irony or subversion, and, in an otherwise illuminating analysis of late nineteenth-century gender debates, Grand's sustained enthusiasm for biological determinism, and her class biases, which I examine in Chapters 5 and 6, are overlooked. Murphy notes that issues of class and race have little place in her study which centres, she emphasizes, on gender concerns. She justifies this on the grounds that New Women tended to come from the middle class.[28]

The privileging of issues of gender carries with it the risk of underplaying the social and political concerns that shape, and in some cases

[23] Jane Eldridge Miller, *Rebel Women: Feminism, Modernism and the Edwardian Novel* (London: Virago, 1994).

[24] While the phrase has, from the 1880s onwards, come to denote separate-sphere ideology, Ian Anstruther demonstrates that Coventry Patmore's poem, *The Angel in the House*, 2 vols., *The Betrothed* (1854), and *The Espousals* (1856), from which this phrase derives, was actually received as a fairly liberal statement of Victorian sexual marriage (see Anstruther, *Coventry Patmore's Angel: A Study of Coventry Patmore, his Wife Emily and the Angel in the House* (London: Haggerston Press, 1992), 74–82, 95–103), but was taken out of context by 1880s conservatives and radicals alike who chose to focus on its conservative position. See also John Maynard, 'The Unknown Patmore', *Victorian Poetry*, 36 (1998), 443–55.

[25] Ardis, *New Women*, 3.

[26] Ibid., 106, 109, emphasis in original.

[27] Patricia Murphy, *Time is of the Essence, Temporality, Gender and the New Woman* (State University of New York Press, 2001), 28, 114.

[28] Ibid., 28–9. While Childs acknowledges that a number of women supported eugenics (*Modernism and Eugenics*, 8), he writes 'feminists resisted the suggestion that educated middle-class women who chose careers over childbearing were neglecting their duties to the race' (4). Childs cites Edith Bethune-Baker, herself a eugenist, who argued that the Whetham's concerns over the fall in birth rate among the middle class were 'prejudiced against the woman's movement', letter to the editor, *The Hibbert Journal*, 10 (1912), 474 cited in Childs, 7, n. 23. William and Catherine Whetham co-authored *The Family and the Nation: A Study in Natural Inheritance and Social Responsibility* (London: Longmans, 1909).

even constitute, these issues, and the complex, multifaceted nature of the women who are grouped together under the New Woman umbrella has tended to be obscured by a unifying vision of the New Woman as a figure who privileged independence over family and who rejected social and sexual roles predicated on a politics of sexual difference. *Love and Eugenics* examines the complex and often repressive class politics of the New Women, exploring the relationship between late nineteenth-century feminism and eugenics, and considering ways in which New Women endorsed or reworked, as well as challenged, the ideology of separate spheres that dominated late nineteenth-century sexual and social politics. On this more complex model, issues of gender are cut through by national and imperial concerns, for issues of hierarchy between social and national groups were as pressing as those between the sexes.[29] Equally, the idea that heterosexuality is inevitably constitutive of male control over women has contributed to an oversimplification of the dynamics of heterosexuality, so that particular forms of the heterosexual relation, such as eugenic love, become overlooked.[30] Eugenic love was the politics of the state mapped onto bodies: the replacement of romance

[29] For illuminating discussion of the relations between late nineteenth-century feminism and imperialism, see Ledger, *The New Woman*, ch. 3; Anna Davin, 'Imperialism and Motherhood', *History Workshop*, 5 (1978), 9–65; and Deirdre David, *Rule Britannia: Women, Empire and Victorian Writing* (Ithaca: Cornell University Press, 1995). On Schreiner's relation to empire, see Anne McClintock, *Imperial Leather: Race, Gender and Sexuality in the Colonial Contest* (London: Routledge, 1995), ch. 5, 'Olive Schreiner: The Limits of Colonial Feminism'; and Carolyn Burdett, *Olive Schreiner and the Progress of Feminism: Evolution, Gender, Empire* (Basingstoke: Palgrave, 2001). See also Laura Chrisman, 'Empire, "Race" and Feminism at the *Fin de Siècle*: The Work of George Egerton and Olive Schreiner' in Sally Ledger and Scott McCracken (eds.), *Cultural Politics at the* Fin de Siècle (Cambridge: Cambridge University Press, 1995). For the extent to which notions of civilization and racial hierarchy framed the thinking of the first generation of suffragettes, see Jane Rendall, 'Citizenship, Culture and Civilization: The Languages of British Suffragettes 1866–1874', in Caroline Daley and Melanie Nolan (eds.), *Suffrage and Beyond: International Feminist Perspectives* (Auckland University Press, 1994), 127–50. See also Anne Digby and John Stewart (eds.), *Gender, Health and Welfare* (London: Routledge, 1996). On the ways in which women participate in ethnic and national processes and in state practices in a number of different societies, see Nira Yuval-Davis and Floya Anthias (eds.), *Woman–Nation–State* (Basingstoke: Macmillan, 1989).

[30] See John Kucich's insightful essay 'Heterosexuality Obscured', *Victorian Studies*, 40 (1997), 475–88. Kucich argues that 'in gay/lesbian, feminist, materialist-feminist, and masculinity studies, heterosexuality remains the constant target of a powerful set of critiques, but the full complexity of its social and psychological dynamics rarely emerges' (476); subsequently, ways that heterosexuality could be interrogated as a social institution are obscured (477). He points out that the sort of issues that Leonore Davidoff and Catherine Hall opened up in *Family Fortunes* (1987) have 'languished in recent nineteenth-century work because of reigning notions about heterosexuality and power'; he notes that this is perhaps more true of literary studies than history (486).

with the rational selection of a reproductive partner in order better to serve the state through breeding.[31] I argue that a number of New Women had a maternalist agenda which, in the context of late nineteenth-century British fears of racial decline and imperial loss, developed as eugenic feminism. The central goal of eugenic feminists was the construction of civic motherhood which sought political recognition for reproductive labour; in the wake of new biological knowledge they argued that their contribution to nation and empire might be expanded if they assumed responsibility for the rational selection of reproductive partners.

BIOLOGY

Biology is uniquely positioned among the sciences. As Abraham J. Heschel notes in *Who is Man*? 'A theory about the stars never becomes a part of the being of the stars . . . we become what we think of ourselves'.[32] Biology is not overtly concerned with social transformation but it has the potential to change human self-perception, and to affect social relations. This potential can be seen at work in the biological narratives that developed in the wake of Darwin's *Origin*, as biology became increasingly central to discourses on class and poverty. Pre-Darwinian scientific ideas also persisted, and became crucial to late nineteenth-century debates on the relative influence of nature and the environment which form the focus of this study.[33]

[31] Historical studies of love, for example, Stephen Kern, *The Culture of Love: Victorians to Moderns* (Cambridge, Mass. and London: Harvard University Press, 1992); Denis De Rougemont, *Love in the Western World* (1940; New York: Schoken Books, 1983); and Peter Gay, *The Bourgeois Experience: Victoria to Freud*, 5 vols. ii. *The Tender Passion* (Oxford: Oxford University Press, 1986), overlook ways in which love was taken up and reworked by the eugenists. Gay notes that calls to marry for love from the 1860s onwards seemed to conservative and censorious moralists a sign that the movement for women's emancipation, was getting out of control (Gay, 99–100). This argument overlooks the idea of rational reproduction which emerged in the 1880s with the development of the social purity movement. Gay writes that 'nineteenth-century novelists explored money, class, politics . . . but their main preoccupation was love', but love in several New Woman novels is largely constituted by these very concerns.

[32] Abraham J. Heschel, *Who is Man*? (Stanford: Stanford University Press, 1965), 7.

[33] Donald MacKenzie argues that eugenics and environmentalism are forms of biological engineering, with the common goal of producing a population fit and clever enough to preserve the existing social order, and both sides shared much common ground in the hereditarian and environmentalist sides of the IQ debate of the 1960s and 1970s. (He observes that environmentalism implied more jobs for professionals than did eugenics (MacKenzie, *Statistics in Britain 1865–1930: The Social Construction of Scientific Knowledge* (Edinburgh: Edinburgh University Press, 1981), 48).) In 1904, the biometrician W. F. R. Weldon, Professor of Zoology at University College London from 1890, pointed out that

One of the first people to use the term biology had been the French naturalist and transformist Jean-Baptiste de Lamarck (1744–1829). Abandoning his commitment to the fixity of species at the age of 50, when he was classifying invertebrates at the Muséum d'histoire naturelle,[34] Lamarck's evolutionary treatise, *Philosophie zoologique* (1809), sought to account for the transmutation of species, advancing a *purposive* view of nature, privileging environmental effects. In the words of the biologist and popular writer Grant Allen, Lamarck 'openly proclaimed under the Napoleonic reaction his profound conviction that all species, including man, were descended by modification from one or more primordial forms'.[35] Lamarck had argued for the tendency of living organisms to develop *without* struggle into more complex forms through what he termed 'the inheritance of acquired characteristics', or 'use-inheritance', a modified version of the ancient doctrine of the Great Chain of Being. However, unlike the Chain of Being, which conceived society as rigid and static, and species as the fixed products of single acts of creation, in Lamarck's version organisms were mutable, moving along a branching chain rather than fixed in a linear one. The theory attempted to account for the transmutation of species, and posited that in responding to environmental changes, organisms were constantly susceptible to structural and functional changes. Individual success in adaptation was rewarded with the transmission of desirable qualities, as acquired characteristics, to successive generations.[36] The

heredity and environment were not separable factors (as the eugenists assumed); this apparently annoyed Galton (Weldon to Pearson, 16 October 1904, University College Pearson Papers, 625, cited in MacKenzie, *Statistics in Britain*, 142). Nonetheless, the hereditarian and environmental approaches are clearly distinct, with the former lending itself to social unfreedom. Nikolas Rose points out that 'the strategy of eugenics is segregation; the strategy of environmentalism is socialism, re-attachment of marginal or disaffected groups to the social order. Eugenics seeks control by exclusion and the tightening of boundaries; environmentalists by integration' (N. Rose, 'The Psychological Complex: Mental Measurement and Social Administration', *Ideology and Consciousness*, 5 (1979), cited in MacKenzie, *Statistics in Britain*, 50). See also P. G. Werskey, *The Visible College* (London: Allen Lane, 1978). For the common ground shared by the hereditarian and environmentalist sides of the IQ debate of the 1960s and the 1970s, see L. Levidow, 'A Marxist Critique of the IQ Debate', *Radical Science Journal*, 6:7 (1978), 12–79; and J. Harwood, 'Heredity, Environment, and the Legitimation of Social Policy', in B. Barnes and S. Shapin (eds.), *Natural Order: Historical Studies of Scientific Culture* (Beverly Hills and London: Sage, 1979), 231–48.

[34] Peter Bowler, *Evolution: The History of an Idea* (1983; Berkeley and Los Angeles: University of California Press, 1989), 82.

[35] Grant Allen, *Charles Darwin* (London: Longmans, Green and Co., 1885), 11.

[36] See R. W. Burkhardt, *The Spirit of System: Lamarck and Evolutionary Biology* (Cambridge: Mass.: Harvard University Press, 1977); A. O. Lovejoy, *The Great Chain of Being* (New York: Harper & Row, 1960). Robert Nye notes that while European social theorists

theory foregrounded environmental influence; in the case of humans, this amounted primarily to *education*, which a number of Enlightenment thinkers had accepted in different forms.[37] It suggested that there was authority in nature for the idea that individuals and social groups might work to better themselves, to progress.[38] In the early decades of the nineteenth century, on the edge of the Hungry Forties, the bottom-up idea of evolution—the idea that an animal could transform itself into a higher being and pass on all its gains (without godly intervention)—had appealed to atheistic revolutionaries.

While Darwin is assumed to have discredited Larmarck's theory, the relation between their ideas is complex. Darwin wrote in private letters that Lamarck's work was 'veritable rubbish'; 'absurd though clever'; 'extremely poor', remarking that 'one-half of Lamarck's arguments were obsolete and the other half erroneous', and that *Philosophie zoologique* was 'a wretched book, and one from which (I well remember my surprise) I gained nothing'.[39] However, Darwin credited the environment as a major influence. He opened the *Origin* with the assertion:

paid lip-service to Weismann's germ theory after 1885, they did not decisively break with Lamarckian notions of inheritance. Applied to social theory, Lamarck's concept of heredity had the effect of placing the individual and society on a continuum, wherein individual acquisitions could be fixed and stored in the social organism, and where the evolution of the social unit expressed its growth in the persistent differentiation of individual functions. Until the advent of neoDarwinian genetics just before the First World War sociologists did not make distinctions between individuals and society in such a rigid manner as has been thought: Nye, 'Sociology: the Irony of Progress', in J. Chamberlain and Sander Gilman (eds.), *Degeneration, The Dark Side of Progress* (New York: Columbia University Press, 1985), 50. Nye draws on Georg Simmel, who charts a shift over the century from a kind of indistinguishable and atomistic 'similarity' to a strong valuation of the 'absolute peculiarity' of the individual personality rooted in 'the collective . . . concrete totality of the living species': Georg Simmel, *The Sociology of Georg Simmel*, ed. by Kurt H. Wolff (New York: Free Press, 1950), 80.

37 The eighteenth-century Newtonian Pierre Louise Moreau de Maupertuis, drawing on the Aristotelian idea of 'epigenesis'—the idea that the embryo develops through the sequential addition of parts rather than by the expansion of a preformed miniature—noted that in humans and other animals both parents contributed to the formation of the offspring, and that thus a new characteristic appearing within an individual might be perpetuated through later generations. See *Venus physique* (1745); *Système de la nature* (1751), and, for further discussion of these ideas, Bowler, *Evolution* 70–2.

38 See Adrian Desmond, 'Lamarckianism and Democracy', in J. R. Moore (ed.), *History, Humanity and Evolution* (Cambridge: Cambridge University Press, 1989), 99–130.

39 F. Darwin (ed.), *The Life and Letters of Charles Darwin*, 3 vols. (London: John Murray, 1887), ii. 29, 39, 215, and 189, cited in D. R. Oldroyd, *Darwinian Impacts: An Introduction to the Darwinian Revolution* (1980; Milton Keynes: Open University Press, 1983), 46, n. 4, and Darwin to Lyell, 12 March 1863), iii. p. 14.

When we reflect on the vast diversity of the plants and animals which have been cultivated, and which have varied during all ages under the most different climates and treatment, I think we are driven to conclude that this great variability is simply due to our domestic productions having been raised under conditions of life not so uniform as, and somewhat different from, those to which the parent-species have been exposed under nature.[40]

Equally, Darwin made use of Lamarck's idea of acquired characteristics. In his chapter on the 'Laws of Variation', discussing the 'effects of use and disuse', he stated 'there can be little doubt that use in our domestic animals strengthens and enlarges certain parts, and disuse diminishes them; and that such modifications are inherited'.[41] While Lamarck's peaceful economy was plainly at odds with Darwin's combative world, by the time he wrote *The Variation of Animals and Plants under Domestication* (1868), Darwin was drawing more directly on Lamarckian ideas: here he outlined his own theory of heredity, the concept of 'pangenesis', which held that hereditary material was gathered from all parts of the body and collected into the 'germ cells' from where it was passed on to subsequent generations. In the sixth edition of the *Origin* (1872) he added a new chapter on goal-directed variation, balancing chance with environmental conditions in accounting for variation.[42] As I shall show in Chapter 8, these ideas were taken up by anti-hereditarians, notably Mona Caird, at the end of the nineteenth century.

The real blow to environmental factors in accounting for evolutionary change came not from Darwin but from the German biologist

[40] *The Origin of Species; or, The Preservation of Favoured Races in the Struggle for Life* (1859; Oxford: Oxford University Press, 1996), 8. The first chapter, 'Variation under Domestication', is a development of the idea that plants and animals under cultivation 'generally differ more from each other than do the individuals of any one species or variety in a state of nature' (8).

[41] *Origin*, Darwin, 110. For Galton on the theory of the inheritance of acquired characteristics, see R. S. Cowan, 'Sir Francis and the Continuity of the Germ-Plasm: A Biological Idea with Political Roots', Actes du XIIe Congrès International d'Histoire des *Sciences*, 8 (1968); and 'Nature and Nurture: The Interplay of Biology and Politics in the Work of Francis Galton', *Studies in the History of Biology*, 1 (1977), 133–208. See also E. W. MacBride, *An Introduction to the Study of Heredity* (London: Thornton Butterworth, 1924). MacBride, Professor of Zoology at Imperial College, was both a leading neo-Lamarckian and a eugenist; he saw Lamarckian mechanisms as too slow to be relied on to improve human populations: see MacKenzie, 251 n. 2.

[42] See Bowler, *Evolution*, esp. ch. 3; Oldroyd, chs. 3 and 13; and Morton, *The Vital Science: Beyond the Literary Imagination 1860–1900* (London: George Allen & Unwin, 1984), 1 for further discussion. See also D. Freeman, 'The Evolutionary Theories of Charles Darwin and Herbert Spencer,' *Current Anthropology*, 15 (1974), 211–37.

August Weismann (1834–1914).[43] His *Essays Upon Heredity* (1889) was an indefatigable treatise on the supreme influence of biological 'nature' over 'nurture', to use the twin terms which Galton had coined in 1874.[44] Weismann advanced the idea of two sorts of cell, somatic and germ cells. He held that the protoplasm peculiar to the germ-cell—'germ-plasm'—which bore the factors determining the transmission of characters from parent, was completely isolated from the body of the organism that carried it, and was transmitted unchanged from generation to generation. This isolation was crucial to his theory; it meant that an organism could only pass on to the next generation what it received from its parents, and that the matter which controlled heredity simply passed through the organism, without contributions from the somatic cells, and impervious to environmental influence. In an experiment which involved cutting the tails off mice over a number of generations, he argued that acquired characteristics could not be inherited, for the tails returned to the mice of subsequent generations. While Lamarckians could argue that only those characteristics which were useful to the organism were inherited, Weismann's experiments did prove that mice deprived of their tails still carried the complete germ-plasm for this characteristic, and that, therefore, Lamarckism rested on a theory of soft heredity. Excluding the somatic cells from any role in heredity, Weismann's theory of germ-plasm effectively wrote the role of the environment out of evolutionary narrative, and marked a major coup for hereditarians. 'The germ-plasm is the essential part of the germ-cell, and determines the nature of the individual that arises from it' declared Grant Allen in the *Academy*.[45] The hereditarian line repeatedly surfaces, in varying guises, in the late nineteenth-century debates over gender and poverty.

LONDON'S POOR

In seeking to contribute to national efficiency, several New Women turned their attention to the problem of London's casual poor, reckless in reproduction but idle in production.[46] The casual poor were not a

[43] See Bowler, *Evolution*, 251–3; and Oldroyd, *Darwinian Impacts*, 164–5.

[44] Galton, *English Men of Science: Their Nature and Nurture* (London: Macmillan, 1874).

[45] Grant Allen, 'Essays upon Heredity' (review of Weismann's *Essays*), *Academy*, 37 (1890), 84.

[46] On the tense relationship between the middle and upper classes and the casual poor in nineteenth-century London, see Gareth Stedman Jones's excellent study *Outcast*

new problem. Defined by their unstable relation to the labour market, they were firmly in the public gaze during the second half of the nineteenth century, and two approaches to the problem of poverty vied for supremacy: the environmental and the hereditarian.

In 1857 the *City Press* observed that the Crimean War (1853–6) had directed public attention 'to the physical condition of the masses whence our solders and sailors must be obtained', urging the necessity of 'providing for the people healthy, out of door recreations',[47] and Charles Kingsley remarked that the 'true wealth of a nation is in the health of her masses', pointing out that it was from the city rather than the country that armies were recruited.[48] *The Times* reported in 1859 'the State has a direct interest in guarding against a deterioration of our race',[49] and here, again, the focus was on improving the living conditions of the poor.[50] The National Association for the Promotion of Social Science (1857–85),[51] more commonly known as the Social Science Association, similarly emphasized the environmental causes of poverty, bringing

London: A Study in the Relationship Between Classes in Victorian Society (1971; Harmondsworth: Penguin, 1992).

47 *City Press* (5 Sept. 1857), cited in A. S. Wohl, *The Eternal Slum: Housing and Social Policy in Victorian London* (London: E. Arnold, 1977), 68.

48 Kingsley, *Miscellanies* (London: John W. Parker and Son, 1859), 2 vols. ii. 342.

49 W. Cooper, quoted in *The Times* 1859 and cited in Wohl, *The Eternal Slum*, 68. Contrast Jack London who saw the poor not so much as a threat to empire as wrongfully cut off from imperial profits (see *People of the Abyss* (1903)). For examples of this emphasis on the environment, see *The Times* 'in the great struggle of nations the best won, because goodness was the associate of strength and healthfulness. The maintenance of the sanitary condition of the people was a necessity to the maintenance of a high position among others', *The Times* (26 Sept. 1883), cited in Wohl, *The Eternal Slum*, 68; and Lord Brabazon, 'The Decay of Bodily Strength in Towns', *Nineteenth Century*, 21 (1887), 676. Brabazon urged town improvements for a healthy nation of athletes and soldiers, emphasizing that everyone should have an interest in the health of the city. See also *Hansard*, 133 (1900), cols. 467, 482, 483 on slums not breeding good soldiers.

50 'Deterioration' was an environmental concept which was gradually supplanted by its biological counterpart, 'degeneration', from the 1880s. For an excellent study of the idea of degeneration, see Daniel Pick, *Faces of Degeneration: A European Disorder, c.1848–c.1918* (Cambridge: Cambridge University Press, 1993). See also William Greenslade, *Degeneration, Culture and the Novel 1880–1940* (Cambridge: Cambridge University Press, 1994). Pick notes that the *Lancet* first used degeneration to describe an internal deterioration during the 1850s: *Faces of Degeneration*, 189–90.

51 For detailed accounts of the work of the society see the National Association for the Promotion of Social Science, *Transactions,* ed. by George W. Hastings (London: John Parker Son and Bourne, 1858–85). Among its members were Lord Shaftesbury and Lord John Russell, Edwin Chadwick, Charles Kinglsey, John Stuart Mill, John Ruskin, and James Kay-Shuttleworth. See also Pauline Mazumdar, *Eugenics, Human Genetics and Human Failings: The Eugenics Society, its Sources and Critics in Britain* (London and New York: Routledge, 1992), 10–13.

together people interested in social reform who were working in law, education, punishment and reformation, public health, and social economy.[52] One of the most important agents outside parliament influencing public policy, the association was concerned with the causes and control of crime and pauperism, and worked statistics on crime, education, and sanitation into an argument for legislative changes that were intended to lead to the moral and physical improvement of the working class.[53] The association's *Handbook* (1857) stated:

> While statistics reveal that crime is not the necessary attendant upon poverty or low wages, they show that it is found most abundant in closely crowded houses, in ill-drained localities, while the morals of the poor quickly manifest an improvement when sanitary reform has been carried out in their dwellings.[54]

In 1871, the association reported 'a progressive physical degeneracy' among urban populations.[55] Environmentalist explanations of the problem of the casual poor naturally led to environmental solutions, from education and housing reform to outdoor recreation.[56] The mid-Victorian pioneer of housing reform, Octavia Hill (1838–1912), urged in 1869 that the poor needed to be trained out of the bad ways into which they had fallen before any progress could be made: 'transplant them tomorrow to healthy and commodious homes and they would pollute

[52] Mazumdar, *Eugenics, Human Genetics and Human Failings*, 10. For a history of this Association see Margaret Fison, *Handbook of the National Association for the Promotion of Social Science* (London: Longmans, 1859), ch. 3.

[53] See Mazumdar, *Eugenics, Human Genetics and Human Failings*, 10–12. See also Gertrude Himmelfarb, *The Idea of Poverty: England in the Early Industrial Age* (New York, Vintage, 1985), 371–400 on 'the ragged and dangerous classes'; and Lawrence Ritt, 'The Victorian Conscience in Action: The National Association for the Promotion of Social Science, 1857–1886', Ph.D. dissertation, Columbia University, 1959, Ann Arbor, University Microfilms (1959).

[54] Margaret Fison, *Handbook of the National Association for the Promotion of Social Science* (London: Longmans, 1859), n. 16, pp. 11–12, cited in Mazumdar, *Eugenics, Human Genetics and Human Failings*, 270.

[55] Henry W. Rumsey, 'On a Progressive Physical Degeneracy of Race in the Town Populations of Great Britain', in *Transactions of the National Association for the Promotion of Social Science* (London: Longmans, 1871), 466–72.

[56] Early nineteenth-century evangelical philanthropy had turned on an essentially environmentalist idea that the poor might be remoralized. See, for example, the work of the evangelical reformer Lord Ashley, the seventh earl of Shaftesbury, who pushed for charity schools for 'ragged children' of the labouring and destitute poor, and for the statutory reduction of daily hours worked in factories. See D. Porter, *Health, Civilization and the State: A History of Public Health from Ancient to Modern Times* (London: Routledge, 1998), 115.

and destroy them'.[57] She remarked 'I see no limit to the power of raising even the lowest classes, if we will know and love them, deal with them as human beings, stimulate their hope and energy'.[58] The forced migration to the cities on account of the capitalization of agriculture and industry had cut through ties of community, creating new vertical links, and led to the increasing segregation of the classes throughout Britain. Hill was a founding member of the Charity Organization Society, which was formed in 1869. As I discuss in Chapter 3, the society aimed to bring the classes back in contact, and to end 'indiscriminate' charity.[59] In *Our Common Land* (1877) Hill urged the need 'to bridge over the great chasm which lies open between the classes',[60] but her system of good deeds was insufficient; there was a clear and growing need for subsidized, municipal housing.[61]

57 Octavia Hill, 'The Importance of Aiding the Poor without Almsgiving', *Transactions, National Association for the Promotion of Social Science* (1869), 389, cited in Wohl, *The Eternal Slum*, 186.

58 Cited in Wohl, *The Eternal Slum*, 185. See also Hill, 'Organised Work Among the Poor: Suggestions Founded on Four Years Management of a London Court', *Macmillan's Magazine*, 20 (1869), 219–26. Mid-Victorian philanthropy was often no less than philanthropic capitalism, a strategy for dealing with poverty that failed to address its underlying, socio-economic causes.

59 See also Mazumdar, *Eugenics, Human Genetics and Human Failings*, ch. 1. On the activities of the society see Stedman Jones, *Outcast London*, esp. chs. 15 and 16. Stedman Jones details the society's development of initiatives in the 1870s designed to impose upon the life of the poor a system of sanctions and rewards which would inculcate thrift and hard work. While there were few substantial changes to practices of relief, the COS did secure the passing of the Casual Poor Act in 1882, which laid down that vagrant paupers would not be released from a ward until they had completed their work task (273). However, social unrest in the 1880s countered the work of the COS.

60 Cited in Wohl, *The Eternal Slum*, 198.

61 In 1875 the Artisans and Labourers Dwelling Act (The Cross Act) was passed 'to allow and to encourage slow clearance on a larger scale, the purchases and demolition by the local authority of large areas of "unfit" property' (Fishman, *East End*, 8). Slum clearance led to massive increases in the homeless and dispossessed, and increased overcrowding as the homeless moved into neighbouring streets, subletting from subletters, tied to their place of employment. Fishman notes that, 'on sound *laissez-faire* principles and the economic precept of profitability', parliament would not readily support local or central government responsibility for re-housing and, therefore, opposed public-sector subsidies. Local council apathy, and fear of offending ratepayers, resulted in a significant time lag between demolition and rebuilding (Fishman, *East End*, 9). See the *Nineteenth Century*, 22 (1888), 252; and Enid Gauldie, *Cruel Habitations: A History of Working-Class Housing, 1780–1918* (London: Allen & Unwin, 1974), 276–7. See also Anthony Wohl, 'The Housing of the Working Classes in London, 1815–1914', in S. D. Chapman (ed.), *History of Working-Class Housing: A Symposium* (Newton Abbot: David & Charles, 1971), 27. To Gladstone's dismay, even Queen Victoria got involved with the new schemes for housing; see D. Porter, *Health, Civilization and the State* (London: Routledge, 1998), 242.

The importance of education as a moralizing force is central to George Eliot's 'Address to Working Men', which appeared in the first number of *Blackwood's Magazine* for 1868. Written at the instigation of the editor, John Blackwood, in response to the Second Reform Bill (1867), Eliot reminded working-class men of the weight of their new responsibilities. She spoke through the persona of the eponymous hero of her political novel *Felix Holt, The Radical* (1866), a respectable member of the working class whose face bears the 'stamp of culture' (398): 'roughs are the ugly crop that has sprung up while the stewards have been sleeping; they are the multiplying brood begotten by parents who have been left without all teaching save that of a too craving body'. Identifying the absence of teaching as a factor in the growth of what she referred to as 'the criminal class', she urged trade union members to send their children to school, 'so as not to go on recklessly breeding a moral pestilence among us'. The target of the address were the 'roughs', whom she described as 'the hideous margin of society, at one edge drawing towards it the undesigning ignorant poor, at the other darkening into the lowest criminal class'.[62] This distinction between the respectable or 'deserving' poor[63] and the unrespectable poor was a distinction explored more fully in *Felix Holt*, in which the mob, whose 'mental state' is 'a medley of appetites and confused impressions' (428), consists 'both of the more decent and the rougher sort'. The majority are not local to the previously peaceful, rural Little Treby, but have flocked from neighbouring manufacturing cities (421).[64] Cities, London in particular, were billed as a threat to national order, the breeding ground of deadly diseases and dangerous ideas.[65] The Second Reform Bill (1867), hastily

[62] George Eliot, *Felix Holt, The Radical* (1866; Harmondsworth: Penguin, 1987), 618–19, 618; 624.

[63] On the derivation of the term 'deserving poor' see Gertrude Himmelfarb, *Poverty and Compassion: The Moral Imagination of the Late Victorians* (New York: Knopf, 1991), 12.

[64] For the earlier treatment of the working class in fiction, see Sheila M. Smith, *The Other Nation: The Poor in the English Novels of the 1840s and 1850s* (Oxford: Oxford University Press, 1980). See also P. J. Keating, *The Working Classes in Victorian Fiction* (London: Routledge, 1971).

[65] See D. Porter, *Health, Civilization and the State*, 114. See also Colin Fraser Brockington, *A Short History of Public Health* (London: Churchill, 1956); William Frazer, *History of English Public Health 1834–1939* (London: Ballière, Tindall and Cox, 1950). In 1865 the newspapers registered a new, strikingly anxious response of the middle class to the tens of thousands of working-class Londoners who attended the funeral procession of Tom Sayers, prize-fighting champion. See Chris Brooks, 'Burying Tom Sayers: Heroism, Class and the Victorian Cemetery', *Victorian Society Annual* (1989).

passed in the midst of bread riots, aimed, in part, at keeping apart the respectable working class and the 'undeserving' poor.[66]

By the 1880s, the time of the New Woman and the coining of the term eugenics, the urban poor were in the forefront of the public imagination. The East End, a term invented 'about 1880'[67] had come to symbolize all that was wrong with Britain. In 1883 the living conditions of the urban poor received extensive coverage in the national press, becoming a regular feature in the *Daily News*.[68] The paper created two regular columns 'Homes of the London Poor' and 'Evenings with the Poor'—as well as a letters page devoted to what was now known as the housing question. In June, the illustrated weekly *Pictorial World* published the first instalment of a series of eye-opening articles, 'How the Poor Live', by the popular journalist George Sims.[69] Thomas Hardy has a single and melodramatic diary entry for 5 April 1883: 'London. Four million forlorn hopes.'[70] For Hardy the real problem was rural depopulation. He warned in *Longman's Magazine* later that year of alarming depopulation in rural areas, as the rural poor were forced, through the impact of capitalization and mechanization, to migrate to the towns. 'This process', he wrote, 'which is designated by statisticians as "the tendency of the rural population towards the large towns", is really the tendency of water to flow uphill when forced' [71] (a point he would make again in *Tess of the D'Urbervilles* (1891)).

The story of the East End sold and—as the running success of the BBC soap opera testifies—still sells. Sims continued to tantalize his reader with horrors he rhetorically declared fit only for the specialized medical magazines—'nameless abominations which could only be set forth were they contributing to the *Lancet*'.[72] The poor, he proclaimed,

[66] For a detailed account of attitudes to nineteenth-century poverty, see Himmelfarb *The Idea of Poverty* (1985). See also Porter, *Health, Civilization and the State*, ch. 7. On the political unrest of the Hyde Park Riots earlier this year, which intensified middle-class fears of the working class, see *The Times* (25 July 1866). See also *Reynolds' Newspaper* (29 July 1866); and Leslie Jones, 'Hyde Park and Free Speech', *Hyde Park Socialist*, 34 (Winter, 1976–7).

[67] *Nineteenth Century*, 24 (1888), 262.

[68] *Daily News* was founded by Charles Dickens. As he wrote in the first issue (21 January 1846), it was dedicated to 'the principles of progress and improvement; of education, civil and religious liberty, and equal legislation'.

[69] Sims was the grandson of the Chartist leader John Stephenson.

[70] *The Life of Thomas Hardy*, 2 vols. (1928–30; London: Studio Editions, 1994), 285.

[71] 'The Dorsetshire Labourer', *Longman's Magazine*, 2 (1883), 252–69, reprinted in Harold Orel (ed.), *Thomas Hardy's Personal Writings: Prefaces, Literary Opinions, Reminiscences* (Basingstoke and London: Macmillan, 1968), 188.

[72] Sims, *How the Poor Live, and Horrible London* (London: Chatto and Windus, 1889), 46.

were 'a race so oppressed, so hampered, and so utterly neglected, that its condition has become a national scandal'.[73] They were becoming the subject of a new investigative journalism which challenged existing codes of decorum. Sensationalism sold stories, and turned heads; it was the tone adopted not only by the press but also by more disciplined Christian and socialist reformers. October 1883 saw the publication of an anonymous twenty-page penny pamphlet by the Revd Andrew Mearns, *The Bitter Cry of Outcast London*, subtitled 'An Inquiry into the Condition of the Abject Poor', revealing the appalling effects of overcrowding. It was one of the most important pieces of writing on the poor in Britain to appear in the course of the nineteenth century. The *Pall Mall Gazette* published a long summary of the piece and a crusading leader 'Is it not Time?', which called for more support and action for the poor.[74] The *Lancet* reported that the article 'altered the whole tenor of political controversy', concluding 'one of the most striking events of the year is the prominence given to the housing of the poor'.[75]

The urban crisis deepened. The unusually harsh winter of 1885–6, which was accompanied by reductions in wages, led to planned demonstrations in Trafalgar Square, centre of civic space, and a traditional place for protest. Unrest came to a head in February 1886 (the coldest February in thirty years)[76] as a meeting on 8 February in Trafalgar Square of some 20,000 unemployed dock and building workers,[77] called by the Fair Trade League, broke into an unplanned riot in Hyde Park. Gentlemen looked on and jeered from the Carlton.[78] Agitation in various parts of London continued on a grand scale over the next two days, with

[73] Sims, *How the Poor Live*, cited in Keating, *The Working Classes in Victorian Fiction*, 87.

[74] 'Is it not Time?', *Pall Mall Gazette* (16 October 1883), reprinted in *The Bitter Cry of Outcast London*, ed. by Anthony S. Wohl (Leicester: Leicester University Press, 1970), 81–90. For the concrete effects of *The Bitter Cry*, see Wohl, *Bitter Cry*, intro., 9–37. One major effect was the founding the following year of Toynbee Hall, a settlement in the East End devoted to practical social reform; it in turn inspired Jane Addams's radical Chicago settlement, Hull House, founded in 1889.

[75] *Lancet* (15 Dec. 1883), 1050, cited in Anthony S. Wohl, *The Eternal Slum*, 229. See also *Daily News* (27 Oct 1883). For a discussion on whether the British race was degenerating, see *Lancet* (1 Dec. 1888), 1076–7. See also letter from a Sheffield doctor, C.N. Gwyne, to the *Lancet* (10 December 1888), 1257. Drawing on a report of the Anthropometric Committee of the British Association, the doctor highlighted the threat that London posed to the health of the nation, warning that 'living in towns exercises a deleterious effect, especially upon the poorer populations in the crowded districts'.

[76] Stedman Jones, *Outcast London*, 293.

[77] *The Times* (9 Feb., 1886), 6.

[78] See Fishman, *East End*, 3; and Stedman Jones, *Outcast London*, 291–4.

rumours flying and the West End in a state of panic.[79] Reactions revealed not only the extent to which the casual poor were a real threat, but unprecedented levels of fear among the middle class.[80] On 13 November 1887, less than a week after the police commissioner banned public meetings at Trafalgar Square, there was a series of demonstrations and marches to the square, organized by the Metropolitan Federation of Radical Clubs, to protest against coercion in London. The result was the police violence of 'Bloody Sunday'. Eleanor Marx, Karl Marx's daughter, who was on the march, recorded 'I have never seen anything like the brutality of the police; the Germans and Austrians who know what police brutality can be, said the same to me'; the Victorian *bourgeoisie* really believed that they were 'confronted with the most serious danger to public order which has menaced it since the Chartist rising of 1848'.[81]

Inspired by the riots of February 1886, Charles Booth (1840–1916), the Liverpool shipowner, social investigator, and reformer, began his extensive research into the London poor. The research ran into a seventeen-volume study *Life and Labour of the London Poor*; the first volume was published in 1892.[82] It was the first study to examine the problem of poverty in general, rather than focusing on the distress of individuals or families. According to what Booth termed cold, scientific evidence, based on the years 1887–8, 35 per cent of the total population of Tower Hamlets, or some 120,000 people, lived on or below the margin of subsistence.[83] Booth divided the population into eight classes, with the first two comprising the 'very poor' and the second two the 'poor': class A consisted of the lowest class; B 'casual labour, hand-to-mouth existence, chronic want'; C, 'irregular earning'; and D, 'regular minimum'.[84] In East London, he employed a double method of classification

[79] 'Rioting in the West End', *The Times*, (10 Feb 1886), 5, cited in Stedman Jones, *Outcast London*, 292. See Stedman Jones, 292–4 on the disturbances and on the rumours and panic that ensued, which revealed new levels of fear among the middle class. See also *Origin and Character of the Disturbances in the Metropolis on 8th February, and the Conduct of the Police Authorities*, Parliamentary Papers (1886), XXXIV, LIII.

[80] See Stedman Jones, *Outcast London*, 294–5. For contemporary responses, see William Morris, *Commonweal*, 2:14 (March 1886), 17; and Edward Aveling, *Commonweal*, 2:14 (March 1886), 21.

[81] Quoted in Fishman, *East End*, 3.

[82] On the contemporary impact of this study, see Stedman Jones, *Outcast London*, 320–1, 328.

[83] Fishman, *East End*, 4.

[84] Charles Booth, *Charles Booth's London: A Portrait of the Poor at the turn of the Century, drawn from Life and Labour of the People in London*, ed. by Richard M. Elman and Albert Fried, 17 vols. (1902; London: Hutchinson, 1969), 1st ser., ii. 21.

according to type of labour rather than poverty, with section 1, the lowest, consisting of 'loafers'; section 2, 'casual, day-to-day' (the distinction between the two being a moral rather than economic one); section 3, 'irregular labour'; 4, regular, low pay; and 5, regular, ordinary pay.[85] Booth argued for the segregation of the residuum into labour colonies. This would give the respectable and independent working class—the poor who were deemed *deserving* of public attention—a better chance in the labour market.[86]

In the closing decades of the century, the poor were given extensive treatment in fiction. In 1884 (the year a Royal Commission on the Housing of the Working Classes was established) George Gissing published *The Unclassed*, a grim, naturalist study of slum life in London. The socialist novelist Margaret Harkness (1854–1923), daughter of Robert Harkness, curate of Trinity Chapel, Great Malvern, cousin of Beatrice Webb, and friend of Eleanor Marx and Olive Schreiner, worked among the poor in London's East End during the 1880s. She examined the living conditions she found there in several of her novels (written under the pseudonym John Law). These included *City Girl* (1887), *Out of Work* (1888), and *Captain Lobe* (1889)—later renamed *In Darkest London*.[87] When Harkness sent Engels *City Girl*, he asked her why she had not portrayed the working classes with more of a revolutionary spirit, but added, 'I must own, in your defence, that nowhere in the civilized world are the working people less actively resistant, more passively submitting to fate, more *hébétés* than in the East End of London.'[88] J. H. Mackay, author of *The Anarchists* (1891), described the East End as 'the hell of poverty'; 'like an enormous black, motionless, giant Kraken, the poverty of London lies there in lurking silence and encircles with its mighty tentacles the life and wealth of the City and of the West End.'[89] The biologization of poverty received striking

[85] Booth, *London*, 1st ser., i. 34–5. See Stedman Jones, *Outcast London*, esp. ch. 3, which reproduces Booth's Table of Sections and Classes from East London and Hackney. See Ch. 3 below for further discussion. For similar distinctions, on moral grounds, see William Booth, *In Darkest England, and The Way Out*, pt 1 ch. 3: 'Darkest England may be described as consisting broadly of three circles, one within the other. The outer and widest circle is inhabited by the starving and the homeless, but honest, Poor. The second by those who live by Vice; and the third and innermost region at the centre is peopled by those who exist by Crime. The whole of the three circles is sodden with Drink.'

[86] *London*, Booth, i. 154, cited in Stedman Jones, *Outcast London*, 307.

[87] The title change of this novel drew attention to its links with the social tract *In Darkest England, and The Way Out* (1890).

[88] Engels to Harkness, 1 April 1888, *Selected Correspondence* (Moscow: 1953), repr. in John Law (Margaret Harkness), *A Manchester Shirtmaker*, ed. Trefor Thomas (1890; Rastrick: Northern Herald Books, 2002), 85.

[89] J. H. Mackay, *The Anarchists* (1891).

treatment in H. G. Wells's *The Time Machine* (1895), where the subterranean Morlocks are segregated from the elite Eloi, and in Jack London's sympathetic account of the East End, *People of The Abyss* (1903), the poor are set apart as a separate breed thriving in a space, outside of and other to civilization:

> a new species, a breed of city savages. The streets and houses, alleys and courts, are their hunting grounds. As valley and mountain are to the natural savage, street and building are valley and mountain to them. The slum is their jungle, and they live and prey in the jungle. The dear soft people of the golden theatres and wonder-mansions of the West End do not see these creatures, do not dream that they exist. But they are here, alive, very much alive in their jungle . . .[90]

And, in Galton's eugenic utopia, 'Kantsaywhere', which he first conceived in 1864, but completed in 1910,[91] class is a biological matter, and the unfit are known as The Unclassed—a direct mapping on to the class system:

> A Bureau was charged with looking after the unclassed parents and their offspring, and much was done to make the lot of the unclassed as pleasant as might be, so long as they propagated no children. If they did so kindness was changed into *sharp severity*.[92]

In this way, by the end of the century, the poor of fiction had become a race apart. This racial framing was not in itself new, but had occurred as a trope throughout the second part of the century. For example, Henry Mayhew, in his extensive investigation of the labouring—and unlabouring—poor undertaken during the 1850s, *London Labour and the London Poor*, describes the poor as racially separate:

> The transition from the artisan to the labourer is curious in many respects. In passing from the skilled operative of the West-end to the unskilled workman of the Eastern quarter of London, the moral and intellectual change is so great, that it seems as if we were in a new land, and among another race.[93]

[90] *People of the Abyss* (London: Isbister and Co. Ltd. 1903), 285.

[91] Pearson, *The Life, Letters, and Labours of Francis Galton*, iiia. 412.

[92] Ibid., 416, emphasis in original. The Utopia purports to be 'Extracts from the Journal of the late Professor I. Donoghue, revised and edited in accordance with his request by Sir Francis Galton, F.R.S' (See Pearson, *Life and Letters of Francis Galton*, iiia. 411). Compare Galton's concept of the 'unclassed' with the prevalence of the term 'underclass' in current socio-political discourse.

[93] Henry Mayhew, *London Labour and the London Poor* (London: 1862), iii. 243. See, for further discussion of the development of the idea of the poor as a race apart, Himmelfarb, *The Idea of Poverty* (1985), 307–400.

However, the racial othering of the casual poor gained a new momentum, and a new command and authority with the rapid assimilation of Darwinian ideas. In 1864, for instance, the *Saturday Review* referred to the Bethnal Green poor as 'a caste apart, a race of whom we know nothing, whose lives are of a quite different complexion from ours, persons with whom we have no point of contact'.[94] The term 'residuum', coined by the dissenting liberal MP John Bright (1811–89) in 1867, marked the poor as somehow separate, and suggested that their descent to the bottom of the social ladder was inevitable, or *natural*.[95] In *Culture and Anarchy* (1869) Matthew Arnold characterized the 'Populace' as 'this vast residuum . . . marching where it likes, meeting where it likes, bawling what it likes, breaking what it likes'.[96] 'The residuum' was held to have forfeited social sympathies, having arrived at their lowly position through moral failings—drunkenness, improvidence, gambling, and recklessness in reproducing. And, as morality was increasingly figured as a product of heredity, these vices could be laid at the door of biological determinism.[97]

By the 1880s the idea of demoralization was replaced by the idea of

94 'Slaves and Labourers', *Saturday Review*, 17 (1864), 72 . See also 'Metropolitan Houseless Poor', *Saturday Review*, 318 (1864), 149–50.

95 *The Times* (27 March 1867), 7/4: 'I call this class the residuum, which there is in every constituency, of almost hopeless poverty and dependence' (*OED*). In 'Burying Tom Sayers' Brooks records a shockingly racialized account of the poor in *Croydon Weekly Standard* (25 Nov. 1865), in which the urban poor are 'a multitude from the East', 'slow-eyed', and 'great jawed'. The East here functions as a blanket trope for all that is perceived to be other, and seems to have developed increasing resonance with the arrival of Jews from Eastern Europe and Russia in the last two decades of the century: see Bernard Gainer, *The Alien Invasion: The Origins of the Aliens Act of 1905* (London: Heinemann, 1972); Colin Holmes, *Anti-Semitism in British Society, 1876–1939* (London: Edward Arnold, 1979); and Holmes, *John Bull's Island: Immigration and British Society, 1871–1971* (London: Macmillan, 1988).

96 Matthew Arnold, *Culture and Anarchy*, ed. by John Dover Wilson (1869; Cambridge: Cambridge University Press, 1960), 166, 193.

97 One extreme example of this process was the biologization of crime. In 1876 the influential Italian criminologist and physician Cesare Lombroso published his *L'uomo deliquente*, or *Criminal Man*, in which, through comparative anthropological measurements, he gave apparent scientific authority to the notion of the born criminal. For Lombroso, criminals presented far more bodily, neurological, and psychic abnormalities than did the general population, and these abnormalities, he argued, signalled the sort of criminal behaviour (for example, prostitution) to which the individual in question was predisposed. This concept of crime was one of the many biologizations of social behaviour which proliferated after Darwin. In 1881 the *Atlantic Monthly* posited a biological basis for crime: see Richard L. Dugdale 'Origin of Crime in Society', Part I, *Atlantic Monthly*, 48 (1881); see also Parts II and III, *Atlantic Monthly* 48 (October 1981) and 49 (February 1882). In 1890 the eugenist and sexologist Havelock Ellis published *The Criminal*, outlining European developments in criminal anthropology, particularly in the work of Lombroso.

degeneration, and the political and social were displaced onto the biological. In a process of staged, explanatory moves from the social and moral to the biological, which were intimately linked with developments in scientific thinking, the poor were being cast as victims of their own biology. It followed that if poverty was a biological condition, it was immune to the environmental changes that could be brought about through social reform. In an article on the casual poor in the *Contemporary Review* in 1885, the eugenist and imperialist Arnold White divided the unemployed into three categories: 20 per cent were genuinely unemployed; 40 per cent were 'feckless and incapable'; and the remaining 40 per cent were 'physically, mentally and morally unfit, there is nothing that the nation can do for these men except to let them die out by leaving them alone'.[98] From the hereditarian standpoint, no amount of moralizing the poor, or uplifting their souls, would help; neither God, nor education, nor philanthropy were any use against defective germ-plasm—or ill-judged marriage to a degenerate partner of the kind that proliferates in Grand's fiction.

The othering of the poor along biological or racial lines was eased by the fluidity of the concept of race in nineteenth century. It might be used to denote the human race, different ethnic Europeans, or wider ethnic differences, even differences between species.[99] Racial language was readily used

[98] Arnold White, 'The Nomad Poor of London', *Contemporary Review*, 47 (1885), 714–27, in Stedman Jones, *Outcast London*, 288–9.

[99] In the early nineteenth century issues of race fell into the science of ethnology. However, ethnologists were monogenists, believing in the ultimate unity of humanity, going back to a single set of parents, Adam and Eve. The new science of physical anthropology took a new, polygenic, line. The Anthropological Society of London (1863–71), a stronghold of physical, and polygenist, anthropologists headed by James Hunt, mastered the shift from ethnology to physical anthropology, arguing for the fixity and persistence of racial characteristics, transforming the concept of foreignness. See James Hunt, 'On the Negro's Place in Nature', *Memoirs Read before the Anthropological Society of London*, i. (1863). See also Nancy Stepan's *The Idea of Race in Science: Great Britain 1800–1960* (London: Macmillan, 1982); Douglas A. Lorimer, *Colour, Class and the Victorians* (Leicester: Leicester University Press 1978); and Michael D. Biddis (ed.), *Images of Race* (Leicester: Leicester University Press, 1979). For the best part of the nineteenth century internal division was considered to be of more use to British social order—providing it was peaceable—than national unity, and the discourse of biology or race was more likely to be used in Britain to *separate* than unite the classes—to mark out as different rather than to bring together. See Peter Mandler, ' "Race" and "Nation" in Mid-Victorian Thought', in Stefan Collini, Richards Whatmore, and Brian Young (eds.), *History, Religion and Culture, British Intellectual History 1750–1950* (Cambridge: Cambridge University Press, 2000); in this essay Mandler notes that for the mid-Victorians, racial and national thinking at home threatened to collapse social distinctions, and was impeded by formidable domestic barriers; he points out that such thinking was particularly unattractive to the 'non-democratic majority of the English political and intellectual elite' and that 'post-colonial analysis tends

to distinguish groups of varying social as well as ethnic backgrounds, as exemplified in the study of the popular ethnologist John Beddoe, *The Races of Britain: A Contribution to the Anthropology of Western Europe* (1885). Galton's definition of eugenics as 'the study of agencies under social control that may improve or impair the racial qualities of future generations, either physically or mentally' demonstrates this slippage between class and race, between the social and the natural.

Another factor was the growth of London itself. As the population density and living conditions in London changed beyond recognition, and the city sprawled outwards without visible structure, planning, or parliamentary direction, 'stretching away on all sides from the original confines of the city'[100] it was increasingly figured as a *terra incognita*,[101] informing the racial othering of the poor, and also drawing links between the East End and the foreign fields of the empire. General William Booth, founder of the Salvation Army, opened his exploration of 'the submerged tenth',[102] and his plan for their rehabilitation, *In Darkest England and the Way Out* (1890):

> Darkest England, like Darkest Africa, reeks with malaria. The foul and fetid breath of our slums is almost as poisonous as that of the African swamp . . . A population sodden with drink, steeped in vice, eaten up by every social and physical malady, these are the denizens of Darkest England amidst whom my life has been spent, and to whose rescue I would now summon all that is best in the manhood and womanhood of our land.[103]

to emphasise the value of racial thinking for rallying the classes behind the English Imperial mission—but this again draws attention to the conceptual gulf between imperial and domestic thought, for rallying the classes was as vital overseas as separating them was at home' (232). For discussion of the British preoccupation with class in relation to the British empire, see David Cannadine, *Ornamentalism: How the British Saw their Empire* (Harmondsworth: Penguin, 2001).

100 Charles Manby Smith, *Curiosities of London Life; or, Phases, Physiological and Social of the Great Metropolis* (London: A. W. Bennett, 1853), 367.

101 For an early example of the use of this trope, see Thomas De Quincey, 'The Pleasures of Opium', *Confessions of an English Opium Eater* (1821). See also an account of 'strange tribes of men' to be found within the city in 'Mayhew's Revelations of London', *Eclectic Review*, 94 (1851), 424.

102 On the 'Submerged Tenth', see Booth's ch. 2 (which takes this term as its title) in *In Darkest England, and the Way Out* (London: International Headquarters of the Salvation Army, 1890), 'we have an army of nearly two million belonging to the submerged classes. To this there must be added at the very least, another million, representing those dependent upon the criminal, lunatic and other classes, not enumerated here, and the more or less helpless of the class immediately above the houseless and starving. This brings my total to three million, or, to put it roughly to one-tenth of the population'; 'This Submerged Tenth is it, then, beyond the reach of the nine-tenths in the midst of whom they live' (22, 23).

103 Preface, Booth, *In Darkest England and the Way Out* (1890). Booth lifted chunks from Stead's response to Mearns—the *Pall Mall* leader 'Is it not time?'

To imagine parts of London as outside civilization was to play with the startling idea that the imperial headquarters housed, in its midst, unsurveyed outposts of empire, or territory not yet won. It was also to express a yet more shocking idea; that somehow Britain, home to an imperial race, with an empire to rule, had managed to breed its own savages, and house them, inadequately, in the very heart of civilization. In *Empire and Efficiency* (1901), Arnold White spoke of 'street-bred brains' and 'country-born labourers in the prime of life' becoming 'white-faced workmen living in courts and alleys', warning that 'the Empire will not be maintained by a nation of out-patients' and that 'the marriage of destitute and sickly minors is a fruitful recruiting-ground for the unfit'. [104] He declared:

> For the present we are safe from attack by barbarians from without. Patches of barbarism within require not pity but the knife. What can society do to discharge its duty as trustee for posterity, to preserve the vigour of the race, and to raise the practicable ideals of Anglo-Saxons? If we are to become a healthy people, the permanent segregation of habitual criminals, paupers, drunkards, maniacs, and tramps must be deliberately undertaken.[105]

For eugenists, the solution to Britain's imperial problems lay in supplanting this race. Through rational reproduction a new healthy race might be bred. This, as I shall show, was how eugenic feminists conceived their contribution to the British empire.

While *Love and Eugenics in the Late Nineteenth Century* considers a number of men and women in the debates on gender and reproduction in the late nineteenth century, the central figures are Sarah Grand, George Egerton, and Mona Caird (see chapters on these authors for biographical detail). In different ways, Grand and Egerton combined

[104] Arnold White, *Efficiency and Empire* (1901, Brighton: Harvester Press, 1973), 95, 97, 96, 111, 100. White was equally exercised by immigrants, writing a piece in *The Times* on 13 July 1887, 'England for the English', in which he declared that 'the pauper foreigner' was 'successfully colonising Great Britain under the nose of H.M. Government'. Here, White was concerned mainly with Jewish immigrants. Links between national health and empire were emphasized in the wake of the early reverses of the British in the Second South African War. According to official army statistics that were revealed in 1903 in the *British Medical Journal*, of 679,703 men medically examined for enlistment between 1893 and 1902, 234,914 were rejected as medically unfit, or 34.6 per cent of the total. Of those accepted, some 5,849 'broke down within three months of enlistment' and another 14,259 were discharged as invalids within two years ('National Health and Military Service', 202, in Wohl, *Endangered Lives: Public Health in Victorian Britain* (London: Methuen, 1984), 332.

[105] White, *Efficiency and Empire*, 120.

their commitment to the social and political advancement of women with a belief in biological determinism and eugenics; while Caird adopted a radically different position, arguing for the historically rather than the biologically determined nature of social evolution, and sought to reveal the social biases that made up and motivated biological discourse.

The men and women I consider were connected in several ways. Engaged in the same debates, they were often brought into direct contact through their professional and political affiliations. The Victorians were polymaths, untrammelled by barriers of specialization; the biologist Grant Allen doubled as a prolific novelist, and even Karl Pearson and Galton wrote fiction,[106] while the New Women writers I discuss were well versed in science. Galton worked closely with Pearson, and he was tutored in mathematics at Cambridge by William Hopkins,[107] father of Ellice Hopkins, a leading member of the social purity movement. In 1885 Pearson founded the Men and Women's Club, which aimed at frank discussion of sexual matters. It was attended by several New Women: Olive Schreiner was one of its members and its associates included Caird and Emma Frances Brooke, Dr Elizabeth Blackwell, Jane Hume Clapperton, and Henrietta Muller.[108] Almost all the women involved were also active in philanthropy and feminist reform, serving on the London School Board, the Charity Organization Society, the Fabian Society, and women's suffrage societies.[109] Other societies in which the subjects of this study were involved included the Rational Dress Society, founded in 1881 by Mrs E. M. King, with Viscountess Harberton as president from 1883 (among

[106] Pearson wrote *The New Werther* (1880), a turbulent novel in celebration of solitary idealism, and *The Trinity: A Nineteenth-Century Passion-Play* (1882), an attack on orthodox Christianity. On Galton's fiction, which I discuss further in Ch. 4, see 'Kantsaywhere', in Pearson, *The Life, Letters, and Labours of Francis Galton*, 4 vols. (Cambridge: Cambridge University Press, 1914–30), iiia., 414–25.

[107] 'Memories' MS, 72. On Ellice Hopkins's own early association with scientists see *The Power of Womanhood; or, Mothers and Sons: A Book for Parents and Those in loco parentis* (London: Wells Gardner, Darton & Co. 1899), 156.

[108] See Lucy Bland, *Banishing the Beast, English Feminism & Sexual Morality* (1885–1914) (Harmondsworth: Penguin, 1995), esp ch. 1; and Walkowitz, *City of Dreadful Delight: Narratives of Sexual Danger in Late-Victorian London* (London: Virago, 1992), esp. ch. 5. The club disbanded in 1889.

[109] See Walkowitz, *City of Dreadful Delight*, 66; Annie Marie Turnball, 'So Extremely Like Parliament': The Work of Women Members of the London School Board, 1870–1904', in London Feminist History Group, *Sexual Dynamics of History: Men's Power, Women's Resistance* (London: Pluto, 1983); and Patricia Hollis, *Ladies Elect: Women in English Local Government, 1865–1914* (Oxford: Clarendon Press, 1987), 81.

its members were Sarah Grand, and Charlotte Stopes, Marie Stopes's mother); the Pioneer Club (an upper middle-class women's club founded in 1892 by Emily Massingberd and Wynford Philipps; Sarah Grand, Mona Caird, Jane Brownlow, and L. T. Meade were among its members); the National Council of Women, a non-party political organization founded in 1895; and the Legitimation League, which was founded in London in 1893 to promote the recognition of illegitimate children. About half of its members were women, and included Clapperton.[110] Among the publications of the Legitimation League were E. C. Walker's *What the Young Need to Know: A Primer of Sexual Rationality*, and the *University Magazine and Free Review*, edited by 'Democritus' and billed as 'of the rationalists'. Mona Caird was a member of the Personal Rights Association, established in 1871 by Josephine Butler and other Contagious Diseases Acts repealers as the Vigilance Association for the Defence of Personal Rights and for the Amendment of the Law in Points wherein it is Injurious to Women, and known (until the middle of the following decade) as the 'Vigilance Association'. The Association became increasingly hostile to the National Vigilance Association, the leading social purity organization.[111] In 1907 the feminist Sybil Neville-Rolfe (née Burney) (1886/7–1955),[112] founded the Eugenics Education Society (the Eugenics Society from 1912, and—since 1989—the Galton Institute), which aimed at promoting, in Galton's words, those agencies under social control that would lead to racial improvement. The society had close links with the Committee of the Moral Education League (founded in

[110] See L. Bland, *Banishing the Beast, Eugenic Feminism and Sexual Morality (1885-1914)* (Harmondsworth: Penguin, 1995), 156 and 172.

[111] See Ch. 8 for further discussion of this society. See also Bland, *Banishing the Beast*, ch. 3.

[112] Sybil was the daughter of Admiral Cecil Burney RN (b. 15 May 1858), son of Captain Charles Burney, and Lucinda Marion Burnett, daughter of George Richards Burnett, and granddaughter of Sir Robert Burnett of Mordon Hall, Surrey, a scion of the ancient Scottish family, the Burnetts of Leys. She remained a tireless campaigner for eugenics her whole life, and published *Why Marry?* (London: Faber and Faber, 1935), *Social Biology and Welfare, Together with a Handbook-appendix on Social Problems Edited by Ethel Grant* (London: George Allen & Unwin ltd, 1949) and *Sex in Social life* (London: Allen & Unwin, 1949). She was also centrally involved with the National Council for Combating Venereal Disease, founded in 1914 (in 1926 the title changed to the British Social Hygiene Council), acting as honorary secretary and secretary-general from its inception until her retirement in 1944. The organization worked closely with the Ministry of Health, and produced propaganda, promoting the educational side of VD prevention and sponsoring, for example, the films *Damaged Lives* and *The End of the Road*. For further details, see *Oxford Dictionary of National Biography* entry on Neville-Rolfe.

1898), whose motto was 'character is everything'.[113] In 1905 Galton gave the University of London £1500 to establish a Eugenics Record Office, and, until his death, £500 for eugenic research (Farrall, 1970, 131). The Record Office became known as the Galton Laboratory of National Eugenics. Other societies from which the Eugenics Society drew its members, which had also been founded in the late nineteenth century, included the Charity Organization Society, the Society for the Study of Inebriety (founded in 1884), and the National Association for the Care and Protection of the Feeble Minded (founded in 1896). These societies were united in their interest in the problem and management of pauperism, and they drew on the energies of the men and women of a new highly educated professional middle class. However, the Eugenics Education Society was distinguished from the rest of this middle-class activist network by its commitment to Galtonian hereditarianism: it saw class as a matter of heredity, and inherited defect as underlying all the problems associated with the residuum, including lack of character. For the Eugenics Education Society the solution to the problem of the residuum lay in the control of their excessive fertility, which it held that they were insufficiently responsible to manage themselves.[114] The society had three goals: to break down the 'present conspiracy of silence that envelops the subject of birth and parenthood' in children's education; to raise public opinion on questions of morality; and to 'strengthen public opinion against unhealthy marriages, and a wilful propagation of an unhealthy and suffering race'.[115] Many New Women, and, in particular, Sarah Grand, were already furthering these aims in their fiction and the press in the closing decades of the nineteenth century, as I shall show in later chapters.

Arnold White was among those who devoted himself to popularizing

[113] Mazumdar, *Eugenics, Human Genetics and Human Failings*, 24. By the end of 1907 the society had a staff of four, including a shorthand typist, and the annual report for 1908–9 shows a membership of 341 (ibid., 8), nearly 80 per cent of whom were eminent enough to be included in the *Dictionary of National Biography* (see Lyndsay A. Farrall, *The Origins and Growth of the English Eugenics Movement, 1865-1925* (New York: Garland, 1985). For a comprehensive study of the complex history and affiliations of the Eugenics Society, see, in particular, Mazumdar, ibid. See also Ian Brown, 'Who were the Eugenicists? A Study of the Formation of an Early Twentieth-century Pressure Group', *History of Education*, 17 (1988), 295–307; Greta Jones, *Social Hygiene in Twentieth Century Britain* (London: Croom Helm, 1986), 43–62; and MacKenzie, and membership lists of the Eugenics Society. See also F. Shenk and A. S. Parkes, 'The Activities of the Eugenics Society', *Eugenics Review*, 60 (1968), 142–61.

[114] Mazumdar, *Eugenics, Human Genetics and Human Failings*, 10, 23.

[115] Sybil Gotto, 'Scheme of Organization' (n.d.), Eugenics Society Papers, B1 cited in Mazumdar, ibid., 29.

the cause of eugenics, and Darwin's grandson Major Charles Darwin and the leading social purist Dame Mary Scharlieb were among the society's guides on policy. Links were established with France, Germany, Italy, and the USA, and in 1912 the society, with Neville-Rolfe a driving force, organized the first International Eugenics Congress, which was held in South Kensington under the auspices of London University. Neville-Rolfe records that the society concentrated its efforts on agitating for, and promoting, legislation advocated by the Royal Commission on the Care and Control of the Feeble-Minded, including the compulsory segregation of the 'feeble-minded' and she welcomed the passing of the Mental Deficiency Act of 1913 as 'a practical example of the value of a biological approach to social problems'.[116] By this year women outnumbered men among the society's members and associate members.[117] It remained closely associated with the New Woman, holding lectures on topics such as 'The New Woman and Race Progress', 'Eugenics and Womanhood', and 'The Biological Aspect of Women'.[118]

Several of the feminist and social reform organizations that were established in the late nineteenth century had their own periodicals, ranging from the radical *Personal Rights Journal* (founded in 1881 as the *Journal of the Vigilance Association for the Defence of Personal Rights*) to the *Vigilance Record* (launched in 1887 by the National Vigilance Association) and *The Adult*, founded in 1893 as the organ of the Legitimation League, to the *Eugenics Review* (founded in 1909 by the Eugenics Education Society). The issues of gender and reproduction were also debated in new feminist journals that burgeoned at the *fin de siècle*, such as *Young Woman* and *Woman's Signal*[119] as well as the

[116] Sybil Neville-Rolfe, *Social Biology and Welfare, Together with a Handbook-appendix on Social Problems Edited by Ethel Grant* (London: George Allen & Unwin ltd, 1949), 19. Neville-Rolfe remained the society's honorary secretary until 1920, after which she served on the society's council and as vice-president; she was then elected to the consultative council on which she served until her death.

[117] As Greta Jones notes, the strongest representation of all was in the provincial societies attached to the society. See Jones, 'Women and Eugenics in Britain: The Case of Mary Scharlieb, Elizabeth Sloan Chesser, and Stella Brown', *Annals of Science*, 52 (1995), 482.

[118] See, for example, the society's annual report, 1910–11, 34–5, cited in Kevles, *In the Name of Eugenics: Genetics and the Uses of Human Heredity* (Cambridge, Mass.: Harvard University Press, 1995), 317, n. 34.

[119] The *Young Woman* was founded in 1892 and edited by Frederick A. Atkins. *Woman's Signal* took over from *The Journal* in 1894, with Mrs Henry Somerset and Annie Holdsworth as editors. On feminist periodicals, see David Doughan and Denise Sanchez, (eds.), *Feminist Periodicals, 1855-1984* (Brighton: Harvester, 1987); see also Margaret Beetham and Kay Boardman (eds.), *Women's Magazines: An Anthology* (Manchester: Manchester University Press, 2001).

medical press and more mainstream journals, notably the *Contemporary Review*, and its more progressive counterparts the *Westminster Review* and the newer *Nineteenth Century*.[120] By the *fin de siècle* the Victorian periodical press had achieved a place of unprecedented importance in national social, political, and intellectual debate. It was the age of the sixpenny (or, increasingly, cheaper) magazine such as *Woman at Home*, half the price of existing middle-class monthlies, and catering to a rapidly expanding audience. According to the *Young Woman*, 'journals play a part in national life wholly undreamed of in the days when the realm of letters was governed by the *Edinburgh Review* and *Quarterly*'[121] and, in an Address to the Women Writers' Dinner in 1894, Mary Eliza Haweis remarked: 'the press is taking the place of the pulpit, the rostrum, the judgement seat'.[122] Karl Pearson noted in his essay, 'Woman and Labour' (1894) 'a study of the more advanced woman's journals, both of this country and of America shows how deeply thinking women are interested in the problems of heredity and of the parental responsibility for producing and rearing healthy human beings' (577).

The *fin de siècle* has been characterized as one of sexual anarchy, but the conflict between the sexes was only one part of the story. Another was the debates between the hereditarians and environmentalists, and it is this which is the focus of this study. Chapter 2 explores nineteenth-century discourse on the relation of women to nature and morality, tracing a link between the social purity movement and eugenic feminism, and Chapter 3 considers the emergence of a moral, and gendered, concept of citizenship which, in the wake of Darwin, became underpinned by the authority of biological discourse. Chapter 4 examines changing relations between science and romance, and the development of a new, rational model of reproduction. Chapters 5–8 focus on the expression of—and opposition to—eugenic ideas in fiction and the press by New Woman writers. Chapters 5 and 6 consider ways in which Sarah Grand sought through her writing to address feminist issues and urge the importance of rational reproduction which she saw as crucial to the

120 For an excellent account of the complexities of periodical debates and affiliations, which focuses on 1889, see Laurel Brake, 'Writing Women's History: The Sex Debates of 1889', in Ann Heilmann and Margaret Beetham (eds.), *New Woman Hybridities: Femininity, Feminism, and International Consumer Culture* (London: Routledge, 2004).

121 *Young Woman* (1892), cited in Cynthia White, *Women's Magazines, 1693–1968* (London: Michael Joseph, 1970), 59.

122 Mrs H. R. Haweis, *Words to Women: Addresses and Essays* (London: Burnet and Isbister, 1900), 69–70.

advancement of women. The polemical short-story writer George Egerton, whose work is a complex mixture of the radical and repressive, forms the focus of Chapter 7, and Chapter 8 explores the resistance to eugenics by the polemical humanitarian writer Mona Caird, examining ways in which she drew on ideas of the liberal radical John Stuart Mill, and the scientific ideas of Darwin (as he himself had expressed them), T. H. Huxley, and Peter Kropotkin. Considering the appeal of biological determinism as well as ways in which it was resisted, *Love and Eugenics in the Late Nineteenth Century* establishes the central role played by women in the popularization of eugenics in late Victorian and Edwardian Britain.

2 Women and Nature

> Equality is the mightiest of humbugs—there is no such thing in existence; and the idea of opening the professions and occupations and governments of men to women, seems to us the vainest as well as the vulgarest of chimeras. God has ordained visibly, by all the arrangements of nature and providence, one sphere and kind of work for a man and another for a woman. He has given them different constitutions, different organizations, a perfectly distinct and unmistakable identity.
>
> Margaret Oliphant[1]

> We are of two sexes: and in healthy diversity of sex, pushed to its utmost, lies the greatest strength of all of us. Make your men virile: make your women womanly.
>
> Grant Allen[2]

> To woman was committed 'the preservation of life, the conservation of type, the purity of race'.
>
> Frances Swiney[3]

> Love, birth, and death were all swaddled in a variety of fine phrases. The sexes drew further and further apart. No open conversation was tolerated.
>
> Virginia Woolf[4]

As the nineteenth century progressed, confusion over the social and political role of women was making waves on both sides of the Atlantic and biology was increasingly looked to for clarity and certainties. In 1887 the socialist feminist Annie Besant, who led the Match Girls Strike in Bow, London, the following year, a milestone in the march for equal pay, observed that there was among women a desire 'to emerge from a life

[1] Margaret Oliphant, 'The Condition of Women', *Blackwood's Edinburgh Magazine* 83 (1858), 139–54.

[2] Grant Allen, 'Plain Words on the Woman Question', *Popular Science Monthly*, 36 (1889), 179. The article was first published in the *Fortnightly Review*, 52 (1889) 448–58.

[3] Frances Swiney, *The Awakening of Women; or, Woman's Part in Evolution* (London: William Reeves, 1899), 85.

[4] Virginia Woolf, *Orlando: A Biography* (1928; London: Virago, 1993), 147.

crystallized around the idea of sex, and to find open to them careers other than dependence on a man as a wife or mistress'. She added, 'it is not that they desire to escape wholly from sexual ties, but that they would have those ties voluntarily assumed and not imposed by necessity'.[5] In 1888, an anonymous writer in the *Westminster Review* described the situation in Darwinian terms, pointing out that women would be affected by environmental change but confessing uncertainty as to what the precise effects might be:

> It is clear that women are in a time of transition. Transitions must come, but woe unto them to whom they come! They must ever be seasons of trial. As environment changes, the organism adapts itself or perishes. The change may be gradual and adaptation easy, or it may be swift and out of step with surrounding evolution—when the adaptation will be attended with effort and pain. How woman's environment has changed, research and observation tell us; how the change must be met, it is the work of deduction and experiment to show.[6]

A new and radical uncertainty was emerging. What constituted the nature of woman? What was her status and role? What difference did class make? What was the relationship of women to men, to education, labour, and citizenship? And what was her destiny? These questions, collectively known as the Woman Question, were fiercely debated and, as with the other most pressing question of the day, the problem of London's casual poor, they were underpinned by post-*Origin* preoccupations with social change, progress, and direction. In both cases biology was looked to for explanation and solution, but with the Woman Question, which cut across class divisions, the permutations were significantly more variable. The solution to the problem of poverty was simply to erase it, although how was less clear. The Woman Question was infinitely more complicated; biological and social measures presented themselves, but the questions were many and varied, and the answers even greater in number.

Several competing narratives emerged. One was that men and women were fundamentally, innately, different, and that social organization was an expression of this fundamental and fixed biological difference. Within this framework, sex difference was *naturalized* and feminism, the

[5] Annie Besant, 'The Economic Position of Women', *Our Corner*, 10 (1887), 99. Cf. 'A Woman of the Day' who suggested in the *Saturday Review* in 1895 that women were less inclined to be a 'mere breeding machine', quoted in Richard Allen Soloway, *Birth Control and the Population Question in England, 1877–1930* (Chapel Hill: North Carolina University Press, 1982), 135.

[6] 'Female Poaching on Male Preserves', *Westminster Review*, 129 (1888), 290–7.

sexual and social emancipation of women, was a violation of the natural order, challenging, as it did, women's central reproductive function. The second position held that social fixity was the result of social rather than biological organization. This position fed both a progressive argument in favour of social change, and a conservative argument that, given the mutable nature of human nature, social change might have undesired mental and psychological effects. A third position argued that sex and society were biologically determined, but that change might be induced through biological rather than social means. This position lent support to the idea that feminism might work *with* rather than against nature, intervening in the process of biological evolution in order to alter biological destiny: this was eugenic feminism.

NATURE AND THE SURPLUS

The census of 1851 had revealed that nearly one half of the adult women in Britain had no spouse to support them, giving a 'surplus', as it was termed, of 400,000.[7] In the same year the *Journal of Psychological Medicine and Mental Pathology* expressed fears that would proliferate over the following decades, namely that there was a growing imbalance in the class and sex make-up of society, with the poor surviving in greater numbers, and a surplus of women: 'more than two million unmarried [women], of whom only one in seventeen is married annually'.[8] The anonymous author supported his premiss that 'whatever may be said of the *rights* of woman, it is her allotted *duty* to marry and bear children' by a forceful appeal to nature:

> the order of nature is, that the woman shall be devoted to the cares of maternity and the domestic duties of life; the order of society is, that millions shall have no husband, and therefore, legitimately, no children . . . the order of nature seems to be, that as maternal cares occupy the woman exclusively, her sustenance and

[7] Judith Worsnop, 'A Re-evaluation of "the Problem of Surplus Women" in 19th-century England: The Case of the 1851 Census', *Women's Studies International Forum*, 13 (1990), 21–31. On contemporary response to the surplus, and its relation to conceptions of middle-class femininity, see Poovey, *Uneven Developments: The Ideological Work of Gender in Mid-Victorian England* (London: Virago, 1989), esp. chs. 1 and 5. For one early response to the surplus woman question, see Margaret Oliphant, 'The Condition of Women', *Blackwood's Edinburgh Magazine*, 83 (1858) 139–54.

[8] Anon., 'Woman in her Psychological Relations', *Journal of Psychological Medicine and Mental Pathology*, 4 (1851), 42. To have published in a medical journal at this time the author is likely to have been male.

protection, and the sustenance and protection of her children, should devolve upon man; the order of society deprives millions of women of a mate and a protector.[9]

The position of women in society was increasingly considered in terms of what was natural. By extension and association, surplus women, cut off from their ordained social and sexual duties, were themselves perceived to be unnatural, pathologized, labelled 'odd', the latter term neatly conflating excess with abnormality, pathology, even. In 'Why are Women Redundant?' (1862) in the *National Review*, W. R. Greg stressed that the surplus was unnatural, and that nature should be consulted for ways to restore a natural balance. Recommending that surplus women be shipped off to the colonies, where they were in short supply, he remarked: 'nature makes no mistakes and creates no redundancies. Nature, honestly and courageously interrogated, gives no erroneous or ambiguous replies'.[10] Such conservative reactions were shared by women. Ellice Hopkins, doyenne of social purity, lamented, 'Nature has carefully provided for the equality of the sexes by sending rather more boys than girls into the world, since fewer boys are reared; but we have managed to derange this order.'[11]

In 1865, Charlotte Yonge explored the question of the surplus in her novel *The Clever Woman of the Family*, focusing on the struggles and successes of seven single—or widowed—women in a small seaside community. The numerical imbalance, and its literary appeal, persisted, with Rhoda Nunn in George Gissing's *The Odd Women* (1893), declaring 'so many *odd* women—no making a pair with them. The pessimists call them useless, lost, futile lives. I, naturally—being one of them myself—take another view. I look upon them as a great reserve.'[12] *Tess of the D'Urbervilles* (1891) alludes more obliquely to the surplus: as Tess peels buds known as 'lords and ladies' she concludes 'there are always more

9 Anon., 'Woman in her Psychological Relations', 42.

10 W. R. Greg, 'Why are Women Redundant?', *National Review*, 14 (1862), 459. The census report of 1861 saw the unequal ratio as the result of male emigration. Worsnop writes: 'it would seem that this article was written in response to the flood of writings by women in the years 1859 through 1861': 'A Re-evaluation of "The Problem of Surplus Women" in 19th-century England: The Case of the 1851 Census', 27. As Mary Poovey notes, Greg conceived of the sexual double standard as inevitable, on account of male irrepressible sexual desire, and urged for women to be removed to the colonies to reduce prostitution.

11 Ellice Hopkins, *The Power of Womanhood; or, Mothers and Sons: A Book for Parents and Those* in loco parentis (London: Wells Gardner, Darton & Co., 1899), 154.

12 George Gissing, *The Odd Women* (1893; Harmondsworth: Penguin, 1993), 41, emphasis in original.

ladies than lords when you come to peel them'.[13] By this year, 4.5 million (out of 13 million) women were in the workforce,[14] 2 million in domestic service, 1.5 million in textiles and clothing, 264,000 in the professions (teachers and nurses), and 80,000 in agriculture.[15] The Tory *Quarterly Review* lamented in 1894 'women are now graduates in half a dozen professions, and disciples in all. They practise medicine as well as novel-writing; the forceps is familiar to them no less than the bicycle; even dress-cutting advertises itself as "scientific" at six guineas the course.'[16]

For many, there was much to gain from the surplus. Just as sheer weight of numbers lay behind the Malthusian idea of existence as struggle, which inspired Darwin's theory of natural selection, so the surplus of women led to the creation of new discourses on femininity and contributed directly to feminism. In the mid-century, single working-class women were increasingly employed in manufacturing or domestic service, but social decorum, at odds with economic realities, held that middle-class women should not work to support themselves. Thus, the surplus woman question was conceived as an essentially middle-class problem. It was deployed by radical women as an argument for the necessity of training and employment for women. The Langham Place circle, active from the mid-1850s to 1870 and led by Bessie Parkes (1829–1925), Barbara Bodichon (1827–1891), and Emily Davies (1831–1921), organized the Victoria Press, the Female Middle-Class Emigration Society, and the Society for Promoting the Employment of Women (SPEW).[17] In the words of the political economist Harriet Martineau, writing in 1859:

> A social organization framed for a community of which half stayed at home, while the other half went out to work, cannot answer the purposes of a society, of which a quarter remains at home while three quarters go out to work. This seems clear enough. It does not follow that extensive changes in the law are

[13] T. Hardy, *Tess of the D'Urbervilles* (1891; Harmondsworth: Penguin, 1986), 182.

[14] For agitation for changes in legislation, see Matilda Blake, 'Are Women Protected?', *Westminster Review*, 137 (1892), 43–8; 'The Lady and the Law', *Westminster Review*, 137 (1892), 364–70. See Davin, 'Imperialism and Motherhood', *History Workshop*, 5 (1978), 23, for proposals for the 'endowment of motherhood.' In 1911 a maternity insurance was incorporated in health provisions.

[15] Janet Howarth, 'Gender, Domesticity, and Sexual Politics', in Colin Matthew (ed.), *The Nineteenth Century: The British Isles 1815–1901* (Oxford: Oxford University Press, 2000), 184–5.

[16] William Barry, 'The Strike of a Sex', *Quarterly Review*, 179 (1894), 294.

[17] See Cadida Lacey (ed.), *Barbara Leigh Smith Bodichon and the Langham Place Group* (London: Routledge & Kegan Paul, 1987).

needed; or that anybody is called upon to revolutionize his thoughts or his proceedings. The natural laws of society will do whatever has to be done, when once recognized and allowed to act. They will settle all considerable social points,—all the controversies of the labour-market, and the strifes about consideration and honour.[18]

At the century's close, Lady Jeune praised the positive effects which the surplus had on female nature in *The Modern Marriage Market* (1897):

in a community where the female element is largely in excess of the male, and where modern thought and education have raised them intellectually on a more equal basis, it was not possible for women to remain the colourless, dependent creatures of the past. And as they have become emancipated they have more or less chosen their own careers, and thousands of women are now living proofs of the advantages of a change that has given them an aim in life which they can pursue successfully.[19]

In her study *Women in Transition* (1907), the British feminist and travel writer Annette Meakin perceived a clear connection between superfluity and feminism: 'as the family could no longer support the steadily increasing number of superfluous members and endeavoured to push them off, the Woman Question arose'. She urged that it was not the unmarried state *per se* but economic factors that caused unhappiness among surplus women, and called into question the prohibitive theories of 'medical men' and 'plodding and conscientious biologists'.[20]

Support for the emancipation of women did not fall neatly into gendered camps but persisted among freethinking radicals of both sexes. There had been a degree of male support for female emancipation and enfranchisement from early in the century. For example, during the 1820s and 1830s Owenite Socialists, inspired by Mary Wollstonecraft and Robert Owen, argued that the abolition of private property would end the status of women as property. John Stuart Mill introduced female suffrage into the Representation of the People Bill that would become the Second Reform Act in 1867, suggesting that the clause containing the term 'man' be amended to read 'person'. *Punch* was horrified, reacting

[18] Harriet Martineau, 'Female Industry', *Edinburgh Review*, 109 (1859), 293–336. See also the 'Report of the Society for Promoting the Employment of Women,' *English Woman's Journal* 8 (1861), 73–5.

[19] Marie Corelli, Flora Annie Steel, Lady Jeune, and Susan, Countess of Malmesbury, *The Modern Marriage Market* (London: Hutchinson & Co. 1897), 70–1.

[20] Annette Meakin, *Women in Transition* (London: Methuen, 1907), 13.

with articles such as 'Shall Lovely Woman Vote?'[21] So were a number of liberal women.[22] The amendment was defeated by 196 votes to 73. In 1869, Mill published his trenchant plea for female enfranchisement, *The Subjection of Women*.[23]

THE BIOLOGY OF MORALITY

Over the course of the nineteenth century the sexes were increasingly differentiated along biological lines.[24] In the early decades, some medical men had argued in favour of female education for preserving and developing female mental strength. The phrenologist and physician Andrew Combe had urged that middle-class women were most at risk to 'mental sloth and nervous weakness'[25] for want of mental exertion; he warned

[21] See, for example, 'Womanhood Suffrage', *Punch* (30 March 1867); 'Shall Lovely Woman Vote?', *Punch*, 4 May 1867, and 'Mill's Logic; or, Franchise for Females', *Punch* (1 June 1867).

[22] On the complexities of responses to female suffrage, see Martin Pugh, *The March of the Women. A Revisionist Analysis of the Campaign for Women's Suffrage, 1866–1914* (Oxford: Oxford University Press, 2000), ch. 6. See also Brian Harrison, *Separate Spheres. The Opposition to Women's Suffrage in Britain* (London: Croom Helm, 1978). For an exemplary discussion of the complex relation between citizenship, nationhood, and empire, see Catherine Hall, Keith McClelland, and Jane Rendall, *Defining the Victorian Nation: Class, Race, Gender and the Reform Act of 1867* (Cambridge: Cambridge University Press, 2000).

[23] On the influence of Mill, see, for example, T. Stanton (ed.), *The Woman Question in Europe* (London: G. P. Putnam's Sons, 1884), 377–8.

[24] See Thomas Laqueur, *Making Sex: Body and Gender from the Greeks to Freud* (Cambridge, Mass. and London: Harvard University Press, 1990). Laqueur argues for a gradual shift from a one-sex model of humanity, which held that the sexes were on a continuum, and that woman was merely an inferior version of man, to a two-sex model which held that the sexes were fundamentally different. See also Angus McLaren, 'The Pleasures of Procreation: Traditional and Biomedical Theories of conception', W. F. Bynum and Roy Porter (eds.), *William Hunter and the Eighteenth-Century Medical World* (Cambridge: Cambridge University Press, 1985), 323–41. On the gendered biases of science, see Cynthia Eagle Russett, *Sexual Science: The Victorian Construction of Womanhood* (1989; Cambridge, Mass. and London: Harvard University Press, 1991); and Londa Schiebinger, *Nature's Body, Sexual Politics and the Making of Modern Science* (London: Pandora, 1993); and *The Mind has No Sex? Women and the Origins of Modern Science* (Cambridge, Mass. and London: Harvard University Press, 1989).

[25] Andrew Combe, *Observations on Mental Derangement: Being an Application of the Principles of Phrenology to the Elucidation of the Causes, Symptoms, Nature, and Treatment of Insanity* (Edinburgh: John Aderson, 1831), 116, repr. in Jenny Bourne Taylor and Sally Shuttleworth (eds.), *Embodied Selves: An Anthology of Psychological Texts, 1830–1890* (Oxford: Oxford University Press, 1998), 43.

against a system of 'ill-directed education' which led to 'nothing more solid than mere accomplishments' and brains which were 'half asleep'.[26] However, in the second half of the nineteenth century, as various reforms in education[27] threatened to undermine 'separate spheres' for men and women—the central tenet of Victorian domestic ideology, embodied by Dickens's Esther Summerson in *Bleak House*, with her self-effacing narrative voice and jangling house keys—conservative arguments in support of natural difference intensified. A new biology of sex was emerging, in opposition to campaigns for social equality. Herbert Spencer argued that excessive education was detrimental to a woman's reproductive health.[28] In the *Descent of Man*, Darwin came out in support of fundamental sex difference, positing that 'with woman the powers of intuition, of rapid perception, and perhaps of imitation, are more strongly marked than in man', powers which he considered inferior, while man, by contrast, was 'more courageous, pugnacious, and energetic' with 'a more energetic genius'.[29] In spite of his earlier emphasis in the *Origin* on change and mutability, his study of humans offered no challenge to sexual stereotyping. Nonetheless, Darwin did not rule out possibilities for social change; it was his followers who became increasingly inflexible.

In 1874 the debates over biology and female education received a transatlantic fillip with the publication of *Sex in Education* by the Harvard physician Edward H. Clarke. *Sex in Education* offered an emphatic warning that girls were reaching breaking point on account of intellectual work—a warning which was developed by the neurologist Henry Maudsley in the *Fortnightly Review*. Arguing that there was 'sex in mind as distinctly as there is sex in body', Maudsley stated categorically, 'sex is fundamental, lies deeper than culture, cannot be ignored or defied

[26] Combe, *Observations*, 17, in Bourne Taylor and Shuttleworth, *Embodied Selves*, 43. See Russett, *Sexual Science*, 19–22, on the support of phrenologists for female education.

[27] See Carol Dyhouse, *Girls Growing Up in Late Victorian and Edwardian England* (London: Routledge & Kegan Paul; Boston Mass., Broadway House, 1981); Felicity Hunt (ed.), *Lessons for Life, the Schooling of Girls and Women, 1850–1950* (Oxford: Basil Blackwell, 1987); Joan Burstyn, *Victorian Education and the Ideal of Womanhood* (London: Croom Helm, 1980); Jane McDermid, 'Women and Education', in Jane Purvis (ed.), *Women's History in Britain*, 1850–1945 (London: UCL Press, 1995). For a comprehensive treatment of women in higher education, see Dyhouse, *No Distinction of Sex? Women in British Universities 1870–1939* (London: UCL Press, 1995).

[28] H. Spencer, *Education: Intellectual, Moral, and Physical* (London: Williams & Norgate, 1861), 186–8.

[29] *The Descent of Man, and Selection in Relation to Sex*, 2 vols. (1871; Chichester: Princeton University Press, 1981), ii. 326–7.

with impunity'.[30] He made America an example of the ill effects of educating girls along the same lines as boys,[31] and, quoting Clarke, warned that if the strain of education on the 'reproductive apparatus and its functions' were to continue at the present rate 'the Sons of the New World will have to re-act, on a magnificent scale, the old story of unwived Rome and the Sabines'.[32] Elizabeth Garrett Anderson, a defining voice in the campaigns for women's access to higher education and the professions, especially medicine, and the first female member of the British Medical Association, offered a cogent reply to these views, but the arguments against educating women on grounds of biology, and support for the idea of fundamental differences between the sexes, intensified in the late nineteenth century.[33] Cesare Lombroso pronounced with authority in the *Contemporary Review*, a publication with an established Christian outlook: 'in figure, in size of brain, in strength, in intelligence, woman comes nearer to the animal and the child'; he proceeded to emphasize her reproductive function and value: 'on the other hand in the distribution of the hair, in the shape of the pelvis, she is certainly more highly developed than man'.[34]

For those who saw differences between the sexes as fundamental, the erosion of difference was not only unnatural, but could be seen as an evolutionary falling away from a higher organization. Sexual differentiation was

[30] Henry Maudsley, 'Sex in Mind and Education', *Fortnightly Review*, 21 (1874), 468, 477. This marks a departure in Maudsley's thinking; he had warned earlier of the dangers of nurturing feminine passivity, reminding his readers in *The Physiology and Pathology of Mind* (1867) that women were the moral and physiological guardians of future generations: see Taylor and Shuttleworth (eds.), *Embodied Selves*, 379.

[31] Maudsley drew on the authority of the American physiologist Weir Mitchell. Charlotte Perkins Gilman underwent Mitchell's 'rest cure' and emphasizes its debilitating effects in her short story 'The Yellow Wall-paper'. See 'The Yellow Wallpaper' and 'Why I Wrote the Yellow Wallpaper', in Angelique Richardson (ed.), *Women Who Did: Stories by Men and Women, 1890–1914* (Harmondsworth: Penguin, 2002), 31–47; 398–9. Sarah Grand also underwent the Weir Mitchell treatment; see Ann Heilmann and Stephanie Forward (eds.), *Sex, Social Purity and Sarah Grand*, 3 vols. (London: Routledge, 2001), ii. 2, 7.

[32] E. H. Clarke, *Sex in Education, or, a fair Chance for Girls* (Boston, Mass., 1874), quoted by Maudsley, 'Sex in Mind and Education', 474.

[33] For a further negative response to female education, see Eliza Lynn Linton, 'The Higher Education of Woman', *Fortnightly Review* 40 (1886). On male and female differences see, for example, James McGrigor Allan (anthropologist), 'On the Real Differences in the Minds of Men and Women', *Anthropological Review*, 7 (1869), 195–219; Benjamin Ward Richardson (physician, 1828–96), 'Woman's Work in Creation', *Longman's*, 8 (1886), 604–19; George Romanes (evolutionist and popularizer of Darwin's ideas, 1848–94), 'Mental Differences Between Men and Women', *Nineteenth Century*, 21 (1887), 654–72; Harry Campbell, *Differences in the Nervous Organization of Man and Woman, Physiological and Pathological* (London: Lewis, 1891); and Henry Havelock Ellis, *Man and Woman: A Study of Human Sexual Secondary Characters* (London: Walter Scott Ltd, 1894).

[34] Cesare Lombroso, 'Atavism and Evolution', *Contemporary Review*, 63 (July 1895), 48.

increasingly seen as a marker of evolutionary *progress*; humans had left hermaphroditism behind. In 1878, *Popular Science Monthly* reported:

> among the humbler groups of the animal kingdom the whole reproductive task is performed by all members of the species. In other words hermaphroditism prevails. As we ascend to higher groups the sexes are separate, and the species becomes dimorphous.[35]

Within this framing, a healthy body was a biologically distinctive one and a natural sphere was a separate one. As Darwin wrote in the *Descent*, 'some extremely remote progenitor of the whole vertebrate kingdom appears to have been hermaphrodite or androgynous'. The Darwinian idea that development might move in a direction that could be conceived as backward—that humans might reel back to their primordial ancestors—posed a terrifying threat to the Victorian narrative of progress, and proved an equally forceful argument to wield against female emancipation. Grant Allen observed 'the lower animals in every great group are, almost without exception, hermaphrodites: the first comer of their kind, without distinction of sex, suffices to satisfy them'.[36] Sexual proximity suggested a reversal of progress—a form of regression. Maudsley argued that the undoing of sex differences would be the undoing of history itself: 'does it not appear that in order to assimilate the female to the male mind it would be necessary to undo the life-history of mankind from its earliest commencement?'[37]

In 1891 the philosopher and barrister Frederic Harrison, George Eliot's friend, denounced the idea of sexual proximity: 'androgynous ignorance has gone about claiming for women a life of toil, pain, and danger' for which 'every husband, every biologist, every physician, every mother—every true woman—knows that women are, by the law of nature, unfit', and concluded: 'to leave women free to go about, in men's clothes and men free to adopt women's clothes would be to introduce unimaginative coarseness, vice, and brutalization'. He urged the need to 'hold fast by the organic difference implanted by Nature between Man and Woman.'[38] In 'Plain Words on the Woman Question', Allen warned that emancipation would leave woman 'a dulled and spiritless epicene

[35] Anon., 'Our Six-Footed Rivals', *Popular Science Monthly*, 12 (1878), quoted in Cynthia Eagle Russett, *Sexual Science*, 136.

[36] Grant Allen, 'Is it Degradation? A Reply to Professor Mivart', *Humanitarian*, 9 (1896), 344.

[37] 'Sex in Mind and Education', *Fortnightly Review*, 21 (1874), 471.

[38] 'The Emancipation of Women', *Fortnightly Review*, 56 (1891), 444.

automaton', observing that healthy girls who embarked upon higher education ('mannish training') became unattractive and unsexed; 'both in England and America, the women of the cultivated classes are becoming unfit to be wives or mothers. Their sexuality (which lies at the basis of everything) is enfeebled or destroyed.'[39] He warned in the *Universal Review* that the 'girl of the future' would soon be 'as flat as a pancake' and 'as dry as a broomstick';[40] a stark contrast to the buxom women who people Galton's eugenic romance, 'Kantsaywhere'. Allen couched his arguments in terms at once feminist and nationalist, arguing that it was women's *racial* duty to liberate themselves from social convention and follow natural dictates—a line that some of his female compatriots, notably George Egerton, would also pursue:

> I am an enthusiast on the Woman Question. Indeed, so far am I from wishing to keep her in subjection to man, that I should like to see her a great deal more emancipated than she herself as yet at all desires. Only, her emancipation must not be of a sort that interferes in any way with this prime natural necessity. To the end of all time, it is mathematically demonstrable that most women must become the mothers of at least four children, or else the race must cease to exist.[41]

For Karl Pearson 'the race must degenerate if greater and greater stress be brought to force woman during the years of child-bearing into active and unlimited compeitition with man'.[42] In 1904, the year of an official inquiry into the physical deterioration of the British race, the *British Medical Journal* remarked that women were becoming masculine through cycling, playing golf, hockey, and other sports, 'which increased her muscles while diminishing her pelvis'.[43] And, as the sun set on Edwardian England, the social purist Mary Scharlieb warned against the effect of learning on the constitution of girls, fearing it would lead to nervous disorders.[44]

Fears of the masculinization of women were accompanied by a corresponding fear of effeminacy in men: both were expressions of degeneration. Both the manly woman and the womanly man were an affront to

[39] Grant Allen, 'Plain Words on the Woman Question', *Popular Science Monthly*, 36 (1889), 179.

[40] Allen, 'The Girl of the Future', *Universal Review*, 7 (1890), 57.

[41] Allen, 'Plain Words on the Woman Question', 173.

[42] 'Woman and Labour', *Fortnightly Review*, 61 (1894), 569–70. See, also Mary Scharlieb, 'Adolescent Girlhood under Modern Conditions', *Eugenics Review*, I (1909), 183.

[43] *British Medical Journal* (5 March 1904), 578, quoted in Richard Soloway, *Birth Control and the Population Question in England, 1877–1930* (Chapel Hill: North Carolina University Press, 1982), 146.

[44] Mary Scharlieb, 'Adolescent Girlhood under Modern Conditions', *Eugenics Review*, I (1909), 183.

evolutionary progress, and to civilization. In *Confidential Talks with Husband and Wife: A Book of Information and Advice for the Married and the Marriageable* (1900) Lyman B. Sperry grouped effeminates with other degenerates whom he declared to be anathema to social or racial progress:

> eunuchs, effeminates and the sexually abused and mutilated are, in the nature of things, mentally and morally defective; they are cynical, selfish, grovelling and unfit for the kingdom of God,—certainly in so far as that kingdom relates to this world.[45]

However, some opposition to these ideas also continued throughout the second half of the century. In 1869, in *The Subjection of Women*, Mill exposed the social and political underpinnings of discourses on the natural: 'what is now called the nature of women is an eminently artificial thing—the result of forced repression in some directions, unnatural stimulation in others' (238). Hardy, a follower of Mill, likewise spoke out against the new emphasis on sexual difference in *Desperate Remedies* (1871), his story of lesbian and heterosexual love, remarking: 'in spite of a fashion which pervades the whole community at the present day—the habit of exclaiming that woman is not undeveloped man, but diverse, the fact remains that, after all, women are Mankind, and that in many of the sentiments of life the difference of sex is but a difference of degree'.[46] And, as I shall show in Chapter 8, Mona Caird too provided an important voice of opposition, drawing on evolutionary biology to argue against fundamental sex difference. In her short story of 1891, 'The Yellow Drawing Room', Vanora Haydon stands in direct opposition to the Victorian ideal of separate spheres. When the narrator warns her: 'The sacred realms where woman is queen will soon be forbidden to you if you consistently continue to think and act in disharmony with the feminine nature and genius', she responds: 'I rather prefer the realms where woman is *not* queen', adding: 'my father never sought to arrange a "sphere" for me, and in my case instinct seems at fault'.[47]

[45] Sperry, *Confidential Talks with Husband and Wife, A Book of Information and Advice for the Married and the Marriageable* (Edinburgh and London: Oliphant, Anderson and Ferrier, 1990) 21.

[46] *Desperate Remedies* (1871; Penguin, 1998), 183.

[47] In A. Richardson (ed.), *Women Who Did*, 26.

THE BIOLOGY OF MORALITY

Women had long been associated with moral virtue in evangelical and medical discourse.[48] In 1803 the medical doctor William Buchan, author of the popular handbook *Domestic Medicine; or, A Treatise on the Prevention and Cure of Diseases* (1772), remarked in his *Advice to Mothers* 'the more I reflect on the situation of a mother, the more I am struck with the extent of her powers, and the inestimable value of her services. In the language of love, women are called angels.'[49] Likewise, Sarah Lewis's highly influential *Woman's Mission* (1839), based on *De l'éducation des mères de famille, ou la civilisation du genre humain par les femmes* (1834) by Louis Aimé Martin, a follower of Rousseau, defined women as morally superior, arguing that they belonged firmly in the domestic sphere where it was their duty to exert a special feminine power through maternal influence.[50] With its broad transatlantic readership, *Woman's Mission* helped to shape and reinforce separate sphere ideology.[51]

As ideological discourses on the biomedical determinants of social relations grew, morality was *biologized* as the basis of morality was altered from 'duty' or mission to 'instinct'. In 1851 the author of 'Woman in her Psychological Relations' declared:

> the relations of woman are twofold; material and spiritual—corporeal and moral. By her corporeal nature she is the type and model of BEAUTY, by her spiritual of GRACE, by her moral, of LOVE.[52]

Purity was so innate in women, he urged, that in even the most abandoned specimen 'the natural sentiment of modesty does not appear to be banished'. Empirical research in the brothels of Paris led him to conclude that 'the instinct to love, in all its relations, is very strong'; even the most brutalized of women are still, by virtue of their biology, 'singularly kind

[48] On evangelical attitudes to femininity, see Jocelyn Murray, 'Gender Attitudes and the Contribution of Women to Evangelism and Ministry in the Nineteenth Century', in John Wolfe (ed.), *Evangelical Faith and Public Zeal: Evangelicals and Society in Britain, 1780–1980* (London: SPCK, 1995).

[49] William Buchan, *Advice to Mothers on the Subject of their own Health and on the Means of Promoting the Health, Strength and Beauty of their Offspring* (1803; Boston: J. Bumstead, 1809), 7.

[50] Elizabeth K. Helsinger, Robin Lauterbach Sheets, and William Veeder, *The Woman Question, Society and Literature in Britain and America 1837–1883*, 3 vols. (Chicago: Chicago University Press, 1983), i. 6.

[51] Within three years it went through ten editions in Britain and four in America, with another seven editions in Britain by 1854.

[52] Anon., 'Woman in her Psychological Relations', 18.

and charitable to each other'. Biology determined and ensured female virtue: 'the bust expresses the sentiment of love'[53]. If women were biologically moral, charitable, and kind, then what was considered their moral 'duty' was really their biological 'instinct'. As I shall show in the chapters that follow, this viewpoint gained medical and more general credence as the century progressed.[54] By the time of the *Descent*, Darwin observed:

> woman seems to differ from man in mental disposition, chiefly in her greater tenderness and less selfishness; and this holds good even with savages ... Woman, owing to her maternal instincts, displays these qualities towards her fellow-creatures.[55]

SOCIAL PURITY AND SEXUAL SELECTION

The idea of rational reproduction has its origins in the social purity movement which developed apace in the 1880s. Prior to this, feminist energies had been focused on the campaign to repeal the Contagious Diseases Acts (CDA) of 1864, 1866, and 1869, which began in the late 1860s under the leadership of Josephine Butler. These acts were introduced as exceptional legislation to control the spread of venereal disease in garrison towns and ports. Demanding the registration and compulsory examination of suspected female prostitutes in these areas, the acts effectively gave state backing to the sexual double standard, legitimizing male promiscuity. They were repealed in 1886. By this time the social purity movement, a loose association of religious and moral crusaders, had become increasingly interventionist, adopting a new, more coercive, policy towards the residuum, and becoming more likely to use the instruments of the state to enforce their moral code.[56] Following W. T.

[53] Anon., 'Woman in her Psychological Relations', 43. See Poovey, *Uneven Developments*, ch. 1, on the early nineteenth-century association of women with moral virtue, and its centrality to the consolidation of middle-class power, as virtue was increasingly articulated on gender rather than inherited class position. Poovey also explores the coexistence of this idea with contradictory conceptions of female sexuality.

[54] See, for example, *Woman and her Era*, by the American feminist reformer Eliza W. Farnham. Farnham argued that women were meant to occupy a higher station from which their moral influence would shape the course of events. She concluded with the assertion that 'Man is the degrader of the Love-relations; Woman their elevator', Eliza W. Farnham, *Woman and her Era*, 2 vols. (New York, 1864), ii. 75, quoted in Helsinger, *et al.*, *The Woman Question*, ii. 203.

[55] Darwin, *Descent*, ii. 326.

[56] See Bland, *Banishing the Beast, English Feminism & Sexual Morality* (1885–1914) (Harmondsworth: Penguin, 1995), 97; and Judith Walkowitz, *Prostitution and Victorian*

Stead's sensational exposure of juvenile prostitution, or 'white slavery', in the *Pall Mall Gazette* earlier that year,[57] the 1885 Criminal Law Amendment Act was passed. It raised the law of consent from 13—to which it had been raised in 1875—to 16, and reformed the law on sexual assault. The act was hedged with moral opprobrium, coming down harshly on brothels and prostitutes and criminalizing 'acts of gross indecency' between men. While it was supposed to raise the age of consent, in practice it was directed at working-class sexual behaviour.[58] A National Vigilance Association was formed with the initial function of ensuring the local enforcement of the act, but, in keeping with the increasingly hostile approach to working-class culture that was developing in the 1880s, it turned its attention to burning 'obscene' books, and attacking music halls, theatres, and bogus registration offices.[59] Social purity groups began to distribute prescriptive literature on morals and child-rearing.[60]

Leading figures in this movement were Ellice Hopkins (1836–1904), Frances Swiney (1847–1922), Laura Ormiston Chant (1848–1923), and Sarah Grand. Hopkins published *The Power of Womanhood; or, Mothers and Sons: A Book for Parents and Those in loco parentis* (1899) and countless didactic pamphlets on social purity, including 'On the Early Training

Society: Women, Class, and the State (Cambridge: Cambridge University Press, 1980), 251. Walkowitz offers an excellent account of the repeal of the CDA. For an informative treatment of the response to venereal disease from 1870 in Britain and several other European countries, which explores links between VD control, colonialism, and imperialism, see Roger Davidson and Lesley Hall (eds.), *Sex, Sin and Suffering, Venereal Disease and European Society since 1870* (London and New York: Routledge, 2001). The collection also explores ways in which a new preventative public health response had notably different national histories. In Britain the First World War Royal Commission on VD led to the institution of a clinic system based on voluntary, open, and confidential access; in France, by contrast, police regulation of prostitution continued until 1960. For an account of how fears about the effect of venereal disease on the family led physicians in the USA to ally with the nascent eugenics movement in the first decades of the twentieth century, see Allan Brandt, *No Magic Bullet* (New York and Oxford: Oxford University Press, 1987), esp. ch. 1. For an interpretation of the American social purity movement, see David Pivar, *Purity Crusade: Sexual Morality and Social Control, 1868–1900* (Westport, Conn: Greenwood Press, 1973).

57 Stead, 'Maiden Tribute of Modern Babylon', *Pall Mall Gazette* (6 July 1885).

58 Walkowitz, *Prostitution*, 250.

59 Ibid., 251, and W. A. Coote, *A Romance of Philanthropy: Being a Record of Some of the Principal Incidents Connected with the Exceptionally Successful Thirty Years of the National Vigilance Association* (London, 1916), chs. 2–9.

60 On opposition to the repressive elements of this movement, from, among others, Josephine Butler, see Walkowitz, *Prostitution*, 252. Walkowitz also notes the latent coercive impulses of the Butlerite feminists in their responses to working-class girls (249).

of Girls and Boys' (1882), and 'The Purity Movement' (1886); she established a number of social purity groups, including the White Cross Society, which solicited pledges of chastity from young men. Swiney wrote several books on the role played by women in evolutionary development, including *The Awakening of Women; or, Woman's Part in Evolution* (1899) and *The Cosmic Procession; or, the Feminine Principle in Evolution* (1906). She was president of the Cheltenham branch of the National Union of Women's Suffrage Societies, vice-president of the Cheltenham Food Reform and Health Association, a member of the Women's Branch of the Malthusian League from 1904, and, from 1907, a leading light in the theosophist group 'The League of Isis'. Chant led a successful opposition in 1894 to the renewal of the Leicester Square Empire Theatre's licence, on the grounds that it was frequented by soliciting prostitutes. She was editor of the *Vigilance Record* and author of the White Cross League pamphlet 'Chastity in Men and Women' (1895),[61] which found later resonance in Cristabel Pankhurst's *The Great Scourge and How to End it; or, Plain Facts About a Great Evil* (1913), with its slogan 'Votes for Women and Chastity for Men'.

While the purity movement gained its early impetus from the challenge to the sexual double standard that the repealers had mounted, by the 1880s it was adopting the very ideas it had sought to challenge, and played a significant role in the post-Darwinian biologization, and feminization, of morality.[62] Turning its attentions to male promiscuity, and endorsing fundamental sexual difference, social purity began to feed off discourses of degeneration, biologizing male sexuality as brutish if left unchecked.[63]

[61] See Chant, *Why We Attacked the Empire* (London: Horace Marshall & Son, 1895). See also Lucy Bland, 'Feminist Vigilantes in Late-Victorian England', in Carol Smart (ed.), *Regulating Womanhood: Historical Essays on Marriage, Motherhood and Sexuality* (London: Routledge, 1992); and Judith Walkowitz, 'Male Vice and Feminist Virtue: Feminism and the Politics of Prostitution in Nineteenth-Century Britain', *History Workshop Journal*, 13 (1982), 77–93.

[62] While Olive Banks and Sheila Jeffreys provide histories of social purity, they pay little attention to connections between social purity and biological essentialism, or to the class and race biases of the movement: O. Banks, *Faces of Feminism* (Oxford: Martin Robertson & Co. Ltd, 1981); and S. Jeffreys, *The Spinster and Her Enemies: Feminism and Sexuality 1880–1930* (London: Pandora Press, 1985). See Walkowitz, *Prostitution*, ch. 3, on ways in which social science was mobilized by the concern over venereal disease. For an illuminating discussion of ways in which medicine played an important role in bringing working-class women into the sphere of state control, see Lynda Nead, *Myths of Sexuality: Representations of Women in Victorian Britain* (Oxford: Blackwell, 1988), ch. 5.

[63] On working-class internalization of social purity values, see Edward J. Bristow, *Vice and Vigilance: Purity Movements in Britain Since 1700* (Dublin: Gill and Macmillan and Totowa, NJ: Rowen and Littlefield, 1978), 103–6. As Bristow notes, thousands of working

The conflation of the medical and the moral, which developed during the eighteenth century,[64] finds clear and dramatic expression in social purity. Grand's eponymous heroine, Ideala, declares: 'the future of the race has come to be a question of morality and a question of health. Perhaps I should reverse it, and say a question of health and morality, since the latter is so dependent on the former'.[65] Herbert Spencer urged the idea of a 'physical morality' in his 1861 treatise on education, arguing that 'all breaches of the laws of health are *physical sins*,[66] and the eugenic feminist Swiney urged: 'women must realise more and more that health and morality are synonymous terms'.[67] Impurity would have moral *and* physical consequences: 'the various hideous forms of disease under which the Nemesis of sin displays its malignant vitality,—scrofula, syphilis, blindness, deafness, paralysis—are the fatal heritages of past *impurity*, of shameless deeds done in the flesh.'[68] Venereal disease, which motivated the social purists, makes clear the persistent association of disease with uncleanliness and impurity, revealing pervasive cultural attitudes and values. The term which the venereal disease control movement took in the twentieth century—'social hygiene'—makes explicit this association.[69]

Given the unhealthy tendency of men to promiscuity and vice, and the natural instinct of women to virtue, social purists and eugenic feminists increasingly emphasized the importance of female choice of a reproductive partner, replacing male passion with rational female selection.

men were recruited into white cross armies throughout the nation and dedicated themselves to promoting the single standard of chastity and attacking private and public vice.

[64] See Roy Porter, 'Diseases of Civilization', in W. F. Bynum and R. Porter (eds.), *Companion Encyclopedia of the History of Medicine*, 2 vols. (London and New York: Routledge, 1993), i. For the evolutionary function of morality, and hence its interest to scientists, see Darwin, *Descent*, i. 97, 98, 103.

[65] *Ideala*, 289.

[66] Spencer, *Education: Intellectual, Moral, and Physical* (London: Williams & Norgate, 1861), 177.

[67] Frances Swiney, *The Awakening of Women*, 125. Ian Hacking in *The Taming of Chance* notes that health and morality were always combined in the utilitarian mind but observes although it appears to be 'a structural device by which the rich were able to regulate the behaviour of the poor ... regimes that scarcely distinguish health from morality are applied to the prosperous too' (Ian Hacking, *The Taming of Chance* (Cambridge: Cambridge University Press, 1990), 120). While this is evident, there is a fundamental difference for the middle class and the working class, for it was the middle class that, particularly in the case of eugenics, governed one such regime. It would therefore have been seen as capable of self-management, while the working class needed to be regulated by a class that knew better.

[68] *The Awakening of Women*, 87.

[69] Allan Brandt, *No Magic Bullet* (New York and Oxford: Oxford University Press, 1987), 5.

Women could become managers of male passion, and agents of regeneration,[70] and so introduce the idea of direction and progress into human development. In emphasizing the importance of reason in the selection of a reproductive partner, social purists and eugenic feminists drew on earlier traditions. Mary Wollstonecraft's *A Vindication of the Rights of Women* (1792), the founding text of Anglo-American feminism, provides an early example of the association of feminism and reason, calling upon women to rediscover their rational selves. The idea of rational reproduction provided a new way of allying feminism and reason.

Frances Swiney took up and reconfigured the ahistoric, essentialist doctrines of the evolutionary biologists Patrick Geddes and J. Arthur Thomson, authors of *The Evolution of Sex* (1889):

> the contrast between the elements is that between the sexes. The large, passive, highly nourished anabolic ovum, the small active katabolic sperm. The losing game of life is what we call a katabolic habit, tendency, or diathesis; the converse gaining one being, of course, the anabolic habit, temperament, tendency, or diathesis.[71]

She made these observations serve the status of women as agents of change, arguing that men were degenerate and largely redundant: 'the ovum always absorbs the sperm. Anabolism implies growth, concentration, conservation, unification, cohesion and solidarity. Katabolism, on the other hand, signifies division, dispersion, disintegration, decay and death.'[72] Therefore, she wrote, 'women are always the pioneers to the humaner and nobler civilisation'.[73] As she saw it, 'from the time that woman lost her power of selection, and man exercised upon her the abuse of sexual excesses, the race began to degenerate'.[74] She urged women to choose life partners 'as to character rather than talent, to healthiness and purity of body and mind, rather than to affluence of position and station'.[75]

In 1896, the eugenist physician and novelist Arabella Kenealy pointed

[70] Laqueur, *Making Sex*, 150, 201. Laqueur discusses the early socialism of Anne Wheeler, through the radical liberalism of Mary Wollstonecraft, to the domestic ideology of the conservative Hannah More and the progressive Sarah Ellis. For Wheeler's devaluation of female (pre-Enlightenment) passion, see Barbara Taylor, *Eve and the New Jerusalem: Socialism and Feminism in the Nineteenth Century* (New York: Pantheon, 1983), esp. ch. 2.

[71] Geddes and Thomson, *The Evolution of Sex* (London: Walter Scott, 1889), quoted in Swiney, *The Awakening of Women*, 20.

[72] Swiney, *The Awakening of Women*, 20.

[73] *The Mystery of the Circle and the Cross*, 29.

[74] Ibid., 45.

[75] *The Awakening of Women*, 91.

out that economic conditions—in particular the surplus—were distorting sexual relations[76] and having a negative impact on racial quality:

the abasement of motherhood has been largely of course a result of economic conditions which have precluded woman from exercising much selection—consequently much emotion—in the matter of a mate. Marriage has been to her who has had no other means of livelihood, no other scope for her faculties, the sole profession or refuge. Such charms and talent as she has possessed have become mere marketable commodities. So artificial indeed are our marriage customs, so little selection has the average woman, that there is not one in five hundred in whom her lover's or her husband's kiss wakes any of the higher emotion latent in every heart.[77]

In 'A New View of the Surplus of Women' in the *Westminster Review*, Kenealy emphasized that women were far more capable of choosing a suitable reproductive partner than men, and that, because the surplus had considerably reduced their capacity to choose, 'the choice is so much the more frequently, therefore, a mistaken one'.[78] Male and female eugenists alike urged the importance of female selection. The physician Caleb William Saleeby, a prominent member of the Eugenics Education Society, stressed 'a girl may be a good mother, in the highest sense, in her choice of a mate'.[79] According to the social purists, civilization meant increasing feminization. It was a sign, Swiney argued, that racial advancement would follow necessarily from social advancement: 'the decrease of hairiness is only one of the many signs of the growing feminization of the race'.[80] Likewise, 'women are naturally more gifted than men, they possess at the outset of life a lever towards the regeneration of mankind'.[81] While Grant Allen granted men an active role in racially improving sexual selection, he also recognized the importance of female choice, reading feminine passivity as the outward—and desirable—manifestation of feminine discrimination:

[desired females] however, as Darwin showed, are not in every way mere passive spectators. They accept and admire the conqueror; but they select even so among many competitors. Galton has pointed out that coyness and daintiness in the

76 As I discuss in the following chapter, Galton had first sketched out this argument in the 1860s. This idea lies at the heart of Charlotte Perkins Gilman's *Women and Economics. A Study of the Economic Relations Between Men and Women as a Factor in Social Evolution* (1898).

77 Arabella Kenealy, 'The Dignity of Love', *Humanitarian*, 8 (1896), 437.

78 'A New View of the Surplus of Women', *Westminster Review*, 136 (1891), 471.

79 *Woman and Womanhood*, 194.

80 Swiney, *The Awakening*, 20.

81 Ibid., 69.

female is as necessary a part of sexual selection as strength or beauty in the male. The higher up we go in the scale of being, the more do we find such selectiveness prevailing. Physiologically speaking, I should say, it is in most cases the duty of the male to be aggressive and eager, the duty of the female to be coy and discriminating.[82]

Social purists biologized vice as male and virtue as female. Swiney's contentions that 'the degeneracy we deplore lies at the door of a selfish, lustful, diseased manhood';[83] and that the 'deleterious factors' of 'greater variability, activity, and exhaustive energy' ('inherent and fundamental' to men) were 'working for male degeneracy' reveal the extent to which social purity was informed by biological determinism. Swiney cited August Weismann as evidence: 'in *The Germ-Plasm* the male is but a disintegrated part of the female'—a gendered reworking of Weismann which would have been a great surprise to him.[84] Men were potential agents of degeneration, biologically designed for *immorality*; if the future were left to them, the inevitable result would be racial degeneration.

Thus, degeneration was a masculine narrative, while regeneration, which reversed its plot, was feminine. The narrative of degeneration found in, for instance, Emile Zola's Rougon-Macquart novels is reversed in Sarah Grand's novels, which suggest ways in which the downward slide of humanity could be halted by placing women in the vanguard of social and biological change. In the words of Ellice Hopkins 'it is this great upward movement, lifting man to a higher level, which is given into the hands of us women, touching, as it does, all the great trusts of our womanhood'; 'a man is what a woman makes him'.[85] This was a direct reversal of the argument advanced by male eugenists such as Allen and Pearson, who assumed that emancipated women would renounce motherhood and femininity, becoming agents of racial degeneration. Social purists turned from the pessimistic narrative of degeneration to its counternarrative, regeneration or racial purification. Like Swiney, Clapperton argued that women were innately more racially aware than

[82] *Grant Allen*, 'Is it Degradation? A Reply to Professor Mivart', *Humanitarian*, 89 (1896), 345.

[83] *The Bar of Isis* (London: Open Road Publishing Company, 1907), 39.

[84] *Awakening*, 20, 39. Weismann explored his theory of germ-plasm in *Essays upon Heredity and Kindred Biological Problems* (Oxford: Clarendon Press, 1889); and *The Germ-Plasm: A Theory of Heredity* (London: Scott, 1893).

[85] *The Power of Womanhood*, 182; 'On the Early Training of Girls and Boys: An Appeal to Working Women Especially Intended for Mothers' Meetings' (London: Hatchards, 1882), 39.

men, who, 'on the contrary, think little of racial or social distinctions in their fugitive connections'.[86]

The idea of a *planned* society underpinned the concept of civic motherhood on which eugenic feminism was based. On this point, male eugenists were in agreement. In *Confidential Talks with Husband and Wife* Sperry wrote:

> the time may come—and many thoughtful people believe it ought to come—when woman shall habitually take the initiative, and man shall be the one to accept or reject. There are several good reasons for believing that in some respects a change would be an improvement. The subject is a debatable one. At least, it is highly desirable that civilised and intelligent women shall have a better chance to select and secure proper conjugal mates.[87]

Likewise, in *Woman and Womanhood*, Saleeby argued that the racial awareness of women was stronger than the 'racial instinct' of men—the will to mate indiscriminately, increasing the quantity but not necessarily the quality of the nation's population. He toed the eugenic line that women's innate moral responsibility and far-sightedness fitted them for sexual selection: 'in the exercise of this function' women are 'naturally more capable, more responsible, less liable to be turned aside by the demands of the moment'.[88] Saleeby was a popular voice among eugenic feminists, arguing that 'the sooner women's political demands were met, the better, because they diverted feminist energies from the much more important racial problems associated with widening differential class fertility'.[89]

Social purists exploited the language of racial hierarchy in urging the importance of morality to the health of the nation. Ellice Hopkins stressed in *The Power of Womanhood*:

> all history teaches us that the welfare and very life of a nation is determined by moral causes; and that it is the pure races—the races that respect their women and guard them jealously from defilement—that are tough, prolific, ascendant races, the noblest in type, the most enduring in progress.

[86] J. H. Clapperton, *A Vision of the Future, Based on the Application of Ethical Principles* (London: Swan Sonnenschein & Co. Ltd, 1904), 159, 121.

[87] *Confidential Talks with Husband and Wife, A Book of Information and Advice for the Married and the Marriageable* (Edinburgh and London: Oliphant, Anderson & Ferrier, 1894), 80–1.

[88] *Woman and Womanhood*, 261.

[89] *Eugenics Review*, 6 (1914), 197, cited in Richard Soloway, *Birth Control and the Population Question in England, 1877–1930* (Chapel Hill: North Carolina University Press, 1982), 144.

Quoting Galton, she warned of the biological consequences of social immorality as women of higher classes neglected their maternal duties and, through lives of sexual excess, became infertile. With the energies of the women of the best stock diverted from reproduction, the race was replenished from the lower classes and declined:

the rapid decadence of Greece, despite her splendid intellectual life, was due to moral causes. Speaking of the decay of the Athenian people, Mr Francis Galton says: 'we know, and may guess something more, of the reason why this marvellously gifted race declined. Social morality grew exceedingly lax; marriage became unfashionable and was avoided; many of the more ambitious and accomplished women were avowed courtesans, and, consequently, infertile and the mothers of the incoming population were of a heterogeneous class.'[90]

The Power of Womanhood was a strident plea to middle-class women to assert their role as moral and physiological guardians of the race. Equally, in the pamphlets she addressed to men, Hopkins posited close relations between social immorality and racial inferiority, overlaying the racial with theological ideas. In 'The British Zulu', she asked: 'are you quite sure that the average Englishman has got much beyond the level of the dirty savage?'; she went on to urge men to 'rise above the "savage"—the lower nature in you'.[91] If you are pure, she promised in 'True Manliness', 'your Eden will have no foul serpent in it . . . and you will hand on an unbroken constitution to your children, and those high traditions which will make them in their turn the pure sons and daughters of a pure father'.[92] Her pamphlets are stamped by class prejudice, and her warnings rest on notions of middle-class purity and working-class impurity (though she concedes that the difference between the two is one of circumstance rather than merit):

Our large houses, our separate bedrooms, our greater education, make us, without any merit on our part, often nicer and more particular in our ways than you; make us feel more the importance of little things, little decent ways, little safeguards, and little constant watchfulness in bringing up our children, which the terrible struggle for existence and the pressure of space but too often make you forget and grow careless about.[93]

90 Galton, *Hereditary Genius*, 331, quoted in *The Power of Womanhood*, 162–3.

91 'The British Zulu', *The White Cross Series* ('for men only') (London: Hatchards, Piccadilly, 1883), 5, 12.

92 'True Manliness', 27.

93 'On the Early Training of Girls and Boys: An Appeal to Working Women Especially Intended for Mothers' Meetings' (London: Hatchards, 1882), 20.

Listing among the sins of the working class 'overcrowding and want of decency in your sleeping accommodations', she warns her readers 'our very existence as a nation is at stake unless you will teach your children, a good deal more than you do, that "obedience" which "is the bond of rule"'.[94]

In 1890, Alfred Russel Wallace, co-discoverer of natural selection, envisioned a time in which women would turn on 'all men who in any way wilfully fail in their duty to society—on idlers and malingerers, on drunkards and liars, on the selfish, the cruel, or the vicious . . . since they will be able to decline, and certainly will not tolerate, any unions other than marriage, all will receive many offers which they can afford to reject'. He proceeded: 'these latter-day Lysistratas will blackmail some of the sexually impetuous males into good conduct, and the residue they will scornfully leave to celibacy and oblivion'; in this way, women would be the agents of eugenic change: 'in such a reformed society the vicious man, the man of degraded taste or of feeble intellect, will have little chance of finding a wife, and his bad qualities will die out with himself'. He concluded: 'we may safely leave the far greater and deeper problem of the improvement of the race to the cultivated minds and pure instincts of the Woman of the Future'.[95]

In the *Origin*, Darwin had outlined two forms of sexual selection, female choice and male choice. He defined sexual selection as dependent on 'the struggle between males for the possession of the females; the result is not death to the unsuccessful competitor but few or no offspring'.[96] In this form of sexual selection, the principles of natural selection were still operative. Darwin outlined a further component to sexual selection: female aesthetic choice. He gave as examples the rock-thrush of Guiana, and birds of Paradise: 'successive males display their gorgeous plumage and perform strange antics before the females, which standing by as spectators, at last choose the most attractive partner' (74). By the time of the *Descent*, Darwin saw sexual selection as playing a greater and more distinct part in the process of evolution. Observing that in almost all species females were the choice-makers, he observed, in keeping with Victorian courting convention, that the dominance of men in the selection of sexual partners made the human love-plot 'exceptional' in the animal kingdom; 'the males, instead of having been

94 'On the Early Training of Girls and Boys', 33.

95 'Human Selection', *Fortnightly Review*, 54 (September 1890), 337.

96 Darwin, *Origin*, 73.

selected, are the selectors'. He explained 'we recognise such cases by the females having been rendered more highly ornamented than the males,—their ornamental characters having been transmitted exclusively or chiefly to their female offspring. One such case has been described in the order to which man belongs, namely, with the Rhesus monkey.'[97] He noted a further difference: 'with civilized people the arbitrament of battle for the possession of the women has long ceased'.[98] While the human romance plot was shown to be motivated by the same reproductive drives, the same striving for survival through progeny as the rest of the animal kingdom, there were two vital differences: men were the choosers, leaving women as the passive embodiments of Victorian femininity; and, among the 'civilized', aesthetic principles overruled physical strength. Highlighting physical and mental differences between the sexes, sexual selection explained these differences as advantageous in finding mates, and thus lent new authority and purpose to Victorian ideas of gender. A woman's beauty would determine her biological destiny.

Social purists were seeking to reverse this androcentric bias of sexual selection, reinvesting women with the agency of selection on the grounds that only they were sufficiently race aware to make responsible sexual choices. Resisting male passion, women, as the bearers of moral biology, would initiate the replacement of romantic love by rational eugenic love—conscious sexual selection. This idea built upon the Malthusian concept that only if passion between the sexes could be regulated might society progress. While Malthusian ideas contained eugenic seeds, targeting the working class as recklessly overproductive, the love now proposed would employ reason not simply *in* but *prior to* the marriage bed, in the process of the selection of a partner. Through the responsible application of reason, racial improvement might occur.

The American psychologist J. W. Slaughter, the first chairman of the organizing committee of the Eugenics Education Society, complained in 1909 of 'the deep-rooted conviction in the popular mind that mating is something spontaneous and undetermined'.[99] The arguments in favour of rational selection which underpinned eugenics were in tune with the general devaluation of passion—or animal behaviour—in favour of reason that had characterized the Enlightenment. However, the situation was arrived at through a complex route. In the wake of Darwin, humans,

97 Darwin, *Descent*, ii. 371.

98 Ibid., ii. 326.

99 'Selection in Marriage', *Eugenics Review*, I (1909), 154.

integrated into the animal economy, were revealed to be motivated more by instinctive patterns of behaviour than by reason. In many ways Darwin was going against the rationalist grain. But, while acknowledging the importance of the part played by passion or instinct—animal behaviour—in human existence, he considered men to be closer to reason than women, thus continuing to privilege rationality. Shot through with sexual hierarchy, his work evidences reluctance in letting go of the reason-passion hierarchy, as he emphasized that men, in their superiority, are more closely associated with reason, women with intuition.

Eugenic feminists emphasized the superior capacity of women for rational selection. Here, they were assisted by the association of women with passionlessness which was fermenting in evangelical and biological discourse. Eugenic love would be the antithesis of passion, a replacement of sexual love, in the name of humanity. Jane Hume Clapperton urged the relevance of sexual selection to culture by demanding 'a law of *social* selection' which would result 'in appropriate birth, or the birth of the socially fit'.[100] In this way, she makes explicit what had been implicit in Darwin's distinction between 'natural' and 'sexual' selection. Clapperton continued: 'the least children can demand of their parents is the birthright of being well-born.' The 'well-born' was to become a catch phrase of eugenics. Francis Swiney emphasized the need for 'careful selection . . . so as to insure to the children born of their union a fair start in life, unhandicapped by baneful hereditary tendencies.'[101]

The characterization of male behaviour as of the moment, less mindful of consequences, of the future, than women's, reinforced the idea that women would make better custodians of the future. The future depended on female virtue, eugenically defined: eugenic virtue. Only through the eugenic intervention of women in the health of the nation might the future of the British race be secured.

[100] *A Vision of the Future*, 159.

[101] *The Awakening of Women*, 129.

3 Charity and Citizenship

The check in the increase of population is applied where it is least likely to be beneficial, for the vacancies in the ranks of humanity, caused by the less prolificness of the higher classes, are rapidly filled up from the ranks below them. Thus the salutary influences which the educated woman might exert as a wife and mother are lost to society, and replaced by the influence of the ungentle, uneducated, and untrained. We think it is also worth consideration whether, if due attention were paid to the *physique* of the middle and higher classes, and a higher standard of corporeal health established, the higher grade of intellectual development, and the finer sensibilities they have acquired, might not be handed down from generation to generation, and the progressive improvement of the *whole* race secured.

Anon.[1]

Even the thoughtless begin to have misgivings as to the efficacy of our charity system. The greed of the idle poor is aroused, parental responsibility annulled, helplessness is fostered, and a cult of ill-health held up to a race that loses Empire when it parts with vigour.

Arnold White[2]

Indiscriminate charity is vicious, say the professional philanthropists.

Jack London[3]

When the vicious and feeble-minded people reproduce, they do so more recklessly.

Marie Stopes[4]

EUGENICS—THE MILK OF HUMAN KINDNESS?

Charity had become pivotal in the question of national efficiency. The hereditarian position was clear and inflexible: no amount of charity in

[1] Anon., 'Woman in her Psychological Relations', *Journal of Psychological Medicine and Mental Pathology*, 4 (1851), 46, emphasis in original.

[2] Arnold White, *Efficiency and Empire* (1901; Brighton: Harvester Press, 1973), 112.

[3] Jack London, *People of the Abyss* (London: Isbister and Co. Ltd, 1903), 83.

[4] Marie Stopes, *Wise Parenthood: A Practical Sequel to Married Love* (1918; London: Putnam, 1931), 26.

the world could undo biology. Malthus had sown the seeds for the eugenic line on charity at the close of the eighteenth century, pinpointing the 'natural tendency of the labouring classes of society to increase beyond the demand for their labour, or the means of their adequate support',[5] and attacking the poor laws which he saw as creating the poor which they maintained, encouraging them to increase their numbers without increasing food for their support (97). In 1800, responding to Malthus, William Pitt the younger, Tory prime minister, withdrew a bill which would have provided allowances from the poor rates to supplement the wages of agricultural workers, based on the size of their families and the current price of bread. The pronouncements of Malthus did not go unchallenged. The radical journalist and politician William Cobbett referred in 1826 to:

> The folly, the stupidity, the inanity, the presumption, the insufferable emptiness and insolence and barbarity, of those numerous wretches, who now have the audacity to propose to *transport* the people of England, upon the principle of the monster Malthus, who has furnished the unfeeling oligarchs and their toad-eaters with the pretence, that man has a natural propensity to breed faster than food can be raised for the increase.[6]

The harvest furnished striking evidence to the contrary, Cobbett noted. But Malthus's ideas gained momentum over the course of the century, informing and in turn finding resonance in developing capitalist practice and evolutionary thought. For Friedrich Engels, the poor law revealed the bourgeois conception of its duties towards the proletariat: 'the non-possessing class exists solely for the purpose of being exploited, and of starving when the property holders can no longer make use of it'.[7] In 1925, looking back over a century, Karl Pearson, Professor of National Eugenics, acknowledged Malthus as 'the strewer of seed which reached its harvest in the ideas of Charles Darwin and Francis Galton'.[8]

In 1851, as Britain presented itself to itself and the world as the workshop of the world at the Great Exhibition, Herbert Spencer published his pioneering work of sociology, *Social Statics; or, The Conditions Essential to Human Happiness Specified and the First of Them Developed.* In this, he

[5] Thomas Malthus, *An Essay on the Principle of Population* (1798; Harmondsworth: Penguin, 1988), 270.

[6] Cobbett, 28 August 1826. *Rural Rides* was first serialized in Cobbett's radical journal *Political Register* before appearing in book form in 1830 (Harmondsworth: Penguin, 2001), 277.

[7] 1892 Preface, *The Condition of the Working Class in England in 1844* (London: Allen & Unwin, 1950), p. viii.

[8] *Annals of Eugenics*, 1 (October 1925), frontispiece.

sketched out a eugenic panacea for poverty and disease, lambasting the idea of charity:

> who, indeed, after pulling off the coloured glasses of prejudice and thrusting out of sight his pet projects can help seeing the folly of these endeavours to protect men against themselves? A sad population of imbeciles would our schemers fill the world with, could their plans last . . . the average effect of the laws of nature is to 'purify' society from those who are, *in some respect or other*, essentially faulty.[9]

For Spencer, elimination through struggle would remove the impure species of a race, and lead to a constantly improving 'type'. Charity eased this struggle and was seriously damaging to the health of the nation. While Darwin would also emphasize the centrality of struggle to existence, he rejected Spencer's belief in the notion of purity, of a 'type' of a species, in favour of the idea of mutability, and was more circumspect on the question of charity, venturing to suggest in the *Descent* that 'the noblest part of our nature' would be lost if 'we were intentionally to neglect the poor and helpless (i. 168, 169). Nonetheless, Spencer continued to wave a public banner of protest against any social alleviation of suffering, arguing that charity, by artificially increasing the lifespan and numbers of inferior stock, was both misplaced and cruel. These ideas proliferated over the second half of the century. The poor were held to have become increasingly dependent on impersonal charity handed out by agencies to whom they felt no sense of personal responsibility. The 'indiscriminate almsgiver' was apparently thriving, as William Guy warned in his *The Plague of Beggars: A Dissuasive from Indiscriminate Almsgiving by a London Physician*, his 1868 write-up of an essay in *Fraser's Magazine*:

> if you will somehow contrive to handcuff the indiscriminate almsgiver, I will promise you for reason I could assign, these inevitable consequences, no destitution, lessened poor rates, prisons emptier, fewer gin shops, less crowded mad houses, sure signs of underpopulation, and an England worth living in.[10]

9 *Social Statics; or, The Conditions Essential to Human Happiness Specified, and the First of Them Developed* (London: Chapman, 1851), 379.

10 William Guy, *The Plague of Beggars: A Dissuasive from Indiscriminate Almsgiving by a London Physician* (London, 1868), cited in Helen Dendy Bosanquet, *Social Work in London 1869–1912: A History of the Charity Organisation Society* (London: J. Murray, 1914), 6. See also Anon., 'London Alms and London Pauperism', *Quarterly Review*, 146 (1876), 376; and Stedman Jones, *Outcast London*, ch. 13, 'The Deformation of the Gift. The problem of the 1860s'.

The ethos of self-help and self-improvement that dominated mid-Victorian Britain provided a hothouse for the flourishing of resistance to charity. In September 1859, shortly before the *Origin* appeared, Samuel Smiles (1812–1904), the cheerful prophet of diligence, industry, and self-denial, self-educated and an opponent of Chartism, published *Self-Help*, which sold 20,000 copies in its first year of publication, and exalted 'youths to apply themselves diligently to right pursuits—sparing neither labour, pains, nor self-denial in prosecuting them—and to rely upon their own efforts in life'.[11] Focusing on the importance of 'self-culture', Smiles's scheme allowed for the possibility of change within a single lifetime, rejecting the strict hereditarian concept of character as fixed before birth, but ignored the social, economic, and political impediments to self-help. Darwin himself considered *Self-Help* 'good-ish'.[12]

W. R. Greg stressed in *Fraser's Magazine* in 1868 that charity would result in national disaster:

> We have kept alive those who, in a more natural and less advanced state, would have died—and who, looking at the physical perfection of the race alone, had better have been left to die . . . In a wild state, by the law of natural selection, only, or chiefly, the sounder and stronger specimens were allowed to continue their species; with us, thousands with tainted constitutions, with frames weakened by malady or waste, with brains bearing subtle and hereditary mischief in their recesses, are suffered to transmit their terrible inheritance of evil to other generations, and to spread it through a whole community.[13]

In 1865, in *Macmillan's Magazine*, Galton expressed to the nation his concerns that money could buy love. Money, he argued, was distorting natural processes of natural and sexual selection and ruining the nation's health, interposing 'her aegis between the law of natural selection and very many of its rightful victims'. As money was buying time—and healthy brides—for the unfit, so charity was needlessly, and heedlessly, preserving them and, potentially, their progeny. In this article Galton recommended a self-conscious programme of human breeding, a process which natural selection would 'powerfully assist . . . by pressing

[11] Samuel Smiles, Preface to 1866 edn., *Self-Help* (1859; London: Institute of Economic Affairs, 1996), p. xii.

[12] 13 May 1860, Notebook, 128, cited in G. Beer, *Darwin's Plots: Evolutionary Narrative in Darwin, George Eliot and Nineteenth-Century Fiction* (1983; Cambridge, Cambridge University Press, 2000), 245.

[13] W. R. Greg, 'On the Failure of "Natural Selection" in the Case of Man', *Fraser's Magazine*, 78 (1868), 359. Darwin cites this article in the *Descent*, i. 173.

heavily on the minority of weakly and incapable men'.[14] The powerful eugenic argument that empathy and charity would result in long-term suffering was emerging.

The Charity Organization Society, formed in 1869, aimed to bring the classes back into contact and put an end to 'indiscriminate' charity. It was, Gareth Stedman-Jones notes, 'a heterogeneous collection of individuals whose reasons for participation varied greatly'[15] and its attempts to moralize the poor were linked to the 'New Liberalism' that emerged in the closing decades of the century, and which sought to reformulate liberalism to accommodate the needs of community. The society would give help only to those who had the strength of character, and the will, to help themselves—the 'deserving' poor—and tried to advise the 'undeserving' poor on how to become deserving and thus eligible for charitable support. The society's Dwellings Committee was active both in investigating the living conditions and in publicizing the needs of the working class, and authorized the construction of dwelling blocks throughout central London.[16]

However, while social reformers increasingly drew attention to the demoralization of the poor, the influence of a strictly hereditarian account of poverty, which identified the condition of the working class as a symptom of too much, not too little, external support, was increasing. Fabians rigidly opposed housing policies that placed a burden on the rates, and gave very little support to the London County Council's development of large suburban housing estates, supporting slum clearance instead. The Liberty and Property Defence League, founded in 1882,

[14] Francis Galton, 'Hereditary Talent and Character', *Macmillan's Magazine*, 12 (1865), 326, 319. Darwin cites this article in the *Descent*, i. 173. See also Galton, *Hereditary Genius: An Inquiry into its Laws and Consequences* (London: Macmillan, 1869), 132–40, which Darwin summarizes thus in the *Descent*: 'The children of parents who have produced single children, are themselves, as Mr Galton has shewn, apt to be sterile; and thus noble families are continually cut off in the direct line, and their wealth flows into some side channel; but unfortunately this channel is not determined by superiority of any kind', Darwin, *Descent*, i. 170.

[15] Stedman Jones, *Outcast London*, 15. Among its diverse members were Octavia Hill, Charles Trevelyan, and Edward Denison. See Calvin S. Woodward, 'The Charity Organization Society and the Rise of the Welfare State', Ph.D. thesis, Cambridge University, 1961).

[16] A. S. Wohl, *The Eternal Slum: Housing and Social Policy in Victorian London* (London: E. Arnold, 1977), 192. See Octavia Hill, *Nineteenth Century*, 30 (1891), 161–70. Hill argues for a system of voluntary inspectors to visit family homes and be in contact with officials, bringing the classes into closer contact. She notes that relief 'is never one-hundredth part the help . . . that self-reliance is' (168). See also Jane Lewis, *Women and Social Action in Victorian and Edwardian England* (Stanford: Stanford University Press, 1991), ch. 1.

played a leading part in supporting self-help over state-help, and the entry of government into the direct provision of working-class housing was slow. Even Edwardian public health reformers, who challenged eugenics through their commitment to environmentalism, conceded that 'the residuum' was a special problem. In 1909 James Niven, medical officer of health for Manchester for over forty years, and one-time president of the Society of Medical Officers of Health, remarked that there would always be 'incurable loafers, incapables, and degenerates' (for these he recommended the workhouse).[17]

In *Social Statics*, Spencer used the notion of selection operating on individuals to justify political *laissez-faire*, on the grounds that state intervention interfered with the destruction of the unfit. Charity was, he argued, worse than ineffectual:

> instead of diminishing suffering, it eventually increases it. It favours the multiplication of those worst fitted for existence, and, by consequence, hinders the multiplication of those best fitted for existence—leaving, as it does, less room for them. It tends to fill the world with those to whom life will bring most pain, and tends to keep out of it those whom life will bring most pleasure. It inflicts positive misery, and prevents positive happiness.[18]

In *Fraser's Magazine* in 1873, Galton warned of the dangers to national health of allowing inferior stock to breed:

> I do not see why any insolence of caste should prevent the gifted class, when they had the power, from treating their compatriots with all kindness, so long as they maintained celibacy. But if these continued to procreate children inferior in moral, intellectual and physical qualities, it is easy to believe the time may come when such persons would be considered as enemies to the State, and to have forfeited all claims to kindness.[19]

Classes were increasingly seen to correspond to biological subtypes that would respond to biological rather than social influences. For all her sympathies towards the poor, they appear as little removed from animals in Margaret Harkness's novels:

> Crouching on the floor, gnawing a bone was a hungry man. His face was sodden with drink. He had swollen features, palsied hands and trembling feet. He had probably begun his life in this Christian country as a homeless boy in the streets

[17] ' "Poverty and Disease": Presidential Address to the Epidemiological Section of the Royal Society of Medicine' (22 October 1900), 41, in Dorothy Porter, ' "Enemies of the Race": Biologism, Environmentalism, and Public Health in Edwardian England', *Victorian Studies*, 34 (1991), 167.

[18] *Social Statics*, 381.

[19] 'Hereditary Improvement', *Fraser's Magazine*, 7 (1873), 129.

and most likely close his days in the casual ward of some workhouse . . . The lodgers threw him scraps, and laughed to see him tearing his food to pieces, devouring it like a dog on the ground.[20]

Jack London was so appalled at the living conditions in the East End that he was moved to reject hereditarianism: 'Indiscriminate charity is vicious, say the professional philanthropists. Well, I resolved to be vicious . . . Out rolled the gold piece, a fortune in their hungry eyes; and away we stampeded for the nearest coffee-house.'[21]

The idea that poverty was the result of *biological* rather than environmental factors which, as I noted in Chapter 1, developed in the closing decades of the century, received widespread middle-class support and was given authoritative backing by Charles Booth, H. Llewellyn Smith, G. A Longstaffe, and Alfred Marshall.[22] Booth's detailed study of the London poor was taken to show that an irreducible fraction of the population was destined to remain in poverty, and thus to confirm the status of the residuum.[23] The idea that national health might be controlled through the regulation of reproduction, and that certain social groups might be eliminated through processes of nature, was gaining momentum, and its popularity rapidly multiplied among eugenists at the *fin de siècle*. The barrister S. A. K. Strahan, author of *Marriage and Disease, a Study of Heredity and the More Important Family Degenerations* (1892) protested at 'the highly artificial life which civilised man has built up or created for himself! Here the weakling, the cripple, and the diseased, which in the natural life would at once succumb, are nursed and protected; they are surrounded with an artificial environment designed to render a continuance of life possible.'[24] Charity went against nature. Eugenics, by contrast, might assist nature.

In a plea for the national importance of rational sexual selection in the *National Review* in 1894, Galton combined Malthusian and eugenic logic in a rejuvenated attack on charitable support for the poor:

[20] John Law [Margaret Harkness], *Out of Work* (London: 1888), 110–11.

[21] *People of the Abyss*, 83.

[22] Stedman Jones, *Outcast London*, 128. See G. A Longstaffe, 'Rural Depopulation', *Journal of the Royal Statistical Society*, 56 (1893), 416; Alfred Marshall, 'The Housing of the London Poor', i. *Contemporary Review*, 45 (1884), 228.

[23] D. Kevles, *In the Name of Eugenics: Genetics and the Uses of Human Heredity* (1985; Cambridge, Mass.: Harvard University Press, 1995), 71.

[24] S. A. K. Strahan, *Marriage and Disease: a Study of Heredity and the More Important Family Degenerations* (London: Kegan Paul, Trench, Trübner, 1892), 2.

The nation is starved and crowded out of the conditions needed for healthy life by the pressure of a huge continent of born weaklings and criminals . . . The course of nature is exceedingly wasteful in every way. It is careless of germs, tens of thousands of pollen grains perishing of which none have had the chance of effecting fertilization, by being transported to the proper spot at the proper moment, by the blind agency of an insect ferreting among the flowers for food . . . The course of nature is also indifferent and ruthless towards our own lives, but reason can teach us to effect with pity, intelligence, and speed many objects that nature would otherwise effect remorselessly, unintelligently, and tediously. By its action, suffering may be minimized and waste diminished. Wherever intelligence chooses to intervene, the struggle for existence ceases . . . a general high level of the qualities that make a good horse has been attained without any aid from natural selection, artificial selection having superseded it.[25]

In his 1901 address to the Anthropological Institute, Galton analysed Booth's eight economic (and moral) classes, quoting extensively from Booth's descriptions of the inhabitants of each class. He mapped Booth's classes onto his own 'natural ones', discussing the members in relation to their 'civic worth', and asserting that 'the brains of our nation lie in the higher of our classes'.[26] Of the lowest group, class A, Booth had noted that the class was diverse, and offered tempered optimism, refusing to homogenize the group entirely; there lingers a sense in which Galton believes there are exceptional cases that might respond to moralization:

I do not mean to say that there are not individuals of every sort to be found in the mass. Those who are able to wash the mud may find some gems in it. There are at any rate many piteous cases . . . it is much to be desired and to be hoped that this class may become less hereditary in its character; there appears to be no doubt that it is now hereditary to a very considerable extent.[27]

Eugenics presented itself as a biological alternative to social charity; it was no less than a new, improved, *biological* philanthropy, which drew on the latest scientific thinking. In the words of the socialist eugenist Jane Hume Clapperton, eugenics made it possible 'to create a painless, instead of a painful, equalization of births and deaths'.[28] The rhetoric of kindness likewise permeated the work of Caleb William Saleeby, who

25 *National Review* (1894), 761–2.

26 29 October 1901, reprinted in Galton, *Essays in Eugenics* (London: Eugenics Education Society, 1909), 11.

27 29 October 1901, repr. in *Essays in Eugenics*, 20.

28 *A Vision of the Future*, 92.

argued that in a generation consisting only of 'babies who were loved before they were born' there would be 'a proportion of sympathy, of tender feeling, and of all those great, abstract, world-creating passions which are evolved from the tender emotion, such as no age hitherto has seen'. He referred to this as his 'eugenic paragraph'.[29] Arnold White was more openly ruthless, demanding that 'heedless pity' for individuals be replaced by 'wise compassion' for the race, redefining kindness as wisdom (with respect to the future), and lambasting indiscriminate kindness as 'sickly emotion' and 'blind mercy'.[30] Galton ended the story of his life celebrating the kindness of eugenics:

> The belief has long been present to my mind that we men may be the chief, ~~and~~ perhaps the only executives on earth and that we are detached on active service with, it may or may not be, only illusory powers of free will. Also that we are in some way accountable for our own success or failure to further certain obscure ends, which have to be guessed at as best we can—that though our instructions are obscure, they are sufficiently clear to justify our interference with the pitiless ~~course~~ routine of Nature, whenever it seems possible to attain the goal towards which it is moving by gentler and kindlier ways.[31]

Eugenics, to a greater degree than social purity, or Social Darwinism, was figured as natural and kind: 'the love of the sexes can harmonize with the highest interests of our collective social life, and eugenics, *not sexual love*, may become paramount in generation'.[32] In *Woman and Womanhood*, Saleeby urged the need for a eugenic feminism, figuring nature (feminized, as usual) as a eugenist; he spoke of 'the eugenic need for love'; adding to Galton's more robust demand for 'physique, ability and energy', he declared 'we also need more love, and we must breed for that',[33] and, writing for the *Contemporary Review*, Blanche Leppington, poet and writer, urged the need to move with the times, arguing that society ought to 'supplement [nature's] mechanism of natural selection by a process of ethical elimination'; eugenic practice is personified as Love, albeit a naive Love, who has 'her work to learn' (the necessity of being cruel to be kind). Through the need for socially responsible marriage, Love would be eugenized; 'her eyes are fixed on the distant generations; the destiny of man is in her heart, and she is hand in hand

[29] C. W. Saleeby, *Woman and Womanhood: A Search for Principles* (London: William Heinemann, 1912), 179.

[30] A. White, *Efficiency and Empire*; 98, 99.

[31] Galton Papers, 57, 'Memories of My Life', 373, Galton's deletions.

[32] *A Vision of the Future*, 113, emphasis in original.

[33] *Woman and Womanhood*, 14, 247, 153.

with Nature'; she comes to realize that her task is 'warfare—not peace, but a sword'.[34]

Jane Hume Clapperton attacked 'individual philanthropy' for 'support[ing] the weak and help[ing] the unfit to survive'. As she saw it, 'individual philanthropy deliberately selected the half-starved, the diseased, the criminals, and enabled them to exist and propagate'; and this led to a gradual '*degenerating* of the race'.[35] In her socialist-eugenic novel *Margaret Dunmore; or, A Socialist Home* (1888) the commune of La Maison decrees: 'there will be no indiscriminate charity, however, with us; no eleemosynary aid that, in supporting individuals, is hurtful to the race'.[36] Eugenists began to redefine kindness: Galton argued in his *Essays in Eugenics* (1909) that it was far more humane to prevent suffering than to alleviate it after it had occurred, and Mrs Alec Tweedie advanced the idea of kindness to the race, asking 'could anything be more philanthropic than to stamp out degeneracy?'[37]

GENDERED CITIZENSHIP AND CIVIC MOTHERHOOD

In 1889 the *Nineteenth Century* published an all-female 'Appeal Against Female Suffrage' drafted by the popular novelist and philanthropist Mrs Humphry Ward. The supporters included public figures such as Lady Stanley of Alderley (wife of the Liberal MP Edward John Stanley), and, as they signed themselves, Mrs Leslie Stephen (Virginia Woolf's mother), and Mrs Matthew Arnold. The appeal was essentially an appeal to biology, an appeal for an overtly *biological* conception of citizenship, which argued that 'disabilities of sex' and habitual practices 'resting ultimately upon physical difference' were inflexible barriers to political equality for women:

[34] Blanche Leppington, 'The Debrutalisation of Man', *Contemporary Review* 67 (1895) 728; 732.

[35] *A Vision of the Future*, 83, emphasis in original. Cf. J. H. Clapperton, *Scientific Meliorism and the Evolution of Happiness* (London: Kegan Paul, Trench & Co., 1885), 365–6: 'the power of nurture is limited. It can direct the forces of nature, but it cannot alter the intrinsic quality of the raw material which nature provides.'

[36] *Margaret Dunmore; or, A Socialist Home* (London: Swan Sonnenschein, Lowrey & Co., 1888), 77.

[37] Strahan, *Marriage and Disease, A Study of Heredity and the More Important Family Degenerations* (London: Kegan Paul, Trench, Trübner, 1892), 2; J. H. Clapperton, *A Vision of the Future, Based on the Application of Ethical Principles* (London: Swan Sonnenschein, 1904), 82; *Pall Mall Gazette* (9 March 1894), 1–2; Tweedie, 'Eugenics', *Eugenics Review*, 9 (1912), 857.

the undersigned protest strongly against the proposed Extension of the Parliamentary Franchise to Women which they believe would be a measure distasteful to the great majority of the women of the country—unnecessary—and mischievous both to themselves and to the State.

Accompanying this statement were twenty-eight double-columned pages of signatures by women, representing some two thousand supporters.[38]

The supporters saw women's sex as a permanent disqualification for the vote, and argued that to proceed in defiance of biology would be injurious to the state. Even those women who entered the debate on the side of the franchise were likely to base their arguments on sexual difference: the following month the journal published responses to the petition from the suffragettes Millicent Garrett Fawcett and Margaret Mary Dilke, with Fawcett (who was president of the National Union of Women's Suffrage Societies (NUWSS) from 1897 to 1919) arguing that the claim of women to representation was predicated on the different service they could provide the state. In turn, Louise Creighton, an opponent of female suffrage and the wife of a Cambridge professor, replied using biology to the opposite end, concluding that sex was a fact which no act of parliament could eliminate.[39] The same rhetoric framed Patrick Geddes and J. Arthur Thomson's influential essentialist tract, *The Evolution of Sex*, which appeared in the same year. In their defence of mental differences between the sexes, its authors remarked 'to obliterate them it would be necessary to have all the evolution over again on a new basis. What was decided among the prehistoric Protozoa cannot be annulled by Act of Parliament.'[40]

Closely informed by shifting attitudes towards charity, health, and empire, a new, gendered, concept of citizenship was emerging. Underpinned by the growing enthusiasm for biological determinism and fundamental sex difference, it was a citizenship of *contribution* rather than political entitlement, predicated on the idea that women were naturally—*biologically*—moral. As biographers of the housing philanthropists Octavia Hill and Louisa Twining, and of Florence Nightingale, have

[38] For a detailed discussion of the suffrage debates in the periodical press in 1889, which draws out complex political alliances, see Laurel Brake, 'Writing Women's History: The Sex Debates of 1889', in Ann Heilmann and Margaret Beetham (eds.), *New Woman Hybridities: Femininity, Feminism, and International Consumer Culture* (London: Routledge, 2003).

[39] Louise Creighton, 'The Appeal Against Female Suffrage: A Rejoinder' [to Fawcett and Dilke in July], *Nineteenth Century*, 26 (1889), 354.

[40] Patrick Geddes and J. Arthur Thomson, *The Evolution of Sex* (London: Walter Scott, 1889), 267.

shown, female philanthropists did not believe that making a contribution should entitle them to the right to vote; instead many were anti-suffragists.[41] In 1867, Barbara Bodichon, active in the Langham Place circle, argued that the enfranchisement of women would enhance public spirit by instilling a 'healthy, lively, intelligent' patriotism, and 'an unselfish devotedness to the public service'.[42] The suffragette Rose Crawshay envisioned that the vote would tend to 'ennoble women's characters' and introduce a higher standard of morality, 'throughout the world'[43] and in 1870, the year of its inception, the *Women's Suffrage Journal* urged that women's suffrage would lead to the moral education of society and should not be reduced to 'what is called a right or an interest'.[44] These ideas were also used to argue against the suffrage.

Offering women a new command of social and sexual relations, gendered citizenship allowed public service to be professionalized as women's work and did not challenge the patriarchal conception of the family;[45] in fact, women began to base their claim to citizenship on their role as bearers and educators of future citizens. From the 1880s to the 1920s welfare and health systems in Europe bore strongly maternalist characteristics, as British feminist historians revealed in the 1990s.[46] Late Victorian and Edwardian women 'domesticated' politics through the language of separate spheres.[47] From the beginning, arguments for

[41] Dorothy Porter, 'Ideologies of Health and Welfare in Northern Europe in the Eighteenth and Nineteenth Centuries', in O. P. Grell, Andrew Cunningham, and Robert Jütte (eds.), *Health Care and Poor Relief in Northern Europe in the Eighteenth and Nineteenth Centuries* (Aldershot: Ashgate, 2002).

[42] Bodichon, *Reasons for the Enfranchisement of Women* (1866; repr. in Jane Lewis (ed.), *Before the Vote was Won: Arguments for and Against Women's Suffrage 1864–1896* (London: Routledge, 1987), 108.

[43] Quoted in Ryland Wallace, *Organize, Organize, Organize! A Study of Reform Agitations in Wales 1840–1886* (Cardiff: University of Wales Press, 1991), 165.

[44] The piece was written by Joseph Mazzini, the Italian nationalist, male supporter of female enfranchisement: 'Mazzini on the Franchise for Women,' *Women's Suffrage Journal* 9 (1871), 95.

[45] For discussion of eugenics and social policy in national context, see Dorothy Porter, *Health, Civilization and the State: A History of Public Health from Ancient to Modern Times* (London: Routledge, 1998), ch. 10.

[46] See Anne Digby and John Stewart (eds.), *Gender, Health and Welfare* (London: Routledge, 1996); see also Seth Koven and Sonya Michel, *Mothers of a New World, Maternalist Politics and the Origins of Welfare States* (London and New York, Routledge, 1993).

[47] See Paula Baker, 'The Domestication of Politics: Women in American Political Society, 1780–1920', *American Historical Review*, 89 (1984), 620–47; and Patricia Hollis, *Ladies Elect: Women in English Local Government, 1865–1914* (Oxford: Clarendon Press, 1987). See also Jane Lewis, *Politics of Motherhood* (London: Croom Helm, 1980).

female enfranchisement had been based on difference, just as they were often informed by conservative and nationalist ideas.[48] Writing in the *North American Review*, the feminist Lydia Lvovna Pimenoff attacked Herbert Spencer's view that women should be denied the voting privilege on the grounds that they could not fight, arguing that this logic would deprive men themselves of the suffrage on the ground that they could not bear children; she concluded 'women *do* furnish contingents to the army and the navy'.[49] Women could contribute to the national and imperial economy through motherhood. In an unpublished manuscript 'Eugenic Advantages, A Forecast', Galton noted:

> the object, briefly, is to call into existence a large contingent of citizens who are naturally endowed above the average of our present nation, with health and vigour of mind and body and of naturally good characters and the question is how to spend money, in the most economical way, in accordance with public sentiment, for doing this.[50]

The first 'naturally' is inserted as a manuscript revision, suggesting Galton's keenness to stress that eugenics was working *with* nature—that the superiority of certain social groups was biologically determined. In another essay, headed 'the money worth to the state of an infant male child of selected parents', Galton asked 'what is the average value to the state of each child, in any large group of them, who are born of parents exceptionally gifted [phrase added] in the qualities that make for civic worth?'[51] Galton repeatedly drew attention to parallels between recruitment for military service and 'recruitment' for marriage: men were recruited into the army, women to marriage; both institutions defend and develop the empire.[52] He urged:

> it is hardly necessary to enter ~~much~~ into detail concerning the medical examination of recruits, which is exacted in order to learn whether or not they are fitted for military service. The methods used, vary somewhat in different countries and they differ much in severity at different ~~times~~ periods, according to the demands of the time . . . it may therefore be taken for granted that an examination of the same general character that recruits to the army undergo, and to which all candidates for the Indian Civil service and certain other public services are subjected, before

[48] For an insightful discussion of this aspect of suffrage rhetoric, see Jane Rendall, 'The Citizenship of Women and the Reform Act of 1867', in Catherine Hall, Keith McClelland, and Jane Rendall (eds.), *Defining the Victorian Nation: Class, Race, Gender and the Reform Act of 1867* (Cambridge: Cambridge University Press, 2000), esp. 163, 169–73.

[49] Lydia Lvovna Pimenoff, 'Science and the Woman's Question', *North American Review*, 156 (1893), 250.

[50] Galton Papers, 138/1.

[51] Galton Papers, 138/1.

[52] See pencil additions to presidential address of 1891, Galton Papers, 138/7 17.

they can be finally received, admits of being instituted, accompanied by what we may call an honour-certificate. Also that there is nothing so deterrent in such an examination as to excite serious repugnance.[53]

In 1891, Galton advocated eugenic strategies for preventing the birth of 'weakly children' who are 'constitutionally incapable of growing up as serviceable citizens and who are a serious encumbrance to the nation'.[54] A decade later, Arnold White declared: 'a medical certificate of physical and mental fitness for the marriage state should be exacted by a wise State before union, in the interest of the unborn, who deserve justice no less than their parents deserve compassion'.[55] And, in *Parenthood and Race Culture: An Outline of Eugenics* (1909), Caleb William Saleeby crystallized the position which social purists and eugenists had come increasingly to adopt: 'we have in marriage not only the greatest instrument of race-culture that has yet been employed—half-consciously—by man, but also an instrument supremely fitted, and indeed without a rival, for the conscious, deliberate, and scientific intentions of modern eugenists.'[56]

The Woman Question and the Housing Question began to serve each other. The idea that the urban poor, as a rapidly increasing expression (moral and physical) of defective biology, constituted a serious internal threat to national health and efficiency coincided with the idea that women might have a new political role in society, based on sex difference, which would allow them to qualify as citizens. Even those suffragettes who were not necessarily hereditarians, such as the Girton lecturer, Julia Wedgwood, and Millicent Fawcett, spoke out against what they held to be sentimental Christian compassion, opposing unsystematic charity which they argued might encourage pauperism, and urging women to gain a more disciplined understanding of national life and political economy.[57] Gendered citizenship could resolve both the uncertainties surrounding the future of the urban poor and the uncertainties

[53] Galton Papers, 138/4, 13–14.

[54] Pencil additions to presidential address of 1891, Galton Papers 138/7, 17.

[55] Arnold White, *Efficiency and Empire*, 120.

[56] *Parenthood and Race Culture: An Outline of Eugenics* (London: Cassell and Company Ltd, 1909), 168. In her discussion of racial degeneration ('such as fell upon the ancient civilizations of the world'), Swiney argued that the only answer is 'legal supervision, and the systematic medical inspection of those of both sexes, who, of their own free-will choose a vicious course of life' (*The Awakening of Women; or, Woman's Part in Evolution* (London: William Reeves, 1899), 219).

[57] See Rendall, 'The Citizenship of Women and the Reform Act of 1867', in Catherine Hall, Keith McClelland, and Jane Rendall (eds.), *Defining the Victorian Nation*, 168. Rendall cites an article by Julia Wedgwood, 'Female Suffrage in its Influence on Married Life',

surrounding the social and political function of women. It provided the framework for a precise form of female participation in national life which did not seek to duplicate masculine service; women might serve the state through reproductive labour. In doing so they would substitute for the indiscriminations of mid-Victorian philanthropy a rational and systematic programme of racial regeneration through the elimination of disease. And, in the hereditarian climate of the 1890s, poverty, immorality, crime, and prostitution were all swept up under the umbrella of disease. Arnold White urged a revival of the patriotism that consisted of 'the production of sound minds in healthy, athletic, and beautiful bodies',[58] warning of the dangers posed to empire by ill self-discipline, ill-health, and charity.[59] He warned that the 'poor law machinery', in treating unavoidable disease, was 'tainting posterity' and was thus 'incompatible with humanity'.[60]

Eugenics and the idea of gendered citizenship, both products of the new will to biologize, bore a vital, reciprocal relation to each other. Reproduction was no longer a sacred, private act, but one of public service, into which one entered from rational choice and a sense of duty. Early manifestations of these ideas can be found, again, in the work of Herbert Spencer. By 1861, Spencer was calling into question the classic understanding of citizenship, which, through its focus on abstract principles, overlooked the family. He noted that 'as the family comes before the State in order of time—as the bringing up of children is possible before the State exists or when it has ceased to be, whereas the State is rendered possible only by the bringing up of children; it follows that the duties of the parent demand further attention than those of the citizen'.[61]

Contemporary Review, 20 (August 1872), 360–70, in which Wedgwood argued that through exercising 'beneficent discipline' and 'intellectual training' women might end 'the rot of pauperism'. See also Wedgwood, 'Female Suffrage, Considered Chiefly with Regard to its Indirect Results', in J. Butler (ed.), *Woman's Work and Woman's Culture* (London: Macmillan, 1869), 247–89. See also Millicent Fawcett, 'Free Education in its Economic Aspects' and 'National Debts and National Prosperity', in Henry Fawcett and Millicent Garrett Fawcett (eds.), *Essays and Lectures on Social and Political Subjects* (London: Macmillan, 1872). Fawcett urged harsh measures to bring out Malthusian self-restraint, referring to the 'luxurious unemployed and the pauperised unemployed' pp. 144–5, cited in Rendall, *Defining the Victorian Nation*, 168; see also Fawcett, *Political Economy for Beginners* (London: Macmillan, 1870), and *Tales in Political Economy* (London: Macmillan, 1874).

58 Arnold White, *Efficiency and Empire*, 121.

59 Ibid., 95, 99.

60 Ibid., 99.

61 Spencer, *Education: Intellectual, Moral, and Physical* (London: Williams & Norgate, 1861), 9.

Spencer reworked the idea of citizenship so that the family was not only a microcosm or symbol of the state, but recognized as bearing an actual relation to the nation state. He argued that:

> since the goodness of a society ultimately depends on the nature of its citizens; and since the nature of its citizens is more modifiable by early training than by anything else, we must conclude that the welfare of the family underlies the welfare of society. And hence knowledge directly conducing to the first, must take precedence of knowledge directly conducing to the last.

This idea was taken up and developed by eugenic feminists who redefined citizenship so that it *began* with the family.

Spencer and eugenists alike had faith in nature. Where they differed was in relation to how nature's goals might be achieved in contemporary society. Eugenists replaced Spencer's faith in political and biological *laissez-faire* with forms of control. According to Spencer:

> happily, that all-important part of education which goes to secure direct self-preservation, is in great part already provided for. Too momentous to be left to our blundering. Nature takes it into her own hands.[62]

By contrast, eugenists thought nature might be given a helping hand: human direction.

Late nineteenth-century emphasis on the civic value of motherhood provided eugenic feminism with firm foundations. The century as a whole also witnessed a gradual shift of emphasis from the importance of wifely duties to those of mothers; a departure from the message of earlier conduct books and advice manuals which warned against too much mothering.[63] 'Maternity', wrote Alexandre Dumas *fils* in his play *Françillon* (1888), is 'women's brand of patriotism'. 'The cradle lies across the door of the polling-booth and bars the way to the senate', declared the anti-feminist Eliza Lynn Linton in 1890, but for a number of women, the cradle was the route to achieve public, civic status.[64] In the *Fortnightly Review*, Frederic Harrison declared that 'to keep the Family true, refined, affectionate, faithful, is a grander task than to govern the State; it is a task which needs the whole energies, the entire

[62] Ibid., 12

[63] See Pykett, *The Sensation Novel from* The Woman in White *to* The Moonstone (Plymouth: Northcote House, 1994), 61.

[64] Eliza Lynn Linton, 'The Wild Women No 1. As Politicians', *Nineteenth Century*, vol 30 (July 1891), 80, p. 79–88 quoted in Claudia Nelson and Ann Sumner Holmes (eds.), *Maternal Instincts: Visions of Motherhood and Sexuality in Britain, 1875–1925* (Basingstoke: Macmillan, 1997), 10.

life of Woman.'[65] The family, the basic building block of society, functioned as a microcosm of empire, fulfilling its duties of citizenship through reproduction.

The fear that emancipated women would renounce motherhood persisted among both sexes and points to the centrality of the maternal function to late nineteenth-century ideas of sexual and social relations. In George Noyes Miller's *The Strike of a Sex* (1891), Rodney Carford, the anthropologist-narrator, records women from all classes uniting in renouncing sex, childrearing, and housework. He learns that the great right which these women are calling their Magna Charta is 'the right to the perfect ownership of their own person'. Carford asks 'if woman is granted this astonishing right to say whether she should bear children or not—will she not seek to escape the burden of maternity to such a degree as to seriously diminish the population?' His interlocutor, Mr Lister, explains that such fears are unnecessary, for women no less than men would resist proposed changes to sex roles : 'if woman is really given her freedom her innate instincts will undoubtedly expand naturally and strongly, and certainly the desire for children is strongly implanted in her'.[66]

In 1890, in an appeal from Frances Russell, wife of the former prime minister John Russell, duty to nature and duty to the *nation* become conflated. A mother to six children, Russell rallied single women to return to motherhood, that 'neglected path to greatness'. Arguing that mothers could give nature a helping hand, Russell argued 'women must learn to think differently about the function of maternity'; 'instead of regarding it, as too many do, as a burden and a trouble to be avoided by every possible means, legitimate or otherwise, it should be considered as one of the most ennobling powers bestowed upon the sex'. Russell concluded her appeal for mothers by urging the literal sense of the proverb 'who rocks the cradle rules the world'.[67] It was no longer simply through 'ties of love and respect' that motherhood laid claim to a central role in the public sphere: national greatness was contingent

[65] Frederic Harrison, 'The Emancipation of Women', *Fortnightly Review*, 56 (1891), 443, 452. Cf. Havelock Ellis, *Man and Woman*. Absent from the 1894 edition, but added to the 7th edition (Boston: Houghton Mifflin, 1929), was an emphasis on the spatial division society predicated on gender (with women being biologically suited to caring for human life in the home); see Cynthia Eagle Russett, *Sexual Science: The Victorian Construction of Womanhood* (1989; Cambridge, Mass. and London: Harvard University Press, 1991), 124.

[66] George Noyes Miller, *The Strike of a Sex* (London: William Reeves, 1891), 55.

[67] Frances Russell, 'A Neglected Path to Greatness', *Westminster Review*, 135 (1890), 395.

upon reproduction. Russell appealed to 'thinking women': 'I desire to interest the mothers, and especially the young mothers, of the race in a question of mental evolution, where they may assist Nature almost as much perhaps as does the gardener in the development of his vegetable creations.'[68]

Responsible motherhood was a moral obligation and a woman's first act of citizenship in late Victorian Britain. It conferred nobility, prestige, and power. At a time of concern over national efficiency and empire, motherhood and imperialism were drawn into an alliance in which the function of reproduction was crucial.[69] 'The great British empire, the greatest civilizing, order-spreading, Christianizing world-power ever known, can only be saved by a solemn league and covenant of her women to bring back simplicity of life . . . reverence for marriage laws, chivalrous respect for all womanhood, and a high standard of purity for men and women alike', declared Ellice Hopkins in *The Power of Womanhood*; 'England, and England alone, is the mighty mother of nations. Three great nations have already sprung from her loins; a fourth in Africa is already in process of consolidation'; 'decay with great empires, as with fish, sets in at the head; and the moral decadence of England will sensibly lower the moral standard of one-fourth of the population of the world. The heart of the nation is still sound. It is not too late'. England was, itself, a trope of motherhood: 'the fruitful mother of nations'.[70]

National health was increasingly a moral matter. Hopkins quoted from James Anthony Froude's seminal history *Oceana; or, England and her Colonies* (1886): 'a sound nation is a nation that is made up of sound human beings, healthy in body, strong of limb, true in word and deed, brave, sober, temperate, and chaste, to whom morals are of more importance than wealth or knowledge' and, correspondingly, motherhood was a moral duty and a public function: 'rarely, indeed, can any public work that [woman] can do for the world equal the value of that priceless work of building up, stone by stone, the temple of a good man's character which falls to the lot of his mother.'[71] Hopkins concluded her tract 'The

[68] Ibid., 392, 393.

[69] See Anna Davin, 'Imperialism and Motherhood', *History Workshop*, 5 (1978), 9–65; see also Marie Corelli, 'Mother-Love', *Windsor Magazine*, 11 (1899–1900), 99: with women 'rest the strength, goodness and greatness of the next generation, in the influence they exercise on their children'.

[70] *The Power of Womanhood; or Mothers and Sons: A Book for Parents and Those in loco parentis* (London: Wells, Gardner, Darton & Co., 1899), 165, 120.

[71] Ibid., 152.

Present Moral Crisis' with the words 'to you, as to woman of old, it is given to save your own nation'.[72] Eugenic love had a strong theological tradition of love as sacrifice on which to draw, as Ellice Hopkins was quick to do:

> Oh, the banner of Love, oh, the banner of Love,
> Will cost you a pang to hold,
> But 'twill float in triumph the field above
> Though your heart's blood stain its fold.[73]

The eugenist Alice Ravenhill, in the first issue of the *Eugenics Review*, noted with some incredulity: 'the intimate connection between home life and national prosperity was hardly perceived sixty years ago.'[74] The Revd Samuel Hemphill made the same intimate connection in his condemnation of women who did not have children in sufficient quantities, though with different emphasis:

> there is a certain publicity, a measure of glory, attaching to this volunteering for your country. But what I will call *the patriotic side of wedlock* is a secret. If you have only one or two children, who is to know whether this be due to the will of God operating through nature, or according to your own perverted will acting in violation of nature? So you build upon the fact that no one can put his finger upon you and your wife and say: 'these are race-murderers'.[75]

According to the social purist Laura Ormiston Chant 'motherhood shall be recognized as the inner sanctuary of all that is holiest on earth, and passion be lifted by the strong and tender hand of mutual love, out of the selfish and base region of mere animalism, into the noble aspiration of noble marriage.'[76] Moral citizenship posed no direct threat to traditional gendered hierarchies, though it could inspire suffragists. In 1909 the suffragists Ethel Hill (author of *The Children of the Abyss* (1905), *The Woman-Friend and the Wife* (1907), and *The Unloved* (1909)), and Olga Fenton Shafer published a collection of essays—*Great Suffragists—and Why: Modern Makers of History* (1909). Among the contributors were Sarah Grand, Olive Schreiner, Millicent Garrett Fawcett, Frances Swiney, Countess Russell and Charlotte Perkins Gilman. Hill concludes her Preface:

[72] 'The Present Moral Crisis' (London: Hatchards, 1886), 24.

[73] Hopkins, 'The Man with the Drawn Sword' (London: Hatchards, 1883), 15.

[74] 'Eugenic Ideals for Womanhood', *The Eugenics Review*, i (April 1909), 269.

[75] The Revd Sam Hemphill, *The Murderess of the Unseen: A Tract on Race Suicide* (Dublin: Hodges, Figgis, & Co., Ltd, 1908), 11, emphasis in original.

[76] 'Chastity in Men and Women: A Woman's Answer to a Woman in Regard to the Equality of the Moral Law' (London: Dyer Brothers, 1885), 11.

I am a Suffragist because I sincerely believe what the 'Antis' are eternally saying with their lips, but do not believe—i.e. that the highest and holiest occupation on earth is the bearing, and rearing, and educating of the succeeding generation. How do I know that they, and all the world, do not believe it? I will tell you. Because this work is relegated to pauper labour. The world pays for what it values. How does it pay its mothers? With board, and lodging, and tips. How does it pay its nursemaids, to whom it entrusts the young? Almost the least of all its servants. How does it pay its teachers, who bend the plastic minds of our children? About as much as our cooks, when you consider living expenses of both. I believe the chief value to the world of the business woman will be to raise the status of the home woman—the mother, to put her work on a more respected basis.

I am the poet of the woman the same as the man,
And I say it is as great to be a woman as to be a man,
And I say there is nothing greater than the mother of men

sang Walt Whitman, and who will say him nay?[77]

As with the question of poverty and the health of the nation, the idea of duty to the race was a determining one, and a substantial number of women underscored the idea of reproduction as woman's central function, recalling independent women to motherhood, and seeking to direct human reproduction through their writing. Autonomy, they argued, was more important than independence, and reproduction was not only compatible with, but the essence of, autonomy.

[77] *Great Suffragists—and Why: Modern Makers of History* (London: Henry J. Drane Ltd, 1909), 18.

4 Science and Love

My dear, romances are pernicious. You do not read them, I hope? . . . The false pictures they give of [love and marriage] cannot be too strongly condemned. They are not like reality.

Charlotte Brontë[1]

The work of art is not its own aim, but it has a specially organic, and a social task.

Max Nordau[2]

What you get married for if you don't want children?

T. S. Eliot[3]

LOVE AMONG THE SCIENTISTS

Around the middle of the nineteenth century, love became less a question of social and scientific debate as the love-plot began to appeal as much to the biologist as to the novelist. In the *Descent of Man*, Darwin justified his new, and extensive, focus on sexual relations, citing Schopenhauer: 'the final aim of all love intrigues, be they comic or tragic, is really of more importance than all other ends in human life . . . it is not the weal or woe of any one individual, but that of the human race to come, which is here at stake'.[4] While the *Origin of Species* had overturned traditional values and beliefs, the *Descent* endorsed many, particularly in relation to the role of women in society. Shifting attention from natural selection, which was *random*, Darwin now gave sexual selection, which was directed by *choice*, a much more important role in his theory of evolution than it had enjoyed in the *Origin*. In so doing, he tacitly granted humans agency in

[1] Charlotte Brontë, *Shirley* (1849; Harmondsworth: Penguin, 1974), 366.

[2] Nordau, *Degeneration* (1892), trans. from the 2nd German edn. (Heinemann 1895; Lincoln and London: University of Nebraska Press, 1968), 336.

[3] T. S. Eliot, 'The Waste Land' (1922).

[4] Darwin took this quotation from Dr David Asher, 'Schopenhauer and Darwinism', *Journal of Anthropology* (January 1871), 323; absent from the 1st edn. of the *Descent*, in which it presumably appeared too late to be included, it is cited in the 2nd edn. (London: John Murray, 1874), 586 (ch. 20).

their own evolutionary development, for if natural selection was selection by nature, then sexual selection invested agency, and agency for change, in individuals. The possibility of sexual selection as a qualitative process had been broached before Darwin; as early as 1853 in a treatise on the management of infancy Thomas John Graham (a popular writer on medical matters) wrote 'it is only by attending to the law of selection, that the organization and qualities of offspring can be improved, and, on the other hand, that the disastrous consequences of improper intermarriages can be avoided'.[5]

In 1864, Galton contemplated writing a eugenic romance: 'let us then give reins to our fancy and imagine a Utopia—or a Laputa if you will.'[6] As Pearson remarked in his discussion of this idea 'a modern Gulliver should start his travels again and seek a bride in Eugenia'.[7] Galton began to see the role that fiction might play in popularizing his ideas. By educating the reading public about the biological impulses that drove the love-plot, as Darwin had done in the *Descent*, the novel might also begin to educate them in the theory and practice of eugenics. He wrote in his notebook in 1888:

> No theme is more trite than that of the sexual instinct. It forms the principal subject of each of the many hundreds, four hundred, I believe, of novels, and of ~~most of the~~ the still more numerous poems that are annually written in England alone, but one of its main peculiarities, has never, so far as I know, been even yet clearly set forth. It is the relation that exists between different degrees of contrast and different degrees of sexual attractiveness. ~~When the fem~~ The male is little ~~if at all~~ attracted by close similarity. The attraction ~~is~~ rapidly increase~~d~~s as the difference in any given respect between the female and the male increases, but only up to a certain point, when this is passed, the attraction again wanes until zero is reached. When the diversity is still greater the attraction becomes negative and passes into a repugnance~~. A modestly fair m~~ such as most fair men ~~might~~ appear to feel ~~towards a woman of a negro tint~~ towards a negress. I have endeavoured to measure the amount of difference that gives rise to the maximum of attractiveness between men and women, both as regards eye-colour and stature, chiefly using for that purpose the data contained in my collection of 'Family Records', and have succeeded in doing so roughly and provisionally.[8]

[5] T. J. Graham, *On the Management and Disorders of Infancy and Childhood* (London: Simpkin, Marshall & Co.), 28, cited in Sally Shuttleworth, 'Demonic Mothers: Ideologies of Bourgeois Motherhood in the Mid-Victorian Era', in Linda M. Shires (ed.), *Rewriting the Victorians: Theory, History and the Politics of Gender* (London: Routledge, 1992), 36.

[6] Karl Pearson, *The Life, Letters, and Labours of Francis Galton* (Cambridge, Cambridge University Press, 1914–1930), ii. 78.

[7] Ibid., iiia. 411.

[8] University College London Library, Galton Papers, 138/3.

Decrying the dysgenic effects of passion he favoured the rational selection of reproductive partners on grounds of their fitness to be parents:

> the causes that lead to marriage are numerous, and of these the blind and passionate influence of love is only one of them, however engrossing at the time. For example, the opportunities of making the acquaintance that led to love have probably nothing to do with love itself. It is therefore not at all impossible that any custom which should succeed in putting men who deserve recognition in a more favourable light than those who do not, thereby indirectly indicating those who, as a class, would be the most appropriate parents of the next generation, might further these marriages to a sensible degree.[9]

As the language of biology was shaping the debates on poverty and the role of women in society, so it underpinned new aesthetic discourses in the second half of the nineteenth century, equating the ugly with disease and the beautiful with health.[10] In an article in the *Leader* in 1854, 'Personal Beauty', Spencer argued a *necessary* relationship 'between ugly features and inferiority of intellect and character', concluding 'the saying that beauty is but skin-deep is but a skin-deep saying'.[11]

Grant Allen was a leading exponent of this new biological narrative. In *Physiological Aesthetics* (1877), dedicated to Herbert Spencer, he set out his object as 'to exhibit the purely physical origin of the sense of beauty, and its relativity to our nervous organization'.[12] Physiological aesthetics joined beauty to function. In an essay for the journal *Mind* (founded in 1876 to serve the rapidly developing science of psychology), Allen argued: 'the facts on which Mr Darwin bases his theory of sexual selection thus become of the first importance for the aesthetic philosopher, because they are really the only solid evidence for the existence of a love for beauty in the infra-human world'.[13] Directing readers to Spencer's essay, 'Personal Beauty', he noted that, while Spencer confined himself to idea and emotion:

> I, in accordance with my general plan, have given greatest prominence to the immediate sensuous effect. At the same time I am most willing to allow that sexual selection and the survival of the fittest will in all probability have produced such an internal consensus that those persons of either sex who will bear outward signs of intellectual, moral, and physical qualities adapted to their circumstances, and who are consequently the most desirable parents for the coming generations, will mutually please the opposite sex.

[9] Galton Papers, 138/4, 10.

[10] See Sander Gilman, *Health and Illness: Images of Difference* (London: Reaktion Books Ltd, 1995).

[11] *Leader* (15 April 1854), 356–7.

[12] Grant Allen, *Physiological Aesthetics* (London: Henry S. King & Co., 1877), 2.

[13] Grant Allen, 'Aesthetic Evolution in Man', *Mind*, 5 (1880), 447.

Noting that sexual selection is 'largely affected by differences of race, class, family, age, sex, and individual peculiarities', Allen remarked 'all that can be said with confidence is this: human beauty is, in part at least, a combination of abstract pleasure in form and colour, with a certain given, relatively rigid, symmetrical, normal healthy type'.[14] Again, aesthetics is returned to the pressing question of health.[15] In his later essay in *Mind* Allen's argument is more overtly eugenic. He declares that there must be 'such an intimate correspondence between the needs and tastes of each species, that the sight and voice of a healthy, normal, well-formed mate must have become intrinsically pleasing for its own sake, as well as indirectly for its associations'. He deduces that

> the heart and core of such a fixed hereditary taste for each species much consist in the appreciation of the pure and healthy typical specific form. The ugly for every kind, in its own eyes, must always be (in the main) the deformed, the aberrant, the weakly, the unnatural, the impotent. The beautiful for every kind must similarly be (in the main) the healthy, the normal the strong, the perfect, and the parentally sound. Were it ever otherwise—did any race or kind ever habitually prefer the morbid to the sound, that race or kind must be on the highroad to extinction.[16]

These ideas were attractive to the Eugenics Society. 'A eugenic girl is a healthy girl, and a healthy girl is an attractive girl', declared the *Eugenics Review* in 1913.[17]

Notwithstanding the potential of the body to express health and disease, exponents of eugenics could not escape the fact that appearances were unreliable. Crucial to eugenics was genealogy, life history; historical records which might overwrite or underwrite the stories the body could tell. After all, hereditary taint might conceal or misrepresent itself.[18] As I show in Chapters 5–8, New Women explored these ideas in

[14] Allen, *Physiological Aesthetics*, 242, 239, 240. Allen directs the reader to ch. 19 of Darwin's *Descent* for a comprehensive discussion of the 'complicated questions of sexual selection' (*Physiological Aesthetics*, 239).

[15] Similarly, Caesare Lombroso linked the idea of racial progress to symmetry, writing in *The White Man and the Coloured Man* (1871) 'Only we White people have reached the most perfect symmetry of bodily form . . .', *L'uomo bianco e l'uomo di colore. Letture sull'origine e le varietà delle razze umane* (Padua, 1871), 222–3, cited in Pick, *Faces of Degeneration: A European Disorder, c.1848–c.1918* (Cambridge: Cambridge University Press, 1993), 126.

[16] Allen, 'Aesthetic Evolution in Man', 448, 449. Sander Gilman's concluding words on the link between sexuality and the beautiful encapsulate Allen's thesis: 'the ugly is anti-erotic rather than merely unaesthetic. It is denied the ability to reproduce' (Gilman, *Health and Illness*, 92).

[17] *Eugenics Review*, 5 (1913), 385–6.

[18] Such fears persisted into the twentieth century: see, for example, the US wartime poster 'She May Look Clean—But,' *c.*1944, Washington, DC: NLM Collection, reproduced in Sander L. Gilman, *Sexuality: An Illustrated History, Representing the Sexual in*

fiction, supplying detailed life histories in novels, but concentrating on moments, appearances, in their short stories. As early as 1882 Galton observed in the *Fortnightly Review* that life histories:

are especially able to forewarn and to encourage us, for they are prophetic of our own futures. If there be such a thing as a natural birthright, I can conceive of none greater than the right of each child to be informed, at first by proxy through his guardians, and afterwards personally, of the life-history, medical and other, of his ancestry. The child is brought into the world without having his voice at all in the matter, and the smallest amends that those who introduced him there can make, is to furnish him with that most serviceable of all information to him, the complete life-histories of his near progenitors.[19]

Later that year, again in the *Fortnightly Review*, Galton made a case for national 'anthropometric laboratories', where 'a man may from time to time get himself and his children weighed, measured, and rightly photographed, and have each to their bodily faculties tested, by the best methods known to modern science'.[20] In thus exhibiting themselves, citizens would be given an account of their state of health and, more importantly, they would be providing posterity with vital health records. Galton urged the centrality of photography for an accurate family record, and signalled ways in which outmoded, inefficient, and incomplete ways of recording family history were on the point of being replaced by widely accessible technological accuracy:

The family Bibles of past generations served as registers of family events. Births, illnesses, marriages, and deaths were chronicled on their fly-leaves, and those ponderous books fulfilled an important function in this incidental way. But they are now becoming generally replaced by more handy volumes, and the family register is disappearing with the old family Bible. In the meantime photography has been discovered and has sprung into universal use, and the hereditary value of what are called 'life-histories' is becoming continually more appreciated. It seems, then, to be an appropriate time to advert the establishment of a new form of family register that shall contain all those notices that were formerly entered in the family Bible and much more besides, namely, a series of photographic studies of the features from childhood onwards, together with facts that shall afford as complete a life-history as is consistent with brevity. ('Photographic Chronicles')

Medicine and Culture from the Middle Ages to the Age of AIDS (London: John Wiley & Sons, 1989).

[19] Galton, 'Photographic Chronicles from Childhood to Age', *Fortnightly Review*, 37 (1882), 26–31.

[20] 'The Anthropometric Laboratory', *Fortnightly Review*, 37 (1882), 332–8.

Alerting his readers to the new possibilities of photography for the family archive, he reveals the extent of his investment in the family as a national, eugenic database. The sentimental, to which he briefly appeals, is overridden by the scientific:

> those who care to initiate and carry on a family chronicle, illustrated by abundant photographic portraiture, will produce a work that they and their children, and their descendants in more remote generations, will assuredly be grateful for. The family tie has a real as well as sentimental significance. The world is beginning to perceive that the life of each individual is in some real sense a prolongation of those of his ancestry. His character, his vigour, and his disease are principally theirs; sometimes his faculties are blends of ancestral qualities, more frequently they are aggregates, veins of resemblance to one or other of them showing now here and now there.

Galton ends on a note of documentary fervour: 'the sum of the statements and recommendations in these pages is to this effect. Obtain photographs periodically of yourselves and of your children, making it a family custom to do so, because unless driven by some custom the act will be postponed until the opportunity is lost' (31).

Rationalized, family history might serve a useful purpose in improving the biological quality of future generations. Galton set up a laboratory at the International Health Exhibition of 1884 (See figures 3 and 4.):

> The measurements instruments dealt with keenness of Sight and of Hearing; Colour sense; Judgment of eye; Breathing power; Reaction Time; Strength of Pull and of Squeeze; Force of Blow; Span of arms; Height, both standing and sitting; and Weight. The ease of working the instruments that were used was so great that an applicant could be measured in all these respects, a card containing the results furnished him, and a duplicate made and kept for statistical purposes, at the total cost of the threepence fee which was charged for admission.[21]

Around 10,000 persons were measured at this laboratory, with Galton assisting: 'four hundred complete sets are published in the *Anthropological Institute Journal*, 1889, and afford good material for future use in many ways'.[22] When the exhibition closed the following year, Galton recorded: 'it seemed a pity that the laboratory should also come to an end, so I asked for and was given a room in the Science Galleries of the South Kensington Museum, where I maintained one during about 6 years' (301). He was even visited by Gladstone:

[21] 'Memories of My Life', ch. on 'The Anthropometric Laboratory', 295–310. On Galton's establishment of a Eugenics Record Office, later to become the Galton Laboratory of National Eugenics, see p. 29.

[22] Ibid., 296.

whose measurements proved very acceptable to Mr Brock the sculptor in making a posthumous statue of him, for Liverpool. Mr Gladstone was amusingly insistent about the size of his head, saying that hatters often told him that he had an Aberdeenshire head 'a fact which you may be sure I do not forget to tell to my Scotch constituents'. It was a beautifully shaped head, though low, but after all it was not so very large in circumference.[23]

In the year of Victoria's death, Galton began a eugenic eutopia, 'Donoghue of Dunno Weir'.[24] It opened with the words 'passion for the good of the society', noting 'love of country is a piety and duty and peremptory law'.[25] Notwithstanding the punning title, the reader is left in no doubt as to the biological identity of the Donoghue family, whose pedigree is meticulously detailed.[26] In 1910, Galton wrote a eugenic romance, though this time with more ambitious intent.[27] As Pearson observed:

We must remember that Galton had set before himself in the last years of his life a definite plan of eugenics propagandism. He wanted to appeal to men of science through his foundation of a Eugenics Laboratory; he had definitely approached separate groups like the Anthropologists in his Huxley Lecture and the Sociologists in his lecture before their Society and in his subsequent essays, he had appealed to the academic world in his Herbert Spencer Lecture at Oxford, and to the world that reads popular quarterlies in his Eugenics Education Society. But there are strata of the community which cannot be caught even by these processes. For these he consented to be interviewed, and for the still less reachable section who read novels and only look at the picture pages of newspapers, he wrote what they needed, a tale, his 'Kantsaywhere'. His scheme for proselytism was a comprehensive one, but I think Galton knew his public better than most men.[28]

The protagonist of Galton's 'Kantsaywhere' is a professor of vital statistics who falls in love with the aptly named Miss Allfancy, a student at the Eugenics College.[29] In 'Kantsaywhere', he records, 'they think much

[23] 'Memories of My Life', 301–2.

[24] 138/5: Galton, MS of 'Donoghue of Dunno Weir' and notes on resemblance traits and biometry (1901).

[25] Galton gives as a source for this quotation William Henry Fitchett, *How England Saved Europe: The Story of the Great War, 1793–1815* (London: 1899), Galton Papers, 138/5, 1.

[26] Galton's own autobiography shares striking parallels with the structure of this romance, as he gives close details of his ancestors, noting which have entries in the *Dictionary of National Biography*.

[27] Galton Papers, 138/6: 'The Eugenic College of Kantsaywhere', enclosed in a letter from Millicent Galton Lethbridge to Edward Galton Wheeler-Galton (*c.*1911). Remains reprinted in Pearson, *The Life, Letters, and Labours of Francis Galton*, iiia. 411–25.

[28] Pearson, *The Life, Letters, and Labours of Francis Galton*, iiia. 412.

[29] See Patrick Parrinder, 'Eugenics and Utopia: Sexual Selection from Galton to Morris', *Utopian Studies*, 8 (1997), 10.

more of the race than of the individual, and on my expressing a faint surprise, the family argued to the following effect: suppose a person to be one of the parents of four children'; 'a person is . . . more important as a probable progenitor of many others more or less like to him in constitution than as a mere individual' (415). Galton defines eugenics as 'all that is transmissible by heredity, whether it be of ancestral origin or a personal sport or mutation' (415). The narrator gets 'a first class PG—Passed in Genetics—degree, and I had to imprint my fingers in their Register, for future identification'. At the core of 'Kantsaywere' lies a new, rationalized love; passion—an inhibitor of rational choice—was edited out of the love-plot.

HEREDITY, HEALTH, AND THE NOVEL

Set in 1829, *The Mill on the Floss* (1860), which George Eliot was writing when the *Origin* appeared,[30] shows the fascination with heredity that ran through the nineteenth century.[31] The laws of heredity that perplex Mr Tulliver—'a pleasant sort o' soft woman may go on breeding you stupid lads and 'cute wenches, till it's as if the world was turned topsy-turvy' gained little illumination from the *Origin*, in which Darwin admitted: 'our ignorance of the laws of variation is profound'.[32] Nonetheless, the novel shows a new interest in evolution. As Tom Tulliver shoots peas at a bluebottle the narrator observes that nature 'had provided Tom and the peas for the speedy destruction of this weak individual'.[33] As I shall show in the following chapters, in the closing decades of the century ideas of heredity and breeding were taken up in the novel with a new urgency by New Woman writers. In an essay 'On the Treatment of Love

[30] The *Origin* went on sale on 22 November 1859 (see Adrian Desmond and James Moore, *Darwin* (Harmondsworth: Penguin, 1992), 477). Eliot was writing the first volume of *The Mill on the Floss* by October 1859 and completed the second volume by 16 January 1860 (see Haight, *George Eliot: A Biography* (Oxford: Oxford University Press, 1968), 308, 319). Eliot felt that the *Origin of Species* was fine, so far as it went, but that it left out the *mystery* of life: 'to me the Development Theory and all other explanations of processes by which things came to be, produce a feeble impression compared with the mystery that lies under the processes' (George S. Haight (ed.), *George Eliot: Letters*, 9 vols. (New Haven: Yale University Press, 1954–78), ii. 227).

[31] See Harriet Ritvo, *The Platypus and the Mermaid and Other Figments of the Classifying Imagination* (Cambridge, Mass.: Harvard University Press, 1997).

[32] Darwin, *The Origin of Species; or, The Preservation of Favoured Races in the Struggle for Life* (1859; Oxford: Oxford University Press, 1996), 137.

[33] *The Mill on the Floss* (1860; Harmondsworth: Penguin, 1985), 68–9, 147.

in Novels' *Fraser's Magazine* had reported in 1856 'every story with love in it is popular. The popularity might be put in another form—there is no story without love in it.' The essay distinguished between 'true stories of life'—or biography—and the novel: 'the interest of the novel terminates with marriage, where the real interest of the biography usually begins'.[34] Eugenic New Woman writers would turn round this emphasis, seeking to provide such 'true stories of life' as they explored, through fiction, the complexities of biological inheritance, turning marriage from narrative *goal* to narrative focus, as part of their programme to educate the public on issues of public and private morality and on the importance of selecting a healthy reproductive partner. The converging ideologies of degeneration and eugenics provided the novel with a new romance plot by replacing 'love and marriage' with marriage as a mediator of genealogy.

However, the novel itself had to be reformed before it could be used to disseminate a new morality, for while Dickens and Eliot had established the moral responsibility of the novelist, the novel was nonetheless intimately bound up with the romance plot that eugenists were seeking to rewrite. In a piece for a collection on Sarah Grand published in 1933, Charles Whitby, Olive Schreiner's cousin, wrote:

> a novel, it was tacitly and well-nigh universally assumed, was a book written to amuse and entertain people, in a mild, unaggressive, superficial way; to titillate their emotions, without troubling the depths; a novel was for pastime, in short, simply and solely.[35]

Sometimes novels did worse than titillate—they were dangerous.[36] In Susan Ferrier's *Marriage* (1818) Miss Grizzy remarks 'I think reading's a very dangerous thing. I'm certain all Mary's bad health is entirely owing to reading. You know, we always thought she read a great deal too much for her good'.[37] Novel-reading functions, in this novel, as a

[34] Anon., 'On the Treatment of Love in Novels', *Fraser's Magazine*, 53 (1856), 411–12.

[35] Charles Whitby, 'Sarah Grand: The Woman and her Work', written for inclusion in the *Sarah Grand Miscellany* (comp. by Gladys Singers-Biggers and published privately under the title *The Breath of Life*); reproduced in Heilmann, *The Late Victorian Marriage Question: A Collection of Key New Woman Texts*, 5 vols. (London and New York: Routledge with Thoemmes Press, 1998), i. 330.

[36] Jenny Bourne Taylor, *In the Secret Theatre of Home: Wilkie Collins, Sensation Narrative, and Nineteenth-Century Psychology* (London: Routledge, 1988); Kate Flint, *The Woman Reader 1837–1914* (Oxford: Clarendon Press, 1993); and Lyn Pykett, *The 'Improper' Feminine: The Women's Sensation Novel and the New Woman Writing* (London and New York: Routledge, 1992) discuss the imagined danger of 'inappropriate' reading material as it was expressed in fiction, the press, and medical and psychological literature.

[37] Susan Ferrier, *Marriage* (1818; Oxford: Oxford University Press, 1997), 179.

symbol of lax moral standards. Lady Juliana's brother lolls dissolutely upon a sofa 'with a new novel in his hand' (150). By the middle of the nineteenth century, even the medical press was seriously considering the effects of novels on women readers. In 1851 the *Journal of Psychological Medicine and Mental Pathology* included novels in a list of dangerous sexual stimuli; writing in fear that woman's natural morality might become diseased by a contaminating environment, it warned against the reading of love-stories, adding parenthetically 'which all novels are'.[38] The central argument of that article was that 'whatever may be said of the rights of woman, it is her allotted duty to marry and bear children'; novels, along with dancing, intimate social intercourse, excessive needle work, and other 'excitants of the sexual feelings' were perceived as a threat to this duty (42, 38). In 1860 Forbes Benignus Winslow, the editor of the same journal, wrote a treatise, *On Obscure Diseases of the Brain, and Disorders of the Mind.* In this, he grouped novels with other written sources of moral pollution (as dangerous as servants) for the minds of innocent middle-class girls, warning of 'vicious books' and 'sensational novels' 'surreptitiously taken into the nursery'.[39]

Eugenic fiction had to distance itself from this form of writing and from the sensation fiction of the 1860s from which it had very different goals—though the genres shared common interests. In Sarah Grand's *The Beth Book*, Beth—who 'always sat on a high chair, that she might not be enervated by lolling'[40] finds her self-discipline start to slip on encountering one of her brutal husband's shilling shockers: 'the story was of an extremely sensational kind, and she found herself being wrought up by it to a high pitch of nervous excitement' (436); sensation fiction was bad for the health. The danger of sensation fiction recurs in social purity writing. 'Our literature is no longer as clean and wholesome as it was', noted Ellice Hopkins in the *Power of Womanhood*.[41] In 'True Manliness' she wrote:

[38] 'Woman in her Psychological Relations', *Journal of Psychological Medicine and Mental Pathology*, 4 (1851), 38.

[39] Jenny Bourne Taylor and Sally Shuttleworth (eds.), *Embodied Selves: An Anthology of Psychological Texts, 1830–1890* (Oxford: Oxford University Press, 1998), 271.

[40] *The Beth Book* (1897; Bristol: Thoemmes Press, 1994), 402; see also Grand's short story 'A New Sensation', first published in 1899 in *Windsor Magazine*, 2 (1899), which highlights the dangers of the pleasure-seeking life, in A. Richardson (ed.), *Women Who Did: Stories by Men and Women, 1890–1920* (Penguin, 2002), 231–43.

[41] *The Power of Womanhood; or, Mothers and Sons: A Book for Parents and Those in loco parentis* (London: Wells Gardner, Darton & Co. 1899), 182.

I am convinced myself, that when health has suffered it has been because the inward law of purity has not been obeyed as well as the outward. Excite yourself by reading trashy, bad novels, by bad talk, by evil imaginations, and you must expect to suffer physically for it, even if you keep pure in act.[42]

Her fellow social purist Laura Ormiston Chant warned:

there is a *danger* in reading low-class books, yellow backed novels, and the whole race of 'Readers' and 'Journals' such as are filled with tales of passion and murder; and there is a danger in reading any sort of book which makes you feel discontented with your lot in life, or that raises impure thoughts in your mind.[43]

Likewise, in his 1894 tract for impressionable girl-readers, *Confidential Talks with Young Women*, Lyman B. Sperry, a popular authority on sex, and self-styled lecturer on 'sanitary science', warned of the dangerous habit of the 'reading of sensational, sentimental novels, or "love stories"' (121). The novel was guilty of promoting romance, passion, and even sexual arousal. In May 1862 *Punch* reported that sensation novels were 'destroying Conventional Moralities, and generally unfitting the Public for the Prosaic Avocations of Life'.[44] Eliot's *Felix Holt, The Radical*, a novel in critical dialogue with sensation fiction, has its own sensational anti-heroine, the adulterous Mrs Transome who has lived the life of 'the clever sinner'; she is 'equipped with the views, the reasons, and the habits which belonged to that character . . . there were secrets which her son must never know' (91).

Sensation novels were practically obsessed with matters of health, or, rather, sickness. They tended to focus on insanity, as the *Spectator* noted with some weariness in an article entitled: 'Madness in Novels'.[45] And

42 'True Manliness' (London: Wells Gardner, Darton & Co., 1883), 18.

43 L. Ormiston Chant, 'Chastity in Men and Momen: A Woman's Answer to a Woman in Regard to the Equality of the Moral Law' (London: Dyer Brothers, 1885), 12.

44 *Punch* (May 1862). The Matrimonial Causes Act of 1857 led to the creation on 1 January 1858 of a Court for Divorce and Matrimonial Causes, which took over the jurisdiction for matrimonial affairs from the church courts and was empowered to deal with child custody, maintenance, and alimony. Many reports of sensational trials were covered in the national newspapers, in particular *The Times*. The *Saturday Review* complained of the divorce court column 'everybody reads it, and everybody comes out of the reading with blushing cheeks and tingling ears' cited in Barbara Leckie, *Culture and Adultery: The Novel, the Newspaper and the Law, 1857–1914* (Philadelphia: Philadelphia University Press, 1999), 94. See Leckie for an excellent exploration of relations between the new emphasis on divorce and the treatment of marriage in fiction. See also 'The Novels and Life', *Saturday Review*, 17 (1864), 188–9 (189).

45 'Madness in Novels', in *The Spectator* (1866), cited in Sally Shuttleworth, '"Preaching to the Nerves": Psychological Disorder in Sensation Fiction', in Marina Benjamin (ed.), *A Question of Identity* (New Brunswick: Rutgers University Press, 1997), 197.

there was madness in abundance; it drove the plot of, to name but a few, Mrs Henry Wood's *St Martin's Eve*, Mary Braddon's *Lady Audley's Secret*, the anonymous *The Clyffords of Clyffe*, and Wilkie Collins's *The Woman in White*.[46] Preoccupied with hereditary taints, fiendish villains, and monstrous mothers they are anxious, troubled, *excessive*, texts, at once setting female sensation, nervousness, and bodily disorder against masculine reason and control, but also calling into question male forms of control, and undermining psychiatric models of explanation.[47] The object of these novels was to create a sensation. They were seen by contemporary reviewers as both the source and symptom of disease. The Dean of St Paul's, Henry Longueville Mansel, declared in the *Quarterly Review* that such 'morbid' works were 'indications of a wide-spread corruption, of which they are in part both the effect and the cause; called into existence to supply the cravings of a diseased appetite, and contributing themselves to foster the disease, and to stimulate the want which they supply'. He concluded that such works, looked at as 'an eruption indicative of the state of health of the body in which they appear . . . are by no means favourable symptoms of the body of society.'[48] Hostile reviews were infused by the language of disease and contamination,[49] and outraged by an absence of moral feeling. In 1881 Leslie Stephen wrote 'the literary equivalent of moral degradation is blunted feeling; the loss of the delicate perception which enables a man to distinguish between exalted passion and brutish appetite. . . . This gives the true meaning, I think, of the modern complaints about what is called sensationalism.'[50] New Woman eugenic writers sought to write in a tradition of moral

[46] At this time, the biologically determined conception of madness, which increased with the pessimism of post-Darwinian psychiatrists such as Henry Maudsley, was still countered by more optimistic ideas. See Roy Porter, *Madness* (Oxford: Oxford University Press, 2002) and *A Social History of Madness* (Phoenix Press, 1996); Andrew Scull (ed.), *Madhouses, Mad-Doctors, and Madmen: The Social History of Psychiatry in the Victorian Era* (University of Pennsylvania Press, 1998); and Andrew Scull, Charlotte MacKenzie, and Nicholas Hervey, *Masters of Bedlam: The Transformation of the Mad-Doctoring Trade* (Princeton : Princeton University Press, 1994). The dominant method of treatment, moral management, worked on the assumption of recovery. Nonetheless, while the positive side of this non-hereditary approach to madness was a belief in recovery, the negative side was the idea that insanity might befall any member of a community, rather than a biologically determined few. This was an idea which sensation novels exploited: see Shuttleworth, '"Preaching to the Nerves"', 201.

[47] H. L. Mansel, 'Sensation Fiction', *Quarterly Review*, 113 (April 1863), 482–3, 512, cited in Sally Shuttleworth, '"Preaching to the Nerves"', 194.

[48] Shuttleworth, '"Preaching to the Nerves"', 194.

[49] Ibid., 194.

[50] Leslie Stephen, 'The Moral Element in Literature', *Cornhill Magazine*, 43 (1881), 47. This piece was the published version of a lecture given in December 1880.

responsibility, but in foregrounding issues of health and disease at times they came perilously close to the novels they were writing against.

The flipside—the necessary double—to the idea that fiction was dangerous was the idea that fiction might have an improving effect on moral standards and on health. Anthony Trollope championed the novel as the 'former of our morals, the code by which we rule ourselves, the mirror in which we dress ourselves'.[51] Here, George Eliot had set a fine example; she had, in the words of Leslie Stephen, 'brought great intellectual powers to setting before us a lofty moral ideal'.[52] In 1861, Dinah Mulock Craik opened an essay on Eliot in the *Cornhill* with an emphatic endorsement of the power of the novel to effect moral and social change:

> The modern novel is one of the most important moral agents of the community. The essayist may write for his hundreds; the preacher preach to his thousands; but the novelist counts his audience by the millions. His power is threefold—over heart, reason, and fancy'.[53]

Charles Whitby observed that the traditional view of women had been

> first seriously challenged by women novelists, rather than by men. I refer to Charlotte Brontë and Emily Brontë, George Eliot, to my cousin, Olive Schreiner, to the authoress of *Robert Ellesmeré* [*sic*], and, last, but by no means least, to Sarah Grand, who, in publishing *The Heavenly Twins*, came right out into the arena, making her heroine the mouthpiece of questions which menaced all the conventions of religion, morality, the social hierarchy and politics.[54]

Fiction and medicine had long been linked through metaphor. For example, Ferrier's *Marriage* (327) takes for an epigram the following extract from *Of Libraries*, by W. Drummond of Hawthornden (1585–1649):

> as in apothecaries' shops all sorts of drugs are permitted to be, so may all sorts of books be in the library; and as they out of vipers and scorpions, and poisonous vegetables, extract often wholesome medicaments for the life of mankind, so out of whatsoever book, good instruction and examples may be acquired.

This idea gathered momentum as the century progressed. In the *Forum*, Hardy likened the reader to a patient, with fiction as a remedy or palliative,

[51] Trollope, 'Novel Reading', *Nineteenth Century*, 5 (1879), 26.
[52] Leslie Stephen, 'George Eliot', *Cornhill Magazine*, 43 (1881), 168.
[53] Craik, 'To Novelists–and a Novelist', *Macmillan's Magazine*, 3 (1861), 442.
[54] Whitby, 'Sarah Grand: The Woman and her Work', reproduced in Ann Heilmann (ed.), *Sex, Social Purity and Sarah Grand* (London: Routledge, 2000).

remarking that reading might be undertaken for 'hygienic', or 'tonic' purposes and that an 'author should be swallowed whole, like any other pill'.[55]

Distancing themselves from the corrupting, the exciting, and the sensational, eugenic writers turned to reason. Cleaned up and rationalized, the novel might become a tool of responsible citizenship, spreading the gospel of Apollo over and against Dionysus, thought over emotion, heads over hearts, redirecting the heart towards eugenic devotion. With its emphasis on reason and responsibility eugenic fiction was the antithesis of the sensation novel, based on secrets and hereditary taint. And, while the novel had much to offer, allowing the effects of heredity to be explored in detail through generations, the short story allowed concentrated snap shots. A short story in the popular monthly magazine the *Ludgate* (1898), 'The Curse of Heredity', by Roslyn Gray, offers a distillation of this new plot.[56] The eyes of the female protagonist—stock emblem of beauty—and allure—in the love-plot, are here a symbol of heredity. Her suitor, Wyndham Grey, conceives of love primarily in terms of sacrifice and responsibility:

> What are the highest examples of love the world knows? Namely, those which show us that love in its best and truest form, is that which unreservedly and unselfishly gives itself for another . . . This is what makes motherhood a sacred thing, and the highest type of love, save one, that the world knows. There is complete surrender of one being for the sake of another.[57]

Religious images are here deftly reworked along biological lines, a practice that was becoming commonplace in eugenic rhetoric. In response to the question 'do you think it right or just, that the children should suffer for the sins of their fathers?' Wyndham replies 'it seems cruel and unjust to us, but it is an inexorable law of nature that the sins of the fathers should be visited on the helpless children they have borne.' At the story's climax, Lois Dering reveals the secrets that would have blighted the heroine of sensational fiction:

> my father died insane; my only brother is at present in a lunatic asylum; the same terrible fate may await me. I have always kept this horrible secret. It was only when you told me of your love that I realised the awfulness of it. (230)

55 'The Profitable Reading of Fiction', *Forum* (1888), in Harold Orel (ed.), *Thomas Hardy's Personal Writings* (London and Basingstoke: Macmillan, 1967), 111–12.

56 Roslyn Gray 'The Curse of Heredity', *The Ludgate*, 45 (July 1898), 223–31.

57 Ibid., 228.

In this story, however, the curse of heredity stops with this confession: Wyndham 'felt calm and strong, and saw my duty plainly. Never would I bring upon one I love such a terrible heritage; I would rather die first.' This conflation of religious and natural imagery, epitomized by the title, is a defining feature of eugenic thinking. The story's ending suggests a reworking of the Fall—instead of a Miltonic expulsion from the paradisal garden, the protagonists dutifully assume their allotted places within the natural scheme: 'she passed under the trees'. The story refuses to entertain the possibility of non-reproductive love. Earlier in the century the idea of mixing biology and love openly would have been unthinkable. Honoré de Balzac had protested in *The Physiology of Marriage* (1829) that

> to apply the word 'love' to the reproduction of the species, is the most odious blasphemy to which modern manners have given utterance. In raising us by the divine gift of thought above the beasts, nature has made us capable of feeling and affection, of desire and passion. There exists in man the double nature of animal and lover. The distinction will throw light on the social problem on which we are engaged.[58]

'Marriage', he continued, 'is the reproduction of the species; it is a guarantee in the bonds of which all men are interested; they have a mother and a father, they will have children.' But 'love is the poetry of the senses'.[59] Eugenic fiction would collapse this division between love (as poetry) and marriage (as sexual reproduction), urging that love was to be no more, and no less, than the rational reproduction of the species. Over the course of the century the biological basis of romance, literature, and life were firmly established so that, by its end, Lyman B. Sperry could draw on scientific authorities to bring home the centrality of biology:

> Says Dr Scott:—'The reason for the existence of love, biologically, is simply to bring about the union of two minute cells—the spermatozoon and the ovum—all other charms and fascinations, which are associated in our minds as belonging to the domain of love, centring in this one deep and natural source.' Dr Maudsley as truly says, 'Were man to be robbed of the instinct of procreation and all that arises from it, mentally, nearly all poetry and, perhaps, the entire moral sense, as well, would be torn from life'.[60]

As the idea of eugenics entered fiction, it came to permeate the writing of New Women. Eugenics pervades the plot of Jane Hume

[58] Honoré de Balzac, *The Physiology of Marriage* (1829; Baltimore and London: Johns Hopkins University, 1997), 60.

[59] Ibid., 60.

[60] Lyman B. Sperry, *Confidential Talks with Young Women* (Edinburgh and London: Oliphant, Anderson & Ferrier, 1894), 84.

Clapperton's novel *Margaret Dunmore* (1888): 'for unhealthy persons to become parents is a crime against Humanity' (127). Joe and Vera study physiology *au serieux*: 'a class for instruction in this science had been organized under the roof of La Maison, and to it outsiders were made freely welcome.' Likewise, Walter Cairns had made a bad marriage 'he mistook a transient passion, indicative merely of virile manhood, for that master passion which diffuses satisfaction throughout the entire complexus of the civilized man, and endures to the end of life' (58).[61] In *Gallia* (1895), Ménie Muriel Dowie's eponymous heroine insists on choosing a partner who is 'fine and strong and healthy, and of a healthy stock'. 'Fired and delighted' by Herbert Spencer (38), Gallia argues that current ideas on health make it inevitable that

> People will see the folly of curing all sorts of ailments that should not have been created, and then they will start at the right end, they will make better people. How can we consider that only one person in ten is handsome and well made, when you reflect that they were most likely haps of hazard, that they were unintended, the offspring of people quite unfitted to have children at all? [. . .] At present half the world is not as well treated as the best class of animals, and there isn't a political economist living who wouldn't say that if the increase of the lower classes could be taken out of their own hands and supervised on scientific lines, crime as well as a number of diseases would be stamped out.[62]

She makes her intentions quite clear: 'I shall marry solely with a view to the child I am going to live for.'[63]

Eugenic love found fine expression through Havelock Ellis. In 'Eugenics and St Valentine', a plea for eugenic certificates, he stressed that St Valentine had for many centuries been 'the patron saint of sexual selection, more especially in England'.[64] So, eugenics had an eminently

[61] In his novel of 1920, *The Coming of Bill*, P. G Wodehouse gave these ideas a parodic spin.

[62] Ménie Muriel Dowie, *Gallia* (1895; J. M. Dent, 1995), 113, 114–15.

[63] Ibid., 129.

[64] Havelock Ellis, 'Eugenics and St Valentine', *Nineteenth Century*, 59 (1906), 779–87. For correspondence from Havelock Ellis to Galton see Galton Papers, 239. On 30 May 1907 Ellis wrote to Galton pledging his support for eugenic certificates, and admitting that while 'some aspects of the scheme' were 'not quite thorough enough', 'I should be very glad indeed to hear that it is likely to move forward in an actual working shape'. On 5 October 1908 he wrote 'as my books have a wide circulation not only in America but in German and French translations I hope to be helpful in spreading the gospel in foreign parts'. Ellis urged Galton to try for a cheap edition of the book on *Human Faculty*, in such a series as 'Longman's Library' as a sort of classic of pioneering work. See also letter to Galton, Galton Papers, 190A, in which Havelock Ellis objected to Galton's 'insistence throughout on achievement' in his plans for eugenic certificates: 'from the eugenic standpoint, it seems to

respectable, romantic, and, importantly, national past. It had been 'by a happy inspiration' that 'Mr Galton chose to make public his programme of eugenic research in a paper read before the Sociological Society on the 14th of February, the festival of St Valentine'. Havelock Ellis asserted that, in keeping with technological progress, 'the new St Valentine will be a saint of science rather than of folklore'. By this deft rhetorical move, he made science and love happy and *natural* bedfellows, revealing that science—specifically calculation—had always played a part in the mating game: 'sexual selection, even when left to random influences, is still not left to chance; it follows definite and ascertainable laws. In that way the free play of love, however free it may appear, is really limited in a number of directions.' He concluded, reassuringly, that 'the eugenic ideal which is now developing is not an artificial product but the reasoned manifestation of a natural instinct'.[65] Three years later, in 1909, he wrote 'The Sterilization of the Unfit' for the first volume of the *Eugenics Review*.

Early in the century, *Frankenstein* had taken science to task, warning of the dangers of human transgression upon the role of the Creator. For eugenists by end of the century, man was the creator, science salvation, and fiction the instrument of salvation.

me more important to ascertain what a man is than what he has done'. He concluded 'the tendency of our civilization has been to sacrifice the man to his work, which seem quite topsy-turvy from the eugenic standpoint.'

[65] Ellis, 'Eugenics and St Valentine', 784, 785, 786.

5 Sarah Grand and Eugenic Love

FN.

> African Negroes, Bushmen of Australia, and, indeed, all low savage races, have broad, flat feet, thick ankles near the ground, low heels, and badly-formed calves to their legs; while in the higher races the feet and legs are well-formed.
>
> She was essentially a modern maiden, richly endowed with all womanly attributes, whose value is further enhanced by the strength which comes of the liberty to think, and of the education out of which is made the material for thought. With such women for the mothers of men, the English speaking races should rule the world.
>
> The marriage certificate should be a certificate of health. Do you not think we might have the law altered to make it so?
>
> Sarah Grand[1]

At Sarah Grand's death in 1943 *The Times* remarked that her bestselling novel of 1893, *The Heavenly Twins*, 'may be said to mark something of an epoch in English fiction . . . Sarah Grand and other writers of the school widened the field of English fiction by freeing it from some of its former limitations as to subject and treatment.'[2] One of the most widely read and talked about of late Victorian novelists, Sarah Grand was a committed exponent of biological determinism and eugenic feminism. In an essay called 'What to Aim at', published in 1894, she gave her readers a degenerate figure running through London:

> a man who, ten chances to one, began life handicapped by his constitution, and never had a chance to repair the error of nature, if, indeed, it could be repaired—one of those who should not have been born. Life for such is of necessity one long illness, full of suffering, mental, moral and physical, dull or acute . . . you

[1] *Two Dear Little Feet* (London: Jarrold and Sons, 1873), 29; Sarah Grand, 'Eugenia: A Modern Maiden and a Man Amazed', in *Our Manifold Nature* (London: William Heinemann, 1894); Grand to Frederick Henry Fisher, 22 March 1894, Special Collections, UCLA.

[2] 'Sarah Grand, Novelist of the Nineties', *The Times*, 13 May 1943, 7 col. e.

support the rotten social system which is responsible for the reckless production of such specimens of humanity, but when one comes as a consequence to trouble you, you evade your responsibility.[3]

For Grand, the question of where responsibility for the poor lay was clear; it lay with those who turned a blind eye to the 'reckless' reproduction of the unfit. She remained wedded to the idea that the middle class was the nation's best stock, urging middle-class women to 'learn to appreciate the value and weight of their own class, the great middle class' and stressing 'it is in the middle class itself that the best breeding, the greatest refinement, the prettiest manners and the highest culture are now to be found'.[4] A century later, interest in her work has revived considerably,[5] but the focus has been on her treatment of sex and gender. Removed, thus, from the issues of national health and class with which she was heavily engaged, she is generally celebrated as a pioneering, and unproblematic, feminist.

Grand was born Frances Elizabeth Bellenden Clarke, the fourth of five children, in 1854 in Donaghadee, Northern Ireland. Her father, Edward John Bellenden Clarke, the son of a lawyer, was a naval lieutenant then serving in Northern Ireland. Her mother, Margaret Bell Sherwood (who had married with a dowry of £6,000)[6] was the sister of the lord of the manor of Rysome Garth in Holderness, Yorkshire (he sold off the family estates in the 1880s).[7] Her stepson Haldane was a keen genealogist with a particular interest in Grand's pedigree which he drew up in elaborate detail. 'To give Madame Grand's lineage would be to raise from the dead a pageant of too many of the great figures in our island's history', he declared, before going on to do so. She was, he concluded:

[3] 'What to Aim at', in Andrew Reid (ed.), *The New Party* (London: Hodder Bros, 1894), 357–8.

[4] 'The Case of the Modern Married Woman, *Pall Mall Gazette* (February 1913), 209.

[5] For an informative biography, see Gillian Kersley, *Darling Madame: Sarah Grand & Devoted Friend* (London: Virago, 1983). See also Teresa Mangum, *Married, Middlebrow, and Militant: Sarah Grand and the New Woman Novel* (Michigan: University of Michigan Press, 1999); and Patricia Murphy, *Time is of the Essence, Temporality, Gender and the New Woman* (State University of New York Press, 2001), ch. 4. *The Heavenly Twins* was republished in 1992 by the University of Michigan Press; *The Beth Book* in 1994 by Thoemmes Press; see also the recent and extensive collection of Grand's essays, letters, and shorter fiction, Ann Heilman and Stephanie Forward (eds.), *Sex, Social Purity and Sarah Grand*, 4 vols. (London: Routledge, 2001).

[6] M. J. Dunn to her sister Charlotte (30 January 1840), quoted in Kersley, *Darling Madame*, 17.

[7] Haldane McFall, 'Madame Sarah Grand', in *Biographist & Review* (July 1902), 81–2.

thrice in the direct descent from the Plantagenet Kings of England, having for forefathers two sons of Edward III . . . She has for ancestors the Norman Kings of England, William the Conqueror, and the Dukes of Normandy—also the early Kings of France, being in the direct line from Hugh Capet and from Charlemagne; and she numbers amongst her forefathers Alfred the Great, and amongst her foremothers the Lady Godiva of Coventry fame, who put herself to shame to save her people. It will thus be seen that Madame Grand's kin have acquired a somewhat pronounced habit of making a noise in the world.[8]

Grand lived in Northern Ireland until the death of her father when she was aged 7; the family then moved to northern England, to a small seaport near Scarborough. In 1868, aged 14, Grand entered the Royal Navy School in Twickenham, followed by a finishing school in Holland Road, Kensington. In 1871, 16, she married Lieutenant-Colonel David Chambers McFall. He was aged 39, widowed, and brigade-surgeon of the Thirty-Fourth Foot, the Indian Border Regiment. His first wife had been the daughter of a colonel; two of the three sons from this marriage survived and after their mother's death they arrived in Ireland aged 10 (Haldane) and 8 (Albert) and fluent in Hindustani.[9] Following the birth of their only child, David Archibald, Grand and McFall spent five years posted at military stations in the East, travelling through Malta, Egypt, and Ceylon (Sri Lanka) to China and Japan.[10] During this time Grand wrote verse and several short stories,[11] and, at 19, she published her first novel, *Two Dear Little Feet* (1873). This work amounted to a tract warning women of the ill-effects of ill-fitting boots and corsets, and thus, more generally, of the effects of vanity on health, emphasizing similarities between Chinese footbinding and Western women's fashion. Heavily informed by the medical knowledge she had acquired from her husband, it contained the seeds of the eugenic ideas which flourished in her later work. Her next novel, *Ideala*, was initially rejected by publishers, including Bentley, with

[8] Ibid., 82. See Matilda Betham-Edwards, *Mid-Victorian Memories* (London: John Murray, 1919); and Sally Mitchell (ed.), intro. to Sarah Grand, *The Beth Book, Being a Study from the Life of Elizabeth Caldwell Maclure, A Woman of Genius* (1897; Bristol: Thoemmes Press, 1994) for further biographical information. For a physiognomical reading of Grand, which noted from the width of her forehead 'that she would reason more from observation and intuition', basing 'her conclusions and her deductions from what she actually sees and knows as facts', see Annie Isabella Oppenheim, *The Face and How to Read it: Scientific Character-Reading from the Face based on Anatomical Values* (London: T. Fisher Unwin, 1907), 165.

[9] Kersley, *Darling Madame*, 32.

[10] 'Sarah Grand and Mr Ruskin', *Woman's Signal* (25 January 1894), 57.

[11] These were rejected and, as she said in an interview with Tooley, she burned them, to her later regret (Tooley, 'Some Women Novelists', *The Women at Home*, 7 (1897), 176).

John Ruskin, reader for George Allen, returning it with the scribbled note that he did not like the title and could not bear queer people however nice.[12] As the *Woman's Signal* noticed, it had 'a pretty strange and rare career for a first novel'; in 1888 Grand published it at her own risk, as a yellow paperback, and it became 'an instant success'.[13] Bentley now took it up and it went through three editions in the first year.[14] With the proceeds, Grand left her husband, moving to Sinclair Road, Kensington.[15] Now in her late thirties, her career as a writer took off. While seeking a publisher for *The Heavenly Twins*, she published two previously rejected books: *A Domestic Experiment* (1891) which told the story of Agatha and Paul Oldham's unhappy marriage;[16] and *Singularly Deluded* (1892), a detective novel in which the heroine Gertrude Somers pursues someone she mistakenly believes to be her husband through a series of nightmarishly unexpected adventures. The *Spectator* remarked 'if her—we conjecture that this pronoun is the right one to use—name should hereafter appear in the front rank of novelists, we shall not be surprised.'[17] With the publication of *The Heavenly Twins* she had adopted the name Sarah Grand (which had come to her in a dream), explaining later to the editor of *Literary World* 'my husband had a great dislike to having his name associated with my ideas, and in order to save him the annoyance, I changed my name.'[18] In addition to eight novels and three short story collections, Grand wrote numerous articles; she was also a popular lecturer, touring Britain and America during the 1890s.[19]

Among her many social and civic duties, Grand served as president of the Writers' Suffrage League, which, founded by Betty Hatton and Cecily Hamilton in June 1908, continued up to the First World War.

[12] 'Sarah Grand and Mr Ruskin', 57.

[13] Ibid., 57.

[14] Kersely, *Darling Madame*, 55–6.

[15] In 1898 Grand moved from Kensington to Tunbridge Wells and, from 1920 to 1926, she lived with her friends William and Rachel Mary Tindall, brother and sister, in their home, Crowe Hall, Bath. Following a fire which effectively destroyed the Hall in January 1926 she moved to her sister's home, also in Bath, where she remained until 1942 when the threat of air raids led her to move to a flat in Calne, Wiltshire.

[16] For contemporary reviews, see *Athenaeum* (28 February 1891), 3305, 278; and J. Barrow Allen, *Academy*, 39 (21 March 1891), 279.

[17] 'Four Good One-Volume Novels', *Spectator*, 70 (18 March 1893), 363. For a less favourable response see *Athenaeum* (18 February 1893), 3408, 215.

[18] Letter to Frederick Henry Fisher, 10 March 1898. Special Collections of UCLA.

[19] For contemporary responses in America, see, for example, the *New York Times* (27 May 1894) 1, col. 5. See also 'New Writers', *Bookman*, 4 (July, 1893), 107–8; 'Sarah Grand', *New York Times* (5 December 1897), 12.

Among its members were Beatrice Harraden, Violet Hunt, Marie Belloc Lowndes (Hilaire Belloc's sister), Christabel Marshall (also known as Christopher St John), Margaret Nevinson, Elizabeth Robins, Olive Schreiner, May Sinclair, and Sarah Tooley. During the last years of the suffrage campaign Grand served as president of the Tunbridge Wells branch of the Women's Constitutional Suffrage Society. She was also a member of the Rational Dress Society, the Pioneer Club, and the National Council of Women. Following her move to Bath in 1920 she was six times mayoress (1923, and again from 1925 to 1929), and became involved with the National Council for Combating Venereal Disease (founded in 1914, the council changed its name to The British Social Hygiene Council in 1926). From its inception it had close ties with the Eugenics Society, and had as its ultimate goal the protection of society from pollution by undesirable elements.[20] Grand died in 1943, Bath's

[20] Social hygiene was 'concerned with the application of the biological sciences to the social problems arising out of man's relationship with man'; it was a subsection of social medicine 'the study and application of the biological sciences directed to the development and conservation of natural resources in the service of the human race' and 'to the improvement of human quality and welfare' (S. Neville-Rolfe, *Social Biology and Welfare, Together with a Handbook-appendix on Social Problems Edited by Ethel Grant* (London: George Allen & Unwin Ltd, 1949), 49). The concept expresses a conflation of the social and the medical which underpinned eugenic thinking. In *The Task of Social Hygiene* (1912) Havelock Ellis argued for the necessity of a Ministry of Health, advocating the duty of the individual to support a scheme whereby the state would take responsibility for the physical well-being of the individual. He argued 'the question of breed, the production of fine individuals, the elevation of the ideal of quality in human production over that of mere quantity, begins to be seen, not merely as a noble ideal in itself, but as the only method by which Socialism can be enabled to continue on its present path' (402). The historian Greta Jones has emphasized the relation between social hygiene and the hereditarian health policies promoted by eugenic bodies and their sympathizers (see *Social Hygiene in Twentieth-Century Britain* (Beckenham: Croom Helm, 1986). Nonetheless, as Dorothy Porter notes, social hygiene in Britain always had a more environmentalist outlook (with its environmentalist public health and eugenic health strands often in open conflict), than in Germany, where the term had originated, coined by the highly influential health reformer Alfred Grotjahn, and where it was a much clearer and exclusive expression of hereditarian ideology (Porter, ' "Enemies of the Race": Biologism, Environmentalism, and Public Health in Edwardian England', *Victorian Studies*, 34 (1991), 162–3). At a meeting of the Social Hygiene Council in Bath Guildhall in June 1928, which Sarah Grand attended, the guest speaker, Miss Hilsdon, spoke on the Hygiene Council's promotion of preventative action in cities. The *Bath and Wilts Chronicle and Herald* reported Hilsdon's speech: 'trained teachers ought to teach biology; the Press should grant fuller publicity on those subjects. She condemned as bad policy the present system which forced people to be criminals or diseased. Especially she stressed the evils of the slums. In Birmingham alone three thousand families each slept in one room, where everything of life and death went on . . .'. The piece concluded 'Mrs Hignett moved a vote of thanks to the Mayoress for the recital of her early experiences. The more they knew of Madame Sarah Grand the more favoured they felt they were in

'most respected citizen', according to the front page of her local paper.[21]

Fifty years earlier, *The Heavenly Twins*, with its forthright treatment of syphilis, had taken Britain and America by storm. The novel explores the disastrous marriages of Evadne Frayling and Edith Beale to degenerates. Upon discovering his wayward past, Evadne refuses to consummate her marriage to Major George Colquhoun, an army surgeon. Following his early death, of degenerative heart disease, she remarries, this time a doctor, with whom she has one child, but her mental health soon begins to fail and she diagnoses herself as insane, considering murdering her child to save it from the possibility of hereditary disease. Galbraith, her husband-doctor (and, by the closing book, the narrator) reassures her that her son is healthy. By contrast, Edith Beale contracts syphilis from her profligate husband, Sir Mosley Menteith, and, entrapped in a highly melodramatic plot, becomes insane and dies, but not before giving birth to a syphilitic child who resembles a speckled toad and also dies. A third story—that of Angelica Hamilton-Wells, one of the heavenly twins—runs alongside these grim stories, culminating in Book IV, 'The Tenor and the Boy.—An Interlude.'

The Heavenly Twins is punctuated with radical ideas—Evadne's abstinence after marriage on health and political grounds, the importance of female education, the cross-dressing scenes of Book IV, and Angelica's early determination to lead a life of freedom and autonomy—and these have been explored in detail by scholars.[22] Equally, the depiction of unhappy marriages that permeates this and several other of Grand's novels and which forms the focus of critical appraisal of her work clearly

having her in their midst': '*The Heavenly Twins*: Bath's mayoress tells their story—Josephine Butler Centenary', *Bath and Wilts Chronicle and Herald* (19 June 1928), 7. See Dorothy Porter and Roy Porter, 'What was Social Medicine? An Historiographical Essay', *Journal of Historical Sociology*, 1 (1988), 95–6; and George Rosen, 'What is Social Medicine? A Genetic Analysis of the Concept', *Bulletin of the History of Medicine*, 21 (1947), 674–733. For the relation in the United States between eugenic ideas and the social hygiene, mental hygiene, birth control, and population control movements, see the papers of the Bureau of Social Hygiene (1911–40), Rockefeller Archive Center; and Allan Chase, *The Legacy of Malthus: The Social Costs of the New Scientific Racism* (New York: Knopf, 1973).

21 'Death of Madame Sarah Grand, Famous Novelist Six Times Mayoress of Bath', *Bath Weekly Chronicle and Herald* (15 May 1943), 1.

22 On ambivalances in Grand, see John Kucich, 'Curious Dualities: *The Heavenly Twins* (1893) and Sarah Grand's Belated Modernist Aesthetics', in Barbara Leah Harman and Susan Meyer (eds.), *The New Nineteenth Century: Feminist Readings of Underread Victorian Fiction* (New York, London: Garland, 1996), 195–204.

shows her to be deeply critical of late nineteenth-century marriage.[23] However, the eugenic discourse which underpins these depictions, and which she expresses unequivocally in her non-fiction, have been overlooked. Grand frequently expressed contradictory ideas in her fiction; she had to fulfil her readers' expectations of entertainment, a factor which complicates the message of her fiction, but her work as a whole shows an overriding commitment to eugenic ideas and it is on this that I shall focus.

Following the death of her husband, Evadne remarks 'he for one should never have been born. With his ancestry, he must have come into the world foredoomed to a life of dissipation and disease' (*Heavenly Twins*, 662). She warns that the consequences of vice 'become hereditary, and continue from generation to generation' (80). Throughout the novel Edith and her short-lived child serve as a harrowing reminder of the incorrigible effects of hereditary disease.[24] 'The Tenor and the Boy. An Interlude' seems to offer respite from the dire sermonizing, and certainly gestures towards social and sexual freedom. As one reviewer noted 'the hilarious doings of the "Twins" and the love-story of "The Tenor and the Boy" are the sugar intended to sweeten the pill of the evils exposed in the tragic stories of Evadne and Edith'.[25] However, this story ultimately also serves as an indictment of pleasure, underlining the overriding importance of duty. It charts the exploits of Angelica, once wedded to the congenial Mr Kilroy, twenty years her senior, in a marriage of uncommon freedom ('Marry me!' said Angelica, stamping her foot at him—'Marry me, *and let me do as I like*' (321, emphasis in original)). Once

[23] For a detailed and illuminating reading of *The Heavenly Twins*, which considers these aspects and discusses the psychological complexity of the novel, see T. Mangum, ch. 3. See also Murphy, *Time is of the Essence*, ch. 4. Focusing on Grand's advocacy of female education in the *Heavenly Twins* and *The Beth Book*, Murphy positions Grand in opposition to dominant male discourse on this issue.

[24] In fact, syphilis is not hereditary, but could be passed from a mother to her unborn child. Fear of the disease seared the pages of late nineteenth-century novels. The following year, Jessamine, Emma Frances Brooke's superfluous woman, dreams of syphilitic children: 'behind lay a Vista of the Ages—the Ages of the future and the unborn. Faces, little faces, came up from them; her ears were full of the tread of little feet; little hands clutched at the veil and dragged it from her; eyes, the eyes of unborn children, looked at her with an awful reproach. They came and touched her with cold hands, and looked, and passed. Little feet and little hands and eyes that were dreadful. Each had the eyes of her suffering boy; each had the impress of her husband' (*A Superfluous Woman* (London: Heinemann, 1894), 275).

[25] Tooley, 'Some Women Novelists', 178. Written while Grand was in Norwich, some years before the novel, in 1899 'The Tenor and the Boy' was published separately as part of a series: 'Heinemann's Popular Novels'.

married, Angelica spends many of her nights wandering the streets dressed as a boy, and in the course of these wanderings she befriends a reclusive tenor. Her spell of cross-dressing ends in disaster when she falls into a river in a boating accident and, to the great distress of Tenor, reveals her true sex. The Tenor dies soon after of pneumonia, and his death catapults Angelica into a life of duty. She returns to her patriarchal, kindly, husband, whom she calls 'Daddy', thankful for the blessing of a good man's love, and determined to 'live for others' (551, 493).

Contemporary response was striking:

> As surely as Tess of the D'Urbervilles swept all before it last year, so surely has Sarah Grand's Heavenly Twins provoked the greatest attention and comment this season. It is a most daringly original work . . . Sarah Grand is a notable Woman's Righter, but her book is the one asked for at every hotel table in the kingdom.[26]

Billed by Arnold Bennett 'the modern equivalent of *Uncle Tom's Cabin*',[27] and by the *Chicago Tribune* 'the most talked-about novel today',[28] even the conservative *Athenaeum* came out in favour: 'it is so full of interest, and the characters are so eccentrically humorous yet true, that one feels inclined to pardon all its faults.[29] For Grand's friend and contemporary Mark Twain it was, in the final analysis, 'a strong, good book' and according to the Irish novelist and critic May Hartley:

> The book should be read by every adult. The function of the novel is now recognised as fully equal to those of the pulpit and the professorial chair and it is the sole recognized means at present for a woman to make her voice and power felt outside the narrow limits of her personal surrounding. I believe that the book will create a *storm* rather than a sensation and that this will be followed by *action* definite and stringent on the part of all *thinking* women. Help can only come from women—Meredith and Hardy have barely touched the fringes of this question . . . both have contented themselves with re-echoing in a modernized form certain views of the 18th Century philosophers. Mrs McFall's book will have a vastly different result.[30]

[26] Extract carried as part of press opinions of *The Heavenly Twins* in *Our Manifold Nature* (London: Heinemann, 1894).

[27] Arnold Bennett, 'The Author of "Babs the Impossible" ', *Academy*, 60 (1901), 347.

[28] 'The Author of "The Heavenly Twins" ', *Chicago Tribune*, repr. in *Critic*, 23 (5 August 1893), 92.

[29] 'New Novels', *Athenaeum* (18 March 1893), 342.

[30] May Hartley, in opinions of literary advisers on *The Heavenly Twins*. Correspondence of Frances Elizabeth McFall, National Library of Scotland, emphasis in original.

Not all responses to *The Heavenly Twins* were so positive. It ended up at the bottom of a lake in Marie Corelli's bestseller of 1895, *The Sorrows of Satan*, thrown there by the hero, Geoffrey Tempest, who finds his young wife reading it;[31] while for George Meredith, who rejected it as reader for Chapman and Hall, it was 'such a very long book' whose author, he remarked, 'is a clever woman and has ideas; for which reason she is hampered at present in the effort to be a novelist.'[32] Notwithstanding reactions such as these, the popularity of *The Heavenly Twins* soared; reviewed by all the major papers and periodicals in Britain and the USA, it was translated into Finnish and Russian.[33] In Britain it was reprinted six times in its first year of publication,[34] with Heinemann reporting a sale of 20,000 within a few weeks.[35] More than five times as many copies were sold in the USA,[36] where it made the overall bestsellers list for the nineties.[37]

W. T. Stead, editor of the *Pall Mall Gazette* and a central figure in the campaigns for sexual reforms, was certainly moved. In his survey 'The Novel of the Modern Woman' (1894), published in the popular *Review of Reviews* in the wake of *The Heavenly Twins*, he wrote:

> the phenomenal sale of her novel is a small thing compared with the result she achieved in breaking up the conspiracy of silence in society on the serious side of marriage. . . . up to that barred and bolted door [of Mrs Grundy's prudish interdict] Sarah Grand stepped with the heroism of a forlorn hope, carrying with her a bomb of dynamite, which she exploded with wonderful results. The heavily-barred gate was blown to atoms, and the conspiracy of silence was at an end. In the last twelve-months, in drawing rooms and in smoking rooms, an astonished and somewhat bewildered society has been busily engaged in discussing the new demand of the new woman.[38]

Thirty years after the publication of *The Heavenly Twins*, in a foreword to a new edition (1923), Grand stated that she had achieved her purpose of outing the sexual double standard and the tabooed diseases it brought with it: 'dinner tables resounded with the controversy, and, in

[31] *The Sorrows of Satan* (Oxford: Oxford University Press, 1996), 245.

[32] 'George Meredith's rejection of *The Heavenly Twins*', Heilmann, *Sex, Social Purity and Sarah Grand*, i. 409.

[33] Heilmann, 'Introduction', *Sex, Social Purity and Sarah Grand*, i. 8.

[34] A fact recalled by *The Times* obituary (24 May 1943), 6 col. d.

[35] 'Sarah Grand, Novelist of the Nineties', *The Times* (13 May 1943), 7 col. e.

[36] Frank Luther Mott, *Golden Multitudes: The Story of Best Sellers in the United States* (New York: R. R. Bowker & Co., 1947), 181–2.

[37] Ibid., 311.

[38] W. T. Stead, 'Book of the Month: The Novel of the Modern Woman', *Review of Reviews*, 10 (1894), 65.

their excitement, those who had most rigorously enjoined silence broke it themselves incontinently'.[39]

ESSENTIAL SEX DIFFERENCES

Sarah Grand believed wholeheartedly that sex difference was fixed and fundamental: 'woman was never meant to be developed man'.[40] In 1892, she wrote to her publisher, John Blackwood, 'my own experience is that in every position women will be women. Womanhood is a constitutional condition which cannot be altered'.[41] The entry of women into the public sphere, the political world, would not eliminate femininity; indeed, Grand argued, it was on account of their femininity that women would be able to serve the nation, and to solve what she termed 'the population difficulty'.[42] Discussing the female franchise in an interview in 1896, she declared 'our influence would be chiefly felt upon questions of morality, and would, I believe, tend to purify the political atmosphere'.[43] She envisaged a separate House of Ladies which 'would be able to discuss many questions which call for reform with greater freedom than women could in a mixed assembly'. Later in the interview she was more explicit—and explicitly eugenist—about what she hoped the vote for women would achieve, echoing Karl Pearson's essay on 'Woman and Labour' of two years earlier:

> women are the proper people to decide on matters of population. Men have not managed to regulate either the population or the social question at all satisfactorily, and it would be well to give us a chance of trying what we can do. We could do much if we had the suffrage; the want of electoral power cripples our efforts.[44]

As she saw women as having a fundamental role in shaping public opinion and thus bringing about social reform, her efforts were all directed towards this end: 'it is women who form public opinion—not in the

[39] Sarah Grand, Foreword, *The Heavenly Twins* (1893; London, Heinemann, 1923), in Heilmann, *Sex, Social Purity and Sarah Grand*, i. 406.

[40] Athol Forbes, 'My Impressions of Sarah Grand', *Lady's World*, 21 (June 1900), 883.

[41] Sarah Grand to John Blackwood (5 December 1892), Letters of Frances Elizabeth McFall, National Library of Scotland.

[42] Grand, 'The Man of the Moment', *North American Review*, 158 (1894), 622.

[43] Sarah A. Tooley, 'The Woman Question: An Interview with Madame Sarah Grand', *Humanitarian*, 8 (1896), 164.

[44] Ibid., 168. See Pearson, 'Woman and Labour', *Fortnightly Review*, 61 (1894), 561–77.

newspaper or on the platform, but in the nursery; what they teach their children in the nursery today will become the public opinion of to-morrow. Women, therefore, are responsible for the subtle change which is already apparent in the views of society on the subject of what a man should be.'[45]

Grand retained her belief in fundamental sex difference and hereditary sex instincts throughout her life. In 1913 in the *Pall Mall Magazine* she observed 'there are two hereditary instincts in the average man, the one urging him to protect the woman, the other impelling him to take advantage of her weakness . . . no woman can judge on merely meeting a man casually which is the predominant force in his character.'[46] As the sage Mr Price had put it in *The Heavenly Twins*:

the thing is so obvious, when one reduces it to words, but yet neither men nor women themselves—for the most part—seem to recognize the fact that womanliness is a matter of sex, not of circumstances, occupation, or clothing; and each sex has instincts and proclivities which are peculiar to it, and do not differ to any remarkable extent even in the most diverse characters'. (197)

Angelica may seem able to move between male and female identities—donning male clothing and bundling up her hair, she temporarily changes her sex and the shape of her head: ' "my head's a queer shape," he said, tapping it'. But we are simultaneously reminded that attempts to alter sex are found out in medical examinations: 'you won't want to examine it phrenologically will you?' (387).[47]

Like many of her contemporaries, Grand believed that civilization itself was predicated on such fixed, or *essential*, sexual difference, and sexual disunion. In her fiction, similarities between the sexes are permitted only in a presexual, child world. In *The Beth Book* (1897), her bestseller follow up to *The Heavenly Twins*, when the young Beth dresses as a boy so that she can accompany Alfred Cayley Pounce and Dicksie Richardson to a menagerie without risk of recognition, it is crucial to Grand's politics that they are still children. It is only Beth's hair that threatens to give the game away, until Dicksie suggests 'turn it up under your cap. These little curls on your neck will look like short hair.' Sexual language is used, emptied of sexual content, to highlight their pre-lapsarian state: 'they

[45] Sarah Grand, 'The Modern Young Man', *Temple Magazine* (1898), 884.

[46] 'The Case of the Modern Spinster', *Pall Mall Magazine* (1913), 52–6.

[47] For evidence of Grand's early interest in phrenology, see *Two Dear Little Feet* (London: Jarrold and Sons, 1873), 20, where she refers to 'a bump of causality'.

were all so delighted with this romantic plan, that they danced about, and hugged each other promiscuously' (254). In an interview for *Woman at Home* in 1895 Grand declared 'the fashion of women dressing in imitation of men' to be 'detestable'.[48]

It was particularly irksome to eugenic feminists that the New Woman was often seen by hostile contemporaries to be promoting proximity between the sexes; it was the last thing they either desired or intended. In an interview in 1900, Grand expressed her regret at being associated with 'the vulgar creature who now passes for the approved type of new woman'.[49] Accepting responsibility for the phrase New Woman, she emphasized that she had envisaged 'a very different being from the caricature of femininity now presented to us under that name, and which the press so often gave me credit for creating'. All she had meant by the New Woman, she pointed out, 'was one who, while retaining all the grace of manner and feminine charm, had thrown off all the silliness and hysterical feebleness of her sex'. As she saw it, the purpose of woman's self-improvement was primarily to serve the marriage relation, and through or in lieu of this—if no suitable partner was to be had—the world: 'so as to be in every way the best companion for man, and without him, the best fitted for a place of usefulness in the world'.

As social purists and eugenists stressed the importance of womanly women, so they emphasized the importance of masculinity to national efficiency and empire. The anti-heroes of Grand's fiction are often military men who abuse their position of defenders of empire, and threaten to weaken the imperial race through sexual immorality. They show, above all, a lack of self-discipline. In 1894 Grand warned in the *North American Review* that men in general were unable to see ways in which to address the problem of the 'superfluous population'; 'the man of the moment does anything but aspire, and it is the low moral tone which he cultivates that threatens to enervate the race. In fact, were it not for the hard fight women will make to prevent it, there would be small hope of saving us from flickering out like all older peoples'.[50] Ellice Hopkins harked back to an age of chivalry in her didactic social purity pamphlets, and equally Sarah Grand urged its importance:

[48] Jane T. Stoddart, 'Illustrated Interview: Sarah Grand', *Woman at Home*, 3 (1895), in Heilmann, *Sex, Social Purity and Sarah Grand*, i. 214.

[49] Forbes, 'My Impressions of Sarah Grand', 883.

[50] 'The Man of the Moment', *North American Review*, 158 (1894), 621, 622.

when invitations were being sent out the other day for a great public function, there was a question as to which regiments should be asked in order to secure the best set of officers, and it was found afterwards that in every instance the regiment chosen was distinguished for the chivalrous loyalty of its tone in regard to women.[51]

Men, she concluded, instead of serving the empire, were, by and large, at the end of the century, 'in mischief—or else in bed', so that 'the man at the head of affairs is beginning to ask seriously if a great war might not help them to pull themselves together' (626) (within two decades this vision was, of course, realized). Such 'flabby' men, as she called them, their bodies showing signs of their mental ill-discipline, were being rejected by the 'modern girl', who was motivated in her choosing by 'the instinct of natural selection' (626). Training men for empire had to begin in the nursery, and with women: she concluded her article on the upbeat note that it was not a time to despair: 'if there is little hope for the present generation, they can spank proper principles into the next in the nursery' (627). A few years later Grand repeated her message in the *Temple Magazine*, voicing serious concern that men were going to university at a time in their lives when they should be out defending the empire and that, worse still, they were receiving an education that unfitted them for a military career:

there are to-day two very marked types in what is known as society—the military and the university, or the kempt and the unkempt . . . A young university man is undisciplined, he is apt to leave his room late in the morning and leave it all in disorder. He never seems to know when his hair should be cut, and his clothes are often but imperfectly brushed. There is much to be desired in the cut of them too, and he puts them on slouchily.[52]

Timing, for Grand, had a lot to do with it: in the old days students went to universities as boys 'and left them on the threshold of manhood; today they enter at a time of life when they should be going out into the world to make careers for themselves—a time when the conceit of adolescence, instead of being brought under the chastening restraint of

[51] Ibid., 623. The feminism of J. S. Mill and Mona Caird took an opposing view. As early as 1826 Mill, aged 19, diagnosed one of the problems of the age as exaggerated chivalry. He saw the age of chivalry as one of 'false refinement', an age 'situated halfway between savage and civilized life': (95) 'Modern French Historical Works—Age of Chivalry', *Westminster Review*, 6 (July 1826) 62–103. Some three decades later, in the *Subjection of Women*, he underlined the negative social effects of chivalry which, he observed, works to keep women in their submissive position, substituting symbolic power for real power.

[52] 'The Modern Young Man', *Temple Magazine*, 2 (1898), 886.

the discipline it so much requires, is rather fostered than cured by the academic atmosphere'. Thus, it was, that many a youth might be found 'idling about the colleges, playing at life and giving opinions that no one wants, whilst elsewhere mere boys are helping to consolidate the empire and to defend and extend our frontiers.' Grand's conclusion is an illuminating one, underlining the importance she attached to self-discipline and national service:

> One could wish for all young men something of the soldier's training. A compulsory two or three years of the Sandhurst system would be of enormous benefit to most of them. There is nothing like it for discipline, for polishing, for physical development, and for the teaching of self-reliance and self-respect. It is surprising that people who can afford to do it do not oftener send their sons to a military college, just to have them set up and to make men of them, whether they destine them for the army subsequently or not.[53]

Even the cross-dressing heavenly twin Angelica fantasizes that she is going to sit Sandhurst exams (387).

EFFEMINACY: *THE BETH BOOK*

The Beth Book, which charts the transport of the young Beth from Ireland to northern England, and her subsequent marriage to the brutal lockhospital surgeon Dan McClure, offers a complex study of Beth's psychological development, exploring her unhappy marriage to a degenerate, her development as an artist, and her eventual release, in the third phase of the novel, when she leaves her husband, moving to a garret in London. Here she writes her first book and meets the American male artist who will become her lover, becoming a public speaker on feminist issues by the novel's close. The powerful feminist politics and psychological richness of the novel have been well documented.[54] However, coexisting with these progressive aspects is a eugenic subtext. At times the progressive and the repressive undermine each other, testifying to Grand's competing aims, as she attempts to keep the reader entertained for the length of the novel; to explore the development of a feminist artist; and to instil in her readers a new

[53] 'The Modern Young Man', 884, 885.

[54] See, for example, Mangum, ch. 5; see also Murphy, ch. 4, on ways in which Grand reworks late nineteenth-century evolutionary psychology, turning female essentialized traits into strengths.

morality. Contemporary reception reflected this confusion. The *Athenaeum* declared itself bemused 'vague rodomontade about—well, that is the trouble; it is difficult to know exactly what about,[55] and *The Dial* followed suit: '*The Beth Book* is clearly a book with a purpose, although it is difficult to state just what purpose.'[56] *Review of Reviews* declared: 'so keenly sensitive is she to the resentment of the reader against sermons in fiction that she conceals her moral so carefully that many who do not think over what they read will miss it altogether.'[57] Nonetheless, contemporary critics were also hostile to the novel's didacticism. *The Dial* lamented its railing 'at the social ideas of the mid-Victorian period', a railing which kept the story going 'for many long chapters after it has ceased to have any human interest',[58] and the *Saturday Review* remarked:

> She *must* jumble up medical and moral questions in one inharmonious whole, she *must* ruin her own works of art and deface them, with iconoclastic fervour, by all the refuse of the controversies that raged twenty years ago around the dead C.D Acts . . . if only—but of course this begs the whole question—it were possible for some philanthropist or some physician to clear the cobweb from her brain and show her, if not the banality of her attacks on beneficent institutions for the cure or alleviation of hereditary disease, at least the folly of dragging them in, like the head of Charles I in 'Mr Dick's' MSS, to the absolute destruction of the sanity and interest of her wonderful novels.[59]

While, as critics have noted, *The Beth Book* offers an attack on the Contagious Diseases Acts,[60] it is equally critical of effeminacy and medical help for the unfit. They all constituted an affront to responsible reproductive relations, and an obstacle to the biological salvation and improvement of the British race. Beth adopts the standard eugenic line on charity and condemns medical treatment for the 'unfit', which she considers an unwelcome endeavour to hinder nature's good work,

[55] 'New Novels: *The Beth Book*', *Athenaeum* (27 November, 1897), 743.

[56] W. M. Payne, *The Dial*, 24 (1898), 78. Others used the confusion her work generated to pathologize her: 'The Strange Case of Sarah Grand is as baffling to the reviewers as it is probably full of interest to the alienist' remarked Danby in Frank Harris and Frank Danby, 'Sarah Grand's latest book', *Saturday Review* (20 November 1895), 578. Frank Danby was the pseudonym for the novelist Julia Frankau (1859–1916); Frank Harris was editor of the *Fortnightly Review* from 1886 to 1894 and friend of Oscar Wilde.

[57] 'Some Books of the Month: "The Beth Book" ', *Review of Reviews*, 16 (1897), 618.

[58] W. M. Payne, *Dial*, 24 (1898), 78.

[59] Frank Harris and Frank Danby, 'Sarah Grand's latest book', *Saturday Review* (20 November 1895), 578. Mr Dick is a character in Dickens's *David Copperfield*.

[60] For discussion of *The Beth Book* in relation to the Contagious Diseases Acts, see Mangum, 165–72.

presenting negative eugenics as an act of *kindness*—a way of making the fit happy and the unfit extinct. This was the eugenic creed. The discourses of health and pronatalism are powerfully present in the novel in other ways. We learn of Beth that

there was to be no atrophy of one side of her being in order that the other might be abnormally developed. Her chest was not to be flattened because her skull bulged with the big brain beneath. Rather the contrary. For mind and body acted and reacted on each other favourably, in so far as the conditions of her life were favourable. (164)

Her abundance of health is thrown into sharp relief in a brief encounter with the proletariat—her skin 'so different in colour and texture from their own, drew from them the most candid expressions of admiration' (271). The regenerative 'modern girl' was an embodiment of moral and physical health and selection know-how. In Beth 'youth and sex already began to hang out their signals—clear skin, slim figure, light step, white teeth, thick hair, bright eyes'; we learn 'there comes a time to all healthy young people when Nature says: "mate, my children, and be happy" ' (233, 234). 'Mate' is a carefully chosen word; cutting through notions of romance and sentiment, it locates the reproductive drive in the (opposing) realm of health and nature. Conversely, passion is pathologized: 'I would rather die of passion myself, as I might of any other disease, than live to be bound by it' (471). The same register was struck by Sperry:

The love of the truly mated husband and wife is more comprehensive, more intense and more enduring that any other sentiment that is awakened by our earthly life and human relationships—unless, perhaps, it be the love of a mother for her child.[61]

Dan Maclure in *The Beth Book* is a physically ambivalent specimen: 'a woman with as much colour would have been accused of painting; in him it gave to some people the idea of superabundant health, to others it suggested a phthisical tendency' (257–8). As if further signs are needed that all is not well, Maclure has defective teeth. As the narrative unfolds, he succumbs to 'fatty degeneration'. Like Evadne and Edith, Beth suffers because she has not been sufficiently rigorous in her selection of a sexual partner. The novel couches effeminacy in the language of contagious disease, and is clearly in dialogue with decadent writers such as Joris-Karl

[61] Lyman B. Sperry, *Confidential Talks with Husband and Wife, A Book of Information and Advice for the Married and the Marriageable* (Edinburgh and London: Oliphant Anderson and Ferrier, 1900), 24.

Huysman, who offered a triumphant celebration of the aesthete in *A Rebours* (1884). According to Mr Kilroy 'there is a perfect epidemic of that kind of assurance among the clever young men of the day, and it's wrecking half of them' (452). Pounce (also known as 'Pointed Beard' (450)), is a case in point. His name signals 'ponce',[62] linking him to a world of sexual transgression. (He delights in the fact that his father named him Alfred, making 'A Pounce'.) As a boy, we learn, he had the makings of a degenerate—his hands are 'long, delicate and nervous' and his 'somewhat sallow complexion looked smooth to effeminacy' (237). He was, according to Charles Whitby, writing in the 1930s, 'a mordant study of a type singularly prevalent in those naughty nineties, and not even yet wholly extinct.'[63] Descriptions of Pounce offer a relentless catalogue of tell-tale signs of male hysteria:

> the light shone on his bald forehead and accentuated the lines which wounded vanity, petty purposes thwarted, and an ignoble life had written prematurely on his face, and his attitude emphasized the attenuation of his body. He looked a poor, peevish, neurotic specimen. (477)[64]

Pounce is suffering from atrophy: in Max Nordau's diagnosis, this was a sign of supreme atavism.[65] He is certain that 'for a man of my temperament there is nothing but celibacy' (478). He represents the unproductive, and the unreproductive. For Beth, Grand, and eugenists more generally, as discussed in Chapter 7, reproductive relations are essential to a fulfilled adult life: 'celibacy is an attempt to curb a healthy instinct with a morbid idea. He is the best man and the truest gentleman who

[62] Although the *OED* does not record 'ponce' being used before 1932 to mean a homosexual or effeminate man, it cites Mayhew using 'pounceys' interchangeably with 'fancy men', meaning pimp (1861 *London Labour*, iii. 354: 1). Pounce reappears as the name of Ella's housekeeper in *The Winged Victory*, thus socially 'downgraded' and sexually transformed. The name also reappears as Pointz in Grand's last two novels *Adnam's Orchard: A Prologue* and *The Winged Victory*: the Pointz family are rapidly degenerating.

[63] Charles Whitby, 'Sarah Grand: The Woman and her Work', written for inclusion in the *Sarah Grand Miscellany* (comp. by Gladys Singers-Biggers and published privately under the title *The Breath of Life*); reproduced in Heilmann, *Sex, Social Purity and Sarah Grand*, i. 330.

[64] See T. D. Savill, 'Hysterical Skin Symptoms and Eruptions', *Lancet* (30 January 1904). See also Vernon Rosario (ed.), *Science and Homosexualities* (New York and London: Routledge, 1997), 91–2. Cf. Colin Drindon, in *The Winged Victory*, a decadent poetaster who wrote under the pseudonym of Joyday Flowers. Drindon later makes a concerted effort to change. For Grand on manliness, see *The Modern Man and Maid* (London: Horace Marshall & Son, 1898). Applauding the 'manly dignity' of 'well bred' young gentlemen, Grand remarks: 'it is easy to see why we are the dominant race' (30).

[65] Nordau, *Degeneration* (1892), trans. from the 2nd German edn., (Heinemann 1895; Lincoln and London: University of Nebraska Press, 1968).

honourably fulfils every function of life' (478). Equally, Grand wrote of woman: 'mateless, she is lonesome; childish, she is incomplete; and the more womanly she is, the greater is her lonesomeness, the more sorrowful the sense of her incompleteness'; the state of celibacy was an unnatural state for normal people.[66]

LOVE AND MARRIAGE

A discussion in the *Westminster Review* in 1899 on the respective merits of marriage and free love opened with the words 'so long as the generative instinct forms the basis of Evolution, so long must the question of Marriage be of paramount importance to civilisation'.[67] The institution of marriage was crucial to eugenic thought, offering the potential for regulating reproduction and optimizing selection. As Nordau observed, 'the institution of matrimony is founded altogether upon the supposition or knowledge of the fact that the interests of the perpetuating and perfecting of the race require a certain supervision by the community, of the impulse of procreation.'[68] According to the Revd Hemphill 'married people are doing their duty, and a religious duty. They are also doing a duty to the State, and to the Race.'[69] As encouragement he suggested 'immunity from taxation, or a handsome *bonus*, to those who have brought forth a numerous progeny'.[70] The state had shares in marriage. As Clapperton marked: 'the marriage-rate for each year may be called the pulse or indicator of the nation's economic well-being'.[71] Swiney looked back to a lost past, and to 'the Greek system of State artificial selection and supervision', arguing for a reinstatement of state control: 'it is already being reborn in Brazil, where anyone considering marriage must come with a health certificate, certifying their freedom from diseases of a certain class, and of others that are hereditary or transmissible' (*The Awakening of Women*, pt. 4). Like Galton, Saleeby, and Arnold White, as I discussed in Chapter 3, Grand drew an analogy

[66] Sarah Grand, 'The Case of the Modern Spinster', *Pall Mall Magazine*, 51 (1913), 56.

[67] Effie Johnson [Euphemia J. Richmond], 'Marriage or Free Love', *Westminster Review*, 152 (1899), 91.

[68] Nordau, 'The Matrimonial Lie', in *Conventional Lies of our Civilization* (London: William Heinemann, 1895), 290.

[69] Hemphill, 'Murderess of the Unseen', (Dublin: Hodgers, Figgis, & Co., Ltd; London: Simkin, Marshall, & Co., Ltd, 1908), 5.

[70] Ibid., 16.

[71] *A Vision of the Future, Based on The Application of Ethical Principles* (London: Swan Sonnenschein & Co. Limited, 1904), 87.

between recruitment for military service and 'recruitment' for marriage,[72] consistently stressing that marriage was to serve not the individual but the race. She saw that marriage law needed reforming, and argued for the divorce law to be applied equally to husband and wife; men could divorce adulterous wives; but husbands had also to be guilty of cruelty before wives could sue for divorce.[73] However, she repeatedly stressed that marriage was racially responsible mating,[74] and a lifelong commitment: 'only by making the supreme relation of man and woman indissoluble is the advance of the race secured'.[75] Drawing on evolutionary language, her novels set out to explore the unhappiness of marrying without rational selection. She devised a hierarchy of forms of love which she linked to the idea of evolutionary progress: 'love, like passion, may have its stages, but they are always from the lower to the higher. And as it is in the particular so it is in the general; it prefers the good of the community at large to its own immediate advantage.'[76] Like Galton, Grand saw passion as anathema to responsible marriage, arguing 'free love is free lust, and its liberty is licence. The higher natures all abandon the cant of passion for the cult of love eventually.'[77] Love, for Grand, 'lives on duty alone, on care bestowed, on kindly little sacrifices of self in daily life, in the continual essentially human effort to make others happy'.[78] In the *New Review* she stated that young people 'should learn the facts of life and be trained not to think anything about them, and this can only be done by early familiarity with the subject, and by removing all sentimentality from it'.[79]

[72] See, for example, Galton Papers, 138/4, 13–14.

[73] Tooley, 'The Woman Question', 167.

[74] Grand's praise of the institution of marriage tends to be papered over, on the grounds that it is a concession to a reading audience less radical than she was: as Jane Eldridge Miller puts it, Grand exhorted feminists to be feminine 'so as not to alienate potential supporters'; likewise, the fact she did not reject love and marriage was, for Miller, apologetic on Grand's behalf, her 'concession to her reading audience', Jane Eldridge Miller, *Rebel Women: Feminism, Modernism and the Edwardian Novel* (London: Virago, 1994), 18, 20. Cf. also Sally Mitchell's assertion, in her introduction to *The Beth Book*, that 'the idealized New Woman was single', *The Beth Book* (Thoemmes), p. vii.

[75] 'Marriage Questions in Fiction', *Fortnightly Review*, 63 (1898), 387, 386.

[76] Ibid., 386.

[77] Ibid., 386. In his satire on eugenics, *The Coming of Bill* (1920), P. G. Wodehouse notes 'passion and eugenics don't go together. The violent trembling fit which assailed him he attributed to general organic weakness' (31).

[78] 'Marriage Questions in Fiction', 386.

[79] 'The Tree of Knowledge', *New Review*, 10 (1894), 680. Frances Swiney urged, also in the 1890s, that 'the most vital interests of life, health, and happiness are at stake in the possession of a right or a wrong introduction to the knowledge of human physiology' (Swiney, *The Awakening of Women*, 35).

Literature, she argued, had to own the part it played in disseminating unhappy, unhealthy, forms of love:

the apotheosis of passion in literature and by tradition has had more to do with making unhappy households than any other preventable cause. In literature as in life, by calling passion love, and giving it precedence over every other consideration, one gets a cheap and easy, but primitive and false effect. It is well for the story of Romeo and Juliet that it ends where it does. Of course such a passion might have led to love, but it does not generally, as every one knows who has had experience of Romeos and Juliets. In such cases the beautiful poetry is only too apt to resolve itself into pitiful prose.[80]

In 1898 Grand warned in *Young Woman* that the happiness of countless generations depended upon the thorough pre-marital scrutiny of a potential life-partner[81] and in a later issue that year she advised women not to marry before 25—an age which many eugenists considered the optimum for reproductivity.

In his discussion of Grand and *The Heavenly Twins*, W. T. Stead declared the novel to be the most distinctively characteristic of all the novels of the modern woman. Observing that the 'new demand of the new woman' was 'that woman, equally with man, is entitled to object to second-hand goods in the marriage market',[82] he drew attention to a fundamental shift in late nineteenth-century attitudes towards marriage. It was no longer 'a mere affair of *trousseaux* and of bridesmaids, of finding an eligible *parti*'; instead it had become 'an affair of cradles and of nurseries, a question involving grim and terrible questions of heredity, and imposing weighty responsibilities of training and education. "Therefore," cried the modern woman, "let me know and understand, and allow me at least an equal right in deciding upon shaping the conditions of the new life, which I have to take a predominant share in fashioning before birth and in training afterwards" '.[83]

[80] 'Marriage Questions in Fiction', 385–6. Cf. 'Emotional Moments', where a fickle, sentimental woman is rebuked by her rational male counterpart: 'Those fever-fits of passion, such as you describe, are a disease of the moral nature—the disease of natures which have departed from the principles that would have balanced them', *Emotional Moments* (London: Hurst and Blackett, Limited, 1908), 25.

[81] Sarah Grand, 'On the Choice of a Husband', *Young Woman*, 7 (1898–9), 3. Cf. Ruth Bannister's declaration, 'I mean my baby to be the most splendid baby that was ever born. He's going to be strong and straight and clever and handsome, and—oh, everything else you can think of. That's why I'm waiting for the ideal young man', in Wodehouse, *The Coming of Bill* (London : Herbert Jenkins, 1920), 25.

[82] W. T. Stead, 'The Novel of the Modern Woman', *Review of Reviews*, 10 (1894), 66, 67, 68.

[83] 'The Novel of the Modern Woman', 65.

This demand was central to the concept of gendered citizenship which did not challenge patriarchal hierarchy. This gendered concept of civic virtue makes apparent ideological inconsistencies in Grand's work both explicable and consistent. 'The influence of a mother is paramount', urged Grand: 'I do not think that a woman can be better engaged anywhere than in her own nursery.'[84]

Grand was full of praise for Elizabeth Rachel Chapman's maternalist *Marriage Questions in Modern Fiction* (1897), in which Chapman celebrated 'thinking women' who put 'the honour of [their] country' and 'the welfare of the race' before their own happiness.[85] Grand recommended it 'especially for young people who would arrive at the highest ideal of marriage, parenthood and citizenship'. In a letter of 1896 she wrote:

> at one time, the subjects of vice and immorality were shunned altogether, now we are beginning to face them boldly, and to deal with them in fiction, not as they do for love of them, but in order to expose the evils, mental, physical and social, which they then entail both on individuals and the community at large. Personally I believe that the woman movement is a great effort of the human race, an evolutionary effort, to raise itself a step higher in the scale of development: and this conviction forced itself upon me when I found that, beneath the surface, earnest and intelligent women were everywhere expressing great dissatisfaction at the present haphazard of marriage and maternity. Emancipated, women consider motherhood the most important function of their lives, and the first thing they ask on obtaining their freedom is whether they ought not . . . to become mothers except under the conditions that are the most favourable to the health, beauty, intelligence and character of their children.

Grand made it quite clear that it was 'for this reason that they have begun to demand a much higher standard of morals and physique than usual to satisfy them in their husbands, and to demand every advantage in every way of education and civil rights for themselves': their demands for social and political change were predicated on selfless feminine citizenship. She concluded her letter:

> I think further that it is in the action of woman in this particular matter, i.e. in regard to the improvement of the race,—that the one hope lies of saving our

84 Tooley, 'The Woman Question', 166.

85 Elizabeth Rachel Chapman, *Marriage Questions in Modern Fiction, and Other Essays on Kindred Subjects* (London and New York: John Lane, 1897), p. xiii. As Grand noted, Nordau held the book to be 'remarkable. It is one of the most suggestive contributions to the much-debated woman question' ('Marriage Questions', 379, 389, 379). For the enduring nature of Grand's beliefs, see L. A. M. Priestley McCracken, 'Madame Sarah Grand and Women's Emancipation', *The Vote* (25 August 1933), 1–2, in which she praised women who showed 'unostentatious initiative' and 'selfless devotion'.

present civilization from the extinction which has overtaken the civilization of all previous peoples; and all I write is for the purpose of spreading this opinion and opening up these subjects to discussion.[86]

This is the message that lies at the heart of Grand's complex fictional studies of married life. 'I hope that we shall soon see the marriage of certain men made a criminal offence. This is one of the things which, as women, we must press forward', declares Beth.[87]

Critics objected to the form of love expressed in *The Beth Book*. The *Young Woman* declared:

in the end of the day, the one thing needful to a woman is to have had a genius for loving, and to have followed it—to have had an instinct burning within her, a fine clear flame, and never let the wind blow it out. When the heroine of a story is terribly wanting in this instinct, one is scarcely able to forgive her.[88]

The New York magazine *Bookman* found Beth an altogether objectionable figure for 'holding a lifelong grudge against her mother for having more children than she can care for, and never trying to help her; by being without affection for her brothers and sisters, regarding them as usurpers of her own rights; by being disliked by her schoolmates and dreaded by her teachers; by never having a friend of her own sex; and by making her interest in the "problem" offensively evident through her earliest association with boys . . .'. Her greatest sin was to be 'absolutely without the capacity for loving'.[89] With a rhythm resonant of 1 Corinthians, *Review of Reviews* declared:

let her be as advanced as she pleases, speak on platforms till she brings the house down with applause, write novels, or study the higher mathematics, but unless love plays a greater part in her existence than it does in Beth's, the Tree of Life will yield for her but Dead Sea fruit, the ashes of which are very bitter.[90]

A NEW AESTHETIC

While Beth's assertion: 'I'm going to write for women, not for men' (376) can be seen as belonging to the novel's development of a female

[86] Letter to Professor Viëter, Nizza (15 December 1896), repr. in Heilmann, *The Late-Victorian Marriage Question*, v. See also Grand to John Blackwood, 5 December 1892, National Library of Scotland, and, for the public expression of these ideas, 'Marriage Questions.'

[87] *The Beth Book*, 442.

[88] Deas Cromarty, 'To the Author of "Beth" ', *Young Woman*, 65 (1898), 235.

[89] '*The Beth Book*', *Bookman*, 6 (1897), 364.

[90] 'Some Books of the Month: "The Beth Book" ', *Review of Reviews*, 16 (1897), 620.

aesthetic,[91] it also signals her intention to educate women eugenically through focusing on matters of health. As Grand saw it, it was the duty of women to rewrite the novel and cure civilization of its love-madness. Through Beth, Grand makes a distinction between male and female writing (143). This distinction finds satirical treatment in Sydney Grundy's West End hit of 1894, *The New Woman*. Lamenting the failure of the stage to broach the 'sexual problem', the Doctor comments: 'the novel will sweep everything before it.' Tellingly, Sylvester adds: 'You mean, the female novel?'; the Doctor acquiesces: 'Nothing can stop it'. 'No, it stops at nothing', continues Sylvester, and the Doctor concludes with approval 'Nor will it, till the problem is solved.'[92] The transformative powers of the *female* novel are perceived as paramount, both by New Woman writers and their critics. This contemporary concept of female writing is crucial for an understanding both of the social role which Grand felt fiction should fulfil, and of the vices she sought, through her writing, to check. Ideala recounts how a friend showed her these two types of fiction in a public library, and how the public had gone to the useful books, and stamped them with their approval:

> we spent a long time among the books, looking especially at the ones that had been greatly read, and at the queer marks in them, the emphatic strokes of approval, the notes of admiration, the ohs! of enthusiasm, the ahs! of agreement. At the end of one volume someone had written: 'this book has done me good.' It was all very touching to me, very human, very instructive. I never quite realized before what books might be to people. (460–1)

Conversely, those books which privileged form over function showed 'no signs of wear and tear'. Serving no useful purpose they have no place in the public sphere. Beth concedes that novel-reading can be a vice, but insists on its capacity for moral influence and reform. As Dr Galbraith contends, if author and reader make the sufficiently great effort required for instructive reading, then 'fiction may do more to improve the mind, enlarge the sympathies, and develop the judgement than any other form of literature—partly because it looks into the hidden springs of action,

[91] See Showalter, *Sexual Anarchy: Gender and Culture at the fin de siècle* (London: Virago, 1991), 66; Sally Mitchell, intro. to *The Beth Book* (Bristol: Thoemmes Press, 1994), p. v. For illuminating discussion of ways in which this novel seeks to develop a feminist aesthetics, see Mangum, ch. 5.

[92] Sydney Grundy, *The New Woman* (Oxford: Oxford University Press, 1998) Act III scene i.

and makes all that is obscure in the way of impulse and motive clear to us'.[93]

For Grand, the novel, to be most effective, must be 'true to life'.[94] However, in *The Beth Book* she stressed, through Galbraith, that the author must take pains to guide the reader:

> When you address the blockhead majority, you must not only give them your text, you must tell them also what to think of it, otherwise there will be fine misinterpretation. You may be sure of the heart of the multitude if you can touch it; but its head, in the present state of its development, is an imperfect machine, manoeuvred for the most part by foolishness. (375)

The publisher and essayist Arthur Waugh's observation on *The Heavenly Twins*—'what has [Grand] told us that we did not all know, or could not learn from medical manuals?'[95]—was inadvertently acute. So too was *The Nation*, responding to the same: 'the author stands in some peril, as a reformer, of trying to cure all maladies with one medicine'.[96] *The Beth Book* equally tried the patience of readers, with the *Bookman* denouncing it as 'an hysterical statement of many undisputed truths relating mainly to the eternal sex problem, and accompanied by statistics belonging to a medical journal rather than to a work of fiction.'[97]

In her 1923 Preface to *The Heavenly Twins*, Grand spoke of her intention to 'compound an allopathic pill' for the general reader and 'gild it so that it would be mistaken for a bonbon and swallowed without a suspicion of its medicinal properties'.[98] Indeed, her methods translated, in medical terms, as allopathy.[99] Orthodox practitioners prescribe drugs not on the basis of *similia*, but on that of *alla*, signifying *other* systems.[100] According to Samuel Hahnemann (1755–1833), founder of homeopathy, the first law of homeopathy was the law of similars, *similia similibus curantur*: like is cured by like.[101] Allopathy controls illness by suppression;

93 *The Beth Book*, 372.

94 Tooley, 'The Woman Question', 161.

95 Arthur Waugh, 'Reticence in Literature', *Yellow Book* (April 1894), 21.

96 *Nation*, 57 (1893), 375.

97 'The Beth Book', *Bookman*, 6 (1897), 363.

98 Heilmann, *Sex, Social Purity and Sarah Grand*, i. 404.

99 Foreword, *The Heavenly Twins*, in Heilmann, *Sex, Social Purity and Sarah Grand*, i. 404.

100 See Deborah Dwork, 'Homeopathy/Allopathy', in W. F. Bynum, E. J. Browne, and Roy Porter (eds.), *Macmillan Dictionary of the History of Science* (London and Basingstoke: Macmillan, 1981), 189.

101 Samuel Hahnemann, *Organon der rationellen Heilkunde* (Dresden: Arnold, 1810) 1810, cited in Roy Porter, *The Greatest Benefit to Mankind: A Medical History of Humanity from Antiquity to the Present* (London: HarperCollins, 1997), 391.

homeopathy by biological adjustment.[102] In choosing allopathy as her method of treatment, Grand endorses the practice of introducing a foreign body into an organism, which will work through suppression. The analogy can be taken further. Grand sought to enact a controlling force on her reader-patient; to affect the mind of her readers with shocking narratives—to cause short-term disturbance (through, for example, syphilitic babies and brutal experiments on animals) in order to effect change: to effect health with affecting narratives. In 1891 Grand wrote to John Blackwood, who was repulsed by her syphilitic text: 'I rather expected that *The Heavenly Twins* would make your hair stand on end. This is the effect it has upon me when I think of its ever being read by anybody and I ought to be immune to the subject, for I hear it hotly discussed everywhere.'

As the *Manchester Guardian* reported on Grand's death in 1945, 'it is hard to realise now what a shock *The Heavenly Twins* gave the reading public of 1893 or how outraged were the nineties by her conception of the new woman—one of whose characteristics was to be that she had learned about sex before marriage'.[103] *The Times* obituary contrasted her work with that of sensation writers: 'in former years Ouida, Rhoda Broughton and others had shocked their readers in order to amuse them; the writers of the Sarah Grand school shocked theirs in order to improve them';[104] as I noted in Chapter 4, this was a fundamental difference between earlier fictions which engaged with medical ideas, and the eugenic works of the late nineteenth century.

The notion of fiction as an educational treatise, or as a medicinal drug, was at odds with one concept of aesthetics which was coming to dominate the *fin de siècle*. In 1896, Grand claimed that her aesthetics was in the ascendant:

> in England, thanks to our efforts, the 'novel with a purpose' and the 'sex novel' are more powerful at the present time, especially for good, than any other social influence. Great teachers and preachers have a very limited audience compared to the audience of popular writers; and the most influential writers are those who set themselves to do some good in the world . . . for one reader that Robert Louis Stevenson has, Mrs Humphry Ward has a thousand; which shows us that story books no longer satisfy us if they contain nothing more than the story . . . We appreciate art, but not art for art's sake; art for man's sake is what we demand.[105]

[102] Ronald Livingston, *Homeopathy. Evergreen Medicine: Jewel in the Medical Crown* (Poole: Asher and Asher, 1991), 28.

[103] Kersely, *Darling Madame*, 14.

[104] 'Sarah Grand, Novelist of the Nineties', *The Times* (13 May 1943).

[105] Grand, letter to Professor Viëter, Nizza, 15 December 1896, reprinted in Heilmann, *The Late Victorian Marriage Question*, v.

There was already a camp opposing art for art's sake: spearheaded by William Morris, late nineteenth-century socialists stressed the social function and value of art. As Morris had stressed in his lecture of 1884 'Art and Socialism': 'The cause of Art is the cause of the people . . . one day we shall win back Art, that is to say the pleasure of life; win back Art again to our daily labour . . . The aim of art [is] to destroy the curse of labour by making work the pleasurable satisfaction of our impulse towards energy, and giving to that energy hope of producing something worth the exercise.'[106] However, for Grand, art was not to bring about the restoration of pleasure, to end alienated labour, but to be morally improving. In adopting the phrase 'Art for Man's Sake', Grand was adopting socialist rhetoric, but redirecting it towards hereditarian goals. Likewise, in setting herself in opposition to Oscar Wilde's camp, she chose to overlook the humanitarian impulses that motivated Wilde's pronouncements on art and individualism. Socialism, he wrote in *The Soul of Man under Socialism*:

> will restore society to its proper condition of a thoroughly healthy organism, and ensure the material well-being of each member of the community. It will, in fact, give Life its proper basis and its proper environment. But, for the full development of Life to it highest mode of perfection, something more is needed. What is needed is Individualism.[107]

He went on to warn that, without individualism, socialism might become authoritarian, noting that 'many of the socialist views that I have come across seem to me to be tainted with ideas of authority, if not of actual compulsion' (24). By contrast, individualism was Grand's *bête noire*.

Like Grand, Nordau unequivocally condemned the art for art's sake camp: 'these bunglers with pen, brush and modelling spattle, strutting about in cap and doublet, naturally swear by the doctrine of the Aesthetes, carry themselves as if they were the salt of humanity, and make a parade of their contempt for the Philistine'.[108] Grand continually presented herself as writing outside the realms of art, stating with pride in her 1923 Foreword to *The Heavenly Twins* 'this book has never been

[106] Willliam Morris, 'Art and Socialism', Lecture to the Leicester Secular Society, 23 January 1884, cited in Raymond Williams, *Culture and Society* (London: Chatto & Windus, 1960), 154.

[107] Wilde, 'The Soul of Man under Socialism', *Fortnightly Review*, 190 (1891), in *De Profundis and Other Writings* (Harmondsworth: Penguin, 1987), 20–1.

[108] *Degeneration*, 327.

accused of being a work of art'.[109] 'We know it is no good expostulating with Sarah Grand about having a purpose in the sense of a doctrine to preach in her novels; she would say quite frankly that she cares nothing about novel-writing as an art, except in so far as it can be used as a vehicle for her doctrines' observed the *Athenaeum*.[110]

Grand explored in her fiction the theories she expounded in the press. In *The Heavenly Twins*, Evadne rejects sensational novels for medical textbooks which she spends the best part of her adolescence reading: 'after studying anatomy and physiology, she took up pathology as a matter of course, and naturally went from thence to prophylactics and therapeutics'. Significantly, among the books Evadne reads are the works of Galton and Spencer (176). The influence of Galton is stressed from the outset of *The Heavenly Twins*, which is framed by the following quotation from Darwin: 'I am inclined to agree with Francis Galton in believing that education and environment produce only a small effect on the mind of anyone, and that most of our qualities are innate' (1).

Nature is privileged unequivocally over nurture. Book II of *The Heavenly Twins* opens with a quotation from a letter from Darwin to Alfred Wallace:

> the great leading idea is quite new to me, *viz.*, that during late ages the mind will have been modified more than the body: yet I had not got as far as to see with you, that the struggle between the races of man depended entirely on intellectual and *moral* qualities. (171, emphasis in original)

Grand's short story 'Eugenia' (1894), unimpeded by the novel's requirements for the development of characters, functions as a manual on eugenic sexual selection. None of the confusion that met Grand's longer fiction is present with 'Eugenia'. As the *Critic* remarked, 'Eugenia is distinctly a modern product, she is even, perhaps, a twentieth-century girl'.[111] Eugenia is all set for healthy child-production: 'she had never worn a tight or heavy garment in her life, and her figure was perfect'. It is no surprise Brinkhampton was fascinated; the narrator marvels: 'anything more radiantly young and strong and healthy it is impossible

[109] Sarah Grand, Foreword, *The Heavenly Twins* (1893; London, Heinemann, 1923), Heilmann, *Sex, Social Purity and Sarah Grand*, i. 401. For contemporary discussion of these issues, see Hilde Hein, 'The Role of Feminist Aesthetics in Feminist Theory', in Peggy Zeglin Brand and Carolyn Korsmeyer (eds.), *Feminism and Tradition in Aesthetics* (University Park, Pa: Pennsylvania State University Press, 1995); and Hilde Hein and Carolyn Korsmeyer (eds.), *Aesthetics in Feminist Perspective* (Bloomington, Ind., 1993).

[110] 'New Novels: *The Beth Book*', *Athenaeum* (27 November, 1897), 743.

[111] 'Our Manifold Nature: Stories from Life', *Critic* (7 April 1894), 232.

to imagine'.[112] Eugenia observes 'there used to be a superstition in society that a man could at any time repair the errors of his youth by making a good match, and there are women still who will introduce "used up" brothers and so on to their girl friends as eligible husbands'. She declares: 'I belong to the party of progress myself, and would not under any circumstances have done such a thing' (110). From the start she is adamant that 'my man's physique must be self-supporting'. The reader is warned that

> accepting a man in ignorance of everything concerning him except that his social position is satisfactory and his manners and appearance are pleasing, is like picking up a peach and eating it in the dark. Or course, it may be a very good peach, but, on the other hand, it may have a wasp on it, or be rotten. (171)

The image, at once sensuous and repellent, marks a new emphasis in fiction on the link between sexuality and disease, and a new focus on the body as a marker of health. Try as Brinkhampton might, 'no care could conceal the "used up" look about his eyes, nor produce a deceptive tinge of health on the opaque sallow of his cheeks' (109). Worse still, he is packed with toxic agents which are sure to speed up any disease his defective inheritance might have set in train: 'he was reeking of tobacco and stimulants' (108). He deploys the very phrases Grand warned women to guard against.[113]

> I've had a good time, don't you know, rather too much of a good time if anything, and now I feel it would be better for me to settle, and I want something nice and young and fresh, with money, for a wife, so that I may repair all my errors at once; someone who has lived all her life at the back of beyond, never been anywhere nor seen anyone to speak of, and is refreshingly unsophisticated enough to mistake the first man who proposes to her for an unsullied hero of romance.[114]

Grand parades a series of such misconceived heroes: Colquhoun, Menteith, Maclure. Eugenia resists being written into such a narrative:

> do you really think it is romantic to marry a man who has been sedulously deteriorating mentally, morally, and physically, in consequence of his weak-minded self-indulgence, from his earliest youth?—a man who requires to be propped up

[112] 'Eugenia', *Our Manifold Nature* (London: Heinemann, 1894), 131.

[113] See Grand, *The Modern Man and Maid* (London: Horace Marshall & Son, 1898), 88. Josephine Butler warned against phrases such as 'he is only sowing his wild oats' and 'a reformed profligate makes a good husband', exposing proverbial wisdom as sexual vice. Quoted in S. Jeffreys, *The Spinster and Her Enemies: Feminism and Sexuality 1880–1930* (London: Pandora Press, 1985), 9.

[114] 'Eugenia', 110.

on alcohol as soon as he gets out of bed in the morning, and soothed with sedative tobacco for the rest of the day? (169)

'Eugenia' concludes with Eugenia's rational selection of a reproductive partner. On the look out for 'drunkenness, dissipation, extravagance and disease, all the misery-making tendencies they ignored when they chose their husbands', she chooses Saxon Wake. Radiant with health (170), Saxon is a yeoman, old as the English soil; a member of the biological aristocracy, his name testimony to his ancient, English, origins.

In disseminating the new, eugenic love, Grand hailed male literary precedent as a source of contamination that was to be upturned at all costs. Rewriting the love-plot, she exposed the health risks of conventional romance. As a follow-up to her reflective readings, Evadne joins in discussions with her aunt, demythologizing romantic love, and decrying the masculine literature she sees as the source of this ideal of love, urging that it sets a 'bad example' by privileging sentiment and urging imitation (*The Heavenely Twins*, 35). She is disturbed by the 'hopeless passion' of Malory's Elaine (35), outraged by the version of morality paraded by Tobias Smollett's *The Adventures of Roderick Random* (1748), and in Henry Fielding's *Tom Jones, A Foundling* (1749), infuriated to find yet 'another young man steeped in vice'. In *Middlemarch* (1871), set in 1832, *The Adventures of Roderick Random* is deemed acceptable reading for women, or at least married women. Even behind-the-times Mr Brooke says to Casaubon, 'get Dorothea to read you light things—Smollett—*Roderick Random*, *Humphry Clinker*: 'they are a little broad, but she may read anything now she's married, you know'.[115] In the emergent context of eugenic feminism, such dissipated heroes were a serious health risk. Evadne declares:

the hero is a kind of king-can-do-no-wrong young man; if a thing were not right in itself he acted as if the pleasure of doing it sanctified it to his use sufficiently. After a career of vice, in which he revels without any sense of personal degradation, he marries an amiable girl named Narcissa, and everyone seems to expect that such a union of vice and virtue would be productive of the happiest consequences. (19)

She concludes, 'the book cannot be wholesome, and it may be poisonous. The moral is: "be as vicious as you please, but prate of virtue" ' (20). Of *Tom Jones, A Foundling*, she is even more dismissive: 'another

[115] *Middlemarch* (1871; Harmondsworth: Penguin, 1985), 320–1.

young man', she writes, 'steeped in vice, although acquainted with virtue. He also marries a spotless heroine. Such men marrying are a danger to the community at large' (20). The pronouncements of Evadne's father on *Tom Jones* and *Roderick Random* acquire a sadly prophetic significance for Evadne: 'they are true to life in every particular . . . In fact, you feel as you read, that it is not fiction' (19). Grand turns the morally feckless heroes of these novels into anti-heroes in her own and, borrowing the 'spotless' heroine, urged that women become 'spotless' not by ignorance on sexual matters, but by exercising their superior capacity for sexual selection on rational grounds, and in doing so avoiding contamination by 'dirty men' (621, 626).[116] Ellice Hopkins voiced the same concerns: 'the man ascends the drawing-room stairs, and if he be rich or titled, finds anxious mammas, who are only too proud and happy to give him their unspotted girl to be his devoted wife.'[117]

Writing in the *North American Review* in 1894, Grand declared the modern girl's 'commonest expressions' of distaste for the 'man of the moment' to be:

> 'I'm not going to marry a man I can't respect,' 'I shan't marry unless I find a man of honour with no horrid past', and 'Don't offer me the mutilated remains of a man', coupled with the names of Tom Jones and Roderick Random.[118]

Of course, some critics refused to abandon the classics: Hugh Stutfield declared, tacitly targeting Grand, 'I would much rather see a boy or girl reading *Tom Jones* or *Roderick Random* than some of our "modern" works of fiction.'[119] He found little of literary merit in Grand's fiction:

> with her head full of all the 'ologies and 'isms, with sex problems and heredity, and other gleanings from the surgery and the lecture-room, there is no space left

[116] See letter from Esther Longhurst, *Saturday Review* (29 October 1904), 548; and letter from F.A. Steel, *Saturday Review* (5 November 1904), 571, for the contemporary debate as to whether girls should be allowed to read *Tom Jones*.

[117] 'Man and Woman or The Christian Ideal' (London, Hatchards, 1883), 6.

[118] Grand, 'The Man of the Moment'. The title implies the spontaneity—the lack of forethought or afterthought that Grand saw characterizing the New Woman and so has sexual undertone. Cf. Edith Searle Grossmann, 'The New Sex Psychology', *Westminster Review*, 172 (1899), 502; in which Grossmann saw in the theatrical revival of *Tom Jones* a return to the 'eighteenth century views' that the 'sex-relationship is not a friendly one at all'.

[119] Hugh E. M. Stutfield, 'Tommyrotics', *Blackwood's Edinburgh Magazine*, 157 (1895), 836. In 1896 Havelock Ellis noted (with some incredulity), '*Tom Jones* is even yet regarded as unfit to be read in an unabridged form' (Havelock Ellis, 'Concerning *Jude the Obscure*' (October 1896; London: The Ulysses Bookshop, 1931), 21).

for humour, and her novels are for the most part merely pamphlets, sermons, or treatises in disguise.[120]

THE FRENCH NOVEL

Social purists concurred with Nordau in seeing France as a nation in the process of becoming unhealthily feminized—and sterile—through the abandonment of 'traditional discipline' and masculine restraint.[121] Unsurprisingly, French fiction figures in Grand's novels as a particularly unhealthy influence. In *The Heavenly Twins*, in Malta, Colquhoun provides Evadne with the complete—and 'dangerous'—works of Zola, Daudet, and George Sand in the hope that they will entice her to have post-marital sex with him (221). However, her studies in physiology and anatomy leave her impervious to the sensual suggestions of the French novels and her reading of *Nana*, *La Terre*, *Madame Bovary*, and *Sapho* only strengthen her resolve, causing her to cry out against 'the awful, needless suffering' (221).

Grand's Pounce also functions as a gauge of the corrupting influence of literature and, above all, of French novels, by which he is held to have been 'bitten' (475). In the words of the doctor Galbraith, who narrated the last book of *The Heavenly Twins*, and has since been knighted: 'if France is to be judged by the tendency of its literature and art at present, one would suppose it to be dominated and doomed to destruction by a gang of lascivious authors and artists who are sapping the manhood of the country' (*The Beth Book*, 367). Galbraith's indictment of degenerate literature is coated in a language of male honour and vigour. Grand provides an authorial footnote indicting French lack of honour and national bravery (367). Through the use of this footnote she seeks to give her vilification of the French an additional layer of authority—to *direct* the reader as to how to read.

[120] Stutfield, 'Tommyrotics', 837. Arnold Bennett was equally critical of Grand's didactic approach, seeing her fiction as increasingly unpalatable following *The Heavenly Twins*; see 'The Author of "Babs the Impossible": An Inquiry', in Arnold Bennett's *Fame and Fiction: An Enquiry into Certain Popularities* (London: Grant Richards, 1891), 71–9.

[121] Nordau, *Degeneration*, 5. For a discussion of the decline of the birth rate in France from 26 in 1,000 in 1870 to 22 in 1890, 19 in 1911, and the related fears of German invasion that exercised the public authorities from 1870, see Anna Cova, 'French Feminism and Maternity: Theories and Policies 1890–1918', in Gisela Bock and Pat Thane (eds.), *Maternity and Gender Policies: Women and the Rise of the European Welfare States 1880s–1950s* (London and New York: Routledge, 1994).

For eugenists and social purists decadent art was a renunciation of responsibility, an expression of a failure of masculinity, and the French novel was its epitome. Grand conceived of her texts as precisely the opposite, refusing to collude with degenerative narratives. Writing against dysgenic narratives, Grand's eugenic pronatalism manifests itself through the reproductive imagery used to describe the writing of good (that is, civilizing) fiction. We learn that Beth had 'some glorious moments, revelling in the joy of creation. There is a mental analogy to all physical processes. Fertility in life comes of love; and in art the fervour of production is also accompanied by a rapture and preceded by a passion of its own' (394). For Beth, 'art-and-style books' are 'barren' (376). Such texts become metonymic figurings of the impotent male aesthete. Sir George considers French literature 'barren of happy phrases to enrich the mind' (367). Beth declares 'the work of our smartest modern writers, particularly the French, satiate me with their cleverness; but they are vain, hollow, cynical, dyspeptic' (374). The texts are anthropomorphized in order that they may be pathologized.

The rhetoric of fertility which characterizes moral art in *The Beth Book* is forcefully expressed by Nordau:

> the highest work of art can, from its inmost nature, be none other than moral, since it is a manifestation of vital force and health, a revelation of the capacity for evolution of the race; and humanity values it so highly because it divines this circumstance.[122]

In her novels, however, Grand came perilously close to writing the sort of fiction she despised. *Bookman* remarked of *Babs the Impossible* (1901) 'the whole atmosphere of the book is suggestive of sensuality. Few novels of recent years are more thoroughly unwholesome and unhealthy, in tone and tendency',[123] and *The Times* obituary remarked of *The Heavenly Twins* 'it is perhaps curious that the novel was never in trouble with the Libraries, for several of the incidents are, by late Victorian standards, highly flavoured. There are gentlemen of family who return late 'reeking of tobacco and stimulants'; there are bastard babies; there is even a tragic episode of venereal infection'.[124] Charles Whitby considered Grand's work alongside that of British followers of the French school of naturalism, such as George Moore and George Gissing. Of these he wrote:

[122] Nordau, *Degeneration*, 335.
[123] J. E. Hodder Williams, 'Impossible', *Bookman* (May 1901), 55.
[124] *The Times*, obituary (24 May 1943), 6 col. d.

their principal preoccupation was to treat human life as a physiological process and nothing more. No doubt their assumption of this liberty was resented by timid readers, but the naturalists were guiltless of the far more serious offence of openly tampering with or attacking the fundamental principles of ordinary people. For, to the naturalists, those fundamental principles were of no interest, not worth questioning, even; they knew too well that reality consisted merely in the mechanical play of blind atoms: that Man was the chance product of natural selection and the struggle for existence, and that the actions and passions depicted in their novels were consequently of no more intrinsic purport or significance than any other natural phenomena! And so it was that their subtle-nihilistic productions, apart from a certain frankness in handling sex-relations (which had, by the way, its own appeal, even to the most prudish), appeared on the whole to conform pretty well to the view that the novel exists solely for pastime.[125]

The implications of Whitby's remarks are interesting. Grand was guilty of inciting the same prurience as the naturalists and, worse still, of exhibiting a didacticism from which the naturalists, writing without an agenda, were free. The critic William Barry expressed concern over the naturalist preference for the ephemeral, for immediate sensuary pleasure, in the face of past and future uncertainties, suggesting that such writers as Zola and Bourget foretell 'the end of a civilization': 'Zola, following, as he supposes, the prophets of evolution, can find no "species," no fixed quantities whatever in the universe at large. It is to him a perpetual flux, and the one way to render it is by the "photography of the moment." '[126] His remarks illuminate Grand's dilemma. In striking contrast to the naturalists, who had no aim, or belief in the past or future, Grand's aim was future certainty, through the application of knowledge gained through close reading and interpretation of the past. She knew that the 'photography of the moment' was insufficient in seeking to bring about national health; for this, as she strove to show through her fiction, it was necessary to get at the stories behind people; for this reason her novels had, of necessity, to be long, and didactic. Nonetheless, her focus was biology, and she needed to keep a close eye on the bodies of her characters as well as their minds, morals, and histories; to catalogue the physical signs, the stigmata of moral and physical degeneracy; to chart a *physiological aesthetic*. The virulence of her attack on decadent

[125] 'Sarah Grand: The Woman and her Work', in Heilmann, *Sex, Social Purity and Sarah Grand*, i. 330.

[126] William Barry, 'Realism and Decadence in French Fiction', *Quarterly Review*, 171 (1890), 90, 68.

novels suggests the extent to which she needed to show her distance from them as well as her disapproval, but at times her fiction came close to revelling in the secrets and vices she was seeking to expose. *The Critic* remarked: 'through the book, the author condemns the work of Zola, Daudet and other French writers of the realistic school, and yet there is a curious parallel between the character of Evadne and that of the heroine of Zola's last book, *Le Docteur Pascal*. Both are oppressed by the terrible problems of heredity . . .'. So too, the *Nation* was quick to draw negative comparisons between Grand and Zola:

It may suit M. Zola to confound the tragic and the pathological; in art there is a degree of mental as of physical agony which must not be shown, or the audience will turn away their eyes. Let the asylum, the sick-bed, keep its dreadful secrets; the curtain which divides them from the art of literature is, happily, impenetrable.[127]

The *Young Woman* admonished Grand directly:

We don't read Zola, and we think you are too good to waste yourself in following where he goes. There are two Zolas, of course, the author of *Le Rêve* and the author of *Lourdes*. You have a real kinship with the first, which is almost unknown, but you are bitten, too, with the mania for 'revelations' that governs the other man, the Zola of the bookstalls.[128]

Some critics objected to Grand's faith in biological determinism, or called its scientific accuracy into question. The Jewish novelist Israel Zangwill wrote in *Cosmopolitan*:

to be a man at all, is to come under Sarah Grand's suspicion. True, she admits once, boys may be good, and girls bad. But the reason is delicious. 'Girls may inherit their fathers' vices, just as boys may inherit their mothers' virtues.' But then in the next generation what prevents heredity acting through these good sons?[129]

127 'The Heavenly Twins', *Critic*, 23 (1893), in Heilmann, *Sex, Social Purity and Sarah Grand*, i. 437; and 'More Novels', *Nation*, 66 (1 June 1898), 446–7 in Heilmann, i. 501–2.

128 Deas Cromarty, 'To the Author of "Beth" ', *Young Woman*, 65 (1898), 234. *Le Rêve*, one of the twenty novels that constitute the series *Les Rougon-Macquart* (1871–93), was an unusual departure for Zola. Its heroine, Angélique, inhabits a sacred world of dream, experiencing sexual desire as religious exaltation. As she prepares to enter reality, on the threshold of Beaumont Cathedral, having just gone through the ceremony of marriage, she dies, a virgin. *Lourdes* (1894) was of a quite different order. The first of the trilogy *Three Cities* (*Rome* appeared in 1896 and *Paris* in 1898), it centres on the national pilgrimage to Lourdes. Chronicling the promiscuities of the crowded city, and calling into question the miraculous cures performed there, the novel infuriated the religious world.

129 Israel Zangwill, 'The Month in England', *Cosmopolitan*, 24 (1898), 455–6.

The *Catholic World* was particularly struck by *The Beth Book*'s refusal to concede any influence to environmental factors, declaring itself 'unable to accept Beth's development of character in the light of the experiences she undergoes'; 'such a deterministic vision of character as the book expresses is unconvincing and unnecessary', concluding that it was quite simply implausible that she would have 'a noble nature' which is quite unaffected by nurture:

If the basis of her character be a generous temper so defined, the treatment to which she has been subjected would arrest all development; or, if a disposition worked itself out at all, it would be towards a cynical unbelief in good, a contemptuous and bitter estimate of mankind. There are moments when the author, to some extent, sees these effects as probable results of the influences with which she surrounds the childhood and dawning girlhood of Beth, but she modifies their power by accidental counter-influences working like the *deus ex machina* who so conveniently rescues an author from the difficulties of his plot.[130]

This is a fair criticism. For the biological determinist characters remain unchanged by their experiences. However, the form of the novel, and the need to retain the reader's interest and belief, require character development consistent with plot and event. This frequently results in a tension in Grand's novels between science and fiction, opening up spaces of indeterminacy or confusion. The dictum of the Darwinian epigraph of *The Heavenly Twins*, 'education and environment produce only a small effect on the mind of anyone, and . . . most of our qualities are innate', proved neither possible nor desirable to sustain though her lengthy novels, and at times her characters tried the patience of her readers, either refusing to respond to their environment in realistic ways, or changing without due cause. Evadne was singled out by the *Nation* as being particularly inconsistent 'often nothing is so true to nature as inconsistency of character; but it is fair to say that Evadne's inconsistency in this particular, as the heroine of a novel of reform, is a breach of trust with the reader'.[131]

The presence of the twins themselves raises questions in *The Heavenly Twins*. On one hand, they offer an opportunity to play with gender and to chafe against stereotypes, for, as children, they switch gender through cross-dressing (61), alike enough to disguise themselves as each other. On the other hand, the practice ends in disaster for the adult Angelica,

[130] '*The Beth Book*', *Catholic World*, 66 (1898), 560.
[131] Review of *The Heavenly Twins*, *Nation*, 57 (1893), 374.

and we learn early that they are explicitly different: 'Angelica was the dark one, and she was also the elder, taller, stronger, and wickeder of the two, the organizer and commander of every expedition' (7). Grand herself sums up the tension: 'the twins were alike in appearance, but not nearly so much as twins usually are' (7). She seems more interested in demonstrating the persistence of hereditary traits than undermining social constructions of gender.

Twins were a vital testing ground for eugenic ideas. In 1875, Galton had publicized his inquiries into the life histories of twins to a broad audience, using the data he had gathered in his research to argue for the predominance of nature over nurture.[132] As he again explained in 1882:

> I took two categories of twins—those who were closely alike in their infancy and those who were exceedingly unlike—and I traced their histories up to the date of the memoir. It appeared that twins who were closely alike at the first, frequently preserved their resemblance throughout life . . . I found not a few cases in which twins residing apart and following different professions at home and abroad still continued to live parallel lives, ageing in the same way, and preserving all along the same features, voice, gestures, and ways of thought.

Noting that 'as regards those twins who were born very unlike, that in no case did their dissimilarity lessen under the influence of identical nurture' he continued: 'the conclusion to which I was driven by the results of this inquiry was that a surprisingly small margin seemed to be left to the effects of circumstances and education, and to the exercise of what we are accustomed to call "free-will".'[133]

[132] Galton, 'The History of Twins as a Criterion of the Relative Powers of Nature and Nurture', *Journal of Anthropological Institute*, 5 (1875), 391–406; and *Frazer's Magazine*, 12 (1875), 556–76. See Galton Papers, 122/3 for letters Galton received on publication of this essay. See also 122/4 for a review of this paper. For later explorations of heredity and twins, see Nathaniel David Mittron Hirsch, *Twins: Heredity and Environment* (Cambridge, Mass.: Harvard University Press, 1930); and, more recently, Lawrence Wright, *Twins: Genes, Environment and the Mystery of Human Identity* (London: Weiden & Nicolson, 1997).

[133] 'The Anthropometric Laboratory', *Fortnightly Review*, 37 (1882), 332–3. See Galton Papers, 122 on Galton's data and notes on the effects of nature and nurture on the physical and mental characteristics of twins, assembled between 1874 and 1876. His notes and letters are replies to his circular, and there are nineteen letters comparing boys and girls (122/1B). Galton has working papers and a notebook on heredity in fingerprints, dated 1892, which includes work on twins (172/4A). Reviewing *Inquiries into Human Faculty and its Development* in *Nature* (31 May 1883), George J. Romanes commented: 'one of the most interesting chapters in the books is that which next follows on from the History of Twins. It will be remembered that the main fact elicited by this inquiry is that nature counts for much more than nurture; for it is shown that "instances exist of an apparently thorough similarity of nature, in which such difference of external circumstances as may be consistent with the ordinary conditions of the same social rank and country do not create

For the biological determinist the effects of circumstance, education, and free will are negligible, while for the novelist they are vital. Grand's fiction expresses this tension as her characters either remain impervious to their surroundings, passing through the pages of the novel like germ-plasm through the body, or, in the interest of didacticism or entertainment, developing beyond the reaches of either biological determinism or probability. The fictional sugar that sweetened Grand's educational pill could render it ineffective, or, at best, confusing.

dissimilarity." ' For Galton's later reflections on the question of free will, where he concluded that most actions were automatic, the product of heredity or environment, see Galton 'Memories of My Life', Galton Papers, 57, 340.

6 Sarah Grand, the Country, and the City

> The production of sound minds in healthy, athletic, and beautiful bodies is a form of patriotism which must be revised if modern England is not to follow ancient Babylon and Tyre. Unless our town dwellers take heed and recognize that we have begun to rot, our position as a World Power is doomed; our expectancy of life reduced from centuries to a few generations, or even to decades.
>
> Arnold White[1]

> Moral and physical stamina are broken, and the good workman, fresh from the soil, becomes in the first city generation a poor workman; and by the second city generation, devoid of push and go and initiative, and actually unable physically to perform the labour his father did, he is well on the way to the shambles at the bottom of the Abyss.
>
> Jack London[2]

> Our national life is vigorously rooted in the soil and sound enough.
>
> Sarah Grand[3]

At the beginning of the nineteenth century, a third of all workers were employed in agriculture; by the end, less than a tenth.[4] With the transformation of Britain from an agrarian to an urban population over the course of the century, more than three-quarters of the population were classified as urban in the census of 1901, as compared to one-fifth in 1801. The theory of degeneration underpinning analyses of the urban poor came increasingly to focus on the division between country and city, bringing environmental and biological concerns together in the name of regeneration. The narrative of class opposition that underpinned eugenic thinking became overlaid with—and complicated by—this narrative of countryside versus town. These overlapping narratives

[1] Arnold White, *Efficiency and Empire* (1901; Brighton: Harvester Press, 1973), 121.

[2] Jack London, *People of the Abyss*, (London: Isbister and Co. Ltd., 1903), 43–4.

[3] *The Winged Victory* (London: Heinemann, 1916), 471.

[4] Though the figures for 1801 and 1881—1,700,000—did not change; see Raymond Williams, *The Country and the City* (London: Chatto & Windus, 1960), 186.

inform the complex politics of Grand's late novels. While they show a new support for country living, which seems to suggests an attachment to aristocracy, they also gesture towards socialism. However, as I shall show, the socialism that enters these novels is underpinned by eugenic ideas on health, and reveals the ideological complexity and deep-seated class hostility that continued to motivate eugenics in twentieth-century Britain.

Cities were essential to empire but, by the closing decades of the century, cities also posed the single greatest threat to national health. In 1886 Arnold White published *The Problems of a Great City*; imperial eugenists were beginning to consider the benefits of rural life on national health. Working within the conceptual framework of agrarian capitalism, they developed a vision whereby land would be brought under ever tighter social and scientific control and intensively *worked* with the aid of the latest scientific techniques. The newly urban workers in Sarah Grand's last two novels return to the country, their bucolic innocence restored, and breed healthy children in happy harmony with the rhythms of nature, all the while extracting maximum profit from the soil. Adnam, in *Adnam's Orchard* (1912), tending his paradisal orchard, and preaching on the intensive culture of the land, is a post-industrial development of the first Adam.

As London entered its greatest moment as an imperial city, the housing question, the misery and poverty it created at its centre, was a national shame. However, while eugenists objected in the name of national health to the life of the city, the dispossession and despair of the East End was not the only problem. Other developments in the city at the *fin de siècle* were at least as concerning. On one hand, a self-consciously modern, and superbly class-conscious sense of separation and isolation was emerging. London, Hardy wrote in his autobiography in 1887, 'appears not to see itself. Each individual is conscious of himself, but nobody conscious of themselves collectively.'[5] This tendency towards individualism and, by extension, towards solitary pleasure brought with it a new perspective, the perspective of the detached observer, the *flaneur*, which would delight poets such as Baudelaire, and which constituted an affront to eugenic ideas of civic responsibility and social obligation. On the other hand—'murky, swarming and rotting', in the words of Gissing in *The Nether World*—London offered maximum scope for unionism, for radical bottom-up politics, nurturing a radical

[5] Florence Hardy [Thomas Hardy], *The Life of Thomas Hardy*, 2 vols. (1928–30; London: Studio Editions, 1994 i. 271).

political consciousness that brought workers together. At its heart was welling the collective response of workers to capitalist tyranny and exploitation. The 1880s saw the unionization of the gasworkers, and the great strike of the matchgirls and the dockers. In the words of Engels, in his 1892 Preface to the *Condition of the Working Class in England in 1844*:

> That immense haunt of misery is no longer the stagnant pool it was six years ago. It has shaken off its torpid despair, has returned to life, and has become the home of what it called the 'New Unionism'; that is to say, of the organization of 'unskilled' workers . . . Faith in the eternity of the wages system was seriously shaken; their founders and promoters were Socialists either consciously or in feeling.[6]

Early in the twentieth century, eugenists began to consider the effects that environmentalist philanthropy and the Garden City Movement might have on national health. The idea of the Garden City, a small, self-contained, ecologically balanced city, with open spaces, avenues, and large gardens, combining workplaces and homes, was the inspiration of Ebenezer Howard (1850–1928), the son of a shopkeeper. Influenced by the utopian ideas of William Morris and Edward Bellamy, Howard had worked as a parliamentary reporter during the 1880s, at the height of the housing crisis. In 1898 he published *Tomorrow: A Peaceful Path to Real Reform*, which was reissued as a fivepenny paperback, *Garden Cities of Tomorrow*, in 1902, and delivered lectures across England on his detailed plan for housing and environmental reform. Howard's aim was to create co-operative communities, improving the material conditions of working-class lives through the marriage of town and country. He wrote in *Garden Cities of Tomorrow* that as a Garden City grew, 'the free gifts of Nature—fresh air, sunlight, breathing room and playing room—shall be still retained in all needed abundance' (1902, 113). In June 1899 Howard formed the Garden City Association, which became The Garden City Limited in 1900. The first Garden City conference, which received a high profile in the press, was held the following year at Bournville, the site of the Quaker Cadbury brothers' cocoa and chocolate factory just south of Birmingham, which one of the brothers, the manufacturer and social reformer George Cadbury (1839–1922), had established in 1889. On 18 March 1901, on holiday abroad and reading about growing British support for the concept of the Garden City, Galton took a cutting from *The Standard*. Headed 'Bournville', it outlined George Cadbury's scheme for the perfect industrial town:

[6] Williams, *The Country and the City*, 231.

this ought certainly to carry out Mr Cadbury's leading idea of giving the men who are confined in a factory during work hours something to amuse and to occupy them out of doors. This, it is hoped, will greatly help in maintaining the physique of our race, than which few things can be more important to the future of the country.

Writing immediately for more information,[7] Galton was already turning over and adding a eugenic spin to the ideas—the best of the artisan class might be selected for breeding: 'English artisans as a body do not seem to have sufficient capacity to originate or carry out co-operative schemes by themselves', he wrote, adding 'I want to see how a settlement will thrive when its members are selected at about the rate of one in four.' He saw such a settlement as a centre of racial fitness and nationalistic pride, where there would be 'no feckless characters' and 'no low life' (he circled this for emphasis): 'as the social tone of the settlement would be conspicuously higher than that in artisan quarters generally the settlers would soon learn to take a patriotic pride in it.'[8] Expressing his fears that 'English artisans when acting as a body of men with equal voting powers' have an insufficient 'dose of civic capacity for maintaining co-operative', he conceded that:

though the whole body of men is too low an average type to achieve success it is more than probable that a moderate selection from the general body would be sufficiently high in type to carry on by themselves co-operative and other sociological works with success. The existence of a settlement such as that of W. G. Cadbury offers means for the experiment. Here through the munificent philanthropy of a wealthy individual, houses are offered to tenants considerably below their normal rental. Consequently if no deterrent conditions are imposed, there will be many applicants to each house, as it becomes vacant. Select the best.[9]

As Galton saw it, a Garden City would produce optimum conditions for eugenic experimentation. Within such a settlement houses prices

[7] UCL Galton Papers, 138/5, 16. Among the speakers at the 1901 conference were Raymond Unwin, a socialist architect who went on to be the planner of Letchworth, the first Garden City, in 1904, and Hampstead Garden Suburb, in 1906. Unwin was a close friend of William Morris and a member of his Socialist League (which campaigned for healthy housing and decent surroundings), forming its Manchester branch. Other speakers included Bernard Shaw and the Scottish surveyor Thomas Adams, an advocate of rural regeneration. The conference received considerable publicity, and a second conference was held the following year at Port Sunlight near Birkenhead. See Standish Meacham, *Regaining Paradise: Englishness and the Early Garden City Movement* (New Haven, Conn.: Yale University Press, 1999); and Kermit C. Parsons and David Schuyler (eds.), *From Garden City to Green City: The Legacy of Ebenezer Howard* (Baltimore: The Johns Hopkins University Press, 2002).

[8] Galton Papers, 138/5, 17.

[9] Galton Papers, 138/5, 14.

would soon be able to be raised, as the good artisan would show self-improvement—and 'should not the better class of workman form a club settlement?'[10] As he explains why he chose to refer to the settlement as a 'club', the class hostilities that underpin his scheme emerge: 'to belong to the settlement would be like belonging to a good club. They would be secure from the neighbourhood of feckless, feeble, slatternly and low class characters.'[11] He went on to express his confidence that projects such as Bournville would improve the 'breed', providing that 'the condition of selection included that of the couple being young with a promise of a large family'—this, he stressed, was necessary to ensure that 'the natural desire of marriage in early years would not be thwarted'.[12]

Environmentalist philanthropy merged rapidly with ideas for the eugenic improvement of the race in Galton's vision. Both approaches were useful to his plans for social engineering. Later in 1901, in his speech to the Anthropological Institute on 'The Possible Improvement of the Human Breed, under the Existing Conditions of Law and Sentiment', Galton remarked that a scheme might be developed, based on actions which were currently 'commonly but half unconsciously' performed by many great landowners 'whose employments for man and wife, together with good cottages, are given to exceptionally deserving couples . . . there are usually more applicants than vacancies, so selection can be exercised. The consequence is that the class of men found upon these properties is markedly superior to those in similar positions elsewhere.'[13] Galton went on to envisage a society in which it is 'a point of honour, and as much an avowed object, for noble families to gather fine specimens of humanity around them, as it is to procure and maintain fine breeds of cattle and so forth, which are costly, but repay satisfaction' (32). He imagines a 'renewed settlement' in which 'exceptionally promising young couples' are provided with 'healthy and convenient houses at low rentals'. But, he cautions, while it is all very well to contrive Utopias ('and I have indulged in many'), 'the first and pressing point is to thoroughly justify any crusade at all in favour of race improvement' (33).

In 1909 the first issue of the *Eugenics Review* stated, under the heading 'its attitude towards social reforms':

[10] Galton Papers, 138/5, 19.

[11] Galton Papers, 138/5, 20.

[12] Galton Papers, 138/5, 21.

[13] This paper was given as the second Huxley Lecture of the Anthropological Institute, 29 October 1901, and collected in Galton, *Essays in Eugenics* (London: The Eugenics Education Society, 1909), 32.

The Review whilst laying great stress on Heredity, will not ignore the importance of Environment. Environment undoubtedly exerts a potent influence on those individual tendencies which, latent at birth, are capable of being moulded by circumstances after birth. It will, therefore, advocate all social reforms that allow such tendencies free play when they are calculated to be beneficent to the community, and that restrain, or serve to repress, such tendencies when they are calculated to be harmful to the community.[14]

In Edwardian England public health policy and administration were informed by biology and environmentalism, as housing reform campaigns began to embrace the concept of town planning. The appropriation of biology by public health policy could lead either to a concealed version of Lamarckism or a combination of eugenic rhetoric and environmental reformism (exemplified by the evolutionary biologist and sociologist Patrick Geddes, who turned sociology into what he termed 'civics').[15] Geddes shared Cadbury's interest in town planning and health, seeking to explain the implications of urbanization and industrialization in environmental terms. While British architects were trying to promote British expertise in promoting Garden City principles at the Garden Cities and Town Planning Exhibition in London in 1910 (organized by the Royal Institute for British Architects), Geddes was seeking to generate a World Civic Movement which would encourage the pooling of ideas to promote happy and healthy environments and peaceful coexistence.[16] Geddes termed his practical theory 'civics' in order to distance it from more abstract historical sociology. Just as Darwinian sexual selection had grounded aesthetics in biology, so Geddes rethought sociology and architecture along biological lines. Commenting on a local arts and crafts exhibition, held in a new public library under 'civic auspices', Geddes stated in his paper 'Civics: As Applied Sociology' II, that 'the impulse to civic

[14] *The Eugenics Review*, 1 (1909), 4. The concept of nurture is used to serve mainstream, negative, eugenics; the piece proceeds to argue that some conditions are too unfavourable to sustain any form of desirable life, and that it would therefore be better for children not to be born into them: 'our asylums, our hospitals, are crowded with cases in which the pre-natal conditions have been such that any biologist or other expert well acquainted with them beforehand would have been able to predict their natural consequences' (4).

[15] See Dorothy Porter, '"Enemies of the Race": Biologism, Environmentalism, and Public Health in Edwardian England', *Victorian Studies*, 34 (1991), 169. See also Porter, *Health, Civilization and the State: A History of Public Health from Ancient to Modern Times* (London: Routledge, 1998), 77.

[16] See Helen Meller, *Patrick Geddes, Social Evolutionist and City Planner* (London and New York: Routledge, 1990), 178. See also, for example, Havelock Ellis, *The Problem of Race-Regeneration* (London, New York, Toronto, and Melbourne: Cassell and Co., 1911), ch. 1, 'The Improvement of the Environment', 13–24.

betterment' associated with the library 'is no longer merely one of aesthetic purpose, of "art for art's sake", nor its execution that of a cultured minority merely; it announces a reunion of this culture and art with the civic polity.'[17] Art, biology, and civic polity were joining forces.

As early as 1888, Jane Hume Clapperton included reference to Geddes in her eugenic novel *Margaret Dunmore*: in spring 1894 the eugenic community opened a hall 'to the general public for the teaching of scientific meliorism' (set six years into the future, this is a moment of utopian triumph): the 'lines of practical action' adopted by the hall, 'following Mr Patrick Geddes' classification, are in terms of the successive sciences':

(1) physical, concerned with wealth, and the organization of labour;
(2) biological, concerned with health and surroundings;
(3) psychological, concerned with education;
(4) social, and political;
(5) moral.[18]

In August 1904, Israel Zangwill wrote in *Today*:

the sociological society is forging ahead at American speed; the professors jostle one another, and Geddes treads on the heels of Galton. After 'Eugenics' or the Science of Good Births, comes 'Civics' or the Science of Cities. In the former Mr Galton was developing an idea which was in the air, and in Wells. In the latter Professor Geddes has struck out a more novel line, and a still more novel nomenclature. Politography, Politogenics, and EuPoliticogenics, likewise Hebraomorphic and Latino-morphic and Eutopia—quite an opposite idea from Utopia—such are some of the additions to the dictionary which the science of Civics carries in its train. They are all excellent words—with the double-barrelled exception—and still more excellent concepts. But I fancy the general idea of them all could be conveyed to the man in the streets under the covering of 'the human shell'. This shell of ours is the city . . . Professor Geddes, in fact, envisages our civic shell as becomes a brilliant biologist, who also happens to be a man of historic imagination, ethical impulses, and aesthetics perceptions For Eutopia (unlike Utopia, which is really Ou-topia, or no place) is merely your own place perfected. And the duty of working towards its perfection lies directly upon you.[19]

Zangwill's words testify to a turn of the century convergence of aesthetics, art, and biology. Geddes's compound terms, with which Zangwill was so taken, are clear expressions of new conceptual and professional alliances.

In his belief that better citizenship was the key to social progress,

[17] Helen Meller (ed.), *The Ideal City* (Leicester: Leicester University Press, 1979), 164.

[18] Jane Hume Clapperton, *Margaret Dunmore; or, A Socialist Home* (London: Swan Sonnenschein, Lowrey & Co., 1888), 204.

[19] *Today* (10 Aug. 1904), in Meller (ed.), *The Ideal City*, 120.

Geddes was deeply influenced by the concept of community and sought voluntary action by local communities 'for the public good within the framework of the local community of a city.'[20] Civics sat comfortably with emergent concepts of gendered citizenship and, equally, fitted the bill of the wider 'moralizing' of citizenship which had appealed to social purists and eugenists alike. The slippery and elastic term citizenship was invaluable to Geddes, as it had been for social purists and was for eugenists. In fact, his position in the Woman Question debates was, like Sarah Grand's, at once pioneering and conservative: both held women to be the bearers of moral biology. Geddes seized upon women's crucial role in shaping evolutionary trends; through motherhood they would shape the economic and social environment, creating ever higher levels of civilization. However, he did not take his gendered concept of citizenship as far as the ballot box; like eugenic feminists he saw women's ability to transform the world as coming from their biological role in the domestic sphere.[21] Geddes used the term civics to cover all the activities which women could usefully, even essentially, perform for the sake of the urban community as a whole. However, he saw motherhood as the ultimate duty and form of fulfilment for a civilized and educated woman.[22] Geddes claimed that his work was a form of citizenship; he also claimed that it was vital to the evolutionary progress, thus, like eugenic feminists, giving a moral and biological dimension to citizenship.[23] Aiming at the biological improvement of national stock through the scientific control of the environment, the alliance between eugenics and civics was a strong one. Geddes spoke of eugenics as being the whole purpose of civics.[24]

Geddes's desire for a fruitful union between the two found some reciprocation in Galton. At the age of 82, Galton made a plea for the study of eugenics as an important element in sociological studies. Galton's eugenics and Geddes's civics were the main attractions of the first session of the British Sociological Society: 'the social service which was to be the outcome of the Regional social survey was to be a form of planning for the physical and social well-being of individuals, the eugenist objective'.[25] Speaking at this session in the School of Economics and Political Science (University of London) on 19 July 1904, with Charles Booth in the chair, Geddes stressed the importance of tapping eugenic enthusiasm:

[20] Meller (ed.), *The Ideal City*, 12.

[21] Geddes, *The Evolution of Sex* (1889), 267, cited in Meller, *Patrick Geddes*, 83.

[22] Meller, *Patrick Geddes*, 83.

[23] Ibid., 90.

[24] Meller (ed.), *The Ideal City*, 73.

[25] Ibid., 72, 73.

Since Comte's demonstration of the necessity of the preliminary sciences to social studies, and Spencer's development of this, still more since the evolution theory has become generally recognised, no one disputes the applicability of biology to sociology. Many are, indeed, vigorously applying the conceptions of life in evolution, in geographical distribution and environment, in health and disease, to the interpretations of the problems of the times; while with the contemporary rise of eugenics to the first plane of interest, both social and scientific, these lines of thought, bio-social and bio-geographic, must needs be increasingly utilised and developed.[26]

At the same meeting Galton likewise outlined scope for a fusion of eugenic and civic policies in order to optimize racial improvement:

the improvement of the individuals of the community, which is the aim of eugenics, involves a corresponding civic progress. Using (for the moment at least) a parallel nomenclature, we see that the sociologist is concerned not only with 'demography' but with 'politography' and that 'eugenics' is inseparable from 'politogenics'. For the struggle for existence, though observed mainly from the side of its individuals by the demographer, is not only an intra-civic but an inter-civic process; and if so, ameliorative selection, now clearly sought for the individuals in detail as eugenics, is inseparable from a corresponding civic art—a literal 'Eupolitogenics'.[27]

Geddes aimed to build a new civic community based on good breeding, anticipating an environment that allows the new breed to flourish. In this way, environment would be added to evolution as a second stage in the process of building a brave new world: biological determinism was thus extended into beliefs about constructing the environment of the future. This was not environmental determinism, for Geddes, unlike environmentalists, did not believe the environment could improve the biologically 'unfit'; as far as he was concerned they were irredeemable.

SARAH GRAND AND THE CITY

During the 1890s, the height of her writing career, Sarah Grand lived in London. While her flat was in the West End, in salubrious Kensington, the rapidly expanding casual poor that were now in the forefront of the public imagination were not much more than a stone's throw away. It was at this time that the poor begin to enter New Woman fiction,

26 Meller (ed.), *The Ideal City*, 122.
27 'Civics: As Applied Sociology' I, in ibid., 76.

primarily as a problem, or as a threat to the nation's health, productivity, and military strength, and repeatedly surface in Grand's writing. Grand regularly travelled east to Fetter Lane to do charitable work. In 1895, *Woman at Home* noted her keen—if fashionable—interest in 'the poor girls of London'; 'she goes every Thursday evening when in town to Mrs Frederic Harrison's Girls' Guild at Newton Hall, Fetter Lane'; '"This summer," she told me, "we have provided our girls with very pretty uniforms for gymnastics, and many of them look charming in them—you would hardly know them for the pale, pinched-looking London work-girl"'.[28]

Eventually, and in keeping with the shift in thinking among eugenists in the early years of the twentieth century, Grand began to factor the environment into her thinking on racial regeneration. In doing so, she brought her fiction into the long-standing and complex country versus city debate. But, to place her in a tradition of radical nineteenth-century thought on the industrialized city and its discontents, from William Wordsworth and William Cobbett through Elizabeth Gaskell to Karl Marx, William Morris, and Edward Carpenter, or to interpret her work in the light of the environmentalist 'Back to Nature' movement of the late nineteenth century,[29] would be to overlook the idea of racial improvement which motivated her.

In her last two novels Grand became more concerned with the environment's effects on health and efficiency. Joining the ideological camp of Geddes, who embraced eugenics, rather than the environmental determinists, her new interest in the environmental influence of health aligns her with early twentieth-century developments within eugenic thought, and underscores the extent of her commitment to eugenics.

Adnam's Orchard appeared in 1912. Adnam is Grand's health and national efficiency prodigy, not unlike Evadne, who spent her youth in an attic in *The Heavenly Twins* reading medical treatises, twenty years earlier. Adnam is interested not only in human biology but in a more extensive control of nature. The novel was swiftly reviewed by the *Times Literary Supplement*. The hero, it remarked, 'is not much more than a

[28] Jane T. Stoddart, 'Illustrated Interview: Sarah Grand', *Woman at Home*, 3 (1895), 247–52, in Heilmann, *Sex, Social Purity and Sarah Grand*, i. 249–50.

[29] See Peter C. Gould, *Early Green Politics. Back to Nature, Back to the Land, and Socialism in Britain, 1880–1900* (Sussex and New York: Harvester and St Martin's Press, 1988). Gould notes the formation of several societies as part of the 'Back to Nature' movement; for instance, the Edinburgh Environment Society (1884), the Selborne League (1885), the Selborne Society for the Protection of Birds (1988); and the Coal Smoke Abatement Society (1898) (Gould, *Early Green Politics*, 16).

boy when he is discovered lolling among the scented violets, purple and white, beneath the gnarled boughs of his neglected orchard, deep in the inspiration of *Culture des Legumes Intensive et Extensive* . . . All the modern problems flourish here—one or two of them a little damaged by long service, all the cries and causes. The pages throb with their author's irrefragable convictions . . . '.[30] The American journal *Bookman* was eager for the sequel (which would appear four years later), concluding 'if she can continue on the present scale . . . we have no fear for the result. It will be deservedly classified as of the school of "Middlemarch" and, allowing for the difference of standard and achievement, even modified comparison like this is still rare praise.'[31]

Throughout her fiction, Grand urges that pleasure is unacceptable without responsibility. Her insistence upon the usefulness of art expresses this refusal of pleasure that is unaccountable, unproductive, or un*re*productive. As discussed in Chapter 5, Grand set out clearly her theory that art ought to be functional and morally improving.[32] In *Adnam's Orchard*, the well-born Ursula, Adnam's mother, gives voice and validation to Grand's theory of art, declaring that art is only of value 'as a means to an end' (476). Early in the novel the reader is treated to a roseate sunset. But, the narrator questions whether this can really be classed as beauty—for it is not the beauty that signifies, or (re)produces, health. The distinction is crucial for understanding Grand's aesthetics: 'to the eye of the artist the sun, low down in the west, gave the last touch of beauty to the quiet land; but, as to the eye of the physician who knows that some much admired beauty is not the beauty of health but the symptom of a deadly disease, so to the eye of the modern agriculturist those peaceful pastures on either hand, sparsely sprinkled with cattle, were symptomatic of the threatened decay of a great nations' (*Adnam's Orchard*, 155). Health is beauty in the eye of the physician.

Adnam's Orchard signals through its title the analogy between human breeding and the cultivation, more generally, of plants and animals which lies at the heart of the novel; the apocalyptic note on which it ends—'henceforth, Adnam's Orchard was the World' (640)—suggests that Adnam is now ready to cultivate a eugenic family. Throughout, he speaks tirelessly of *Culture Maraîchère* or 'intensive culture': 'the soil will have to be made, of course—it always has to be made for market-

30 'Adnam's Orchard', *Times Literary Supplement* (25 October 1912), 424 b.

31 'Only a Prologue', *Bookman*, 43 (1913), 228.

32 See especially 'Marriage Questions in Fiction', *Fortnightly Review*, 63 (1898), 378–89.

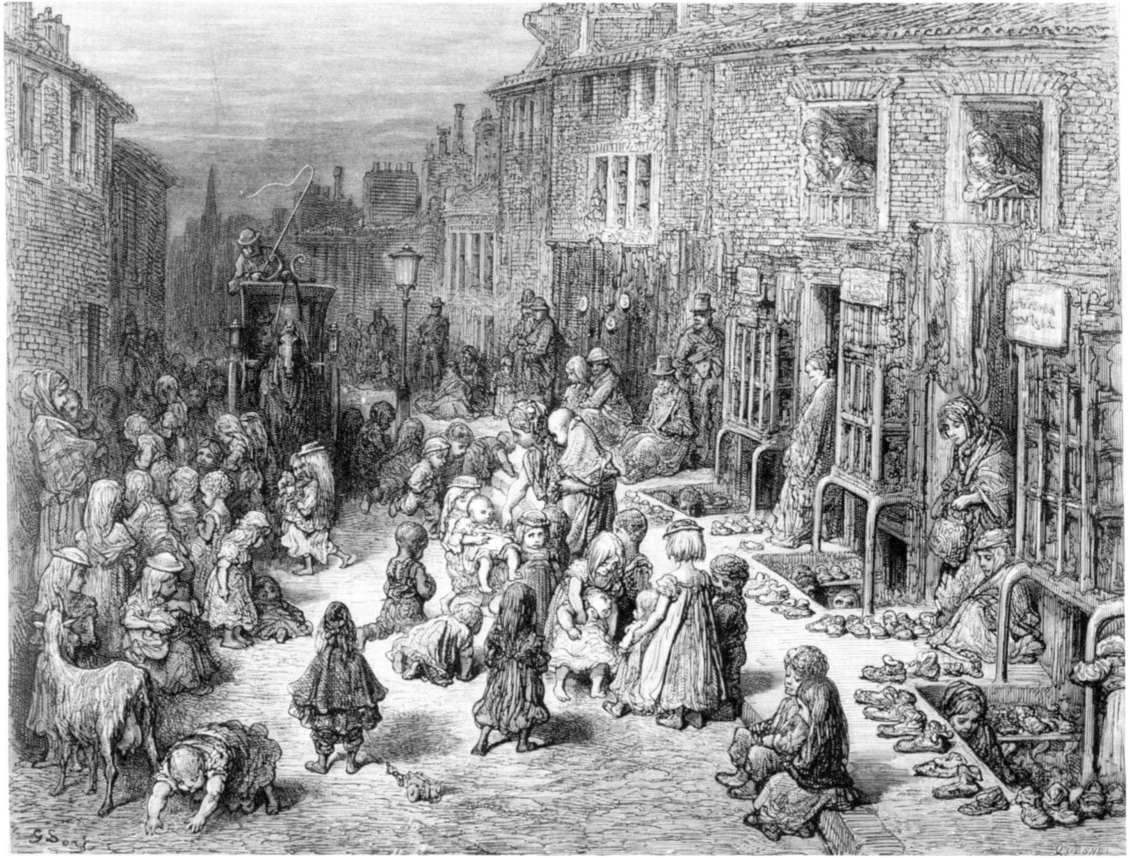

1. Gustave Doré, *Dudley Street, Seven Dials*, from Gustave Doré and Blanchard Jerrold, *London: A Pilgrimage* (London: Grant & Co., 1872). Earlier depictions of the Victorian working class tended to present them as a mob; here, the emphasis on children reflects the century's gradual displacement of the political to the biological.

126 PUNCH, OR THE LONDON CHARIVARI. [March 20, 1880.
HAPPY THOUGHT! LET US ALL HAVE A VOICE IN THE MATTER.
Noble Breeder of Shorthorns. "Well, you *are* a Splendid Fellow, and *no* mistake!"
Prize Bull. "So would *you* be, my Lord, if you could only have chosen your Pa and Ma as carefully and judiciously as you chose Mine!"

2 (*above*). *Happy Thought* (20 March 1880). Three years before Galton coined the term eugenics, the idea of human selective breeding is sufficiently in the air to be the target of satire in *Punch*.

3 (*right*). *Eugenics* (1911). G. K. Chesterton's cartoon dates from eleven years before he published his vehement attack, *Eugenics and Other Evils: An Argument Against the Scientifically Organized State*, which he had put on one side during the war, mistakenly thinking that the loss of enthusiasm for eugenics which occurred in the face of military conflict signalled its demise. Chesterton's understanding of the implications of eugenics was both prescient and profound.

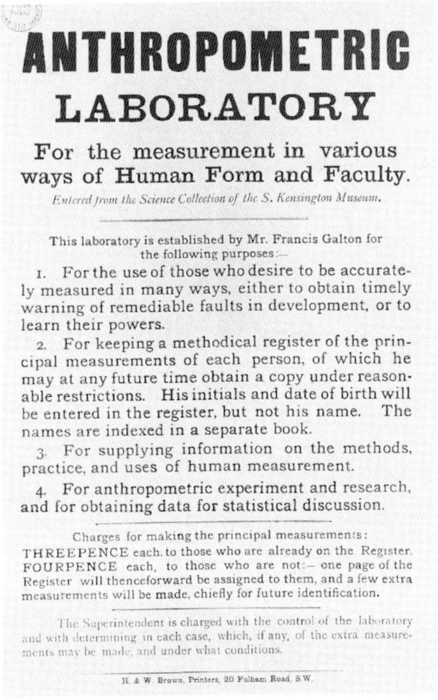

ANTHROPOMETRIC LABORATORY

For the measurement in various ways of Human Form and Faculty.

Entered from the Science Collection of the S. Kensington Museum.

This laboratory is established by Mr. Francis Galton for the following purposes:—

1. For the use of those who desire to be accurately measured in many ways, either to obtain timely warning of remediable faults in development, or to learn their powers.

2. For keeping a methodical register of the principal measurements of each person, of which he may at any future time obtain a copy under reasonable restrictions. His initials and date of birth will be entered in the register, but not his name. The names are indexed in a separate book.

3. For supplying information on the methods, practice, and uses of human measurement.

4. For anthropometric experiment and research, and for obtaining data for statistical discussion.

Charges for making the principal measurements:

THREEPENCE each, to those who are already on the Register.
FOURPENCE each, to those who are not:— one page of the Register will thenceforward be assigned to them, and a few extra measurements will be made, chiefly for future identification.

The Superintendent is charged with the control of the laboratory and with determining in each case, which, if any, of the extra measurements may be made, and under what conditions.

H. & W. Brown, Printers, 20 Fulham Road, S.W.

4 (*above*). Francis Galton's Anthropometric Laboratory at the International Health Exhibition, South Kensington Museum, 1884–5. Two years earlier Galton had urged in the *Fortnightly Review* the importance of such national laboratories, to provide posterity with vital records on national health.

5 (*left*). Advertisement calling for people to be measured at Galton's Laboratory. 10,000 people were measured, including Gladstone, who believed his head to be bigger than it was. When the Exhibition was over, Galton kept a room for these purposes for six more years in the Science Galleries of South Kensington Museum.

6–7. Beardsleyesque illustrations by 'Mortarthurio Whiskersly' (Edward Tennyson Reed) for Owen Seaman's 'She-Notes' (*Punch*, 17 March 1894)—a parody of George Egerton's 'A Cross Line' in *Keynotes*. Seaman was editor of *Punch* from 1906 to 1932. The New Woman is presented as highly sexualized and decadent, her advanced views signalled by her smoking and exotic dress. Labelled 'Japanese Fan de Siècle Illustrations', they signal the current vogue for all things Japanese.

8. *Punch*, 18 April 1894, illustration to a verse parody, 'Donna Quixote': 'you shake your lifted latch-key like a lance! /And shout, "in spite of babies, bonnets, tea, /Creation's heir, I must, I will be—Free!"' The cartoon and verse target Ibsen, Tolstoi, Mill, and *The Yellow Book* as dangerous influences, but the New Women, Egerton, Caird, Grand, Iota, and Dixie, are the most dangerous. Donna Quixote is shown inhabiting a fantastic, or *insane*, world of rational dress, sexual freedom, and broken marriage laws.

9. *Illustrated Police News*, 4 April 1891 (detail). In 1888 Mona Caird's polemical attack on Victorian marriage and enslavement to custom, in the *Westminster Review*, had sparked the biggest newspaper controversy of the century. Three years later, the debate is still clearly writ large in the public imagination. The *Illustrated Police News* (est. 1864), one of the earliest London tabloids, had gained a reputation for sensationalism during the Jack the Ripper murders (1888); this issue included a sensational report of a marriage which had ended with the husband trying to hang his wife. The cover images all point, in different ways, to the economic underpinnings of marriage, juxtaposing upper-class *ennui* with the harsh realities of working-class married life. Cupid in the central image also suggests the abandonment of the child, and can be seen as part of the gradual shift of interest towards the maternal, rather than wifely function, and the welfare of the future generation. The far right depiction of Bill and Nancy Sykes from *Oliver Twist* recalls the centrality of the marriage plot in fiction.

10. The ideas of male degeneration and female regeneration that developed apace in the wake of Darwin, gathering momentum from the social purity movement, were to have a lasting effect. They underpin this 1912 suffragette poster which urges physical and mental health and morality as conditions for the vote, and as part of its ostensibly progressive polemic associates these attributes exclusively with women.

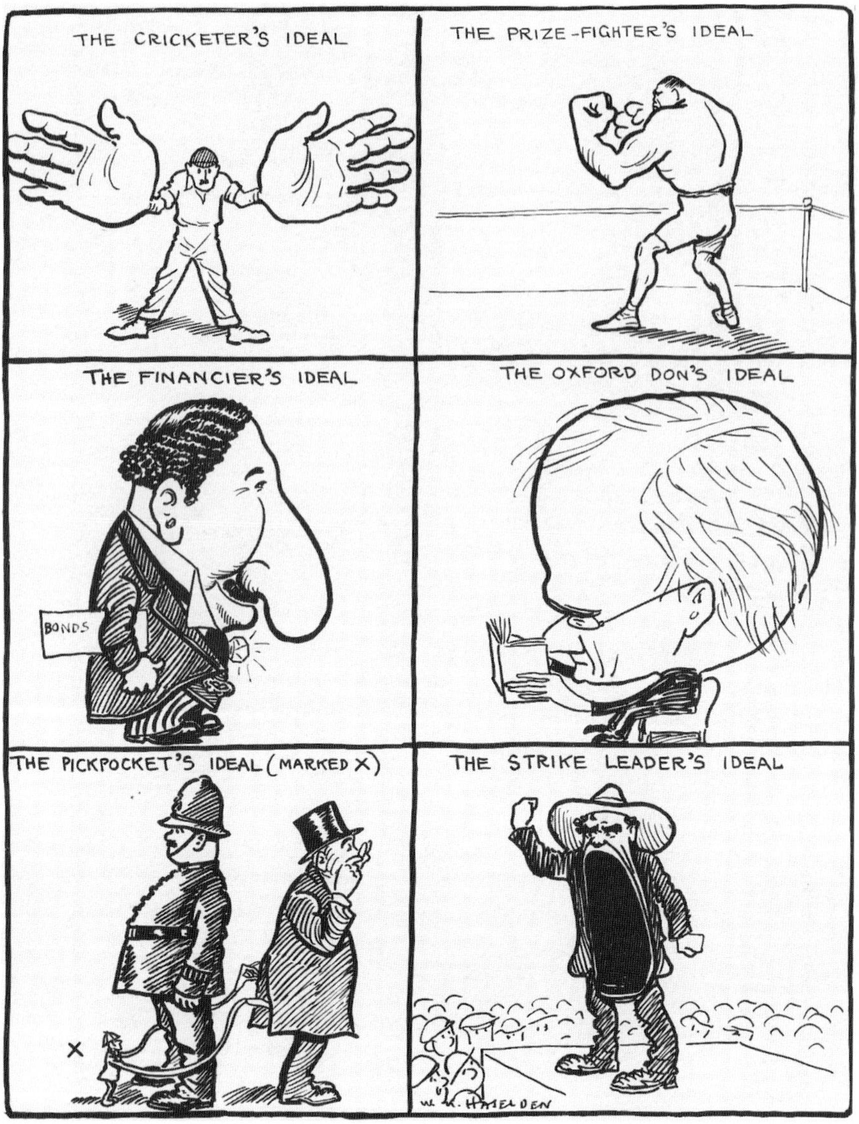

11. *Daily Mirror* cartoon by W. K. Haselden, 1912—the year of the Eugenic Society's first International Congress. The absurdity of Haselden's sketches—in the case of 'the financier's ideal', drawing on anti-Semitic ideas—serves to underscore the absurdity of the eugenic idea.

gardening' (159–60).[33] From the outset the novel privileges the biological; the reader is immediately introduced to Emery Pratt, his eldest son, Seraph, and 'two sporting dogs'. We are told: 'Father and son they undoubtedly were—there was no mistaking the breed—but in this last specimen the strain was no longer pure. The father, a splendid old man, was a thoroughbred of his kind, the son was a mongrel'. If 'man' is being used facetiously of the dog, then it is impossible to tell which of the two pairs, the human or the canine, is the subject of the narrator's gaze. Later, Grand writes, Algernon 'was essentially a mongrel, but not of the genial, intelligent type, with many amusing traits; rather of the objectionable cur-kind'.[34] The confusion seems deliberate, designed to unsettle the reader, and to situate humans within a Darwinian matrix of biological relations. Grand proceeds to describe their limbs as 'large' and in 'perfect proportion', with 'brains well balanced in their ample skull, and colouring rich in health'. But Seraph is degenerating: 'there was a falling off in all these traits. Only in height did he approach his father. For the rest he was a weedy specimen' (3). Seraph speaks like a degenerate. He 'spoke like an underbred man imitating the tone of a gentleman' (3). Negative eugenics is broached at the onset, with Emery Pratt contending that 'the world would not be a worse world if the bad sort was left out altogether'. Adnam is Pratt's younger son, from his second marriage (to Ursula Aubon Strelletzen). Early on the narrator comments he 'had a look of breeding about him which would have been evident to any one who was a judge of breeding' (5). He has 'good strong teeth' (256), and even his sleep is rounded with health: 'he lay in the perfect abandonment of healthy sleep' (149).

Grand's interest in environmental effects finds clear expression in a comparison of Emery's two sons: 'such differences of character do not prove that qualities good or bad are inherent in the blood, things neither

33 *The Observer* observed 'Adnam's intensive culture experiment was so fascinating an experiment that we raged when all his work was trampled down' (*The Winged Victory*, cover). In *Herland*, published in 1915, Charlotte Perkins Gilman draws the same parallels between eugenic breeding and intensive agriculture. For further instances of the connection between the breeding of humans and other species, see 'A New Sensation', which has a market-gardener as its hero (*Windsor Magazine: An Illustrated Monthly for Men and Women*, 2 (1899)); A. Richardson (ed.), *Women Who Did: Stories by Men and Women, 1890–1920* (Penguin, 2002), 231–43. The link between this character, Adam Woven Poleson, and the first Adam is made explicit. By contrast, Mona Caird's novel *The Great Wave* (1931) opposes the practice of intensive culture as invasive and disrespectful of nature.

34 *Adnam's Orchard: A Prologue* (London: Heinemann, 1912), 311.

to be acquired nor eradicated. In childhood heredity may be successfully combated by training and environment; and in later life by knowledge and determination' (22). The emphasis on innate qualities which dominates in her earlier fiction begins to yield.[35] Luke, the novel's urban degenerate, goes further, declaring 'heredity be blowed!' (126), while Ella voices the more moderate position taken by the novel as a whole: 'environment counts' (126).

In *The Winged Victory*, the sequel to *Adnam's Orchard*, these new ideas find further expression in a description of Colin Drindon. Environment could have a negative effect, but if the biological material was sound then the effects might be reversed through transplantation to a new environment:

he was not physically decadent, nor mentally. As a youth he had involuntarily taken on the colour of his surroundings, like an imitative insect. He found himself among degenerates, and conformed without thought to their usages. Had chance thrown him among men of muscle he would have conformed to their standard in like manner. Colin Drindon was enervated by luxury and inaction, but the condition in his case was an acquired condition, the result of a pose, and not yet incurable.[36]

The novel offers a strident denunciation of late nineteenth-century individualism:

Licence had begun to masquerade as progress. 'Liberty to be oneself' was a popular catchword which meant riddance of moral restraint and acceptance of the bondage of vice. Individuals clamouring for the right to lead their own life were for satisfying their baser desires at no matter what cost of suffering to their immediate neighbour, or to the community at large. (568)

In *Adnam's Orchard*, Grand hails a new hierarchy based not on social but biologial qualities:

in the days to come, 'low-born' will be applied to the degenerate offspring of an exhausted stock, regardless of social position; and the high-born to the inheritors of health and strength, mental, moral, and physical. (401)

It is an idea she restates in *The Winged Victory*: 'the fetish of class has been pulled to pieces of late years, and personality has come into its own' (204). However, her own fiction resists this idea: these last two novels are

[35] Contrast Mangum, who sees the novel as Grand's only overtly eugenic book: Teresa Mangum, *Married, Middlebrow, and Militant: Sarah Grand and the New Woman Novel* (Michigan: University of Michigan Press, 1999), 203–11.

[36] *The Winged Victory* (London: Heinemann, 1916), 318.

steeped in class politics. Ella, a member of the labour aristocracy, is constantly described as a class misfit, considered to show exceptional physical and mental traits for her social—or biological—group. Of Ella and Ellery, who is apparently her father, the reader learns: 'they not only looked as if they belonged to different classes and different centuries, but to different nations; she to some fine-featured, clear-skinned classic race, he a nondescript Norman-Saxon-and-Dane are we' (*Adnam's Orchard*, 42; the allusion is to Tennyson's patriotic poem 'A Welcome to Alexandra' (1863)). Class receives its most racial description in this passage. Belonging to the working class, Ellery is a model of ill health; Grand notes in parenthesis: 'he had been nicknamed Flipperty because of these jerky ways of his' (43).

Adulation of Ella continues in *The Winged Victory*: 'her feeling for the beautiful was innate, her perception and discrimination wonderful considering her heredity. She had come to London ignorant of every art but her own, yet her taste was never at fault' (48). Taste, Grand implies, is the product not of nurture but nature, and here—unaccountably—it is possessed by a member of the working class. Even Ella's manners ill fit her class: 'you would think she had been prepared to be presented at Court' (85). 'She's not a common work girl', Mr Harkles corrects Lord Terry. 'That's just the puzzle. She's uncommon. She'd be uncommon put her where you like' (99). Likewise, 'that high head of hers and her step showed pedigree. Daughters of common farmers may be beautiful, but they don't have that air!' announces one of several 'gossips' (117). The healthy environmental influence of the country was part of the early twentieth-century eugenic recipe for health; good breeding was the other. The highest praise that the novel can offer a working-class character is to distance her, biologically, from her class.

Ella is keen to maintain her physical fitness, declaring to the duke: 'I want exercise all over' (*The Winged Victory*, 247). 'Of course', he replies. 'Very natural. Other girls go to balls. Ride, dance, shoot, fence, gymnastics "all over". Spirit of the day. Comes out even in seclusion.' He is Grand's mouthpiece for physical efficiency and a health-based citizenship: 'must take care of that splendid physique. Health before everything. What the nation wants is health. The parents of healthy children are good patriots' (248). As living proof of the wisdom of the duke's words, Adnam (like Beth and Eugenia), is one of Grand's eugenic models:

> he had balanced his life with nice attention to the development of body as well as of mind, and had made good muscle by varying his hours of sedentary study with active outdoor pursuits. He was good at cricket, football, rowing and riding. (28)

This, Grand remarks, is what British public schools have in their favour: 'games for the development of physique and for the discipline of fair play' (*Adnam's Orchard*, 157).

A newly regenerated Colin Drindon biologizes Ella's talents: '"She's a gentlewoman to the tips of her fingers. Show me a better bred!" "She certainly has all the air" said Bratasby reflexively. "Interesting that, considering her origin. Breeding is implicit, I suppose, in phenomenal beauty"' (*The Winged Victory*, 418). Even the narrator pretends not be able to fathom her breeding: 'in spite of her peasant blood,—or possibly because of it—she had in perfection that finest finishing touch of gentlehood, gentlewomanly self-control' (294). By the close of the novel the mystery is solved: Ella is revealed to be the illegitimate daughter of the duke.

The eugenic union between the duke and Ella's mother is one that Grand endorses on grounds of race improvement, even if it means she must accept bastardy. And in doing so she toes the eugenic line: illegitimacy was preferable to race suicide, and was actively embraced by some exponents of race improvement, such as George Egerton, for whom, as I explore in Chapter 7, considerations of race overrode conventional morality. In *Adnam's Orchard* the narrator lends tacit support to a new morality of illegitimacy:

> the Brabants had always been conspicuous for their family pride. They considered their blood the best in the country, that of Royalty of necessity not excepted, Royalty having originally founded the family with some of its own, and up to the present generation they had pretty nearly all been for improving the race with it whenever they found a woman willing; as must have been evident to any nice observer moving about on the family estates and in the villages tenanted by the Duke's people, where, among red-haired, fair-haired, brown-haired and neutral tinted families with plebeian features, the soft black hair, the patrician delicacy of skin, and the refined traits which distinguished the Brabants, continually reappeared in some mother's Benjamin boy or darling girl, conspicuously. (63)

While the idea that extramarital liaisons might improve the race is not without irony, the suggestion is that rational cross-class alliances could be beneficial to the race.

URBAN DEGENERATION

In *Adnam's Orchard* the effects of London life on Luke Banks, Ella's half-brother, are striking, and entirely in keeping with contemporary attitudes towards the connection between the city and ill health. Luke returns from 'the foetid atmosphere, moral and physical, of the London slums' (135) on the brink of moral and physical degeneration: 'he missed the turmoil of the London streets, the moving multitudes, the possibility of excitement'. The streets of London are the place for sensation, for sensual pleasure, for pleasures of the moment. Luke has developed a taste for alcohol: 'his short cut to a happy frame of mind he had learnt in the slums of London, where the value of salt to improve a man's appetite for beer is so well understood and pleasant sensations are rare' (135). But clean country living reverses the degenerative effects of the city:

> physically, the wholesome country air and the quiet life were gradually restoring him to his right mind. As his debilitated nerves recovered from the vitiating effects of his town life, he lost his craving for tobacco and alcohol and recovered his appetite for food; he was less irritable although unhappier; he ceased to be in opposition to everything, his temper improved, and he became a pleasanter man to deal with. (401)

The same idea of rural regeneration underpins *The Winged Victory*. Ella blossoms in the countryside:

> she haled deep draughts of [air], and soon her blood, refreshed, was coursing merrily through her veins. The physical sense of well-being eased her mind. In and out among the trees she sped buoyantly, glorying in her youth and health and strength, not thinking at all. (399)

She is a 'girl, fresh from country solitudes and with senses healthily acute' (48). This adulation of rural virtue was central to the mythology of nature that peaked in Edwardian Britain, drawing on Victorian fears of urban unrest and ill health. It permeates, for example, E. M. Forster's *Howards End* (1910). When Leonard Bast, a lower middle-class inhabitant of London who bears all the early signs of degeneration, takes the train out of Hilton, he finds the country populated by working men who, ruled by the natural rhythms of nature, are 'England's hope'; in the right environment, biological strengths from previous generations might come to the fore, and flourish: 'they can still throw back to a nobler stock, and breed yeomen'.[37]

Adnam's Orchard opens with a eulogy of reproductive love: 'love and hope were voiced in low sweet notes, in passionate trills'; 'all over the countryside the first fragrant promise of spring—wrought happy trouble in the blood of sentient things'. The novel's eugenic message is laboured

[37] *Howards End* ch. 41. See also D. H Lawrence, *England, My England* (1922).

home: 'nature calls to the birds, and the birds obey her, and she gives them joy unmarred; but man makes it his duty to thwart nature' (1). There is a sense that the inhabitants of the country live in a healthy obedience to nature.

Adnam has to choose between city and country:

> he was confronted with the choice of barren bachelorhood and the third of a rafted room in his father's house, or he might take his chance of being able to support a wife and family by precarious work in a town, work for which he was not fitted, and must in any case wrest from other men. Probably he would find himself condemned to surroundings where men swarmed like maggots in cheese, with the horrible stench of the crowd in their nostrils, their vitality sapped by the vitiated air, their flesh wasting for want of proper nourishment, and even the best of them driven by exhaustion to find fictitious strength to continue the struggle in the fatal poison of the public house. Adnam might have thought in this strain had he known enough. But he did not know enough. (154).

The passage expresses the polarized attitudes towards the country and the city that had been in the ascendant from the 1880s. Reminiscent of Galton's private attack on 'low life', it reveals the extent to which Grand was repelled by the material reality of urban poverty. Adnam, however, is fortunate. Unlike the dispossessed, rural labourers, forced off the land by machinery, by the capitalization of agriculture, and evicted from their cottages, he has property. He has options.

Nonetheless, Grand reads the move to the city in terms of degeneration, interpreting urbanization as a wilful abdication of the duties of rural life. She observes that migration to the city is part of a wider social and political picture, centring on the decline of an agrarian economy which she sees as a symptom of the degeneration of the aristocracy. The rural poor are simply aping their social betters: as the duke puts it, 'the workpeople themselves have degenerated . . . too keen on amusement. That is why the towns attract them. They are for shirking work and playing all the time . . . filters through from the top. Like master, like man' (*The Winged Victory*, 390). Zooming in on an unsuspecting assortment of rustic poor assembled in the Brabant Arms, the narrator of *Adnam's Orchard* tells us that:

> such yokels, lineal descendants of Shakespeare's, have been preserved for us in fine spirits by Mr Thomas Hardy, but he captured almost the last living examples. Any decayed specimens still to be found lingering amid the general decay in remote country districts are survivals from the day before the schools were opened and set to extinguish the race.

'Yokels' are extinct in the country, owing to the combined effects of urbanization and education; conversely the urban poor are expanding.

In 1916, when *The Winged Victory* appeared, the *Times Literary Supplement* remarked:

> Ella Banks, a lacemaker, enjoys the patronage of a Duke and Duchess who live in the countryside where she was born and bred. Ella is a girl of extraordinary attainments—how come by remains inexplicable. She speaks irreproachable English, dresses in impeccable taste, has a knowledge of French and German, quotes abundantly from the poets, summons a little Latin when she chooses, and is possessed of an imperishable *sang-froid*. Nothing is told us to explain how the young cottager came by all these virtues.[38]

The novel holds the reader's attention through the secret of Ella's birth. Ella falls secretly in love with the duke's heir; the duke and duchess set her up in business in London where 'the town dower-house is made over to her, together with a complete inventory of crystal chandeliers, inset Lancrets, Adams carvings, spending equipage, major-domo, and family solicitor'.[39] The duke is behind all this—the duchess in fact dislikes her—and the two often spend fond evenings together. Ella is a social reformer; she seeks to re-establish the lace-making industry, with a fair wage for the workers. As the *Times Literary Supplement* notes, 'the girl is in no wise meant to be the bucolic *ingénue* of a false tradition; she is a practical, potentially discerning, and, above all, unimpeachable decorous young woman'. In the last quarter of the book, following detailed documentation of conversations between Ella and the duke:

> the pace quickens. An attack is made on Ella's honour; she shoots the assailant, her friends contrive a verdict of death by misadventure; the Duke sends her to recuperate in his yacht, with a stringed band in attendance . . . Society . . . is so low-minded as to conclude, once for all, that Ella must be the Duke's mistress. Ella returns, hears the rumours at last, infers that the Duke is seeking to justify them, consents in her indignation to a clandestine marriage with the ducal heir, and then the truth is sprung upon her: she is the Duke's daughter; she has married her brother. Her bridegroom kills himself, and the book ends—a sequel plainly in view—with a reconciliation between the father and daughter.

Grand's attempts to explicate an increasingly complicated politics and retain the reader's interest make for a highly improbable plot. *The Winged Victory* was, the *Times Literary Supplement* concluded, 'a preposterous story, preposterously related'.[40]

[38] *Times Literary Supplement* (24 August 1916), 404.
[39] Ibid.
[40] Ibid.

The class politics of *The Winged Victory* may seem novel. Ella's sojourn in London allows the reader on a tour through the streets of London and learns that, like that of their mothers:

> the endurance of the children was also wonderful. Ill-clad, half-starved, sickly, still they shouted and laughed, played in the gutter, squabbled and fought—fought for their lives after their kind. The children of the slums are of their mothers' breed, and their mothers are heroic. (396)[41]

Here, Grand recognizes the strength of these working-class women and, conceiving of them as a 'breed', seems to distance them from the rest of their class. Ella 'saw the potential beauty under the dirt on the faces of little children, faces that should have been round and rosy but were sharpened by want—as were their wits—and horribly matured by suffering. She saw the sweetness pathetically surviving in the smile of the prematurely aged and haggard young woman.' The moment registers the ambivalence found in Grand's last two novels. While there is a sense that certain members of the working class might be rescued from their degrading living conditions and restored to health, the novels are pervaded by ideas of fitness, and biological determinism—in the form of class biology—triumphs. Ella appears to have made good her working-class potential, but Grand, by giving her an aristocratic pedigree, stops short of allowing this to be a possibility.

FAILING ARISTOCRATS

In *Hereditary Genius* (1869), Galton declared the hereditary aristocracy were a 'disastrous institution' for 'our valuable races'; the younger sons of the peerage, unable to maintain their status as well as afford a family, tended either not to marry, or to marry heiresses, many of whom were infertile.[42] Henry Maudsley in *Body and Will*

[41] This quotation found its way into a local collection of short extracts from Grand's work 'The Breath of Life: A Short Anthology of Quotations for Days & Months from the Works of Sarah Grand', comp. by her devoted friend Gladys Singers-Bigger. Selling at 1 shilling, profits were to go to 'The Mayoress Fresh Air Fund' at Bath, as the front cover announced, giving a health gloss to the seemingly metaphysical title (The Sarah Grand archive, Bath County Library).

[42] Galton, *Hereditary Genius: An Inquiry into its Laws and Consequences* (1869; London: Watts & Co., 1892), 335; Maudsley, *Body and Will* (London: Kegan Paul, Trench, 1883), 14. Cf. Pearson, *The Chances of Death and Other Studies in Evolution*, 2 vols. (London and New York, 1897), 100: 'we must conclude that society after all recruits itself from below'. Later, even Maudsley was to admit that the concept of degeneracy had gone too far, becoming an

(1883) argued that degeneration could occur from the top downwards, and the eugenist Arnold White was more vocal in his denunciation of the British aristocracy, insisting in *Efficiency and Empire* (1901), that society was 'rotten at the top' and that 'the first step, therefore, towards obtaining an efficient people is to eliminate from among our rulers all those who are themselves physically and mentally inefficient'.[43] The inheritance of wealth, combined with the rule of primogeniture, operated in a dysgenic way, protecting the old aristocracy from the laws of natural selection. Increasingly seen as sham, its stock was further degraded by attempts to revive failing fortunes through marriage with rich heiresses from 'dubious' social backgrounds.[44] The issue was discussed in national newspapers, notably the *Guardian* and *Daily News*.[45]

Adnam's Orchard expresses an ambivalence towards the aristocracy, as Grand equivocates over their fate and fortunes. The squire explains to Lena, who believes that the landed classes form the backbone of Britain: 'you can't have two backbones, my dear. Ours is another function. We are the nerve, the governing power. We keep the kingdom together. Without us it would have gone to pieces long ago.' However, while the novel enjoys a nostalgic attachment to the aristocracy, Grand concedes that the upper classes are degenerating and, in line with eugenic thinking, looks forward to their extinction. Their physical ill health and want of moral fibre permeates her last novels. Early in *Adnam's Orchard*, we learn (not without a degree of humour) that:

> the Brabant head had come to be noticeably small, natural selection having acted without question on the conventional fallacy that a small head is a thing to be desired. 'The beautiful little head' of fiction is responsible for a tendency to breed small skulls in which there is no room for a useful supply of brains. (75)

In *The Winged Victory*, we meet Miss Kedlock; her mother was a Brabant, a cousin of the present Duke of Castlefield Saye. She is a classic example of her class:

ideological weapon: Maudsley, 'Insanity in Relation to Criminal Responsibility', *Alienist and Neurologist* 17 (17 April 1896), 175.

[43] *Efficiency and Empire* (1901; Brighton: Harvester Press, 1973), 108. See also W. C. D. Whetham, 'The Extinction of the Upper-classes', *Nineteenth Century and After*, 66 (1909).

[44] Karl Pearson, 'The Groundwork of Eugenics', *Eugenics Laboratory Lecture Series* II (London: Dulau, 1909), quoted in G. R. Searle, 'Eugenics and Class', in Charles Webster (ed.), *Biology, Medicine and Society 1840–1940* (Cambridge: Cambridge University Press, 1981), 218.

[45] See, for example, the *Guardian* (23 March 1870). In 1870 the *Graphic* reviewed *Hereditary Genius*, reporting that one-fifth of heiresses have no male children at all: *Graphic* (22 January 1870) Galton Papers, 120/5, 179.

degeneration showed in her hands and feet, which were somewhat too small for her height, but both were beautifully formed, and the whiteness of her well-kept hands betokened a fastidious physical refinement; she came of the ruling caste. (34)

The eugenically minded Duke Brabant is only too anxious to admit that his class is degenerating; he wishes to reverse the trend through biological regeneration.[46] Addressing the 'Land and Leisure Club', he states:

Heredity. Greatly interested in the subject. We pride ourselves on a long line of descent and remain culpably careless of the breed. Good blood, uncontaminated blood—what does that mean in men's mouths? A mass of disease very often, at the end of a long line of noble ancestors. (245)

He lectures his sons on the necessity of eugenic marriage, stressing the importance of informed sexual selection. 'None of your noble dames with hereditary disease in their families. Degenerate specimens. I'll talk to him about that. A fine intelligent country girl, of good sound stock, that's the thing for a wife' (246).[47] (Two decades earlier these ideas motivated the plot of *Tess of the D'Urbervilles*, as Hardy conflates the two inheritances. Angel assumes Tess to be such a country girl, and it is true that she inherits her beauty from her mother, but Angel later uses her aristocratic paternal inheritance to account for what he sees as moral weakness.) The duke perseveres:

[he] had been descanting lately in the language of the stockyard on the necessity of getting good new blood by marriage into degenerate old families, and the recollection was reassuring. Melton had it in his mind that new blood was badly wanted in his own family, as indeed it was, the fluid having been much thinned in the course of ages by marriages with cousins, and vitiated by alcohol and other excesses; but this is not the sort of thing a young man in love can discuss with a young girl, though it may be the best reason he has to ground hope upon that their marriage will be sanctioned. The subject has begun to be dangerous, too, for another reason even then. The modern woman has rebelled against nothing more passionately than the evils which have resulted from her sexual subjection. (329)

By contrast, the duke's own (illegitimate) union with Ella's mother has been a way of serving his country. The features of Melton and Ella are

[46] Contrast Mangum, who sees this novel as rejecting eugenics by exposing the ill health of the aristocracy, *Married, Middlebrow, and Militant*, 210.

[47] For further treatment of this subject in fiction, see Hardy's *Group of Noble Dames* (1891; Stroud: Alan Sutton Publishing, 1993). For discussion of this work in relation to heredity and eugenic discourse, see Angelique Richardson, ' "How I Mismated Myself for Love of You!": The Biologization of Romance in Hardy's *A Group of Noble Dames*', *Thomas Hardy Journal*, 14 (1998), 59–76.

'refined to perfection, their clear delicate skins, the clean symmetry of the racehorse breed in their limbs, were so much of a type as almost to suggest a likeness; but the girl was incomparably the nobler specimen—the abler, the more alive of the two' (*The Winged Victory*, 546).[48] Paralleling the eugenic match between Saxon Wake the Yeoman and Eugenia—a member of the declining aristocracy—in 'Eugenia', yeoman (country) added to aristocracy (nation) turns out well in Ella's case. Grand takes great care to stipulate that such a mixed class union is to be undertaken only in exceptional circumstances. '"I'm for early marriages"', Mr Strangeworth tells the duke, ushering in a painfully didactic eugenic exchange. '"I don't think a man's age so much matters", said the Duke. "His choice is the important thing. I am for recommending young men to marry women on their merits, mental and moral, of course, but also, and particularly, physical." "Regardless of caste?" Colin Drindon asked eagerly. "In exceptional cases" was the Duke's cautious reply' (*The Winged Victory*, 355). The caution was Grand's.

Melton allows romantic love to triumph over a more disinterested study of Ella's pedigree, which would have revealed the unfitness of their union. He is bewildered when his father forbids him to marry Ella: 'you have always insisted that I should marry "good blood" in the sense of physical fitness. My choice is physically as well as mentally splendid—without a flaw—very beautiful' (*The Winged Victory*, 635). Melton tells Ella:

> You're splendidly born—a high-born favourite of nature, richly endowed in all that is essential to human happiness. It is just the kind of marriage [the duke] has always advocated for me. Time after time, he has entreated me to bring good new blood into the family, to save it from decadence. (*The Winged Victory*, 548)

Here, class is biologized to such an extent that its social meaning is eclipsed by an emphasis on nature. The passage offers Grand's most explicit validation of new blood. In the words of Adnam's mother, who professes an allegiance to socialism, 'the more workers there are for the community at large, the less there will be for each individual to do, and the more leisure for him to be himself' (*Adnam's Orchard*, 170). She continues 'a man should give his services, himself, to the community at large' (173); the same concept of sacrifice to the community which permeates Grand's earlier writing is at work in these novels. Using the language of disease, Ursula tells Adnam that 'conservatism is the canker

[48] On symmetry and health, see Grant Allen, *Physiological Aesthetics* (London: Henry S. King & Co., 1877), 240.

of society'. The socialism towards which the novel gestures finds expression through a member of the erstwhile ruling classes, and is more a form of social imperialism, explaining the duke's apparent political volte-face. 'Henceforth, I follow the banner of the Sociocrat' (*The Winged Victory*, 239). A tension between socialism and Social Darwinism surfaces in the late novels: early on in *The Winged Victory* the narrator hails 'this new age, with its new dawning heroes of altruistic co-operation, of noble aspiration, of self-sacrificing love' (58), but we are also told that 'the battle is to the strong, and life is a battle' (51). Here was a form of socialism that was compatible with eugenics, and which aimed ultimately at the demise of the working classes. H. G. Wells, for example, 'always insisted that the aim of socialism was to abolish the working class as he knew it, not to give it power.'[49]

The shift towards socialism in Grand's last novels coexists with eugenic commitment. Both *Adnam's Orchard* and *The Winged Victory* stress the importance of heritage. The Pratts, labourers on the land, have a pedigree longer even than the Brabants: 'the Pratts also had a family pew. They were the oldest family in the neighbourhood, and it had been theirs before the Brabants came' (*Adnam's Orchard*, 213). By contrast, the Pointzs are socially inferior—a condition explained along biological lines:

> all their actions were instinctive, and all the outcome of the primary instinct of self-preservation; but for lack of foresight they were wanton of the means, and for lack of adaptability incapable of saving themselves from the effects of their own idleness, extravagance, and waste. It was cross-bred, this last generation . . . a bad cross which had destroyed in them the graces of the finer strain. (427)

The notion of a finer strain colours Grand's portrayal of the duke, and in Ella it would seem her ducal heritage is her saving grace. Even when Melton kills himself, Grand is able to praise Ella's self restraint: 'good blood makes no outcry' (*The Winged Victory*, 647). In *Adnam's Orchard*, we are told:

> loyalty and long-suffering are characteristic of the English. The people believed in their gentry and were proud of them. By heredity they were prone and by habit they were accustomed to look up to them, and they preferred them for rulers. (354)

While she was politically committed to the eugenically promising middle classes, Grand's residual romantic attachment to aristocracy testifies to

[49] Norman Mackenzie and Jeanne MacKenzie, *The Life of H. G. Wells: The Time Traveller* (1973; London: The Hogarth Press, 1987), 185.

the complexity of eugenic motivation. Nonetheless, when it came to overtly degenerate specimens, Grand had no such misgivings. In her short story 'Boomellen' (1894), the eponymous anti-hero (who is named on account of his tendency to loiter (256)):

> had arrived at the weary end of his ancestry, being the last male representative and heir of two used-up races. His father had been 'wild' in his youth, but his degrading habits were cut short by something which suspiciously resembled epilepsy. He married the daughter of a drunken father and an arrogant, nervous, irritable, self-indulgent mother. The consequences of this combination in Boomellen's mother were markedly neurotic.[50]

Grand warns her readers about the deceptiveness of appearances: 'no one would have supposed for a moment that his impressively handsome husk contained not a tithe of the immortal soul which animated their obviously inferior clay'; she compares his body to 'the irregular profiles' (257) of his working-class companions. While a vestigial attachment to aristocracy shows through, the story ends unequivocally with the drowning of the degenerate Boomellen: 'ineffectual life, ineffectual death' (271). The story, like all Grand's fiction, argues for the importance of effective lives, warning of the consequences of a life without duty, lived without rational thought and planning for the future. As Boomellen joins the ranks of Grand's male degenerates we are left wondering if such specimens have a chance—it seems necessary for Grand's social message that they play out pre-ordained patterns of behaviour and succumb, inevitably, to their biological fate. Certainly, they are to be avoided at all costs as reproductive partners.

50 'Boomellen', *Our Manifold Nature* (London: Heinemann, 1894), 257.

7 George Egerton and Eugenic Morality

> I wonder how many childless women go to sleep with a dream child cuddled in the round of their arms? and yet I meet more women every day who shrink from mothering, or who are indifferent to it, if they don't actually dislike children. Perhaps the terrible object-lesson over-population offers has something to do with it—for one cannot but shudder, if one has to pass through poor streets, at the scores of sickly ugly urchins rolling in the gutter, yelling at one another with hideous distorted speech. The stoned prophet of one generation may become the tutelary genius of another; so perhaps a statue of the apostle of limitation may be erected in the market-place of every town some day.[1]

> Woman is, if she could only realise it, man's superior by reason of her maternity—the negation of that is her greatest cowardice. They have gone on wrong lines in trying to force themselves into man's place as an industrial worker. The varying cycle of their physical being unfits them for steady labour.—I am with them every time they try to advance on the line of their own sex needs, the consolidation of their rights as separate individuals, as owner of the child, as embryo mothers [. . .] Our new women are merely units out of place.—The industrial conditions of our time produce them; they cannot fulfil their proper place in the economy of nature—there are not enough men to go round.[2]

The writer George Egerton, popular, polemical, and best known—then as now—for her experimental short stories, openly celebrated female sexuality, upturning conventional morality concerning marriage and monogamy and redeeming illegitimacy. Her most notorious story, 'A

[1] Egerton, *Rosa Amorosa: The Love Letters of a Woman* (London: Grant Richards, 1901), 112.

[2] Egerton to Ernst Foerster, London (1 July 1900), in Ernst Foerster, *Die Frauenfrage in den Romanen Englischer Schriftstellerinnen der Gegenwart* (Marburg: N. G. Elwert'sche Verlagsbuchhandlung, 1907), 46–8, repr. in Heilmann, *The Late Victorian Marriage Debate: A Collection of Key New Woman Texts*, vol. V (London and New York: Routledge with Thoemmes Press, 1998).

Cross-Line', a dramatic exposition of female sexual freedom, was published in *Keynotes* (1893). The reader gains access to the inner life of the story's female subject, a married woman engaged in an adulterous liaison, and known only as Gypsy:

> she can see herself with parted lips and panting, rounded breasts, and a dancing devil in each glowing eyes, sway voluptuously to the wild music that rises, now slow, now fast, now deliriously wild, seductive, intoxicating, with a human note of passion in its strain. She can feel the answering shiver of feeling that quivers up to her from the dense audience . . .[3]

While the moment unequivocally celebrates female sexual desire and autonomy, it also places Gypsy in a world outside civilization, connecting her to the rhythms of nature, to the instinctive and primal. Throughout Egerton's fiction, such emancipatory moments coexist with, or at times express, a more repressive ideology. Her evocation of women's spiritual and genetic otherness, their unknowability, which has appealed to late twentieth-century feminist scholars as an early example of radical, or difference, feminism, made common cause with eugenic feminism and complicates her relationship to freedom.[4] While Egerton speaks out in her fiction against the social and sexual repression of women, her writing as a whole foregrounds the maternal function, equating women with primary impulses and instincts. In 'The Regeneration of Two', Fruen declares 'we are always battling with some

[3] A. Richardson (ed.) *Women Who Did: Stories by Men and Women, 1890–1914* (Harmondsworth: Penguin, 2002), 57.

[4] For recent exponents of difference feminism, see Luce Irigaray, *Je, tu, nous: Towards a Culture of Difference*, trans. by Alison Martin (London: Routledge, 1993); Hélène Cixous, 'Sorties' (1975), in Hélène Cixous and Catherine Clement, *The Newly Born Woman* (Manchester: Manchester University Press, 1986), 66–79; 'The Laugh of the Medusa' (1975), in Robyn R. Warhol and Diane Price Herndl, *Feminisms: An Anthology of Literary Theory and Criticism* (New Brunswick, NJ: Rutgers University Press, 1991); and Irigaray, *This Sex Which is Not One* (Ithaca, NY: Cornell University Press, 1985). Eve Kosofsky Kristeva also invokes the idea of feminine 'otherness'. See also Rosi Briadotti, 'Sexual Difference Theory', in Alison M. Jaggar and Iris Marion Young (eds.), *A Companion to Feminist Philosophy* (Oxford: Blackwell, 1998), 298–306. In *Why Feminism? Gender, Psychology, Politics* (Cambridge: Polity Press, 1999), Lynn Segal outlines the attack of 'difference feminism' on the 'spurious unity or wholeness of the Western subject, which urges the need to attend to the repressed "feminine" ', and which urges that women speak and write their sexuality, which is always 'plural, circular, and aimless, in contrast to all existing singular, linear and phallocentric, masculine forms of symbolization'. Segal notes that this position nonetheless posits a *universal* corporeal subjectivity for women (30, 53). Alison Jaggar writes that a commitment to biological determinism grounded in human sexes with distinct essences as the explanation of gender differences is a characteristic defect of radical feminist thought: Jaggar, *Feminist Politics and Human Nature* (Totowa, NJ: Rowman and Allanheld, 1983).

bottom layer of real womanhood that we may not reveal; the primary impulses of our original destiny keep shooting out mimosa-like threads of natural feeling through the outside husk of our artificial selves, producing complex creatures' (198).

Of all late nineteenth-century feminists, Egerton bore the brunt of press attention, finding herself a favourite target in the satirical pages of *Punch* (see figure 6). In 1894, writing under the pseudonym 'Borgia Smudgiton', Owen Seaman, later editor of *Punch* (1906–1932), published a parody of *Keynotes*' 'A Cross-Line', calling it 'She-Notes' (see figures 7 and 8),[5] highlighting what was perceived by contemporaries to be novel, and threatening, about this short story: 'in a twinkling her wild, free instinct doubles at a tangent. With a supple bound she is on his shoulders curling her lithe fishing boots into one of its waistcoat pockets. Surely gypsy blood runs in her veins!' The parody is of the following:

> You seem amused, Gypsy!
> She springs out of her chair and seizes book and pipe; he follows the latter anxiously with his eyes until he sees it laid safely on the table. Then she perches herself, resting her knees against one of his legs, whilst she hooks her feet back under the other—[6]

Emphasizing, through caricature, the novelty of Egerton's writing, *Punch* focused on the disruptive elements in her writing; this focus has been maintained by recent critical interest which has concentrated on her development of a modernist aesthetics, and on the psychological complexity of her characters.[7] Egerton was as interested in the physiological as the psychological, but the latter has received most critical

[5] Borgia Smudgiton [Owen Seaman], 'She-Notes', in A. Richardson (ed.) *Women Who Did*, 73–7.

[6] A. Richardson (ed.), *Women Who Did*, 74, 55.

[7] See Sally Ledger, introduction to *Keynotes and Discords* (1893 and 1894; Birmingham: Birmingham University Press, 2003) on Egerton's emergent modernist aesthetics. Recent appraisal of Egerton has focused on her experimentation with literary form. See, for example, Lyn Pykett, *Engendering Fictions: The English Novel in the Early Twentieth Century* (London: Edward Arnold, 1995), 165–74; Jane Eldridge Miller, *Rebel Women: Feminism, Modernism and the Edwardian Novel* (London: Virago, 1994), 199; Sally Ledger, *The New Woman: Fiction and Feminism at the Fin de Siècle* (Manchester: Manchester University Press, 1997), 192. Celebrated as an early exponent of self-consciously *gendered* writing—what Hélène Cixous has termed *écriture feminine*—Egerton has attracted attention largely as a precursor of modernism: see also Miller, *Rebel Women*, 27; Pykett, *The Improper Feminine*, 95, 196, 213; and Pykett, *Engendering Fictions*, 38, 61, 73. See Laura Chrisman, 'Empire, "Race" and Feminism at the *fin de siècle*: The Work of George Egerton and Olive Schreiner', in Sally Ledger and Scott McCracken (eds.), *Cultural Politics at the fin de siècle* (Cambridge: Cambridge University Press, 1995); and Ledger, *The New Woman*, 192, for Egerton's uneasy relations with feminism.

attention. Exploring the interiority of her female subjects, and mapping the uncharted landscapes of female desire, her fiction offers an example of ways in which literary experimentalism and the celebration of sexuality and freedom can coexist with repressive ideologies, and it is on these that I shall focus.

George Egerton was born Mary Chavelita Dunne in 1859, in Melbourne, Australia, the oldest daughter of a Welsh mother (née George), and an Irish army officer, John J. Dunne.[8] Like Sarah Grand, she spent most of her childhood in Ireland, but also spent time in New Zealand, Chile, Wales, and Germany. When she was 14, her mother died and the family began to break up. Egerton trained as a nurse, and in 1887 she eloped to Norway with a married man and friend of her father, Henry Higginson, who turned out to be violent and an alcoholic.[9] Egerton left him after a year, returning to England and, in 1891, marrying Egerton Clairmonte 'an idle and penniless Newfoundlander'.[10] She settled in Cork, Ireland, and wrote her first and most renowned collection of short stories, *Keynotes*, for John Lane and Elkin Matthews at the Bodley Head.[11] The collection sold over 6,000 copies in its first year alone, was translated into seven languages, and went though eight editions by 1898. The second edition, issued in 1894, was used by John Lane to launch his Keynote Series of novels and short story collections. Egerton's second collection of stories, *Discords* (1894), bleaker in outlook—as the name suggests—than *Keynotes*, was published as the sixth volume of the Keynote Series.[12] Soon after the birth of a son in 1895 Egerton's marriage came to an end; divorce followed in 1901, when she married Reginald Golding Bright, fifteen years her junior, a literary agent and, in the 1920s, Hardy's dramatic agent. Egerton herself became a dramatic agent for, among others, G. B. Shaw and Somerset Maugham. Egerton produced a further collection of short stories, *Symphonies* (1897), a full-length autobiographical novel, *The Wheel of God* (1898),

[8] Terence de Vere White (ed.), *A Leaf from the Yellow Book: The Correspondence of George Egerton* (London: The Richards Press, 1958), 12, quoted in Martha Vicinus (ed.), Introduction to George Egerton, *Keynotes and Discords* (1893 and 1894; London: Virago, 1983), p. x.

[9] Egerton recorded this in 'Under Northern Sky', in *Keynotes*.

[10] Vicinus (ed.), Introduction, p. xiii.

[11] For an extensive consideration of Egerton's life and work see, in addition to de Vere White, Margaret Diane Stetz, ' "George Egerton", Woman and Writer of the Eighteen-Nineties', Ph.D. dissertation, Harvard University, 1982.

[12] On the publication of, and contemporary response to, *Keynotes*, see Rosie Miles, 'George Egerton, Bitextuality and Cultural (Re)Production in the 1890s', in *Women's Writing*, 3 (1996), 243–60.

and *Rosa Amorosa* (1901), an epistolary novel which celebrated her own brief affair with a Norwegian man. Egerton's choice of George as a pseudonym, and her initials, GE, mirror the greatest of her literary foremothers, George Eliot.

NATURE AND THE CITY

'Books with "morals" at the end of each tale; how she detested "moral"! What was moral? it spoiled a story anyway, and she always skipped it.'[13] So begins *The Wheel of God* (1898), Egerton's most autobiographical novel. In direct contrast to the social purity writers, Egerton aligned herself with the aesthetics which found its most famous expression in Oscar Wilde's dictum: 'There is no such thing as a moral or an immoral book. Books are well written, or badly written. That is all.'[14] The young Mary, central character of *The Wheel of God*, and a voracious reader, falls victim to strict domestic codes of propriety:

> Aunt Frances, too, had taken one of Aphra Behn's plays from her, and told her she must not read such things; they were unfit for her; and *Tristram Shandy* too; she had thought Uncle Toby entertaining, and she could not remember ever to have seen one bad thing in any book. Even if she had, one never need remember horrid things![15]

Some years later, when asked to name her favourite author, she replies, wearily 'Thomas Hardy'. Her audience is shocked:

> 'You think his *Jude the Obscure* a fit book for family reading?' 'You don't object', replied Mary, 'to having the story of David on your table; and though David was what you call a success and "got there every time" to use a slang term, and poor Jude was a failure, yet I always think they were not so unlike in their erotics'. (228)[16]

In her epistolary novel *Rosa Amorosa* (1901) Egerton entered the ongoing debate on the potential of fiction to affect the moral life of the nation. On the question of the eighteenth-century novel, the free-spirited Italian Rosa Amorosa takes an opposite view to Grand's, and points up late Victorian hypocricies:

[13] George Egerton, *The Wheel of God* (London: Grant Richards, 1898), 5.

[14] Preface to *Dorian Gray* (1891; Harmondsworth, Penguin, 1985), 21.

[15] *The Wheel of God*, 44.

[16] For Egerton's praise of the character of Sue Bridehead, as a 'temperament less rare than the ordinary male observer supposes', see Egerton to Hardy (22 November 1895), Dorchester County Museum.

if your moral conscience as a nation were not always in the way of your intellectual conscience, a true transcript of your manners would oust the French novel from the shelves of the collector of *contes salés*. Your novels are not readable, because they are written with an eye to a bookstall-monopolist's censorship, whilst the materials for a modern 'Tom Jones' or 'Roderick Random', chronicles of the flesh and blood of today, are lost to posterity; and a faithful picture of the life of our time will be better gleaned from the files of the divorce and police reports and the maunderings of the ladies' papers than from the pages of contemporary fiction.[17]

Like Grand, Egerton celebrated the reproductive goal of heterosexual relations, but while for Grand these relations needed to be brought in line with concepts of civic responsibility, for Egerton natural impulse and social law were often at odds, with marriage and morality potential obstacles to racial regeneration. In *Rosa Amorosa* she spoke out against art which failed to be true to life, but which satisfied the demands of publishers and the circulating libraries or complied with the fashions of the day:

in England everything is run, even law and religion, on trade principles . . . Neither literature nor Art is a component part of the life of people here. The great bulk of the moneyed middle class do not look upon them as in any measure necessary to finer living; and if they have any books in their houses, they will either be well-bound editions of such authors as have become classics by the suffrage of time, and which they have never read or probably forgotten; or such books as are in vogue in Mudie's, or are having a boom in the papers. Of one thing you can be sure in such a house—no book will be judged on its merits as a work of art. (143–5)[18]

Like Grand, Egerton was concerned with the effects of the urban environment on health, and the spectre of urban degeneration haunts her writing: 'the new generation [of vagabonds] are seldom anything more than objectionable, low offshoots from London with an eye to gain' (*Rosa Amorosa*, 107). London is 'perhaps the wickedest, most complex city of any time' (143). Much of her work serves as a eulogy to nature, offering a concomitant diatribe against the city, which she sees as a place both of unnecessary human suffering and also of the kind of excesses

[17] Egerton, *Rosa Amorosa*, 11.

[18] Egerton made common cause with contemporary opponents of literary censorship, notably George Moore, author of the polemical treatise *Literature at Nurse; or, Circulating Morals* (1885). Moore was outraged by the strict moral censure exercised by Charles Edward Mudie (1818–90), founder of the famous circulating library, the main branch of which was opened in Oxford Street in 1852.

and recreations that blunted the reproductive drive and impaired the maternal function.

As part of this polar vision, Egerton sets up an opposition between healthy reading and novel reading, emphasizing, like her social purist contemporaries, the need to replace the romance narrative with a frank, and practically instructive, representation of human and, in particular, sexual, relations. It was, she held, crucial to racial progress that this new representation be readily available to young people. She shared with several New Women the belief that fiction was the most readily available, and digestible, form in which to disseminate these ideas, and sought, through her own, hybrid texts, to bridge the literary and the medical. The stories in *Keynotes* and *Discords*, set in rural Ireland, the fjords of Norway, and the English countryside, are as far way from the moral pollution of London as Egerton can imagine, without having to leave Europe, which, given the racial strategy of her work, would have defeated the object.

In 'The Heart of the Apple', in Egerton's 1897 collection *Symphonies*, the teenage heroine Evir lives on an island on the south coast of Norway. A quaint, scarcely human figure, known as 'Little Elf',[19] she is, quite literally, made for mothering and she bristles with reproductive health: 'she had developed early, and showed every sign of precocious womanhood. Amongst the anaemic, retarded girls of a city, she might have passed easily for a woman grown' (183). Crucially, in her library there was 'not one novel, not one romance' (183); instead she has 'books on birds and beasts and fishes and plants'—books which would convey the facts of life without the fiction of romance. We learn 'the miracle of sex, underlying every natural law, its individual working in the propagation of the young, was no mystery to her, and consequently no subject for prurient musing'. It is a theme to which Egerton returns with greater gusto the following year in *The Wheel of God*. Mary, we are told, 'had books, school books, on botany and zoology; and yet it was a sin to think of quite natural things if they touched on men and women' (44). Until novels could treat the facts of life with the same matter-of-factness as a zoological treatise, it was best to steer clear of them and look, instead, to nature, teeming with models of pronatal triumph: 'a whole choir of birds intoning matins, no solemn Gregorian chants, but a gracious joyance in the world's beauty and the delight of mating and nestmaking' (*Rosa Amorosa*, 88).

[19] 'The Heart of the Apple', *Symphonies* (London and New York: John Lane, 1897), 168.

Like Grand's Beth and Eugenia, Evir is a perfect eugenic specimen, an evolutionary success story: 'she was a thing of absolute health, every muscle, every fibre sound, every nerve strung to the right key,—a creature of instinct, pure and simple . . . a young female animal with her basic instincts intact' (184). Egerton's women are at once made fully animal, *and* spiritualized, by their maternity. Inspired by the sight of a baby, Evir is filled with 'unrest and vague desires' which make her venture further from the island in a rowing boat. As suddenly as the frost king loosens his grip on the island, 'causing the ice to cry out with a sharp, crackling rend, that told of its rapid dissolution', Evir, at the age of 15, after a brief scuffle in the woods, loses her virginity to a male artist. Her fitness for motherhood is reiterated; she is

> a child woman, with her absolutely fresh, unspoiled nature, all her basic instincts intact; a genetic creature, fashioned of the right ground-stuff for the renewal of life in man by the formation of new strong individuals; a thing of perfect health, sound in mind and body, all her apperceptions unconfused by the scrapment system of modern education.[20]

Evir's purity and simplicity have remained intact largely through her isolation from the unreformed, and unrepentant, novel. Once his brief spell as a mate has passed, the artist drops out of the story. Predictably, Evir gives birth to a healthy baby (212). Some years later, the artist returns to the island, only to be told by Evir: 'I am one of the race of women, and there are many, to whom the child is first—the man always second. He fills life for me, and I should be jealous of your claim on him' (216). The story ends with her son's undivided cry—'mother!'—echoing from the rocks (218). There are a number of parallels between this story and Grant Allen's notorious *The Woman Who Did*, in which the heroine, Herminia Barton, Cambridge-educated daughter of the Dean of Dunwich, and a eugenic feminist, regards herself as 'living proof of the doctrine of heredity'. In contrast to 'a town-bred girl' she is a 'natural' woman who has devoted herself to 'this one great question of a woman's

[20] Ibid., 206, 207. Darwin introduced the use of 'genetic' in its biological sense in a late edition of the *Origin*—'It is incredible that the descendants of two organisms, which had originally differed in a marked manner, should ever afterwards converge so closely as to lead to a near approach to identity throughout their whole organization. If this had occurred, we should meet with the same form, independently of genetic connection, recurring in widely separated geological formations; and the balance of evidence is opposed to any such an admission' (ch. 4, 6th edn.). However, the use of the term in this sense was still relatively unusual; it was more commonly used simply in relation to origin (see *OED*).

duty to herself and her sex and her unborn children', and concluded that she can only love, and bear children, outside of marriage.[21]

SEX DIFFERENCE

Although contemporary readers saw Egerton as a New Woman *par excellence*, she, like Sarah Grand, sought to dissociate herself from popular representations of the New Woman, which focused on a cultural convergence of the sexes rather than on unalterable biological differences. In 1900 she wrote:

I am embarrassed at the outset by the term 'New Woman.'—I have never yet replied to myself in a satisfactory way—to the question what is she?—I have never met one—never written about one. My women were all the eternally feminine—old as Eve—the term seemed to me to be one of those loose, cheap, journalistic catch words [. . .] To bracket me with Madame Sarah Grand or Mrs Mona Caird is all right from the point of view of differentiation—wrong from any other.—I never aim at any 'equality' theory because I hold that there is no inequality. We are different animals that is all—'the end aim of our creation is a different one'.[22]

Egerton's fiction foregrounds woman as a natural enigma, *closed* to masculine scrutiny:

she laughs, laughs softly to herself because the denseness of man, his chivalrous devotion to the female idea he has created blinds him, perhaps happily, to the problems of her complex nature. Ay, she mutters musingly, the wisest of them can only say we are enigmas.[23]

By arguing for her enigmatic status, Egerton underlined the status of woman as *other*. Writing for the *Ludgat*e in 1898 she stated: 'I am not greatly concerned in the social, so-called educational, or political

[21] Grant Allen, *The Woman Who Did* (1895; Oxford: Oxford University Press, 1995), 30, 39, 41.

[22] Egerton to Ernst Foerster, London (1 July 1900), in Ernst Foerster, *Die Frauenfrage in den Romanen Englischer Schriftstellerinnen der Gegenwart* (Marburg: N. G. Elwert'sche Verlagsbuchhandlung, 1907), 46–8, reproduced in Heilmann, the *Late Victorian Marriage Debate*, v. In recognizing the animal nature of humans, Egerton was clearly a contemporary of Freud, as she later noted: 'if I did not know the technical jargon current today of Freud and the psychoanalysts, I did know something of complexes and inhibitions, repressions and the subconscious impulses that determine actions and reactions. I used them in my stories.' ('A Keynote to *Keynotes*' (1932), Heilmann v.).

[23] 'A Cross Line', A. Richardson (ed.), *Women Who Did*, 58.

advancement of women. They are exotics—what interests me is her development from within out as a female.'[24]

Nonetheless, celebrating the enigma of woman also offered a way of celebrating difference and autonomy, and thus may be seen as a genuinely ambivalent strain in her work. Egerton was ultimately uninterested in the political participation of women in the life of the nation; her belief in the fundamental importance of biology meant that she saw any shift towards political equality as damaging to racial improvement. Through Rosa Amorosa, she expressed her concern that the suffrage would bring with it a threat of the erosion of sexual difference, on which the possibility of racial regeneration was premised: 'the one dominant fact in a woman's life' is 'her need to love and be loved'; and stressed:

> [woman] imagines universal suffrage will be a step on the way to removing woman's disabilities: woman's biggest disability is, as it always has been, herself. She talks of equal rights for women, by which she either means continence for the man, in a way which can only be called *diablement idéal*, and not supported by the history of evolution; or equal licence for the woman, forgetting that she has had that from time immemorial, except when it was repugnant to her as an individual. (*Rosa*, 78)

The idea of fundamental sex difference dominates Egerton's work:

> broadly speaking, woman has given most of her energy to a development of masculine qualities, instead of a cultivation to the utmost of the best in herself—as woman—with the object of producing the finest type of womanhood (80).[25]

Likewise, the journalist in *The Wheel of God* urges of woman: 'let her develop herself to the uttermost as a woman, not as an atrophied animal, with a degenerate leaning to hybridism. Your way leads to three sexes—man, half-man, and what is left over' (309). The fear of sexual loss that was an overriding anxiety of the *fin de siècle*, and a symptom of the discourse of degeneration, penetrates Egerton's work. Through *Rosa Amorosa*, Egerton enlarges on this:

[24] 'Women in the Queen's Reign: Some Notable Opinions, Illustrated with Photographs', *Ludgate*, 45 (1898), 216. For Hardy's ambivalent response to Egerton's evocation of women's psychological and physical otherness, see his comments in his copy of *Keynotes* (annotated both by him and Florence Henniker), quoted in Michael Millgate, *Thomas Hardy: A Biography* (Oxford: Oxford University Press, 1982), 356–7.

[25] Later in the novel, Rosa states, 'I am not a modern woman for nothing' (*Rosa*, 179) before declaring unequivocally: 'I don't want to be like you nor any man, except in such ways as I might imitate you with advantage to myself; your code of honour with one another, your *esprit de corps* is worth taking a lesson from' (*Rosa*, 179).

a male spirit may be accidentally held in a perfect female body and vice versa—and that such a combination may explain the—I use the word resignedly—anomaly of genius in a woman. The *vice versa* is more disastrous. In the case of the woman, she may, if the body holding the spirit be sound, turn out a satisfactory mother, though I think her functions would possibly be limited; and she would at worst be a trouble to herself and a puzzle to man; but in his case he will probably be a species of intellectual eunuch—the male in him feminized and the female of no sex whatever. The decadent proper rather belongs here. (83–4)

The city, civilization, and the romance plot were grouped together as enemies of nature and of national health. The city is repeatedly figured in Egerton's work as a place where sexual relations are distorted, unnatural, unreproductive. 'Gone Under', from *Discords*, tells the harrowing tale of Edith, a woman whose illegitimate child has been murdered, and who, abandoned by the child's father, is forced into a life of prostitution. The reader is pulled through the city in search of the destitute woman, who is glimpsed, for a moment, in Compton Street:

What a wreck! What a face! What a mask of the tragedy of passion, and sin, and the anguish of despair! Phthisis and drink have run riot together; have wasted her frame, hollowed her cheeks, puffed her eyelids, dried the dreadful purple lips and saddened the soul within. The girl follows the shambling steps with dry wide eyes and painful heart thud. A loafer at the other corner says something to the woman as she passes, she answers him with a toss of head, and a peal of ribald laughter, that is worse to hear than a tortured cry.[26]

The woman hurries on, screaming at a policeman 'with the defiance of reckless despair, twice, thrice, never slackening her speed; further on, at a turning near Gray's Inn Road, she stumbles, and falls heavily, but she picks herself up with lightning speed and scuds on again . . .'. Egerton's night-time city becomes a symbol of death: 'she has disappeared into the night as she came, into the night of despair that leads to death' (113). Profoundly connected to—if removed from—this image of destitution is the artifice of Leicester Square, where relations are casual and sex a barren commodity:

That rendezvous of leering, silk-hatted satyrs and flaunting nymphs of the pavement, where the frou-frou of silk mingles with the ring of artificial laughter, the glitter of paste with the hectic of paint, where the very air is tainted with patchouli, and souls sensitive to the psychometry of things shiver with the feel of passional atoms vibrating through the atmosphere of the great pairing ground of this city of smug outer propriety [. . .] where the foot-walk is crowded with the

[26] 'Gone Under', *Discords*, 112.

'fallen leaves' of fairest and frailest womanhood, like wild rose leaves blown by a wanton wind into a sty.[27]

This sense of the futility, the empty, unnatural rhythms of the city, recurs in 'A Psychological Moment at Three Periods', in the same collection: London is both a place of ennui, of excess, and of lack—the west is emasculated, the east overpopulated:

London that is west of Piccadilly Circus is virtually empty; town looks jaded; the very mansions wear a day-after-the-fête air. The men who look some way so effete, so weak-kneed in their town dress, have gone to shoot grouse or lure a salmon, gone in obedience to the only honest passion left in them—the lust to kill. The stalls in such theatres as are open have a show of soiled frocks, and the jaded young women of the big shops grow paler in the chaos of the autumn sales.[28]

The anxiety surrounding loss of sexual difference, which Huysman and Wilde turned on its head, creating men of decadent excess, in Duc Jean Floressas des Esseintes (1884) and Dorian Gray (1891), essentially womanly men, resurfaces in 'The Regeneration of Two', when Fruen remarks to her male interlocutor:

'so much'—with bitterness—'for the dolls, as you call them, . . . and the desexualized half man, with a pride in the absence of sex feeling, reckoning it as the sublimest virtue to have none, what is she but the outcome of centuries of patient repression? Repress and repress—how many generations has it gone on? You must expect some return for it—if you get the man-woman as a result! Well, I have known some feminine men too. Isn't feminization a result of all civilization, and isn't'—with desperation—'it that perhaps you resent most?'[29]

Part of Fruen's concern is over 'the fragile latter-day product with the disinclination to burden itself with motherhood'.

The epigram Egerton gives to 'The Regeneration of Two'—'love is the supreme factor in the evolution of the world' (163)—is from Henry Jones Drummond (1851–97), a Scottish evolutionary theologian whose work was underpinned by a firm belief in fundamental sex difference and the efficiency of natural selection in weeding out the unfit. Drummond delivered a hugely popular series of lectures in Boston in 1894, which were published the same year as *The Lowell Lectures on the Ascent of Man*

[27] Ibid., 109–10.
[28] 'A Psychological Moment at Three Periods', *Discords*, 20.
[29] 'The Regeneration of Two', *Discords*, 199. On the desire of women for masculine men, see also 'A Cross Line'.

and which presented motherhood as the pinnacle of evolution: 'the Pisces, then the Amphibia, then the Reptilia, then the Aves, then—What? The Mammalia, THE MOTHERS. There the series stops. Nature has never made anything since.'[30]

The Wheel of God begins as Mary concludes her reading of *Jane Eyre*. She asks: 'what was this love of which all the poets sang; that made men set out on ventures bold; and women sit and weep at lonely casements; that ran like a magic golden thread through every tale of romance and chivalry?' (3). Like many of her contemporaries, Egerton chose to make the idea of love central to her work and, in doing so, sought to redefine it. In this novel 'John Morton', a worldly woman journalist who separates sexual relations from conventional, and, in particular, social purity, notions of morality, declares of woman:

> 'she cares more about being loved than she does for all the triumphs of science, or legislation, or morals; at heart, you know', smiling wickedly, 'she isn't much of a moralist. The tragedy comes, when she happens to be a monogamic woman—oh, there are plenty of polygamic ones knocking round—and she won't realise that on the whole, natural man is congenitally built that way'. (308)

Rosa Amorosa forms Egerton's most lengthy exposition on love; in a letter of 1900 she wrote: 'what I thought of love I tried to convey in my *Rosa Amorosa*'.[31] Declaring 'love is a religion' (12), Rosa Amorosa stresses 'life is a golden book, and the letters of the poem it holds are magic runes, with colours and fragrance and melody, so that the reading is everlasting delight, and the subject is eternally old and ever new—just love, love, love!'

> Remember—and it is that you are in danger of forgetting—the more absolutely unlike you remain to him, the greater your power! You have competed now in all the academies, stormed most of the closed doors of male enterprise, held your own in all the callings of life—the one thing you *haven't done* is learned to *love better*, and when all is said and done, cry as you may against it, Love is the one thing needful for you.[32]

Like several contemporary thinkers, notably Karl Marx, Friedrich Engels, and Mona Caird, Egerton traced the history of marriage, emphasizing the economic conditions which had given rise to marriage law, and which continued to underpin hierarchies of power within conventional romance. Rosa Amorosa writes: 'the English marriage law, for

[30] *The Lowell Lectures on the Ascent of Man* (London: Hodder and Stoughton, 1894), 343.

[31] Egerton to Foerster, Heilmann, *The Late Victorian Marriage Debate*, vol. V.

[32] *Rosa Amorosa*, 16–17, emphasis in the original.

instance, is based on Canon law, with amplification in deference to the entailing of property' (133). Egerton's unsettling short story 'Virgin Soil' (1894) exposes a secret side to marriage. Florence berates her mother for not equipping her with the facts of life:

> Marriage becomes for many women a legal prostitution, a nightly degradation, a hateful yoke under which they age, mere bearers of children conceived in a sense of duty, not love. They bear them, birth them, nurse them, and begin again without choice in the matter, growing old, unlovely, with all joy of living swallowed in a senseless burden of reckless maternity, until their love, granted they started with that, the mystery glory of their lives, is turned into a duty they submit to with distaste instead of a favour granted to a husband who must become a new lover to obtain it.[33]

But the eugenic values that lead her to take up this radical position bleed through into her language, finding expression here in the eugenic keyword 'reckless'.[34]

In 'A Cross Line', Gypsy renounces her defiant disregard for conventional sexual mores, content, once she is pregnant, to give up her illicit affair and settle into a life of domestic regularity. While the story has celebrated the protagonist's lifestyle and erotic fantasies, it closes as she sets about turning her unused clothes into clothes for her baby: 'too fine for every day . . . [W]hy, one nightgown will make a dozen little shirts' (she is assisted by her working-class maid, whose own, illegitimate, baby is dead). The nightgown signals her sensual side (35–6); an aspect of her character which has now served its reproductive purpose.

Other eugenic thinkers also questioned monogamous sexual patterns. Grant Allen, for example, while firmly in favour of exploiting sexual selection to achieve 'sound and efficient citizens', argued that 'no mere

[33] 'Virgin Soil', in A. Richardson (ed.), *Women Who Did*, 103–14.

[34] A similar ideological hybridity is to be found in William Morris's *News From Nowhere*; in his chapter on love he has Old Hammond lament the fruits of 'the respectable commercial marriage bed', which he claims tend to be less healthy and beautiful than the offspring which result from love that is 'natural and healthy' even if transient. Morris refers here to a central tenet of The Manifesto of the Socialist League, which he presented for adoption on 5 July 1885: 'our modern bourgeois property-marriage, maintained as it is by its necessary complement, universal venal prostitution, would give place to kindly and human relations between the sexes' (1890; Harmondsworth: Penguin, 1993), 96. Jane Hume Clapperton's work draws on the same ideas. In *A Vision of the Future: Based on The Application of Ethical Principles* (1904), she lamented that 'children of the comparatively superior types are becoming numerically weaker than children of the thoughtless, reckless members of society who exercise their reproductive powers to the utmost'; 'slum-children show no tendency to proportionately diminish in number' (152, 151).

"eugenic" system of marriage—that is to say, of permanent and strictly monogamous union' would ever achieve the 'admirable and varied results we can get by infinite varying of the conditions of the experiment'.[35] Likewise, Jane Hume Clapperton questioned the economic basis on which monogamy was founded:

> in appraising the value of our much-vaunted monogamy, we must clearly understand that its legal basis is not, and never was, a strong personal adhesion of sympathy and affection, but a compact respecting personal property, involving in the cases where the 'contracting parties are possessed of wealth, both property in person and in thing' . . . it is to monogamy that we owe the typical domestic tyrant and many tyrannous attributes that survive in modern masculine human nature. Monogamy, too, has always been accompanied by other sexual relations in which both sexes are degraded and one sex is socially and physically ruined. As Mr W. E. H. Lecky has pointed out, 'monogamy on one side of the shield implies prostitution on the other'.[36]

The social purists chose a different route to race regeneration. In the words of Ellice Hopkins:

> It is becoming an impossible for intelligent women with a knowledge of physiology and an added sense of their own dignity to accept the lower moral standard for men, which exposes them to the risk of exchanging monogamy for a peculiarly vile polygamy—polygamy with its sensuality, but without its duties—bringing physical risks to their children and the terrible likelihood of an inherited moral taint to their sons.[37]

WRITING LIKE A WOMAN

Of the female artist, Egerton wrote in 1900:

> I had only one aim in my writing—to put myself as woman into my writing—my thoughts, my views, my sentiments.—Up to [this] time all the writing women had [done] seemed to me to vice or to echo man. They donned breeches when wielding their pen.—In my opinion—Man had done everything in art and literature immeasurably better than woman could ever hope to do. There was only one thing she had not done, only one thing she could do—put her own sex into it. I tried to do that. I had, contrary to opinion, no propaganda in view—no emancipation theory to propound, no equality to illumine. I chose

[35] Grant Allen, 'The Girl of the Future', *Universal Review*, 7 (1890), 49, 54.

[36] *A Vision*, 135, 138. W. E. H. Lecky (1838–1903) was an Irish essayist and historian.

[37] *The Power of Womanhood; or, Mothers and Sons: A Book for Parents and Those in loco parentis* (London: Wells Gardner, Darton & Co. 1899), 182.

my characters with a view to exposing some side of womanhood, some freak, some hidden trait, some secret emotion.[38]

'Haven't you ever thought that one's brain is a store of negatives—negatives that give all the past of each individual through each link of the chain right to the first origin?', asks Rosa Amorosa the following year. Writing becomes the expression of the unconscious, the mind biologized, instinctive, and primal, tending backwards, to first causes. It becomes 'a form of "printing off" from the plates stored in ourselves'.[39] Egerton posits that the troubled life of women allows, necessitates, even, a mirroring, fragmented art form. She suggests, and seeks to develop through her own work, an art form for women that expresses sociobiological differences between the sexes. Rosa writes:

that the male is the greater artist—(by that I do not mean a man who has exhibited in academies, but the being endowed with a faculty for the revelation of intrinsic beauty for its own sake alone, without reference to its mere utility)—is perhaps only because his store of inherited memories has been less blurred by physical disturbance, than is the case of the woman. Fathering is joy, relief; in fact all his sexual life is, in its best regulated order, helpful to him. That is scarcely so with the woman. For her, the struggle to work with head and produce with body at the same time is often fruitful of harm. (81–2)

This equation of 'fathering' with relief, and its relation to the 'sexual life' suggests that parenthood for men is little more than an untroubled physical act. Mirroring parenting, writing is, for Egerton, intrinsically sexed. She conceives of male narrative as the product of inherited memory (or mind) combined with (healthy, bodily) experience; thus it constitutes *organic* art, while female narrative is born of struggle. She further suggests that women's place in biological narrative determines their relation to beauty. Beauty is theirs to *trade* within the evolutionary market; thus they are distanced from the ideal of disinterestedness. This difference, which is an expression of seemingly inseparable social and biological factors, showed through in women's writing, and might, she suggests, be turned to creative advantage. While Grand saw civilization as the highest point of evolution, and Mona Caird saw nature as largely a social construct, Egerton posits a primal, *natural*, self which she seeks to express through her writing, reaching *beyond* the social.

These gendered theories of art motivate Egerton's preference for the

[38] Egerton to Ernst Foerster, London (1 July 1900), Heilmann, *The Late Victorian Marriage Debate*, vol. V.

[39] *Rosa Amorosa*, 80–1.

intrinsically fragmented form of the epistolary novel, and of the short story, which reached its heyday in the 1890s,[40] over linear and leisurely novels. In *Rosa Amorosa* the restless, threatened and disrupted nature of female narrative is signalled through the letter. In the following passage, for example, the disrupted subject of Rosa's narration is further disrupted by the form its retelling takes:

> Now, I am not telling you all of the adventure which gave rise to all this disrupted disquisition; but I must send it to the post if it is to reach the 'little village' tonight and cross the Channel on the first stage of its way to you. It is strange to think of it whirling down through the marsh lands of Essex, lying in its sealed bag in the scarlet mail-car as it dashes through the crowded streets, to more train and the chopping swing of the Channel. (100)

With its high claims to truth, and inherently disrupted form, the epistolary novel embodies the tensions which Egerton posited as intrinsic to female experience and narrative. Equally, she saw the short story as inherently suited to the working conditions enjoyed by women writers, remarking in 1932:

> I was a short story, at most a long short story writer. For years they came in droves and said themselves, leaving no scope for padding or altered endings; the long book was not my pigeon . . . Publishers told me bluntly: 'There is no market for short stories'. . . It is easier now than it was then, but there is still, I fancy, a snag for women. Art is a jealous and arbitrary mistress and brooks no rival. . . . Until woman makes as deliberate a choice as a nun, who never bungles her job because she accepts the sacrifice her vocation demands, she will never meet man, at his best, on equal terms as a writer—and perhaps not then.[41]

For Egerton, writing women were circumscribed by their biology, and the way round this was new, short forms of fiction that would fit with the rhythms of motherhood.

Equally, the short story closely fitted eugenic emphasis on the visual. The visual provided an index to health. In Egerton's stories, the body takes centre stage, and she privileges images, snapshots, impressions, the image over the written narrative. She urges that the hermeneutics of the

[40] See Bliss Perry, 'The Short Story', *Atlantic Monthly*, 90 (1902) 241–52. Henry Duff Traill, *The New Fiction: And Other Essays on Literary Subjects* (London: Hurst and Blackett, 1897); Henry Seidel Canby, *The Short Story* (New York, Henry Holt, 1902); Wendell V. Harris, 'English Short Fiction in the Nineteenth Century, III. The Rise of the Short Story in England', *Studies in Short Fiction*, 6: 1 (Fall, 1968), 45–57.

[41] Egerton, 'A Keynote to *Keynotes*', in John Gawsworth (ed.), *Ten Contemporaries: Notes Towards their Definitive Bibliography* (London: Ernest Benn, 1932), 58–60, repr. in Heilmann, vol. V.

body be simplified. The implication is that the fit and unfit ought to be easily identified,[42] and that the trappings of civilization were impediments to assessing health. 'The whole world of men and women would suddenly stand in nudity, the moral effect would be colossal', declares Rosa Amorosa in a moment of seeming sexual liberation, but a vision of a totalitarian health regime quickly follows:

all false shame would die a summary death, and the exigencies of continuing the ordinary duties of life would compel people to cast all consideration of it aside. The common idea of beauty would be entirely revolutionized; the human face would lose its undue prominence and become a mere detail in a whole; straight, clean limbs and a beautiful form be the only thing admirable; disease and bodily blemishes the one right cause for shame, and, as a result, concealment. (83)

Disease is linked with shame, and health with innocence, in this telling conflation of the moral and the physical. Embracing her relation to Eve, the first mother, Rosa Amorosa writes 'it is the red clay in me, unbroken through all the ages from time primeval to me; the spirit which will save me ever from becoming the cow-like mother of mediocrities, fathered by habit, out of duty' (104). She declares:

I never could see any merit in a quiver full of congenital semi-idiots. The man and woman who give one or two beautiful sound-limbed, healthy-souled children to the world are surely more praiseworthy. Do you remember how I shocked that very select supper party of 'rights' when they were discussing the claim of one of your dialect poets for the yearly State Grant, by saying I thought any woman who had produced a prize child had a much greater right to apply for it? (104)

In a later letter she urges:

it is no woman's part in life to play the *rôle* of relieving officer for the preservation of wastrels—to heart-starve while she pours the treasures of her nature into a man with the receptivity of a sieve—any more than it is her duty to go on mothering children to an inheritance of disease or insanity . . . these are matters every thinking woman of today must decide for herself, without reference to priest or judge—if she only has courage enough to do so. (181)

[42] The arguments have not been absent from debates surrounding AIDS and public awareness. See, for example, Elaine Showalter's discussion of parallels between responses to syphilis in the late nineteenth century and AIDS in the late twentieth. While Victorians called for the branding of syphilitics, William F. Buckley advised that 'everyone detected with AIDS should be tattooed in the upper fore-arm, to protect common needle-users, and on the buttocks, to prevent the victimization of other homosexuals', 'Identify all the Carriers,' *New York Times* (18 March 1986), section A, 27, quoted in Showalter, *Sexual Anarchy: Gender and Culture at the Fin de Siècle* (1990; London: Virago, 1992), 191.

Here, Rosa joins the eugenist rejection of charity as going *against* nature, and working against national efficiency.

Egerton strove to write the *pronatal* fiction that she thought was a woman's duty to produce. The term 'philoprogenitiveness' recurs several times in her work. It was a term used within phrenological discourse[43] to denote the faculty of the brain for affection for children. The term contained an etymological ambivalence of which Johann Gaspar Spurzheim, who popularized the science in Britain, had been conscious when he adopted it in 1815: 'I am aware that the name ought to indicate love of producing offspring. As, however, "progeny" means offspring; philoprogeny, love of offspring, and Philoprogenitiveness the faculty of producing love of offspring, I have adopted the term.'[44] This semantic confusion would prove useful to the eugenists. Imbued with the authority of the scientific, philoprogenitiveness was a term which lent itself readily to the project of eugenic feminism, which conflated 'love of children' with 'love of producing children', though Spurzheim had disowned this sense.[45] The eugenists' embrace of philoprogenitiveness underscores this proximity.

Clapperton noted 'this sentiment of love of offspring or philoprogenitiveness, is well established in the British race';[46] observing

> in view of the law of population, and the fact that science has made plain how practically to separate the amative from the reproductive conditions of physical union, the love of the sexes can harmonize with the highest interests of our collective social life, and eugenics, *not sexual love*, may become paramount in generation. What social morality requires is that the forces of philoprogenitiveness and

[43] See Roger Cooter, *The Cultural Meaning of Popular Science. Phrenology and the Organization of Consent in Nineteenth-Century Britain* (Cambridge, Cambridge University Press, 1984). See also Robert M. Young, *Mind, Brain and Adaptation in the Nineteenth Century: Cerebral Localisation and its Biological Context from Gall to Ferrier* (Oxford: Oxford University Press, 1970). For instances of the use in the word by other supporters of eugenics, see H. G. Wells, *Anticipations*, 174, and the epigraph to Grand's *The Winged Victory*: ' "I call you philoprogenitive mad, Ninny" said Lord Terry de Beach. " '*Voyez-vous, nos enfants nous sont bien necessaries, Seigneur*.' Victor Hugo, eh?" said the Duke.' The word also forms the compound of the first line of T. S. Eliot's 'Mr Eliot's Sunday Morning Service' (1920), 'Polyphiloprogenitive'.

[44] Spurzheim, *The Physiognomical System of Drs Gall and Spurzheim: founded on an anatomical and physiological examination of the nervous system in general and brain in particular; and indicating the dispositions and manifestations of the mind* (London: Baldwin, Cradock and Joy, 1815), Preface (dated December 1814), 10 (*OED*). Its organ is located by phrenology just above the middle of the cerebellum.

[45] Greta Jones notes that the proximity of Galton's work not to modern theories of heredity but to Gall, Lavater, and the tradition of reading character in physical signs tends to be forgotten: *Social Darwinism*, p. viii.

[46] Clapperton *A Vision*, 154.

a public conscience combined should dominate the function of reproduction, while love is left free from coercive control in the sphere of individual life.[47]

For Clapperton, philoprogenitiveness was the key to rational reproduction, and would ensure the health of future generations:

science points to philoprogenitiveness, or love of off-spring, as the proper motor force in reproduction. Were this force the antecedent cause of parentage throughout the nation, disease and premature death would be undermined and gradually subside. 'Indiscriminate survival' gives way before that 'rational selection and birth of the fit' which is a fundamental condition of social well-being—the master-spring to a rapid evolution of general happiness.[48]

In Egerton's 'The Spell of The White Elf', in *Keynotes*, the desire for a child overrides the desire for a lover. Belinda is described as 'one bump of philo-progenitiveness, but she hates men' (80).[49] The narrator remarks:

Do you know I think it is not an uncommon feeling amongst a certain number of women. I have often drawn her out on the subject. It struck me, because I have known many, particularly older women, who would give anything in God's world to have a child of 'their own' if it could be got just as Belinda says, 'without the horrid man or the shame.' It seems congenital with some women to have deeply rooted in their innermost nature a smouldering enmity, ay, sometimes a physical disgust to men, it is a kind of kin feeling to the race dislike of white men to black. (80)[50]

Privately, Egerton declared:

I would do away with all absurdities such as disgrace attending the birth of a child out of wedlock—the absurd illogical laws as to illegitimacy—allowing every woman to mother a child if she wishes, a child in honour bearing her name, for the welfare of which she would be responsible to the state. I would give her greater rights over her children, but I would demand a closer attention to [her] duty as a mother citizen.—The same moral licence as man, no.—There are the same physiological reasons why she should remain pure, as [there are] for preserving a mare or a bitch untainted.—She is only of value in as far as she is a vessel for the mothering of healthy men and women. Logically ground down to its ultimate solution that is the reason for her existence—and the only one . . . [51]

[47] Ibid., emphasis in original.

[48] Clapperton, *A Vision*, 333.

[49] Stutfield singled out this passage in 'Book of the Month: The Novel of the Modern Woman', *Review of Reviews*, 10 (1894), 68–9.

[50] Cf. 'a few women absolutely devoid of philo-progenitiveness proper have a mothering quality in their love for man' (*Rosa*, 124). For a further example of a woman who wants a child but not a partner, see Rudolph Dircks, 'Ellen' (1896), in A. Richardson (ed.), *Women Who Did*, 181–6.

[51] Egerton to Ernst Foerster, London (1 July 1900), in Heilmann, vol. V.

In 1895, Ménie Muriel Dowie's Gallia remarked: 'a woman gets a good deal out of motherhood; more than she does out of marriage: motherhood is, on the whole, better suited to her than marriage, I believe.'[52] Likewise, the narrator in 'Gone Under' argues that the health of a child must be put before all other considerations. Declaring 'the *only divine* fibre in a woman is her maternal instinct', she consoles Edith Grey, whose illegitimate child seems to have been murdered. It is through changing attitudes towards biology that Egerton seeks to intervene in the social. The narrator remarks

> I have often thought that a woman who mothers a bastard, and endeavours bravely to rear it decently, is more to be commended than the society wife who contrives to shirk her motherhood. *She* is at least loyal to the finest fibre of her being, the deep, underlying generic instinct, the 'mutterdrang' that lifts her above and beyond all animalism, and fosters the sublimest qualities of unselfishness and devotion. No, indeed, you poor woman, you are not bad, you are perhaps just as God intended![53]

Rosa Amorosa concludes with a letter to Egerton herself, in which Rosa reminds her of the 'face in a picture in a chapel' that they had seen together, 'telling us of the dream-children unborn in us, stirring all that was best in us both, and sent us out into the solid world again with a fresh vow of fine womanhood in our life's intention' (*Rosa*, 249).

In 'A Psychological Moment at Three Periods', the narrator remarks

> it used to be a fancy of mine that if I were unfortunate enough to bring an illegitimate child into the world I would never disown it or put it away. I suppose it is my lack of orthodox belief which makes me unable to see that a bastard is less the fruit of a man and woman's mating than the child of a marriage blessed by priest or parson.[54]

The use of the word 'mating' at once desentimentalizes and doubly validates the procreative act, removing it from a matrix of conventional social relations, and situating it in the animal economy of Darwinian evolutionary narrative. She continues:

> to my poor woman's logic the words of the clergy have nothing to do with the begetting. I know men think differently; they don't seem to realise that their physical and mental peculiarities, their likeness, body and soul, is stamped on the

[52] Ménie Muriel Dowie, *Gallia* (1895; London: J. M. Dent, 1995), 91–2.

[53] 'Gone Under', 101, emphasis in original.

[54] George Egerton, 'A Psychological Moment', in *Keynotes and Discords* (1893 and 1894; London: Virago, 1983), 59.

one as well as on the other. They rarely give them so much as a thought, at best seven shillings a week.[55]

Speaking from a hereditarian position, the narrator argues that women see and value children differently from men, aware that through children their own biological and spiritual life is extended. She points to a tension between social law and eugenic virtue, lamenting that men 'will strive and toil, love, ay, sin, for the puniest specimen of humanity assigned to them by religion and law. If I had such a child', she adds, with a lightening of eyes, 'I would call it mine before the whole world and tack no Mrs to my name either' ('A Psychological Moment', 59). In the same year that this story was published the Legitimation League was founded in London to promote the recognition of illegitimate children.[56] The goals of the league shifted, and in 1897, when it launched its journal *The Adult*, it formally adopted as its primary aim the education of public opinion 'in the direction of freedom in sexual relationships'.[57] The May issue of 1898 advertised a competition, offering prizes of 100 guineas and 50 guineas, 'for the two best works on the psychological, physiological and pathological effects of celibacy on women'. Eugenists decried the effects of female chastity as injurious; the recognition of illegitimate children was not without eugenic motivation. The same issue of *The Adult* noted:

the thoughtful author of 'The Strike of a Sex', Mr Noyes Miller, is strongly of opinion that celibacy has even worse consequences for women than for men. All authors on lunacy agree that enforced celibacy gives us more lunacy victims than any other cause. Certainly no one can doubt that hysteria in its many forms, which perhaps is a worse social evil than lunacy, very largely results from the unhealthy and unnatural condition of celibacy.[58]

In 'The Regeneration of Two', the narrator observes:

a futile code of morality—a code that makes the natural workings of sex a vile thing to be ashamed of; the healthy delight in the cultivation of one's body as the beautiful sheath of one's soul and spirit, with no shame in any part of it, all alike being clean, a sin of the flesh, a carnal conception to be opposed by asceticism; a code that has thrown man out of balance and made sexual love play far too prominent a part in life—(it ought to be one note, not even a dominant note, in the chord of human love) [. . .] factory doors open and troops of men and

[55] Ibid., 59.

[56] See Bland, *Banishing the Beast, English Feminism & Sexual Morality (1885–1914)* (Harmondsworth: Penguin, 1995), 156 and 172.

[57] Gerald Moore, *The Adult*, i. (September 1898).

[58] Dora F. Kerr, 'The Conversion of Mrs Grundy', *The Adult*, 2 (May 1898), 100.

women and children, apologies for human beings, narrow-chested, stunted, with the pallor of lead-poison in their haggard faces, troop out of them; and as they laugh wearily their teeth shake loosely in their blue-white gums, and they are too tired to wash the poison off their hands before their scanty meals. And I see great monopolies eating away the substance of the people, and magnificent chapels built in the memory of railway kings who ruined thousands of women and children, and I say, 'so much for the rulers.' And I said to myself 'salvation lies with the women and the new race they are to mother'.[59]

[59] 'The Regeneration of Two', 189–90, 192.

8 Mona Caird: Individual Liberty and the Challenge to Eugenics

> The Feminist Movement, called in those ancient days the 'Revolt of Women', was just beginning to express itself. Mona Caird had thrown a flaming bomb into the camp of the thoroughly smug and respectable ranks . . . Violent correspondence raged round that for months, even years, and she was banned and shunned like the plague in certain circles.
>
> Charles Whitby[1]

> Not all the Mona Cairds and Olive Schreiners that ever lisped Greek can fight against the force of natural selection. Survival of the fittest is stronger than Miss Buss, and Miss Pipe, and Miss Helen Gladstone, and the staff of the Girls' Public Day School Company, Limited, all put together.
>
> Grant Allen[2]

When Mona Caird declared in 1888 in the *Westminster Review* that marriage in its present form was 'a vexatious failure',[3] she sparked the

[1] Charles Whitby, 'Sarah Grand: The Woman and her Work', written for inclusion in the *Sarah Grand Miscellany* (compiled by Gladys Singers-Biggers and published privately under the title *The Breath of Life*); reproduced in Ann Heilmann and Stephanie Forward, *Sex, Social Purity and Sarah Grand*, 4 vols. (Routledge, 2001), i. 345.

[2] Grant Allen, 'The Girl of the Future', *Universal Review*, 7 (1890), 52.

[3] Caird noted that legal redress for the habitual forms of oppression that characterized the marriage relation was virtually impossible, and the reforms that were most needed were ones not merely of the penal system but of social convention: 'Marriage', Independent Section, *Westminster Review*, 130 (1888), reprinted in *The Morality of Marriage, and Other Essays on the Status and Destiny of Woman* (London: George Redway, 1897), 105, 106. *The Morality of Marriage* is reprinted in Ann Heilmann, *The Late Victorian Marriage Debate: A Collection of Key New Woman Texts* (London and New York: Routledge and Thoemmes Press, 1998), vol. 1; all subsequent page references are to this collection. In the same article, Caird wrote: 'as the monogamic ideal becomes more and more realised and followed, not from force but from conviction, increasing freedom in the form of marriage must—paradox as it sounds—be looked for among a developing people. Greater respect for the liberties of the individual would alone dictate a system less barbaric, and would secure it from danger of abuse' ('Marriage', *The Morality of Marriage*, 109).

most famous newspaper controversy of the nineteenth century. She was not opposed to marriage *per se*, but urged its development along lines which paid greater respect to the freedom of the individual. In response, Edwin Arnold, editor of the *Daily Telegraph*, posed the question 'Is Marriage a Failure?' At this time the paper boasted an average daily circulation of 'in excess of 500,000', and could claim the 'largest circulation in the world';[4] it received 27,000 letters in response to the question, from all corners of the world. 'England stood aghast at the mass of correspondence which, like a snowball, grew in size as it rolled along', observed Harry Quilter in his introduction to a selection of the letters:

> Wives and mothers, maids and bachelors, spinsters and husbands, clerks and curates, priests and publicans, saints and sinners, gathered themselves into one compact mass of respondents, and hurled their woes, their joys, their experiences, their doctrines, and themselves at the head of the *Daily Telegraph* . . . 'seasons changed, summer passed away.' Baldwin fell from the clouds, and Edison's voice was brought us in a box, Imperial diaries came out and were suppressed, grouse were cleared from the moors, and partridges shot in the stubble, but still with the inevitability of fate, the regularity of time, and the persistency of a Scotch lawyer, the three columns of perplexed curates, city barmaids, observant bachelors, and glorified spinsters maintained their hold upon the journal, and their claim on the public attention.[5]

In *The Diary of A Nobody* Mr Pooter, who made his first appearance in *Punch* in the year of the marriage controversy, recorded 'we had a most pleasant chat about the letters on "Is Marriage a Failure?" It has been no failure in our case'.[6]

Mona Caird (née Alice Mona Alison) was born on the Isle of Wight in 1854.[7] Her landowning father, John Alison, was an engineer and inventor. Her mother, Matilda Jane Hector, had been born in Schleswig-Holstein,

4 The *Daily Telegraph* advertised these as its figures for 1887. Information provided by Phil Broad, *Telegraph*.

5 Harry Quilter (ed.), *Is Marriage a Failure*? (London: Swan Sonnenschein & Co., 1888), 2. Quilter dedicated the volume (which formed part of his *Universal Review Library* series) to Edwin Arnold 'in admiration of the enterprise of that journal which originated, of the discretion with which it conducted, and of the firmness with which it terminated the greatest newspaper controversy of modern times'.

6 George and Weedon Grossmith, 'The Diary of a Nobody', *Punch* (17 November 1888), 233.

7 For further biographical information, see Ann Heilmann, 'Mona Caird (1854–1932): Wild Woman, New Woman, and Early Radical Feminist Critic of Marriage and Motherhood', *Women's History Review*, 5 (1996), 67–95; and Margaret Morganroth Gullette, afterword to Mona Caird, *The Daughters of Danaus* (New York: Feminist Press, 1989), 493–534.

then part of Denmark, and—since 1946—a state of Germany. At the age of 23 she married James Alexander Henryson-Caird, a 31-year old landowner from an established Scottish family. They seem to have spent much of their married life apart, with James spending most of the year on his estate, and Caird spending one or two months there each year, and the rest of the time in London or abroad. At the age of 30 she became a mother and, like Grand and Egerton, she had one son, Alister James. A leading figure in the late nineteenth-century press debates on women and on science, her essays denouncing Victorian moralities and biological determinism appeared transatlantically between 1888 and 1894 in the *North American Review*, the *Fortnightly Review*, the *Nineteenth Century*, and the *Westminster Review*. This last, pillar of the middle class, though with a progressive bent, distanced itself from the content of her essays by placing them in its quarantined Independent Section.[8]

Caird was also the author of six novels, a number of short stories, a travel book, and number of pamphlets protesting against vivisection. She published her first novel, *Whom Nature Leadeth*, in 1883, under the name G. Noel Hatton; its successor, *One that Wins: The Story of a Holiday in Italy*, appeared in 1887. With her third novel, *The Wing of Azrael*, published the year following the newspaper controversy, her fiction began to attract serious attention, and her polemical novel *The Daughters of Danaus* (1894) was an immediate bestseller. The poet Elizabeth Sharp dedicated her anthology, *Women Poets of the Victorian Era* (1890), to Mona Caird, designating her 'the most loyal and devoted advocate of the cause of woman'.[9] Sharp noted that although Caird's opinions were met with acute hostility at the time, they contributed a great deal to 'altering the attitude of the public mind in its approach to and examination of [the woman question]'.[10] Among those troubled by her outspoken views were social purity feminists. For example, Ellice Hopkins remarked rather curtly in her maternalist tract *The Power of Womanhood* (1899):

> I am aware that neither Mr Grant Allen with his 'hill-top' novels, nor Mrs Mona Caird need be taken too seriously, but when the latter says, 'there is something pathetically absurd in this sacrifice to their children of generation after generation of grown people' I would suggest that it would be still more pathetically absurd to

[8] These essays were drawn together in a single volume in 1897 by George Redway.

[9] *Women Poets of the Victorian Era* (London: Walter Scott, 1890). Caird dedicated *The Wing of Azrael* (1889) to Sharp 'with grateful and admiring affection'.

[10] Elizabeth A. Sharp, *William Sharp (Fiona Macleod): A Memoir* (London: Heinemann, 1912), i. 207, cited in Heilmann, 'Mona Caird', 87, n. 3.

see the whole upward-striving past, the whole noble future of the human race, sacrificed to their unruly wills and affections, their passions and desires.[11]

Interest in Caird began to revive in the late twentieth century, but the extent of her dissent from the social purists, and her active and sustained attack on late nineteenth-century eugenics, remain largely overlooked.[12] Caird appropriated the scientific rhetoric of the social purists and eugenists in order to rework their arguments, exposing the biases inherent in the new discourse of biology and reclaiming the importance of environment and culture in shaping individuals. In interrogating contemporary enthusiasm for biological determinism, she offered an environmentalist challenge to the idea that nature determined the development of individuals or the development of society. For Caird the development of the individual was social; the development of society was historical. She argued that evolution was not deterministic, and that individuals might—and should strive to—change themselves during the course of their lives: after all, Darwin had put change at the very heart of evolution. Equally, she questioned the matrix of power relations that lay at the heart of eugenic feminism, following Darwin's rejection of teleology in her argument that evolution did not intend for motherhood to be the natural function of all women—'how false are all the inferences of phrases such as "Nature intends", "Nature desires". She intends and desires nothing—she is an abject slave.'[13]

[11] *The Power of Womanhood; or, Mothers and Sons: A Book for Parents and Those in loco parentis* (London: Wells Gardner, Darton & Co., 1899), 149. The quotation from Caird is from 'A Defence of the So-called "Wild Woman" ', *Nineteenth Century*, 31 (1892), 811–29.

[12] While some studies of late nineteenth-century feminism refer to Mona Caird, they tend merely to synopsize her views on marriage and summarize the plot of her best-known novel, *The Daughters of Danaus*. See, for instance, Lucy Bland, *Banishing the Beast, English Feminism and Sexual Morality (1885-1914)* (Harmondsworth: Penguin, 1995), 126–30; Sheila Jeffreys, *The Spinster and Her Enemies: Feminism and Sexuality 1880–1930* (London: Pandora Press, 1985), 43. Most accounts group her with the eugenic feminists to whom she was most opposed; see, for example, Gillian Kersley, *Darling Madame: Sarah Grand and Devoted Friend* (London: Virago, 1983), 58; and Marilyn Bonnell, 'The Legacy of Sarah Grand's *The Heavenly Twins*: A Review Essay', *English Literature in Transition*, 36 (1993), 472. Caird herself made it clear that she did not share Grand's views; see, for example 'Ideal Marriage', *Westminster Review*, (Independent Section) 130 (1888), 620. Lucy Bland has taken this homogenizing approach further, assuming Caird shared with her contemporaries 'the imperialist rhetoric of racist "common-sense" ' (*Banishing the Beast*, 130), a view which fails to attend to Caird's strong anti-racist views. Caird's interest in, and subversion of, evolutionary discourses which lay at the heart of her arguments, remain neglected.

[13] 'A Defence of the So-called "Wild Woman" ', *Nineteenth Century*, 31 (1892), 811–29; reprinted in Mora Caird, *The Morality of Marriage, and Other Essays on the Status and Destiny of Woman* (London: George Redway, 1897), 173. Further references to this work will give the title of the essay, followed by *Morality*.

Darwinian anti-teleology forms the bedrock of *The Daughters of Danaus*, a novel which engaged explicitly with contemporary biological discourse on the urban poor. The artistic genius Hadria Fullerton, the novel's central character and one of four Fullerton children, declares that the suffering of women 'is no more "intended" or inherently necessary than that children should be born with curvature of the spine, or rickets' (209). Hadria's older sister, Algitha, leaves Scotland for London, committing her working life to alleviating the suffering of the urban poor. *The Daughters of Danaus* calls into question the eugenic rhetoric of self-sacrifice as well as the idea of biological determinism, and Algitha emphasizes at the outset that she does not belong to the camp of self-sacrificing lady philanthropists: 'the work was really wise, useful work among the poor, which Algitha felt she could do well', but she admits and celebrates the possibility of individual freedom—'I don't want to pose as a philanthropist . . . though I honestly do desire to be of service. I want to spread my wings. And why should I not?'[14] She elects to be '*un*womanly'.[15] After several years working among the London poor, Algitha declares: 'I can't believe, for instance, that among all those millions in the East End, not *one* man or woman, for all these ages, was born with great capacities, which better conditions might have allowed to come to fruition.'[16] Meanwhile, Hadria marries an Englishman, Hubert Temperley, but finds the condition on which she married him—that she should have absolute freedom—ultimately impossible to put into practice in the face of family pressures. She escapes to Paris, where her musical talent can flourish, and for a short while her work as a composer progresses by leaps and bounds, but family pressures force her to return 'to the land of fogs, the land of the *bourgeois*' (335), and she joins the 'accursed list of women who gave up their art for '*la famille*' (333).[17] Monsieur Jouffroy, her mentor and teacher, points out that she is succumbing to an age-old form of oppression, when she returns to save her mother further ignominy (Mrs Fullerton makes herself ill on account of her daughter's wayward behaviour): 'your family has doubtless become ill. Families have that habit when they desire to achieve something. Bah, it is easy to become ill when one is angry, and so to make oneself pitied and obeyed. It is a common

14 *Daughters of Danaus*, 29, 31. 15 Ibid., 31, emphasis in original. 16 Ibid., 462.

17 Emphasis in original. In stressing the importance of unalienated labour, Marx noted that real free labour, such as musical composition 'demands the greatest effort' (*Marx's Grundrisse*, selected and trans. by D. McLellan (London: 1971), 124–5, in Graeme Duncan, *Marx and Mill: Two Views of Social Conflict and Social Harmony* (Cambridge: Cambridge University Press, 1973), 80.

usage' (335). But Hadria feels powerless in the face of the law of custom, and, having believed passionately in the possibility of choice and freedom in her youth, now denies that she has a choice (335). Finding her outlet for her creative genius blocked by the harrassment that kills (321), her creative energies are sublimated—in an interesting reversal of the standard process of sublimation—in an illicit, and ultimately self-destructive, sexual relation with the unprincipled seducer Professor Theobald: 'he did not understand the angry, corroding action of a strong artistic impulse that was incessantly baulked in full tide' (398); the relationship is but an expression of 'this craving to fill the place of her lost art' (419). While she eventually withdraws from the liaison, won over by internal principle, she remains crushed by familial oppression, her genius unfulfilled and her happiness denied.

Caird's concern with the abuse of freedom led her to become increasingly critical of the rise of biological determinism, which was underpinned by the paralysis of the individual. In her sixth novel, *The Stones of Sacrifice* (1915), she focuses almost exclusively on eugenics and, in her late seventies, she was moved to write *The Great Wave* which she published in 1931, the year before her death. Set in Germany at the time of the First World War, the novel exposes the barbarism to be found both within science and nature; the great wave of the title symbolizes the laws of 'Force and Cruelty'. The novel's scientists share a Malthusian view of existence. The novel offers a damning indictment of eugenics, denouncing negative eugenics—the extermination of the unfit—and Nazi science with foreboding urgency, and marks a shift in Caird's work. This shift is from a critique of pronatalism or positive eugenics—aimed at promoting the birth of the 'fit'—to an emphatic indictment of racial hygiene and negative eugenics—which aimed to prevent the birth or survival of the unfit. The shift reflects both the rise of racial hygiene in Germany,[18] and a shift in eugenic thinking in Britain: in the same year that *The Great Wave* was published, Havelock Ellis declared:

[18] See Gisela Bock, 'Antinatalism, Maternity and Paternity in National Socialist Racism', Gisela Bock and Pat Thane (eds.), *Maternity and Gender Policies: Women and the Rise of the European Welfare States 1880s–1950s* (London and New York: Routledge, 1994). For discussion of the emphasis in Third Reich policies on sterilization and euthanasia, see also Kevles, *In the Name of Eugenics: Genetics and the Uses of Human Heredity* (1985; Cambridge, Mass.: Harvard University Press, 1995), 96–112; and Robert N. Proctor, *Racial Hygiene: Medicine under the Nazis* (Cambridge, Mass. and London: Harvard University Press, 1988), 176–221. Negative eugenics was already the focus of political reforms in other countries, such as the United States, Denmark, and Sweden, which established compulsory sterilization before the First World War.

the most urgent eugenic task appears to be, not the propagation of what we imagine to be good stocks, but the elimination of those which, certainly or probably, are injurious to society or to themselves, and that the members of these stocks must sometimes in the last resort be induced by social pressure, and even perhaps by legislation, to undergo sterilisation . . .

In 1901 Galton thought that to increase the productivity of the best stocks was far more important than to repress the productivity of the worst. But seven years later he declared that this latter task of repressing the worst stocks is 'unquestionably the more pressing subject'. It is evident that he was on the way to the conclusion that it is negative eugenics with which alone we can be, directly that is to say, actively concerned.[19]

The idea of promoting the best stock has always been part of aristocratic ideology, but had not previously been accompanied by any notion of eliminating the worst stock. As capitalist forces multiplied, causing maximum social instability and threatening social anarchy, the notion of a natural right to rule (previously held to be the privilege of the aristocracy) was eroded. With the demise of a metaphysical basis for political authority biology was looked to as a new way of establishing a ruling class and the aristocratic ideology of promoting the best stock was transformed into a fascist ideology which aimed at eliminating the worst stock.

The Great Wave does not condemn all science, but carefully separates destructive and creative forms. The most sinister of the German scientists, the chemist Herr Waldheim, cherishes an 'idea of the Fatherland' which serves fascism (445). A follower of Nietzsche, he lectures on 'Evolution and the Superman'. The novel's most responsible scientist, Grierson, regrets 'that human progress was to be promoted by the extinction of all the more generous and civilized impulses of the race' (163). Projecting Darwin's theories of inter- and intra-species conflict onto nations, Waldheim declares that the nation in which the warring spirit does not dominate 'is not apt to be selected for survival' (169), and in a neat and telling conflation of religion and racial hygiene he concludes: 'heaven is not fond of degenerates' (170). Another of the novel's scientists, Professor Windle, sees science and ethics as entirely and necessarily separate, declaring 'my department is physics, not morals'. He sees no limits to the power of science: 'science is moving from victory to victory and is placing in man's hands a power over matter and over his own destiny such as the world has never seen before' (55).

19 Havelock Ellis, 'Eugenics and the Future', *More Essays of Love and Virtue* (London: Constable and Co. Ld., 1931), 185, 204–5.

Dr De Mollyns has a more guarded faith in science: 'how is this tremendous power to be used? Is there to be a standing together of strong and weak, fit and unfit?' Grierson, who is collecting information for a work on sociology by the proprietor of the *Social Science Review* (101), takes this further: through his own scientific practice he seeks to unite ethics and evolution, and he respects the 'ultimate mystery' of life, believing that 'while you can express in an equation the behaviour of many innate objects, you can't do that with living creatures. The equation doesn't come off' (77). Science, in spite of its enormous capacity for harm, is also represented as having the potential to subdue 'the evil elements of "Nature" '; here Grierson determines to 'lend a hand' (515). Envisioning the defeat of Nazi science, the novel concludes by imagining Grierson's return to the laboratory, and to scientific practice that is able to respect the mystery of life.

LIBERTY, INDIVIDUALISM, AND THE INFLUENCE OF JOHN STUART MILL

The liberal philosophy of John Stuart Mill was an inspiration for late nineteenth-century and early twentieth-century opposition to eugenics in Britain, and was central to the liberal challenge to eugenics in the 1912 parliamentary debates over the Mental Deficiency Bill.[20] Both Mill and Caird assert the primary role of ideas, and of those capable of formulating and developing new ideas. While their belief that thought determines action aligns them with Hegel rather than Marx, their distance from Marx should not be overstated. Individualism was not anathema to Marx—in *The German Ideology* he wrote that class 'achieves an independent existence over and against the individuals so that the latter find their conditions of existence predetermined, and hence have their position in life and their personal development assigned to them by their class, become subsumed under it'[21]—and should not be confused with the individualism of the Thatcher years a century later.[22] Education and

[20] Josiah Wedgwood, *The Parliamentary Debates* (House of Commons): *Official Report*, ser. 5, 38, cols. 1467–78.

[21] *The German Ideology* (Moscow, 1874) 60, cited in Graeme Duncan, *Marx and Mill: Two Views of Social Conflict and Social Harmony*, 121.

[22] For a useful account of different models of individualism—the competitive, the materialistic, and the psychological—as they developed in the course of the nineteenth century, see Regenia Gagnier, 'The Law of Progress and the Ironies of Individualism in the Nineteenth Century', *New Literary History*, 31 (2000), 315–36. For contemporary political

enlightened community were central to Mill's thought and he became, according to the new liberal L. T. Hobhouse (1864–1929), an exponent of liberal socialism.[23] Mill shared with Marx a deep commitment to autonomy, activity, true consciousness, and sociality.[24] By contrast, at the close of the nineteenth century, it was the hereditarians who were most vociferous in their denunciation of individualism: Grand, for one, speaking out in the *New York Times*, warned that 'civilization is threatened by the cant of individualism'. She saw ungraciousness, a lack of deference and of manners, as the mark of this individualism, noting that this was not a consequence of a want of altruism, and positing, rather, a 'crude contradiction' between 'our National sentiments, as expressed in our institutions, and our domestic manners'; remarking 'our charities are on a colossal scale. The amenities of civilized warfare are the outcome of our benevolence.'[25]

Mill's ideas on nature, society, and the individual had a formative influence on Caird's thinking, and his thesis—expounded in *The Subjection of Women*—that woman's nature had been artificially manufactured by an oppressive society, also permeates Caird's fiction and essays.[26] Caird opened her polemical article, 'Ideal Marriage', in the *Westminster Review*, with the following words from Mill's *On Liberty*: 'eccentricity has always abounded when and where strength of character has abounded. That so few now dare to be eccentric marks the chief

analysis of the individual and community, see Raymond Plant, *Politics, Theology and History* (Cambridge: Cambridge University Press, 2001), ch. 10. See also E. Fraser, *The Problems of Communitarian Politics* (Oxford: Oxford University Press, 1999); D. Phillips, *Looking Backward: A Critical Appraisal of Communitarian Thought* (Princeton University Press, 1993).

23 In his later years, as he became increasingly concerned by the parasitic relation of the minority upon the wage-earning majority, Mill looked forward to a co-operative organization of society in which 'a man would learn to "dig and weave for his country", as he now is prepared to fight for it, and in which the surplus products of industry would be distributed among the producers'. He recognized that these views ranked him, on the whole, with the Socialists, 'the brief exposition of the Socialist ideal given in his Autobiography remains perhaps the best summary statement of Liberal Socialism that we possess': Hobhouse, *Liberalism* (1911; in James Meadowcroft (ed.), *Liberalism and Other Writings* (Cambridge: Cambridge University Press, 1994), 55).

24 For an excellent comparative study of Marx and Mill, see Graeme Duncan, *Marx and Mill.*

25 'This is an Ungracious Age', *New York Times* (8 January 1905), 8, in Heilmann, *Sex, Social Purity and Sarah Grand*, i. 199.

26 See, for example, 'A Defence of the So-called "Wild Woman" ', *Morality*, 170, and Claudia's remark 'Woman's Nature's manufactured. I've seen it in the loom' (Mona Caird, *The Stones of Sacrifice* (London: Simpkin, Marshall, Hamilton, Kent & Co. Ltd, 1915), 37).

danger of the time.'[27] In *On Liberty*, which appeared in the same year as the *Origin*, Mill wrote: 'no one can be a great thinker who does not recognise that as a thinker it is his first duty to follow his intellect to whatever conclusions it may lead' (95); he continued: 'he who lets the world, or his own portion of it, choose his plan of life for him, has no need of any other faculty than the ape-like one of imitation . . . it is only the cultivation of individuality which produces, or can produce, well-developed human beings' (123, 128).[28] Mill saw that the opinion of the middle class held sway, and highlighted the dangers for society that this posed:

> at present individuals are lost in the crowd. In politics it is almost a triviality to say that public opinion now rules the world. Those whose opinions go by the name of public opinion are not always the same sort of public: in America, they are the whole white population; in England, chiefly the middle class. But they are always a mass, that is to say, collective mediocrity. (131)

Equally, he saw custom as a break on social development and progress, declaring

> It is not only persons of decided mental superiority who have a just claim to carry on their lives in their own way. There is no reason that all human existence should be constructed on some one or some small number of patterns. If a person possesses any tolerable amount of common sense and experience, his own mode of laying out his existence is the best, not because it is the best in itself, but because it is his own mode. Human beings are not like sheep; and even sheep are not indistinguishably alike . . . the despotism of custom is everywhere the standing hindrance to human advancement . . . if resistance waits till life is reduced nearly to one uniform type, all deviations from that type will come to be considered impious, immoral, even monstrous and contrary to nature. Mankind speedily become unable to conceive diversity, when they have been for some time unaccustomed to see it.[29]

Mill opened *On Liberty* with a quotation from *The Sphere and Duties of Government* (1854), by the German liberal political philosopher, Wilhelm von Humboldt: 'the grand, leading principle, towards which every government unfolded in these pages directly converges, is the

[27] John Stuart Mill, *On Liberty* (1859; Harmondsworth, Penguin, 1985), 132, cited in Caird, 'Ideal Marriage', *Westminster Review* reprinted as 'The Future of the Home', in *The Morality of Marriage*, 115.

[28] Hardy considered the chapter from which these quotations are taken, 'Of Individuality', to be a 'cure for despair': Florence Hardy [Thomas Hardy], *The Life of Thomas Hardy*, 2 vols. (1928–30; London: Studio Editions, 1994), i. 76.

[29] *On Liberty*, 132–3, 136.

absolute and essential importance of human development in its richest diversity'.[30] Darwin too would stress the importance of diversity for evolutionary development—a point not lost on Caird.

In 1913, shortly after the Mental Deficiency Act became law, Mona Caird delivered the presidential address to the Personal Rights Association, a rallying cry for the protection of individual freedom. The address entered circulation as a penny pamphlet.[31] The Personal Rights Association had been established in 1871 by Josephine Butler and other Contagious Diseases Acts repealers as the Vigilance Association for the Defence of Personal Rights and for the Amendment of the Law in Points wherein it is Injurious to Women, and was known (until the middle of the following decade) as the 'Vigilance Association'. It became increasingly resistant to Britain's central social purity organization, the National Vigilance Association (NVA), which had stolen its name. The National Vigilance Association established itself in support of the Criminal Law Amendment Act of 1885. In 1889 *The Personal Rights Journal* (founded in 1881 as the *Journal of the Vigilance Association for the Defence of Personal Rights*, with the slogan 'the price of liberty is eternal vigilance') dubbed the NVA 'vigilant stampers on the feeble' and questioned the nature of the 'protection' offered by the association, which 'cramm[ed] homeless and helpless girls into a hospital where surgical outrage . . . awaits them'.[32] In the liberal tradition of Mill, the Personal Rights Association held on to its goal, the resistance to encroachments upon individual liberty. Caird's impassioned speech to the society was dominated by an insistence on the need for collective resistance to the growth of state power. She declared that in protecting 'inalienable personal rights':

> we render increasingly possible all that makes life interesting, dramatic, and truly worth the living: all adventures of the human spirit. A vista of possibilities is thus opened which promises an enrichment in all relations of life, an enlargement of the range of consciousness, and therefore of progress, to which we can actually

[30] Humboldt was also author of *The Limits of State Action* (1791). Mill acknowledges his debt to Humboldt in his autobiography. According to the *Westminster Review, The Limits of State Action* 'ushered in a new era' in political theory (Richard Miniter, 'Wilhelm von Humboldt: German Classical Liberal', *The Freeman*, 41 (1991), 2). For further contemporary discussion of the relation of the state and the individual see Matthew Arnold's *Culture and Anarchy* (1869), esp. ch. 3.

[31] 'Personal Rights: A Personal Address delivered to the Forty-first Annual Meeting of the Personal Rights Association on 6th June 1913 by Mrs Mona Caird' (London: The Personal Rights Association, 1913).

[32] *Personal Rights Journal* (1889), 4.

set no limits. Compare this with the unspeakable boredom of the hurdy-gurdy existence of a State-dominated community! (10)

Caird decried the growing belief in 'the idea of *numbers*', an idea which 'enters largely into the popular idea of right and wrong—what I call arithmetical morality',[33] remarking 'the ancient idea of vicarious sacrifice is as rampant today as it was when the groves of ancient temples echoed with the cries of human victims, burnt on the altars, for the appeasement of the Gods and the good of the community' (4).[34] Caird warned that these ideas, underpinned by nationalist and racist ideologies, would lead logically and rapidly to eugenics. In *The Pathway of the Gods* (1898) Anna muses: 'after all, what did it matter what became of so paltry a creature as a mere individual? She tried always to bear in mind that it was not the individual, but the race that was of consequence.' In response, Julian 'made some scornful suggestions about a happy race composed of disconsolate individuals':

'The one must suffer for the many: it is the law of nature,' she said. 'It is thus that humanity progresses. . . . You are a perverse creature! But what is to be done, in one's hopelessness of any sort of result from one's own frustrated life, unless one's dreams can be transferred to the race? Ah, don't rob me of that, Julian, or what should I have left in the horrible loneliness?'[35]

Julian refuses her consolation: 'the individual is bullied to the suicidal point. Some day, perhaps, the race will cease to produce individuals differing sufficiently from the rest for the majority to call mad. Then woe to the majority!' (140). In *The Stones of Sacrifice*, the staunch eugenist Swainson Stubbs demonstrates the usefulness of sacrificing the individual to eugenic discourse: 'the Race, not the liberty of the unimportant unit, was what mattered' (154).

[33] 'Personal Rights', 4, emphasis in original. This utilitarian morality underpinned the politics of eugenics. See, for example Grand, 'Marriage Questions', *Fortnightly Review*, 63 (1898), 386. For a parody of these ideas, see, for example, Caird, *The Great Wave*: 'if we could but get rid of our clamorous *personal* demands . . . our yearning for happiness and companionship and love—old Schopenhauer and the Easterns saw that. If we could realize the end of our troubled dreams promised by the absorption into the One, the Great Unconscious' (511).

[34] In one version of the classical tale from which *The Daughters of Danaus* receives its name, all but one of Danaus's fifty daughters are punished (for killing their husbands on their wedding night) by being given the task of filling leaking jars with water. The punishment captures the sense of futile self-sacrifice that Caird saw applauded by contemporary emphasis on an abstract, impersonal, greater good: in the words of Hadria (472): 'women will go on patiently drawing water in sieves, and pretend they are usefully employed because it tires them!'

[35] Caird, *The Pathway of the Gods* (London: Skeffington and Son, 1898), 125–6.

In *The Great Wave*, the idea of self-sacrifice to the community is taken to its logical conclusion—war: '"All working together for good", the orthodox in religion and in science (in slightly different phraseology) piously insisted. It was God's (or Nature's) way of achieving the Great Purpose of the Ages' (503). 'My two sons have come back permanently crippled. So the war hasn't spared me. Yet I regard it from the point of view of the community', explains Dr Knowles (506).

In her speech on Personal Rights, Caird called into question the eugenist interpretation of charity (5–7). As discussed in Chapter 3, in the name of kindness to the race, eugenists were opposed to supporting the poor and vulnerable.[36] In 1894 in the *Westminster Review* Caird had spoken out on this point:

> there are, however, some who go even to this length: holding that we suffer from over-civilization, and that it is folly to protect the weak against the strong, since this policy confuses natural selection and enfeebles the race.[37]

The same year, in *The Daughters of Danaus*, Professor Fortescue makes the same point: 'it is not the protection of the weak, but the evil and stupid deeds that have made them so, that we have to thank for the miseries of disease.' The remedy he proposes is 'a more faithful holding together of all who are defenceless, a more faithful holding together among ourselves—weak and strong, favoured and luckless . . . the weak are not born, they are made' (104). The following year, Ménie Muriel Dowie's Gallia argued for the reverse, for 'making better people rather than people better'.[38]

Drawing to public attention misuses of the idea of community, Caird's personal rights speech culminated in a moving plea against eugenics:

> a recent medical proposal to dissect criminals alive in the interests of the Community—another collective-term fetish [which] reveals, in typical form, the line of sentiment (I can scarcely call it thought) against which we have to contend . . . Is it quite impossible to awaken the public to the awful and innumerable dangers which confront us all, as soon as the protection of personal

[36] See, in particular, Arnold White, *Problems of a Great City* (London: Remington, 1886; repr. New York, 1985), and *Efficiency and Empire* (London: 1901).

[37] 'Phases of Human Development', *Marriage*, 233. This idea underpinned Herbert Spencer's social theory; see, for example, *Social Statics; or, The Conditions Essential to Human Happiness Specified*. Windle in *The Great Wave*: 'stupid humanitarianism is interfering with natural selection. Preserving the unfit. Midsummer madness!' (232), and Waldheim's powerful demand for the elimination of weaker individuals (315).

[38] *Gallia* (1895; London, J. M. Dent, 1995), 113.

rights is withdrawn? . . . Can we not persuade our contemporaries to ask themselves if, for instance, the apostles of eugenics have shrunk from any measure, however outrageous, which they thought promised the desired results? Provided the end is gained, the individual must pay the price. It seems to be thought unworthy of him to object. Thus he is placed at the mercy of every wind and tide of popular opinion, or, what is worse, at the mercy of the views of experts who naturally tend to think all things lawful which benefit their particular branch of knowledge. If vaccination is approved of, vaccinated the individual must be. If science demands human vivisection, he must submit even to that outrage.[39]

Caird explained that her decision to take the chair on this occasion was in part owing to a lack of other willing candidates. Concerned by the collusion of her female compatriots with invasive forms of state control, including eugenics, she suggested that their unwillingness to speak out against encroachments upon freedom reflected an internalization of their own oppression, an argument which helps to explain the growth of eugenic feminism:

I felt moved to accept the honour on account of the scarcity of wholehearted champions, especially—I regret to hear—among the sex which has always been deprived of personal rights . . . Perhaps that is just why they *are* lacking in respect

[39] Cf. Grierson's protest in *The Great Wave*: 'our right even over our own bodies is denied us: compulsory inoculations, and heaven knows what fantastic rite of the medical priesthood . . . You were eloquently commenting on it yourself the other day. Never *submit*! At the bidding of what we are pleased to call Science, the public is increasingly ready to submit to anything under heaven—or hell, preferably hell!' (322). In 1853 the British state had made vaccination for smallpox compulsory for all children within the first year; a new, more stringent Vaccination Act was passed in 1867. See Dorothy Porter, *Health, Civilization and the State: A History of Public Health from Ancient to Modern Times* (London: Routledge, 1998), ch. 8. The compulsory inspection of prostitutes was the next step taken by the state in its attempt to control disease; the third was the Infectious Disease (Notification) Acts of 1889 and 1899 (Porter, 129). Mid-century advocates of 'state medicine', such as Dr Henry W. Rumsey (1809–76), Cheltenham doctor and author of *Essays in State Medicine* (1855) and Dr John Simon (1816–1904), lecturer in pathology at St Thomas's Hospital Medical School and president of the Metropolitan Association of Medical Officers of Health from its inception in 1855, argued that the right of the individual to contract, spread, and die of infectious disease was subordinate to the rights of the health of the community as a whole (Porter, *Health, Civilization and the State*, 129; see especially ch. 7). The Anti-Compulsory Vaccination League was founded in 1867 by, Richard Gibbs, with various Boards of Guardians refusing to implement the law on vaccination. In 1879 Gibbs's cousin, William Tebb, launched a journal, *The Vaccination Inquirer*, and founded the London Society for the Abolition of Compulsory Vaccination the following year. In 1896 Tebb amalgamated the provincial and London organizations into one National Anti-Vaccination League (see Roy Porter and Dorothy Porter, *In Sickness and In Health: The British Experience 1650-1850* (London: Fourth Estate 1988). On opposition to vivisection, see also Sarah Grand, *The Beth Book*. While Grand opposed this form of encroachment by science, she failed to see its connections with, and logical extension to, eugenics.

for them! And what a warning this is! The spirit of liberty, it would appear, can be starved to death . . . The career of women having depended not on right but on favour, they have learnt to care for an abstract idea which has no bearing on their lives. Only the exceptional mind cares for that. (3–4)[40]

In the *Westminster Review* Caird remarked there was 'doubtless an instinctive desire on the part of many women, who were brought up in the old faith, to prevent their sisters from moving beyond the lines that bounded female existence in the earlier half of the century'.[41] In positing this notion of the bullied bully, she resists the notion that women are innately moral, which had proliferated in the nineteenth century and would revive within some strands of feminist thinking in the late twentieth century.

NATURE AND HISTORY

From its inception in 1877 the *Nineteenth Century* was celebrated for its new and accessible style of writing, and, in encouraging genuine debate through symposia, it remained the most widely respected of the monthly reviews for the rest of the century.[42] The founder, James Knowles (co-founder, with Tennyson, of the Metaphysical Society in 1869), had previously—and briefly—edited the *Contemporary Review*, but had felt reined in by its religious constraints. The *Contemporary Review* rejected an article by Caird on evolution in marriage.[43] By contrast, the *Nineteenth*

[40] Caird also addresses this issue in 'The Lot of Woman under the Rule of Man', *The Morality of Marriage and Other Essays on the Status and Destiny of Women* (London: George Redway, 1897), 95, and in several of her novels, notably *The Daughters of Danaus* and *The Great Wave*.

[41] For this reason, Caird was particularly critical of Grand's fiction: see 'The Future of the Home', *Morality*, 118. In her fiction, Caird extended her observations on women's capacity to oppress others as well as themselves to the appeal of the masculine man to women. See *Daughters of Danaus*, 201, and *The Great Wave*, 358 for suffragette support for the sinister eugenist scientist Waldheim. Cf. Frances Swiney's argument, drawing on laws of sexual selection, that woman 'has perfected in man all the virile virtues, the best and fairest of womanhood having ever fallen a spoil to the conqueror during the reign of sheer force' (*The Awakening of Women; or, Woman's Part in Evolution* (London: William Reeves, 1899), 72).

[42] Robert M. Young, *Darwin's Metaphor: Nature's Place in Victorian Culture* (Cambridge: Cambridge University Press, 1985), 160.

[43] In 1890, and even with a positive—and placatory—recommendation from Caird's friend and advocate Thomas Hardy ('my impression', he had reassured the editor Percy Bunting, 'is that there is nothing heterodox in it: & you will find her amenable to reasonable suggestions'), the *Contemporary* declined to publish the piece. Thomas Hardy to Percy Bunting, editor of the *Contemporary Review* (13 January 1990), *The Collected Letters of Thomas Hardy*, ed. by Richard Little Purdy and Michael Millgate (Clarendon Press: Oxford, 1978–88), i. 207–8.

Century, with its penchant for fiery debate, was delighted to publicize Caird's work, balancing it alongside such pieces as 'The Wild Women as Politicians', an attack by the patriarchal journalist Eliza Lynn Linton upon progressive feminists.[44] Like the older *Fortnightly*, it expressed a Hegelian commitment to 'the natural emergence of truth by free expression and interplay of as many points of view as possible', privileging rationalism, and foregrounding evidence.[45] Seeking to maintain freedom from political affiliation, it soon outstripped the *Fortnightly* in terms of both sales and progressive reputation, and made waves in popularizing science, carrying accessible pieces by eminent and polemical thinkers such as Thomas Huxley. In 1892 it published Caird's infamous essay 'A Defence of the So-called "Wild Woman" ' in which she entered into battle with Eliza Lynn Linton, warning that science was being used to bolster rather than question outmoded, and barbaric, notions of nature, declaring contemporary 'worship of "Nature" ' to be 'a strange survival in a scientific age of the old image-worship of our ancestors . . . this is a subtle form of superstition which has cunningly nestled among the folds of the garment of Science'.[46] 'Nature', as popularly understood, was no more than the projection onto the external world of primal prejudices and laws 'unmodified by human intelligence or moral development'; it is not, she urged, 'our master but our slave, having no mercy for those who yield themselves to her dominion'.[47] Again, in the *Westminster Review*, in 'Phases of Human Development', Caird exposed ways in which the pliable concept of nature was used to justify barbaric social practices. The main thrust of her argument, which bears a close relation to the position Huxley took in *Evolution and Ethics*, also published in 1894, is that to avoid degeneracy society and the state must depart from nature. Huxley pointed out that one function of the gardener was to create conditions more favourable than those of the state of nature.[48] Caird asserted:

[44] *Nineteenth Century*, 30 (1891), 79–88. See also 'The Wild Women as Social Insurgents', *Nineteenth Century*, 30 (1891), 596–605; and 'The Partisans of the Wild Women', *Nineteenth Century*, 31 (1892), 454–64.

[45] D. A. Hamer, *John Morley: Liberal Intellectual in Politics* (Oxford: Clarendon Press, 1968), 73–4. On the treatment of science in the periodical press see Louise Henson, Geoffrey Cantor, Gowan Dawson, Richard Noakes, Salley Shuttleworth, and Jonathan R. Topham (eds.), *Culture and Science in the Nineteenth-Century Media* (Aldershot: Ashgate, 2003).

[46] 'A Defence of the So-called "Wild Women" ', 175. The article offers a sustained exposition of the social construction of both 'nature' and the 'nature' of women.

[47] 'Phases of Human Development', *Morality*, 231, 232.

[48] T. H. Huxley, *Evolution and Ethics*, ed. by James Paradis and George C. Williams (1893; Princeton, NJ: Princeton University Press, 1989), 72.

[man] indolently justifies the cruelties of life,—the torture of the weak by the strong, the rule of man over woman, the oppression of animals by mankind,—by the authority of Nature. It does not disturb him that the existence of the State, as such, depends upon a *departure* from Nature. Throughout the universe, he urges, the same eternal law holds sway; let not the weak, above all let not women, seek to evade it. But that is exactly what every progressive being *has* to do, if he wishes to avoid degeneration . . . In opposition to the widely-accepted theory that whatever is natural is always right, it would be almost safe to assert, that whatever is natural is certain to be wrong. It is unquestionably by becoming less and less 'natural' that the human being becomes more and more tolerable. It is by presenting to the imagination, a new method of diverging from the tame and barren wastes of 'Nature' unredeemed, that a new step of progress is begun.[49]

In an essay, 'On Nature' (1854), which forms part of his *Nature, The Utility of Religion and Theism*, Mill negotiates a midway path between the need to control, and, alternatively, emulate nature, concluding that 'the duty of man is to cooperate with the beneficent powers, not by imitating, but by perpetually striving to amend, the course of nature—and bringing that part of it over which we can exercise control more nearly into conformity with a high standard of justice and goodness'. In this essay Mill consistently exposes the social and economic concerns which underpin discourses on the natural. His argument was that society should depart from nature, which was, in any case, largely an artificial construct, and he noted that for the most part even those who sought to oppose nature, or intervene in its course:

rather endeavour to show that they have as much right to the religious argument as their opponents, and that, if the course they recommend seems to conflict with some part of the ways of Providence, there is some other part with which it agrees better than what is contended for on the other side. (16)

He stressed:

There is a sphere of action in which society, as distinguished from the individual, has, if any, only an indirect interest; comprehending all that portion of a person's life and conduct which affects only himself, or if it also affects others, only with their free, voluntary, and undeceived consent and participation.[50]

Caird shared Mill's view that the state was a necessary departure from the state of nature[51] and opposed the right of the state to interfere in the life of an individual unless the individual had impinged on another's

[49] 'Phases of Human Development', 232. Emphasis in original.
[50] *On Liberty*, 80.
[51] See 'The Human Element in Man', *Morality*, 232.

freedom. Her prose and fiction are permeated with Mill's ideas on liberty, but she is equally aware of the political importance of collective action: 'a conquering race, if it is wise, governs its subjects largely through their internecine squabbles and jealousies. *But what if they combine?*', asks Algitha in *The Daughters of Danaus* (473).

Like Mill and Darwin, Caird historicizes nature. In *Whom Nature Leadeth* (1883), Leonore positions nature within a temporal continuum: 'Nature not only as she seems at this moment, but as she has been, is, and may be.' At the heart of the novel lies the idea that patterns of existence might be changed—and within a single lifetime—and that what was considered to be nature was more often than not merely a matter of habit: 'alter the balance of your nature; overcome the force of unopposed instinct, and thus change the very nature of Nature'. [52] This idea was crucial to the resistance to biological determinism: 'all history proves that society is in a state of perpetual motion, and that there is, perhaps, no set of ideas so fundamental that human beings have not somewhere, at some period in the world, lived in direct contradiction to them'.[53] It was also central to Mill's philosophy, which offered a sustained challenge to the idea that existing human nature, and existing relations, were universal and inevitable. In *Auguste Comte and Positivism* (1865), he wrote:

> The principal error of narrowness with which they are frequently chargeable, is that of regarding not any economical doctrine, but their present experience of mankind, as of universal validity; mistaking temporary or local phases of human character for human nature itself; having no faith in the wonderful pliability of the human mind; deeming it impossible, in spite of the strongest evidence, that the earth can produce human beings of a different type from that which is familiar to them in their own age, or even, perhaps, in their own country.[54]

In the *Westminster Review*, Caird drew on these ideas in her challenge to racial thinking. She underscored the determining influence of the environment, and the negligible influence of biology: for Caird 'the race' was not a fixed biological category but a fluid social grouping: 'the race, therefore, even more than the individual, is clay in the hands of the potter: Circumstance';[55] 'we must on no account admit . . . local "human

[52] Caird, *Whom Nature Leadeth* (London: Longmans, Green), 294, 293.

[53] *North American Review*, 150 (1890), 692–705, and 151 (1890), 22–37, repr. in *Morality*, 23.

[54] Mill, *Auguste Comte and Positivism* (1865; Ann Arbor: University of Michigan Press, 1961), 82–3.

[55] 'Suppression of Variant Types', in 'Phases of Human Development', *Westminster Review* (Jan. 1894), 141, 162–79, repr. in *Morality*, 196.

nature" as a constant factor, but must regard it as a mere register of the forces that chance to be at work at the moment, and of the forces that have been at work in the past. Different centuries produce different types of humanity, though born of the same race.'[56]

BIOLOGY AND THE INDIVIDUAL

Darwin had acknowledged the crucial importance of the individual in the process of evolution, writing in his chapter on variation and nature in the *Origin*: 'individual differences are highly important for us, as they afford materials for natural selection to accumulate'.[57] Individual difference was the risk on which evolutionary development was predicated; the individual might die as a result of its difference, or bring about a new direction, a new variety, or, ultimately, species.

As part of her anti-eugenic feminist project, Caird drew on both Darwinian and Lamarckian ideas, following their emphasis on the importance of environmental factors in producing evolutionary change, and taking up Lamarck's theory of 'use-inheritance'. In doing so, she co-opted evolutionary biology into an alternative narrative which did not give to women the role of policing society as evolution's 'consciousness', but which demonstrated that they themselves were subject to evolutionary change, and that their functions and uses might be modified in such a way as to reduce the imperative of the maternal role. Likewise, she challenged the idea that women were destined for evolutionary stasis, an idea which was prevalent in hereditarian discourse. She wrote in *The Daughters of Danaus*: 'women are the wild rice of the modern philosophical world. They are treated as if they alone were exempt from the influences of natural selection, of the well-known effects upon organs and aptitudes of continued use or disuse.'[58] And, in 'A Defence of the So-called "Wild Woman" ', she observed that if modern women really were 'insurgents against evolutionary human nature, instead of being the indications of a new social development, then their fatal error will assuredly prove itself in a very short time'.[59] Returning to Mill's warning against the growing tendency of the nineteenth century to suppress individual difference, she warned in the *Westminster Review* 'the present

[56] 'Suppression of Variant Types', in 'Phases of Human Development', 197–8.
[57] *Origin* (1996 edn.), 39.
[58] 'Marriage', *Morality*, 63.
[59] 'A Defence of the So-called "Wild Woman" ', *Morality*, 169.

organisation of society is not conducive to race progress: unusual natures, when they *did* appear, would be likely to be destroyed or neutralised'.[60]

Lamarckism gave the environment a leading role in the evolutionary drama. For Caleb William Saleeby it was the greatest bugbear of the eugenists: 'the advocates of eugenics or race-culture have to recognise that, so long as the Lamarckian idea obtains, their crusade will fail to find a hearing'.[61] Lamarckism persisted in promoting education and social reform as the solution to the problem of national decline. It lies at the core of *The Daughters of Danaus*. Mrs Fullerton sees 'her lost aptitudes', acquired in her own life, but fallen into disuse, resurface in the next generation: 'the buried impulses had broken out, like a half-smothered flame, in her children, especially in her younger daughter. Singularly enough, the mother regarded these qualities, partly inherited from herself, as erratic and annoying' (33).[62] Early on the reader learns that 'Mrs Fullerton showed signs of incomplete development. The shape of the head and brow promised many faculties that the expression of the face did not encourage one to expect' (32). Mrs Fullerton is degenerating: 'a few volumes of poetry, and other works of imagination, bore testimony to the lost sides of her nature' (33). Her nervous system is wrecked, 'not by one shock or event, but by the accumulated strains of a lifetime. The constitution was broken up, once and for all' (366). Hadria realizes now, 'with agonising vividness, the sadness of her mother's life, the long stagnation, the slow decay of disused faculties, and the ache that accompanies

[60] 'Phases', 202, emphasis in original. Caird uses the term genius to denote the ability to resist the pull of convention. For discussion of genius in relation to women and late nineteenth-century fiction, see Penny Boumelha, 'The Woman of Genius and the Woman of Grub Street: Figures of the Female Writer in British *Fin de Siècle* Fiction', *English Literature in Transition*, 40 (1997), 164–80.

[61] *Parenthood and Race Culture*, 134.

[62] In his detailed (and incredulous) account of the contemporary belief in the transmission of acquired characteristics, Strahan rejects the theory that germ cells can 'lie apart, dormant and unimpressionable' within a human until it reaches the procreative period when 'they wake up and are ready to be passed on to the next generation, there to light up life' (*Marriage and Disease, A Study of Heredity and the More Important Family Degenerations* (London: Kegan Paul, Trench, Trübner, & Co. Ltd, 1892), 35). As Peter Bowler points out, as part of the elimination of teleology 'vestigial organs had to be those that had once been of some use but which now were degenerating because they served no purpose and were a waste of energy for the organism to produce'. Bowler notes that Darwin 'was prepared to consider that the degeneration might be produced by the inherited effects of disuse, because he always admitted that Lamarckism might play a subordinate role in evolution' (Bowler, *Evolution, The History of an Idea* (1983; Berkeley and Los Angeles: University of California Press, 1989), 178).

all processes of decay, physical or moral' (362).[63] Hadria suffers a similar decline to her mother, falling victim to Lamarckian disuse: 'the neglected gift was beginning to show signs of decay and enfeeblement. It had given fair warning for many a year, by the persistent appeal that it made' (477). It is their surroundings, not their constitutions, which must bear responsibility for the decline of Hadria and Mrs Fullerton.

One of the most persuasive exponents of Lamarckism in the late nineteenth century was the Russian anarchist and evolutionary sociologist Prince Peter Kropotkin, to whom Caird refers directly in *The Great Wave*. Kropotkin argued that characteristics developed successfully in a group of animals could be passed on in the successive generation and intensified in later generations. In his essays in the *Nineteenth Century*, collected in *Mutual Aid* (1902), he argued that Lamarck had been unjustly passed over in the matter of the direct effect of environment on the development of plans and animals, and that adaptation provided relief from competition, remarking:

each species is continually tending to enlarge its abode . . . as Wallace himself shows . . . in forming new habits, moving to new abodes, and taking to new sorts of food. In all such cases there will be no extermination, even no competition—the new adaptation being a relief from competition, if it ever existed; and yet there will be, after a time, an absence of intermediate links, in consequence of a mere survival of those which are best fitted for the new conditions—as surely as under the hypothesis of extermination of the parental form. It hardly need be added that if we admit, with Spencer, all the Lamarckians, and Darwin himself, the modifying influence of the surroundings upon the species, there remains still less necessity for the extermination of the intermediate forms.[64]

[63] Cf. Caird's criticism of the woman who 'voluntarily permits herself—a unit of society—to degenerate in mind or body'; degeneration was the result of 'self-immolation' ('Children of the Future', *Morality*, 156).

[64] *Mutual Aid: A Factor of Evolution* (1902; London: Freedom Press, 1998), 66. Kropotkin refers here to Darwin's frequent mention in the *Origin* of 'the extermination of transitional varieties' (paragraph on 'extinction', *Origin*, 1996 edn., 90–1). He notes that Darwin is deploying the term 'extermination' metaphorically (*Origin*, 1996 edn., 53) and that, 'with his usual fairness' Darwin was able to admit that 'probably in no case could we precisely say why one species has been victorious over another in the great battle of life' (*Origin*, 1996 edn., 64). Kropotkin notes that while in an area stocked with animals to its fullest capacity, the appearance of new varieties would mean in many cases the appearance of individuals able to seize more than their fair share of the means of existence, and starve both the parental form and those intermediate forms which do not possess it in the same degree, both Darwin and Wallace 'knew nature too well not to perceive that this is by no means the only possible and necessary course of affairs' (*Mutual Aid*, 64–6). Kropotkin's ideas of co-operation might be seen as an early version of what would now be called 'group selection'—an idea which challenges the argument that natural selection works against the production of any instinct that would lead an individual to sacrifice their own good for

Kropotkin argued co-operation was just as necessary to the evolutionary scheme as struggle.[65] Although Caird departed from his view that a basis for morality was to be found in nature, sharing Huxley's belief that a humane society would necessarily depart from nature,[66] she concurred with Kropotkin, and Huxley, in opposing the idea of the 'survival of the

that of others (see Richard Dawkins, *The Selfish Gene* (London: Oxford University Press, 1976); and *The Extended Phenotype: The Gene as the Unit of Selection* (Oxford: Freeman, 1982). For further discussion of these ideas see V. C. Wynne-Edwards, *Animal Dispersion in Relation to Social Behaviour* (Edinburgh: Oliver and Boyd, 1962); G. C. Williams, *Adaptation and Natural Selection* (Princeton: Princeton University Press, 1966); S. A. Boorman and P. R. Levitt, *The Genetics of Altruism* (New York: Academic Press, 1980); N. Eldredge, *Reinventing Darwin: The Great Evolutionary Debate* (London: Weidenfeld and Nicolson, 1995); and Alexander J. Field, *Altruistically Inclined? The Behavioral Sciences, Evolutionary Theory, and the Origins of Reciprocity* (Ann Arbor: The University of Michigan Press, 2001). As Peter Bowler notes (*Evolution*, 235; see also 329), Darwin himself had drawn upon the idea of group selection, appealing to an idea which Alfred Wallace had first suggested, which held that in animals where the parent must care for the young, the family group will become important and selection may well favour the instinct to defend that group. See *Descent*, i. 97 and 165, where Darwin draws on Wallace's *Contributions to the Theory of Natural Selection* (1870). Darwin concludes that 'there can be no doubt that a tribe including many members who, from possessing in a high degree the spirit of patriotism, fidelity, obedience, courage, and sympathy, were always ready to give aid to each other and to sacrifice themselves for the common good, would be victorious over most other tribes; and this would be natural selection. At all times throughout the world tribes have supplanted other tribes; and as morality is one element in their success, the standard of morality and the number of well-endowed men will thus everywhere tend to rise and increase' (i. 166). However, the difficulty of identifying genuinely altruistic behaviour, coupled with the fact that group selection can always be undermined by individual selection, has proved problematic for exponents of group selection (see Bowler, *Evolution*, 329). Bowler notes that Lamarckism ensured that Kropotkin's theory of co-operation would not degenerate into a version of Social Darwinism in which successful groups eliminated those with a lesser degree of co-operation in the struggle for existence (*Evolution*, 228).

65 For other exponents of co-operation rather than struggle, see the vitalists who believed, with Henri Bergson, in supremacy of a creative Vital Spirit, a quality of insurgence inherent in every particle of life. See David E. Allen, *The Naturalist in Britain: A Social History* (1976; Princeton NJ: Princeton University Press, 1994) 180–1. See also Ruskin's *Modern Painters* (London: Smith Elder; 1851–60) v (1860).

66 Huxley argued that nature was not to be looked to for a system of ethics, and that far from being a model to emulate, or assist, nature was to be combated, just as instincts and unconscious impulses were to be interrogated and resisted. See 'The Struggle for Existence: A Programme', in the *Nineteenth Century*, 23 (February 1888) 161–80, republished as 'The Struggle for Existence in Human Society', in Huxley, *Collected Essays*, 9 vols. (London: Macmillan, 1893–4), 199–200. See also *Evolution and Ethics* (1894). On the question of morality and nature, Kropotkin and Huxley were to reach loggerheads in the periodical press, with Kropotkin responding to Huxley's views through eight articles in the *Nineteenth Century* between 1890 and 1896, and positing collaboration as a universal adaptive strategy; these articles were collected and published in 1902 as *Mutual Aid: A Factor of Evolution*. In the first, he refuted Huxley's view of nature as a scientific deduction ('Mutual Aid Among Animals', *Mutual Aid*, 23).

fittest'. In *Ethics: Origin and Development*, Kropotkin objected to Spencer's exclusive focus on the competitive elements of nature, arguing that Spencer saw in the 'struggle for existence' only the *extermination* of the non-adapted, whereas its principal feature should be seen in the survival of those who adapt themselves to the changing conditions of life. He urged that 'anyone who will attentively observe the actual life of animals (as was done, for example, by Brehm, whom Darwin rightly called a great naturalist) will see what a vast part is played by *sociality in the struggle for existence*.'[67]

Within biological discourse the boundary between the individual and environment raised complex issues. In her article in the *Westminster Review*, 'The Power of Heredity', the hereditarian and New Woman novelist Isabella Ford drew on the work of Dr Harry Campbell, author of *Differences in the Nervous Organism of Man and Woman, Physiological and Pathological* (1891). In 'Marriage of the Unfit: What is Life?' Campbell observed:

> Life is an interaction between the individual and his environment, therefore disease is an abnormal interaction between the two. It proves that you cannot possibly eliminate the part played by the individual from the causation of any disease, since it is his structure which determines whether he shall or shall not react abnormally to a given environment. Now his structure is essentially determined by heredity.[68]

In this passage the relation between the organism and the environment is not one of dialogue, of interaction, but of *reaction* on the part of the organism. Likewise, Clapperton defined health as 'the consequence and evidence of a successful adaptation to the conditions of existence'; it 'implied the preservation, well-being and development of the organism; while disease marks a failure in organic adaptation to external conditions, and leads to disorder, decay and death.'[69] In keeping with hereditarian policy, both these arguments laid the blame for disease on the individual; it is a defective organism that is to blame for ill-health. In the *Origin*, Darwin had emphasized the profound reciprocity between organism and environment. Equally, the theorist of degeneration Ray Lankester defined degeneration as 'a gradual change of structure by

[67] Peter Kropotkin, *Ethics, Origin and Development*, ed. by George Woodcock, trans. by Louis S. Friedland and Joseph R. Piroshnikoff (1922; Montreal and New York: Black Rose Books, 1992), 320–1, emphasis in original. The manuscript was incomplete at Kropotkin's death in 1921, see George Woodcock, introduction, p. x.

[68] Cited in Ford, 'The Power of Heredity', *Westminster Review*, 151 (1899), 543.

[69] *A Vision of the Future*, 116–17.

which the organism becomes adapted to less varied and less complex conditions of life'.[70] Hereditarian discourses were moving away from Darwin, and increasingly underplayed environmental factors, coming to focus on the biology and biological history of the individual. Caird sought to reverse this trend, arguing that degeneration was not a biological but a social or *environmental* disease, and substituting for 'race-regeneration' the idea of social regeneration.[71] While her hereditarian opponents had biologized the social, Caird deftly returns the biological to the social, calling into question the analogies between society and biology which Herbert Spencer had popularized:

> I utterly disbelieve in the facile and misleading analogy of the 'social *organism*'. Societies do indeed change, but they do *not* go through an exactly-repeated series of stages after the fashion of 'organisms'. It is quite unproved that there is any inherent 'principle of decay.' What, in fact, *is* a principle of decay?[72]

In her 1888 article on marriage in the *Westminster Review*, Caird went as far as to claim that marriage in its present form was 'a melancholy instance of this communal form of degeneration'; 'in undermining marriage we are contemplating a stupendous step of racial progress'.[73] In limiting women's activities to motherhood, society had 'deprived children of the benefits of possessing really *efficient* mothers'.[74] In a later essay in the *Fortnightly Review*, she again engaged head-on with eugenic feminism, and its advocacy of 'perpetual renunciation for a race that never comes'; she opens with a quotation from Jane Hume Clapperton on the 'Humanity of the Future', and attacks the privileging of the unborn; of 'children of the future' (*Morality*, 150). Two years later she

[70] Quoted in Eugene S. Talbot, *Degeneracy, its Causes, Signs and Results* (London: Walter Scott Ltd, 1898), 14.

[71] Introduction to *Morality*, 17. Caird took issue with Nordau's conception of degeneration as 'a morbid deviation from an original type' (*Degeneration*, 16). Nordau quotes Morel, *Traité des Dégénéresences* (Paris, 1857), 5, arguing that the term might be employed more accurately in describing his support for vivisection. For Cairdr, Nordau bore 'the truly degenerate self-contradictory "sign of degeneracy" in his simultaneous condemnation of the immorality of his day, and his own lack of compassion'. For further examples of Caird's redefining of degeneration and progress along social lines, see 'Early History of the Family', *Morality*, 35.

[72] 'Personal Rights', 11, emphasis in original.

[73] 'Marriage', *Morality*, 105, 111.

[74] 'Phases of Human Development', *Morality*, 180. Annette Meakin made the same argument in *Woman in Transition* (London: Methuen, 1907), see esp. 41–2, 83, 86. Attacking Saleeby's virulent pronatalism, Meakin cited Col. Higginson: 'children are not the sole evidence of service rendered to the State': ' "the very fact," he remarks, "that during one half of the years of a woman's average life, she is made incapable of child-bearing, show that there are, even for the most prolific and devoted mothers, duties other than the maternal" ' (83).

pointed out that the rights of the present race were 'at least as great as those of the coming one'.[75]

Caird emphasized that the environment was a genuinely *interactive* force—'the chemical union of native bias with daily circumstance which has for product a human character'.[76] Thus, the line between individual and environment is blurred, complicating issues of responsibility in relation to poverty and disease. If the environment had a significant part to play, then the division of the poor into the deserving and undeserving was facile and redundant, and the idea of eugenics fundamentally flawed.

VARIATION

The incessant construction of variety for survival is deterministic, but determined, itself, by chance. Darwin placed variation at the centre of his account of the origin, and preservation, of species:

> owing to [the] struggle for life, any variation, however slight and from whatever cause proceeding, if it be in any degree profitable to an individual of any species, in its infinitely complex relations to other organic beings and to external nature, will tend to the preservation of that individual, and will generally be inherited by its offspring.[77]

In fact, natural selection amounted to the preservation of these slight variations.[78] Darwin wrote conclusively in *Variation of Plants and Animals under Domestication* (1868):

> no shadow of reason can be assigned for the belief that variations, alike in nature and the result of the same general laws, which have been the groundwork

[75] 'A Defence of the So-called "Wild Woman" ', *Nineteenth Century*, 31 (1892), 811–29; repr. in *The Morality of Marriage*, 183. Cf. Henrietta Muller, 'The Future of Single Women', *Westminster Review*, 65 (1884). In this article, sparked by Caird's *Whom Nature Leadeth*, Muller praises Caird for making unconditional claims on behalf of women, and for not prescribing that they, first and foremost, 'be wives, mothers, homekeepers' (151). Taking the definition of progress of Karl Ernst Von Baer, founder of embryology, Muller proceeded to argue that, on the premiss that organic and social progress were contingent on 'increasing differentiation and specialization of the several parts of the same being', women would cease to be one group with one function but divide into a number of specialized subsections (152). Muller also takes issue with Pearson's essay 'What Woman is Fitted For', *Westminster Review*, 127 (1887), 64–75.

[76] 'Phases of Human Development', *Morality*, 203.

[77] *Origin*, 115. For a discussion of the complexities of variation, see George Romanes, 'Recent Critics of Darwinism', *Contemporary Review*, 53 (1888), 836–54.

[78] *Origin*, 115.

through natural selection of the formation of the most perfectly adapted animals in the world, man included, were intentionally and specially guided. However much we may wish it, we can hardly follow Professor Asa Gray in his belief that 'variation has been led along certain beneficial lines', like a stream 'along definite and useful lines of irrigation'.[79]

In the *Origin*, Darwin had examined the influence of changing living conditions, and while he considered the direct effect of differences in climate, food, etc., to be slim, he argued that these differences affected the reproductive system, thus inducing variation in offspring.[80] Eugenists denied the effects of environmental change in producing variation, focusing on biological endowment, placing responsibility, again, on the individual and his or her family history—redefining as a science what had in past centuries been an aristocratic fallacy. While eugenists, notably Galton, accepted that evolutionary development was predicated on variation, they were uncomfortable with its chancy and unexpected nature. Variation posed a threat to their rational schemes. Where did it come from? The haphazard nature of biological development could, they argued, be offset by artificial sexual selection, which would tame variation.[81] Eugenic thought required that causes and origins were easily identifiable—while Darwin had thought they were infinitely perplexing, and unknowable.

The search for origins becomes, in itself, a theme, in *The Daughters of Danaus*. Valeria du Prel ponders of Hadria:

where *did* you come from? There appeared to be more here than mere heredity could account for. But science had never solved this problem; originality seemed always to enter upon its career, uncaused and unaccountable.[82]

[79] *Variation of Plants and Animals under Domestication*, ii. 428, quoted in Romanes, 'Recent Critics of Darwinism', 851. Romanes directed readers 'specially interested in this subject to a correspondence upon it between the late Professor Asa Gray and myself in the pages of *Nature*, extending from 25 January to 31 May, 1883'.

[80] *Origin*, 108–10.

[81] S. A. K. Strahan, author of the eugenic treatise *Marriage and Disease*, sought to circumvent this by arguing that variation, more often than not, was regression: *Marriage and Disease*, 24–7. Cf. Darwin on reversion in the *Origin*—he records, but does not endorse, the following principle: 'after twelve generations, the proportion of blood, to use a common expression, of any one ancestor, is only 1 in 2048; and yet, as we see, it is generally believed that a tendency to reversion is retained by this very small proportion of foreign blood'. In explaining the apparent resurgence of characteristics, he emphasized the influence of environmental factors over remote ancestors: 'in each successive generation there had been a tendency to reproduce the character in question, which at last, *under unknown favourable conditions*, gains an ascendancy' (196, emphasis added).

[82] *The Daughters of Danaus*, 58.

At the core of *The Daughters of Danaus* lie the vagaries of heredity. Inheritance is almost impossible to predict or explain. The differences between the four Fullerton children housed under one roof are testimony to this—'if it were not that one is born with feelings and energies and ambitions of one's own, parents might treat one as a showman treats his marionettes' (38). The reader learns that 'each member of the Fullerton family had unusual ability of some kind'. It is conceded that 'heredity might have some discoverable part in the apparent marvel', but that part is neither clear nor certain (59). The more complex heredity was, the less useful it was to the eugenists. For the anti-eugenist Professor Fortescue, heredity is not incompatible with choice: 'only after the decision had been made did heredity fix it' (102). He advises Hadria: 'you have peculiar advantages of a hereditary kind, if only you can get a reasonable chance to use them'. Heredity is of no use by itself; its energy potential needs to be unlocked by the environment; but it is inherently unpredictable: 'heredity asserted itself, as it will do, in the midst of the fray, just when its victim seems to have shaken himself free from the mysterious obsession' (260).[83] Heredity could not be counted on.

This was the same line of resistance pursued by G.K. Chesterton. In *Eugenics and Other Evils: An Argument Against the Scientifically Organized State*, his crusading protest against eugenics, which he completed in 1913, he wrote:

> even simple heredity can never be simple; its complexity must be literally unfathomable, for in that field fight unthinkable millions. But yet again it never is simple heredity: for the instant anyone is, he experiences . . . To summarise: you know there is wine in the soup. You do not know how many wines there are in the soup, because you do not know how many wines there are in the world. And you never will know, because all chemists, all cooks, and all common-sense people tell you that the soup is of such a sort that it can never be chemically analysed. That is a perfectly fair parallel to the hereditary element in the human soul.[84]

[83] Cf. Clapperton's *Vision of the Future*, Part II, which has as its epigraph: 'the laws of heredity constitute the most important agency whereby the vital forces, the vigour and soundness of the physical system are changed for better or worse' (77).

[84] *Eugenics and Other Evils: An Argument Against the Scientifically Organized State*, ed. by Micheal W. Perry (1922; Seattle: Inkling, 2000), 52–3. For Chesterton on H. G. Wells and eugenics, and on Wells's point, in *Mankind in the Making*, that the inheritance of health is not easy to predict, because health is not a quality, but a relation, a balance, see *Eugenics and Other Evils*, 54. While Wells allows education more influence in *The Work, The Wealth and Happiness of Mankind* (1931), he still favours isolating and sterilizing the unfit.

Chesterton concluded the discussion 'the Eugenist has to settle, not the result of fixing one steady thing to a second steady thing; but what will happen when one toppling and dizzy equilibrium crashes into another'.[85] In *The Daughters of Danaus*, the Fullerton children are defeated not by heredity but by environment, by their circumstances.[86] In *The Great Wave* de Mollyns declares 'people talk a lot of nonsense about heredity, I maintain it's environment that eventually makes heredity' (43).

Caird was thoroughly versed in Darwin's original ideas, which were far more flexible and accommodating than his hereditarian followers would allow. Caird educated her readers in the complex process of variation as Darwin himself had documented it, repeatedly affirming the importance of chance.[87] She argued that social progress is dependent upon *chance* variation, not artificial selection:

> we have already seen that the health of society depends upon its power of production of variations in the type; the decline of certain races being the result of a failure of this faculty, or the fruits of an organisation which suppresses their development and influence.[88]

In this way, Caird engaged with late nineteenth-century obsession with health, but revealed the social prejudices fuelling the obsession.

Through her fiction and politics, Caird examines the ways in which privileged social groups were using the concepts of health and disease both to construct versions of normality and, in doing so, to exclude those they found it profitable to exclude. She concluded that present codes of morality and living conditions were anything but conducive to health—a conclusion she knew would resonate with contemporary readers:

> strict marriage, prostitution, the cultus of external sanctions, irrespective of spiritual facts; commercialism and competition in the most exaggerated forms, the subjection of women, with their consequent purchase by men, under differing names and conditions throughout society; and finally, the (also consequent) dual moral standard for the two sexes . . . from elements such as these it is morally impossible to produce a healthy society.[89]

85 Chesterton, *Eugenics and Other Evils*, 55.

86 On the overriding emphasis the novel places on the environment, see *The Daughters of Danaus*, 36 and 59. Contrast Ledger who argues that biological determinism ultimately triumphs in this novel: *The New Woman: Fiction and Feminism at the Fin de Siècle* (Manchester: Manchester University Press, 1997), 28.

87 *Origin* (1996 edn.), 52, 108.

88 'Phases of Human Development', *Westminster Review*, 141 (1894), 37–51; 162–79; repr. in *The Morality of Marriage*, 210.

89 'Marriage Before and After the Reformation', *Morality*, 91.

Positioning Mill's ideas on individual liberty in a biological context, she demonstrated that the present arrangement of society would lead, inevitably, to evolutionary degeneration: 'the conditions of life for women have been a national disaster; for no race can afford to risk the results of such paralysing uniformity'. 'The subjection of women', she noted, 'whether it be complete and logical, as in the East, or modified and irrational, as among ourselves, is like a vast machine carefully constructed to stamp out and mangle smooth all varieties and all superiorities in the race.'[90] Society would have to be radically re-organized if it were to remain in existence: in a race where 'half its numbers are placed in similar conditions, trained in the same fashion', the chances of variation, crucial to survival must 'evidently be few'.[91] She returned to the subject in her address to the Personal Rights Association:

> We shall find ourselves in the current of an evolution backwards to the savage state, in which the individual is very like that foolish and much over-rated insect, the bee, hopelessly submerged in the social hive. As the strata of what I call Hive-heredity accumulate, there is always a deeper and deeper soil of Hive-instinct out of which each new generation has to spring. Is it not progressively unlikely, therefore, that 'sports' would appear? And if they did appear, at lengthening intervals, would they not be handicapped by a strong Herd-instinct, impregnably seated in that reservoir of inborn impulse that we now call the 'subconscious'? (9)[92]

Drawing together the ideas of Mill and Darwin, Caird offers a compelling challenge to biological determinism:

> If Society is obsessed by a crude and unproved theory of heredity, how are we to resist interference with our marriages, or being treated as hysterical, or feeble-minded, or degenerate, or insane? Genius and originality generally seem pathological to the majority. ('Personal Rights' 8–9)[93]

[90] 'The Morality of Marriage', *Morality*, 138.

[91] 'Phases of Human Development', *Morality*, 202. See also 'Phases', 234.

[92] Cf. Huxley, *Evolution and Ethics*: in bee society 'the members of the society are each organically predestined to the performance of one particular class of functions only . . . Among mankind, on the contrary, there is no such predestination to a sharply defined place in the social organism. . . . Moreover, with all their enormous differences in natural endowment, men agree in one thing, and that is the innate desire to enjoy the pleasures and to escape the pains of life' (84–5).

[93] In *The Stones of Sacrifice*, Alpin declared of Claudia 'at least there was *one* woman who had escaped the hereditary instinct' (151, emphasis in original). By the hereditary instinct he meant the will to explain the social along biological lines; for Caird, instincts—a key concept for the hereditarians—were largely social habits that might be broken. For further interrogation of the term instinct, see, for example, *Daughters of Danaus*, 341; *The Stones of Sacrifice*, 151; 'Phases of Human Development', 239.

HOMEOPATHIC FICTIONS

'Much has been said for and against the writing of "novels with a purpose." ' So begins Caird's Prologue to *The Wing of Azrael* (1889). Caird devotes the prologue to the question of whether art should have a function, arguing against the instrumentalizing of art:

> the work of fiction whose motive is not the faithful rendering of an impression from without, but the illustration of a thesis—though that thesis be the corner-stone of Truth itself—has adopted the form of a novel for the purposes of an essay, and has no real right to the name.[94]

Her aesthetic principles express the same commitment to freedom that runs through all her work:

> human affairs are too complex, motives too many and too subtle, to allow a small group of persons to become the exponents of a general principle, however true. An argument founded on this narrow basis would be without value, though it were urged with the eloquence of a Demosthenes.[95]

In keeping with the validation of self and the subjective, central to her political vision, Caird validates the individuality of the writing subject.[96] Speaking out against aggressively didactic fiction, Caird does not simply join the art for art's sake camp, but develops her own theory of art. In *The Great Wave*, when the anti-eugenist Elliot Grierson seems to have reached a point of emotional and political hopelessness, the narrator remarks:

> it often happens that the homeopathic principle is useful psychically as well as physically, and Nora had counted upon that fact in letting the talk take this dismal turn. And she had judged correctly. The Schopenhauer form of pessimism, backed up by the doctrine of the degradation of energy, had been too much for Grierson. It caused a reaction. He begins to recover. (512)

In drawing on homeopathic medicine—cure by imitation[97]—Nora becomes an alternative healer, calculating that entering into Grierson's

[94] Caird, Preface to *The Wing of Azrael* (London: Trübner, 1889), p. vii.

[95] Ibid., p. viii.

[96] Contrast Heilmann, who argues that in constructing herself as an artist rather than a feminist, Caird adopted a traditionally gendered discourse which cast the artist as a man: Heilmann, *The Late Victorian Marriage Debate: A Collection of Key New Woman Texts* (London and New York: Routledge (with Thoemmes Press) 1998), v. p. xvii.

[97] See, for example, Ronald Livingston, who refers to homeopathy as 'treatment by analogy or mimicry', *Homeopathy. Evergreen Medicine: Jewel in the Medical Crown* (Poole: Asher and Asher, 1991), p. xxiii.

state of mind—severe post-war depression—holds the key to curing him. This strategy underpins Caird's aesthetics: patients and readers alike ought to be spared authoritarian intervention. In fiction, homeopathy is analogous to the depiction of sameness which aims not at controlling but moving the reader. By contrast, eugenic novels, which Grand had celebrated for their *allopathic* properties, aimed at controlling or suppressing the readers, in keeping with the principles of orthodox medicine. Caird's homeopathic theory not only underpins the themes she explores in her fiction but also operates at the level of language, as she uses the same terms—to different effect—as her hereditarian opponents.

VICTORIAN MOTHERHOOD AND EUGENIC LOVE

Victorian motherhood was an ideological minefield. Looking back from the twentieth century, Virginia Woolf remarks, as Orlando enters the nineteenth century:

> And just as the ivy and the evergreen rioted in the damp earth outside, so did the same fertility show itself within. The life of the average woman was a succession of childbirths. She married at nineteen and had fifteen or eighteen children by the time she was thirty; for twins abounded. Thus the British Empire came into existence; and thus—for there is no stopping damp; it gets into the inkpot as it gets into the woodwork—sentences swelled, adjectives multiplied, lyrics became epics . . .[98]

In 1866, George Eliot wrote:

> The mother's love is at first an absorbing delight, blunting all other sensibilities; it is an expansion of animal existence; it enlarges the imagined range for self to move in, but in after years it can only continue to be joy on the same terms as other long-lived love—that is, by much suppression of self, and power of living in the experience of another. Mrs Transome had darkly felt the pressure of that unchangeable fact. Yet she had clung to the belief that somehow the possession of this son was the best thing she lived for.[99]

While Eliot was more divided on the question of duty and the individual, she addressed the tensions inherent in motherhood that Mona Caird would place under close scrutiny in the climate of scientism and imperi-

[98] Virginia Woolf, *Orlando: A Biography* (1928; London: Virago, 1993), 147–8.

[99] George Eliot, *Felix Holt, The Radical* (1866; Harmondsworth: Penguin, 1987), 98.

alism that marked the closing decades of the century. In the words of Hadria, science wishes things in the maternal department 'left as they are': 'Women are made for purposes of reproduction; let them clearly understand that. No picking and choosing.'[100] 'It may seem paradoxical, but it is nonetheless true', Caird wrote in the *Nineteenth Century*, 'that we shall never have really good mothers, until women cease to make motherhood the central idea of their existence.'[101] She argued that pronatalism was the ultimate disease of civilization:

> through these ages of overstrain of every kind—physical, emotional, nervous—one set of faculties being in perpetual activity while the others lie dormant, woman has fallen into a state that is more or less ailing and diseased; that upon her shoulders has been laid the penalty of the injustice and selfishness of men. Have we not gone far enough along this path of destruction; or must women still make motherhood their chief task, accepting the old sentiment of subservience to man, until they drive yet further into the system the cruel diseases that have punished the insanities of the past; diseases which are taking vengeance upon victims of ill-usage for their submission, and pursuing their children from generation to generation with relentless footsteps? Such is the counsel of Mrs Lynn Linton and her school. Upon the consequences of all this past ill-treatment is founded the pretext for women's disabilities in the present. They are physically weak, nervous, easily unstrung, and for this reason, it is urged, they must continue to pursue the mode of life which has induced these evils.[102]

In her fiction, she made the point even more strenuously: 'the illegal mother is hounded by her fellows in one direction; the legal mother is urged and incited in another: free motherhood is unknown amongst us'; '[motherhood] among civilized people, represents a prostitution of the reproductive powers' (342, 343).

In *The Great Wave* Caird emphasized the centrality of motherhood to eugenic—and, ultimately, Nazi—thought. The Nazi supporter Mrs Verrkker declares that the woman's sphere '*more* than satisfies me'; 'I rest the woman's claim not on citizenship or law-making or anything of that sort—what does a true woman want with these? No, I rest it on something much more fundamental.' She pauses before announcing with reverence and deliberation: 'on the sanctity of motherhood'. Herr Wobster enthuses: 'Ja, Ja, doppel vote mit twins! Zweimal heilig! Gewiss, gewiss, dass is aber gut: dass ist aber furchtbar gut!' (218).

Caird develops an alternative narrative of racial progress; one that is

[100] *Daughters of Danaus*, 257.
[101] 'A Defence of the So-called "Wild Woman" ', 173.
[102] Ibid., 175–6.

non-biological, and egalitarian, and has at its centre a rejection of the idea that motherhood was the most worthwhile occupation for a woman. In 'Motherhood under Conditions of Dependence', for the *Westminster Review*, she wrote: 'a higher race can be produced through the education of women', and took issue with 'men of science, who might be expected to see a little further than their noses for joining in the foolish chorus:—"Women will ruin their constitutions by intellectual efforts" '.[103] In the *Nineteenth Century* she argued that if they continued to be coerced into self-sacrifice, and the 'over-production' of children, then women would 'for ever constitute an element of reaction and decay, which no unaided efforts of men could counteract.'[104]

[103] 'Motherhood under Conditions of Dependence', *Morality*, 135. See also 'Phases of Human Development', *Morality*, 238, on education as a prerequisite for variation.

[104] 'A Defence of the So-called "Wild Woman" ', *Morality*, 187. See also 'Motherhood under Conditions of Dependence', *Morality*, 134–5. Caird turned the eugenic term race-suicide on its head, arguing that pronatal pressures upon women 'nationally speaking, is suicidal' (*Morality*, 138). In keeping with her exposure of the social prejudices underlying biological determinism, Caird took up the term fitness in the periodical press. Darwin wrote in the *Origin* that variations 'would be taken advantage of by natural and sexual selection, in order to fit the several species to their several places in the economy of nature, and likewise to fit the two sexes of the same species to each other, or to fit the males and females to different habitats of life, or the males to struggle with other males for the possession of the females' (*Origin*, 1996 edn., 129). It was Herbert Spencer who detached the term from this sense of environmental interdependence, coining the term 'the survival of the fittest' (*Principles of Biology* (London: Williams and Norgate, 1864–7), ii. 53: 'by the continual survival of the fittest such structures must become established'). Caird redefines fitness as the ability to resist self-sacrifice and argues that by this standard, the average mother 'is totally unfitted for the training of mind or character' ('Marriage', *Morality*, 154); likewise the dedication of 'a whole sex' to 'the exhausting function' of motherhood has meant the work has fallen on 'unfit' shoulders; the woman 'who has no interest larger than the affairs of her children is not a fit person to train them' ('A Defence of the So-called "Wild Woman" ', *Morality*, 172, 173); and those mothers who are interested only in their own children are 'not fit to bring up children at all' ('Marriage', *Morality*, 154). Equally, in *Whom Nature Leadeth*, Caird emphasizes the socially constructed nature of fitness: in a chapter entitled 'The Extinction of the Unfit' the luckless Crawford, convinced he is to become extinct, resorts to killing himself when nature fails to extinguish him. Likewise, Huxley argued that 'those who saw eliminating the unfit as 'the only way of ensuring the progress of the race . . . must rank medicine among the black arts and count the physician a mischievous preserver of the unfit', lamenting the 'unfortunate ambiguity of the phrase "survival of the fittest" ' (*Evolution and Ethics*, 36–7; 80). As he put it, 'in a large proportion of cases, crime and pauperism have nothing to do with heredity; but are the consequence, partly, of circumstances and, partly, of the possession of qualities, which, under different conditions of life, might have excited esteem and even admiration . . . It is fairly probable that the children of a "failure" will receive from their other parent just that little modification of character which makes all the difference. I sometimes wonder whether people, who talk so freely about extirpating the unfit, ever dispassionately consider their own history. Surely one must be very "fit" indeed, not to know of an occasion, or perhaps two, in one's life, when it would have been only too easy to qualify for a place among the "unfit" ' (39).

The body of Caird's writings expose Victorian motherhood as riddled with oppressive laws and ideologies. In 1890 in the *North American Review*, she highlighted the direct relationship between the custody of children and property law, noting that before the Custody of Infants Act of 1886 the father of a legitimate child was, as far as legal rights were concerned, its sole parent:

> whenever we find the father enjoying legal rights over his children superior to those of the mother, we may know, without further proving, that his wife is his property, legally considered, and that he derives his parental privileges from her, exactly in the same way as the owner of a walnut tree derives his ownership of the walnuts from his rights in the tree. Sentiment may gloss over the fact, but that fact remains.[105]

In her fiction her message was the same: 'no woman had yet experienced [motherhood] apart from the enormous pressure of law and opinion that has, always, formed part of its inevitable conditions' (*The Daughters of Danaus*, 342). Try as she might, Hadria in *The Daughters of Danaus* is not a born mother. Her female ward (who turns out to be the illegitimate child of Professor Theobald) consigns her beloved doll to Hadria's care. Only moments later, as Hadria enters a heated discussion of woman's rights, the doll finds itself 'hanging down disconsolately from her elbow, although she was clutching it, with absent-minded anxiety, to her side, in the hope of arresting its threatened fall'. The unfortunate episode culminates in the doll falling 'with a great crash, into the fender among the fire-irons'. Even this pitiful sight does not awaken her maternity; 'there was a little burst of laughter' (349, 350, 354).[106] Unlike her eugenic contemporaries, who focused on motherhood as an ideal, Caird focused on its day-to-day realities, demonstrating that children were often custodians of paralysing custom, 'little ambassadors of the established and expected'.[107]

For Caird, motherhood and the idea of race, twin strategies of the imperial plan, are instruments of oppression which act on and through

[105] 'The End of the Patriarchal System', section 3 of 'The Emancipation of the Family', *Morality*, 50.

[106] Cf. Saleeby, who held that the female sex had a natural addiction to dolls or babies, *Woman and Womanhood*, 167. Having emphasized the naturalness of motherhood, Saleeby curiously remarked: 'we must breed for motherhood'; through artificial selection, motherhood might be made even more natural. On eugenic emphasis on women's inborn tendency to mother, see, for example, Iota's [Kathleen Mannington Caffyn] eugenic novel, *A Yellow Aster* (London: Hutchinson and Co., 1894).

[107] *Daughters of Danaus*, 187

the flesh. She dresses both in the imagery of imprisonment.[108] In *The Daughters of Danaus* motherhood is 'the sign and seal as well as the means and method of a woman's bondage': it 'forges chains of her own flesh and blood; it weaves cords of her own love and instinct' (341). Childcare *per se* did not in itself serve the eugenic plan. In the words of Saleeby, childcare which was not based on direct biological relation was 'a total denial of the value of the psychical aspects of motherhood and fatherhood alike'.[109] In *The Great Wave*, the anti-eugenist Grierson asserts that the maternal instinct is 'the fiercest of all instincts', and proceeds to desentimentalize maternal love:

> in the beginning, it presumably secured the advantage of the race (if that's an advantage), but *now*——! Can one count on it as truly civilizing? Does it make for tolerance, for spacious thinking, for broad sympathy, for understanding and peace and brotherhood? Assuredly not. It makes, as I say, for *its own*. The truly maternal woman scorns the notion of caring for any child not of her own superior flesh and blood. 'What do I care for other people's brats?' I heard a violently maternal woman exclaim, and she gloried in her savagery. (428–9, emphasis in original)

For Caird, mothers who were prejudiced in favour of their biological children risked falling victim to an exploitative maternalist imperialism. They were privileging the future over the present, valuing life only in so far as it signified race continuity.

Caird's views on love were predicated on her belief that the sexual relationship should be grounded in friendship and respect, observing 'in love, there ought to be *at least* as much respect for individuality and freedom as in friendship'. On the matter of sexual difference, she pursues a quite different line from the eugenic feminists. Instead of scapegoating one sex as aggressive and degenerate, and praising the other as biologically destined to regenerate the race, she emphasizes the capacity of men and women alike for both cruelty and compassion. It was not biology but a combination of circumstances and choice that would determine which predominated in any individual. She notes, however, that late nineteenth-century social and economic pressures made this free, and freeing, form of love almost impossible: 'Love comes with a vast bundle

[108] In *The Stones of Sacrifice*, race is 'the chain of life that linked century to century' (207); see also the poem 'To Mothers' by Charlotte Perkins Gilman, supplied by the feminist magazine *Shafts* (1898), 24, in a review of *The Morality of Marriage*: 'We are Mothers. Through us in our bondage, | Through us with a brand in the face | Be we fettered with gold or with iron | Through us comes the race.'

[109] *Parenthood and Race Culture*, 166.

of claims in her hand, and she even passes on these claims to mere kinship, which presses them with the persistency of a Shylock. Freedom in marriage is not for those who understand freedom no better than this.'[110]

In her fiction, Caird took the idea of rational love advocated by eugenists to its logical extreme: in *The Pathway of the Gods* the sage traveller Julian Ford imagines saying to a lover: 'the present combination of circumstances is such as to produce in me a vivid though delusive impression of undying devotion for you. Tell, oh! tell me, that circumstances have induced in you an answering illusion.' 'Would love-making ever be thus reduced to its elements in a scientific age?' (48), he muses.[111] In *The Stones of Sacrifice*, a novel that is concerned primarily with sexual selection, the anti-hero, Thorne, leader of the staunchly eugenic Triumvirate party (his name suggests the capacity of nature to cause pain), proposes 'to regulate marriages scientifically in the interests of the race, and to decide the vexed question of woman's position in strict accordance with her function of producing the largest number of healthy people for the State'. If 'natural instinct' is not enough, then 'they must be coerced into it by law and opinion'. Eugenic love had little to do with the meeting of hearts and minds. The duty of parents, he stresses, was to 'sacrifice themselves for their offspring' (154). The novel declares the obsession with the idea of the survival of the fittest 'primitive savagery made into a cult' (236). In her last novel Caird explored ways in which the discourses of nature and of love were misused to justify barbarism, encapsulating in an illuminating exchange between Dr Wobster and Mrs Verreker a message that lies at the centre of her work:

> '*Ach ja! die Nature!*' cried Doctor Wobster, who cherished a warm enthusiasm for that abstract entity, 'our Great Mother ordains that men must fight with other men. *Ja*, and de women brings always more men into de world for dis purpose. It is beautiful!' . . . Mrs Verreker glowed at the thought that these struggles which seemed to the ordinary mind so dreadful, really were the means of developing our higher natures. So *Love* lay behind all this apparent anomaly.[112]

110 'Married Life, Present and Future', *Morality*, 145, 149.

111 Cf. Sarah Grand, *The Heavenly Twins* (1893; Michigan: University of Michigan Press, 1992): 'Evadne sighed. She was too highly tempered, well-balanced a creature to be the victim of any one passion, and least of all that transient state of feeling miscalled "Love". Physical attraction, moral repulsion: that was what she was suffering from' (226).

112 Caird, *The Great Wave*, 218, emphasis in original.

Afterword

I have argued that eugenic feminism finds repeated expression in both the journalism and fiction of many New Women writers. As they saw it, the women of Britain could best serve the race, the country, and their own interests through the rational selection of a reproductive partner. It was a eugenic programme, calculated to produce a healthy, Anglo-Saxon middle class, and remains a vital chapter in literary history and feminist thought, and a vital part of the story of New Women. Why, we might ask, has it been neglected? As I discussed earlier, eugenic feminism sits uneasily with the generally prevailing notion of the New Woman writer as a free-thinking forerunner of the suffragette, a dangerously radical proto-feminist. More theoretically, the late twentieth-century drift into philosophical relativism must take some responsibility for the obscuring of eugenic fictions, whose authorial intentions have not been acknowledged in the apparently emancipatory climate that privileged the reader as producer, and took pleasure in killing the author.

It is also true to say that the authority of eugenic writers was compromised by the form of their fictions. Eugenic fictions had to be entertaining as well as didactic, and the novel required characters to change, or at least develop, in order to retain the reader's attention; eugenic ideology did not allow such flexibility. As discourses of heredity and degeneration gained an increasing hold on the popular imagination, the idea of rational reproduction proliferated in fiction and the press, but it remained essentially an idea, housed in the polyvocal British periodical press, with the prejudices, opinions, visions, and goals of the various contenders held in dynamic equilibrium.

Unlike so many other Western, Protestant societies Britain never passed a eugenic law.[1] Looking back from the twentieth century, Galton noted how little popular feeling had been 'prepared to consider

[1] For contemporary developments in Europe and America, see Dorothy Porter, *Civilization and the State, A History of Public Health from Ancient to Modern Times* (London: Routledge, 1998), ch. 10; and, in America, Daniel Kevles, *In the Name of Eugenics: Genetics and the Uses of Human Heredity* (1985; Cambridge, Mass.: Harvard University Press, 1995).

dispassionately proposals for any practical action ~~based upon theory~~' when he first introduced the ideas into public circulation in 1865.[2] In 1907, Havelock Ellis wrote to Galton 'in the concluding volume of my Sex "Studies" (which are published in America and translated into French and German) I shall do what I can to insinuate the eugenic attitude. Public opinion is the only lever at present, and legislative action must be impossible—and futile—for a very long time to come.'[3] Galton himself observed in the Preface to his *Essays in Eugenics* (1909) that 'the power by which Eugenic reform must chiefly be effected, is that of Popular Opinion'.[4] And Leonard Darwin, one of Darwin's grandsons, and president of the Eugenics Society from 1911 to 1928, emphasized 'one of the first steps towards eugenic reform must be the education of the public'.[5]

Galton's ideas had been met with resistance from the outset. In 1869, the *Saturday Review* remarked:

[2] 'Memories', 340, Galton's deletions.

[3] Havelock Ellis to Galton, 13 June 1907, Galton Papers, 239. The work of Gregor Mendel, an Augustinian monk and the son of Czech peasants, on inheritance in peas would prove central to the early twentieth-century development of eugenics, as hereditarians divided into biometricians and Mendelians. First published in 1865, it was rediscovered in 1900 by three continental biologists, Hugo de Vries, Carl Correns, and Erich von Tschermak. The Cambridge biologist William Bateson (1861–1926) rapidly became the leading British Mendelian, coining the term 'genetics'. Through elementary probability theory and assumptions about dominance, theoretical accounts of the process of heredity could be produced. Mendelians had a vested interest in defending the value and territory of biology. Bateson himself disliked the narrowly middle-class values of the eugenics movement, and feared that its success might lead to the further success of utilitarian rationalization and modernization (Donald MacKenzie, *Statistics in Britain 1865–1930: The Social Construction of Scientific Knowledge* (Edinburgh: Edinburgh University Press, 1981), 147). By contrast, the biometricians did not have a developed, explicitly theoretical, model of heredity, and in general their reaction to Mendelism was hostile; their key goal was the development of techniques to predict the overall incidence of characteristics within biological populations. For Galton's view of Mendel, see Galton Papers, 138/11 (1909). It was not until the work of R. A. Fisher (1890–1962) that a workable synthesis was achieved between biometrics and Mendelism, in *The Genetical Theory of Natural Selection* (Oxford: Clarendon Press, 1930). Fisher showed that a theoretical account of evolution by natural selection could be erected on the basis of Mendelism. MacKenzie points out that the view of Fisher resolving the biometrician-Mendelian controversy should not overshadow the extent to which his goals were identical to those of Pearson's, and that rather than reconciling Mendelism and biometry, Fisher chose to use Mendelism to vindicate biometric eugenics (189).

[4] Galton, *Essays in Eugenics* (London: The Eugenics Education Society, 1909). C. W. Saleeby also emphasized the importance of public opinion, which he held as capable of controlling marriage and therefore race culture: *Parenthood and Race Culture* (London: Cassell and Company Ltd, 1909), 168.

[5] Leonard Darwin, 'First Steps Towards Eugenic Reform', *Eugenics Review*, 4 (April 1912), 35.

Mr Galton's elaborate figures may be as easily turned to support the very opposite conclusion to that for which he entered upon the compilation [. . .] Why do children of the same parents grow up so widely apart in intellect and character? Why are the great men on Mr Galton's list above their brothers and sisters at all? . . . until we can do infinitely more towards sorting the stores of man's mental growth and experience into what he brings into the world and what he draws from his subsequent surroundings in the world, our minds are in no condition for even the first shadowy conception of a 'law of heredity'.[6]

The following year the Anglican theologian and scholar the Revd Frederic William Farrar raised two central objections to Galton's theory of selective breeding in *Fraser's Magazine*: 'we deliberately believe that, for every thousand men who attain the kind of eminence which in many cases seems to satisfy Mr Galton's requirements, there are many thousands more with equal or superior ability who fail solely from lack of opportunity'; secondly, 'Mr Galton has not sufficiently allowed for the effects of family tradition and surrounding circumstances, and early education'.[7] *The Times* concluded that Galton's ideas could be of little practical value, observing that 'the universal knowledge of reading, writing, and ciphering and the absence of pauperism would raise the national grade of ability far quicker and higher than any system of selected marriage.'[8] In 1872 the *Chamber's Journal* remarked mockingly:

instead of 'marriages of affection' or 'convenience' or of marriages being 'made in heaven' they ought to be arranged by some competent tribunal, who shall decide the case upon its merits: whether Corydon is appropriate to Chloe, and vice versa, and whether their issue is likely to be such as to advantage the general community. Under this happy and philosophic system, we shall no more hear of a lady 'throwing herself away' upon an unworthy object. *Locksley Hall* will have no further interest save as an example of what used to happen in an age of unreason; clever men will no more suffer under the proverbial stigma of 'always marrying stupid women:' . . . It will be no longer a vulgar wish to perpetuate the name of Robinson, but to bequeath to a grateful country in perpetuity the wit, the humour, the administrative talents, or the power of multiplying four figures by four figures in one's head, which is now the attribute of Master Jack Robinson only, and may be lost for ever by a *mésalliance* with a dull heiress!

[6] *Saturday Review* (25 December 1869), Galton Papers, 128/6.

[7] F. W. Farrar, 'Hereditary Genius', *Fraser's Magazine* 2 (1870), 262, 263 Darwin cites this article in the *Descent of Man* (i. 173 n. 18). For further early opposition to eugenic ideas, see *Spectator* (27 November 1869), Galton Papers, 120/5.

[8] *The Times* (7 January 1870), Galton Papers, 120/5.

The journal pronounced decisively that with Galton's conclusions it was 'wholly unable to agree'.[9] Ten years later, the *Guardian* remarked:

when Mr Galton passes from the speculative to the practical region, we find much not only to question, but to condemn. Who is to decide whether a man's issue is not likely to be well fitted 'to play their part as citizens?' Do not weak men have strong children, stupid ones wise, wicked good? The practical inferences which are the outcome of all this odd and very imperfectly worked out speculation are as much opposed to philosophy as they are to common sense and good feeling.[10]

One major source of opposition to eugenics came from the public health service which became rapidly professionalized in the closing years of the century. By 1889 this occupational group consisted of 1500 officers, and had its own journal: *Public Health*. In 1912 Edward Hope, one-time president of the Society of Medical Officers of Health, remarked: 'today we hear a great deal of eugenics and genetics and the impairment of the race, and the mischief which is wrought by the indiscriminate sanitarian who preserves the lives of the weakly and the degenerate'. He warned that 'the eugenists would be well advised to leave alone the criticisms upon sanitation'; they should concentrate not on selective breeding but on eliminating the slum housing that endangered health.[11]

The closest Britain came to passing a eugenic act was the 1912 Mental Deficiency Bill. A key opponent was the libertarian liberal MP Josiah Wedgwood, who entered parliament in the landslide victory of 1906 and led an anti-eugenic parliamentary lobby against it. The lobby decried 'the dictum of the specialist'[12] and denounced the encroachment on individual liberty and the privileging of collectivism above the individual that eugenics entailed. The bill was, in Wedgwood's words, 'a bill of very serious risks and dangers to the people of this country'.[13] The anti-

[9] *Chamber's Journal* (19 February 1870), 119; Galton Papers, 120/5.

[10] *Guardian* (4 July 1883), 1001; Galton Papers, 124.

[11] Edward Hope, 'The Expanding Scope of Sanitary Administration', *Public Health*, 26 (1912–13), 40–1, in Dorothy Porter, ' "Enemies of the Race": Biologism, Environmentalism, and Public Health in Edwardian England', *Victorian Studies*, 34 (1991), 165. Porter concludes that 'for explanations of ill health, preventative medicine looked to the historico-sociological determinants of social developments above and beyond the biological basis to human existence' (173).

[12] *Hansard* (10 June 1912), cols. 642, 643.

[13] *Hansard* (10 June 1912), col. 642. On Labour's opposition to the Mental Deficiency Bill and to the defeated Sterilization Bill of 1931, see Jones, *Social Hygiene*, 43, 58, 103. As Jones notes, C. P. Blacker wrote to J. R. Blacker 'if you want to enlist the help of the dysgenic you are not very likely to enlist their sympathy if you speak about them as dregs and scum', cited in Jones, 103. See Jones, *Social Hygiene*, 58–62 on Socialist support for eugenics.

eugenists succeeded in achieving the removal of a eugenic clause prohibiting marriage and criminalizing procreation among the feeble-minded in 'the interests of the community' before the bill passed into law in 1913.[14] The act empowered a central authority to detain and segregate certain of the 'feeble-minded'. This suggestively vague term included paupers, habitual drunkards, and women on poor relief at the time of giving birth to, or being found pregnant with, an illegitimate child.[15] In the British parliamentary debates over the Mental Deficiency Bill, Leslie Scott, Home Secretary, conceded to the opposition that 'feeble-mindedness' was a broad definition, but followed this admission to argue for 'the importance of utilizing all the existing administrative experience and method of certifying that the country has at present in dealing with this new category of defective persons'.[16] This was a timely development. Between 1900 and 1914 the category of the habitual criminal emerged, and recidivism was turned into a pathology by the hereditarians, for whom socio-economic deprivation counted for next to nothing in accounting for crime. The 1908 Prevention of Crime Act sanctioned the preventative detention of five to ten years for those who had led a 'persistently dishonest life'. The regulatory, and coercive, powers of the state were multiplying rapidly.[17] As the freethinking Catholic G. K. Chesterton put it in *Eugenics and Other Evils: An Argument Against the Scientifically Organized State*, 'feeble-minded' was 'a new phrase under which you might segregate anyone'.[18] Of the Mental Deficiency Bill he wrote: 'I will call it the Feeble-Minded Bill, both for

[14] Josiah Wedgwood, *The Parliamentary Debates* (House of Commons): *Official Report*, ser. 5, 38, cols. 1467–78. See D. Porter, ' "Enemies of the Race" ', 162; Greta Jones, *Social Hygiene in Twentieth-Century Britain* (London: Croom Helm, 1986), 26–41; and Geoffrey Searle, *Eugenics and Politics in Britain, 1900–1914* (Leyden: Noordhoff, 1976), 92–111, for the important role played by Josiah Wedgwood.

[15] See Kevles, *In the Name of Eugenics: Genetics and the Uses of Human Heredity* (1985; Cambridge, Mass.: Harvard University Press, 1995), 99. For a recent study of this act and the development of the idea of mental deficiency, see Mark Jackson, *The Borderland of Imbecility: Medicine, Society, and the Fabrication of the Feeble Mind in late Victorian and Edwardian England* (Manchester: Manchester University Press, 2000). See also Mathew Thomson, *The Problem of Mental Deficiency: Eugenics, Democracy, and Social Policy in Britain c.1870–1959* (Oxford: Clarendon Press, 1998).

[16] *Hansard* 39, col. 637.

[17] V. A. C. Gatrell ' Crime, Authority and the Policeman-state', in F. M. L. Thompson (ed.), *The Cambridge Social History of Britain, 1750–1950* (1989), cited in David Feldman, 'The Importance of Being English: Jewish Immigration and the Decay of Liberal England', *Metropolis London: Histories and Representations* (London: Routledge, 1989), 84.

[18] Chesterton, *Eugenics and Other Evils: An Argument Against the Scientifically Organized State* ed. by Michael W. Parry (1922; Seattle: Inking, 2000), 49.

brevity and because the description is strictly accurate. It is, quite simply and literally, a Bill for incarcerating as madmen those whom no doctor will consent to call mad'.[19] In the year that the Mental Deficiency Bill was introduced, the *Daily News* reported a demand by Leonard Darwin for a national register of the 'naturally unfit'. Among the unfit he included 'all ins-and outs at work-houses, and all convicted prisoners', and looked forward to a system whereby the family history of those on the register would be examined 'especially as regards the criminality, insanity, ill health and pauperism of their relatives'; thus 'many strains would be discovered which no one could deny ought to be made to die out in the interest of the nation; and in this way the necessity for legislation, such as that proposed by the Royal Commission on the care and control of the feeble-minded, would be further emphasised.'[20] Leonard Darwin's enthusiasm increased during the war years, and in 1923 he condemned the effects of social reform as forces encouraging the continuance of race inferiority and deterioration, urging 'to secure human progress the inferior types must be eliminated'.[21]

However, the relationship between the Mental Deficiency Act and eugenics was complex. It provided for many victims of mental deficiency to live outside institutions and, most importantly, it made no mention of sterilization.[22] In fact, the act's association with eugenics ultimately worked to its disadvantage on account of prevailing opposition to the notion of the expert who could decide who fell within its remit.[23] The Eugenics Society itself commanded little real influence in the twentieth century. On the eve of the First World War, it had 634 members; numbers fell during the war and, at its peak in 1932–3, could only boast 768;[24] its impact on social policy was in practice negligible.[25]

Intellectual and moral resistances to eugenics proliferated in the first

[19] Chesterton, *Eugenics and Other Evils*, 25.

[20] Leonard Darwin, 'First Steps Towards Eugenic Reform', 34–5.

[21] The *Daily News* carried the story under the heading 'Major Darwin and Race Inferiority Progress Hindered by Social Reform', reported in *Birth Control News*, 2 (August 1923), 1, reprinted in Chesterton, *Eugenics*, 167.

[22] Kevles, *In the Name of Eugenics*, 99.

[23] Thomson, *The Problem of Mental Deficiency*, 298.

[24] Searle, 'Eugenics, The Early Years', in Robert A. Peel (ed.), *Essays in the History of Eugenics*, Proceedings of a Conference Organized by the Galton Institute (London: Galton Institute, 1997), 30.

[25] Searle, 'Eugenics, The Early Years', 33. See also Porter, ' "Enemies of the Race": Biologism, Environmentalism, and Public Health in Edwardian England', *Victorian Studies*, 34 (1991), 159–78.

decades of the twentieth century.[26] Several of the leading medical journals, including the *British Medical Journal*, were consistently hostile to eugenics,[27] and very few doctors possessed any understanding of genetics. In 1913 the Eugenics Society attempted to get eugenics added to the medical curriculum, but the leaders of the profession rejected this on the grounds that it was already too crowded.[28] Ultimately, eugenics was at odds with the professional ethics of the medical profession, which aimed at relieving suffering without regard to consequences, and family doctors, awed by the specialists' discourses on statistics and genetics, and the idea of pronouncing on fitness for parenthood, were also alienated.[29] Eugenics was also contested by psychology, which was too engaged with philosophical questions about the mind to subscribe to any theory of total hereditary determination of behaviour—and, as the hereditarians and environmentalists reached stalemate, psychoanalysis emerged as a new explanatory model, a means of resisting biology.

Catholic resistance grew with Father Thomas J. Gerrard, Chesterton, and Belloc as key figures. In 1924, the Very Reverend Vincent McNabb wrote an open letter in the *Catholic Times* on welfare centres set up to help the poor:

> Those of us who have lived long within the nidus of the disease realized, as if by intuition, that sooner or later these welfare and kindred centres would move from an economic to an ethical basis. Such a move would mean that their end would contradict their beginning. Having been begun in order to aid the poor, they would end with eugenic schemes to eliminate the poor.[30]

[26] Thomson, *The Problem of Mental Deficiency*, 299.

[27] See Searle, 'Eugenics and Class', in Charles Webster (ed.), *Biology, Medicine and Society 1840–1940* (Cambridge: Cambridge University Press, 1981), 226. Searle cites the *British Medical Journal* (23 August 1913), 508–10.

[28] Searle, 'Eugenics and Class, 227.

[29] Ibid., 228–9. See also Leslie Stephen's objection to the eugenic idea that social institutions reduced the capacity for moral self-realization and rationality: Leslie Stephen, 'Heredity—an Address to Ethical Societies', in *Social Rights and Duties* (1896), ii. 21, cited in Jones, *Social Darwinism and English Thought: The Interaction between Biological and Social Theory* (Brighton: Harvester, 1980), 109. Benjamin Kidd saw Galton's view of civilization as 'so elementary that there was no place in it for moral standards, or for any of those problems of the responsibility of the individual for the universal which have distracted the human mind since the dawn of knowledge', Benjamin Kidd, *The Science of Power* (London: Macmillan, 1918), 77, quoted in Jones, *Social Darwinism and English Thought*, 109.

[30] Cited in *Birth Control News* (April 1924), 3. On the opposition of the Catholic church, see Father Thomas J. Gerrard, 'The Catholic Church and Race Culture', *Dublin Review*, 149 (1911), 55–67; and *The Church and Eugenics* (London: P. S. King, 1912); see also Chesterton, *Eugenics and Other Evils*; and Childs, *Modernism and Eugenics*, 7. Hilaire

The Catholic Church came out in formal opposition, condemning eugenics and associated practices in the encyclical *De Casti Connubii* in 1930.[31]

The debates of the nineteenth century over biology persisted through the twentieth century, with a synthesis of genetics and natural selection through the work of Ronald Fisher, Theodore Dobzhansky, Ernst Mayr, and J. B. S. Haldane emerging during the 1930s. At this time eugenics was resurfacing as reform eugenics, under the leadership of Carlos P. Blacker, president of the Eugenics Society from 1931 to 1952. In *Birth Control and the State* (1926), Blacker had argued that biological explanations needed to be considered in a broader social context.[32] The Eugenics Society introduced into parliament two bills (1931 and 1932) to legalize voluntary sterilization, but these attracted little support.[33] In 1934, the year the Nazi Eugenic Sterilization Law came into effect, the British government set up a Committee on Mental Degeneracy. Its head, Laurence G. Brock, emphasized the uncertainty surrounding the biological cause of mental deficiency. Nonetheless, his committee report fanned a new interest in voluntary sterilization in the case of hereditary disorders which won the endorsement of Julian Huxley and Lancelot Hogben, holder of the new Chair of Social Biology at the London School of Economics, and several Labour groups and women's organizations.[34] However, the British public was divided, and the House of Commons denounced

Belloc's newspaper, *Eyewitness*, ran a fierce campaign against the Mental Deficency Bill; see Jones, *Social Darwinism*, 49. See also Stephen Dedalus's objection to eugenics, and his unhappiness with an evolutionary explanation for female beauty—'it leads to eugenics rather than to esthetic' in the fifth chapter of *A Portrait of the Artist as a Young Man*, which Joyce completed in 1914; see Childs, 12.

[31] See *Casti Connubii* in Claudia Carlen (ed.), *The Papal Encyclicals 1903–1939*, 5 vols. (Raleigh: McGrath, 1981). See Searle, 'Eugenics and Politics in Britain in the 1930s', *Annals of Science*, 36 (1979), 159–69, cited in MacKenzie, *Statistics in Britain, 1865–1930: The Social Construction of Scientific Knowledge* (Edinburgh: Edinburgh University Press, 1981), 47 and 253, n. 27.

[32] See Richard A. Soloway, 'From Mainline to Reform Eugenics—Leonard Darwin and C. P. Blacker', in Robert A. Peel, (ed.), *Essays in the History of Eugenics* (London: The Galton Institute, 1998), 62. For Labour's opposition to campaigns for voluntary sterilization of members of the 'social problem' group during the 1920s and early 1930s, which were seen as fundamentally anti-working class, see John MacNicol, 'Eugenics and the Campaign for Voluntary Sterilization Between the Wars', *Social History of Medicine*, 2 (1989), 147–69. In the light of Labour's opposition, MacNicol warns against overstressing links between eugenics and 'progressivist' thought.

[33] Kevles, *In the Name of Eugenics*, 167.

[34] See ibid., 167. See also H. G. Wells, Julian Huxley, and G. P. Wells, *The Science of Life* (Doubleday, Doran, 1931), 1467–8, cited in Kevles, *In the Name of Eugenics*, 344, n. 10.

such measures as anti-working class.[35] Ultimately, sterilization was defeated because it infringed ideas about individual rights and social responsibilities that were fundamental to British democracy.[36]

During the 1930s eugenics began to be challenged from within the science of human genetics. While Hogben did not renounce his support for racial improvement, he argued that the study of pedigrees needed to be replaced by quantitative analysis,[37] and pointed out that social bias could enter the selection and interpretation of data.[38] The geneticist J. B. S. Haldane objected to the fact that genetics was used against the working class and, in *Heredity and Politics* (1938), concluded 'a consideration of human biology does not, in my opinion, justify the perpetuation of class distinctions'.[39] The Eugenics Society survived attacks such as this from left-wing geneticists, and even the disgrace of German eugenics, but in the new, more egalitarian climate that followed the Second World War, the class bias of eugenics increasingly became both transparent and unacceptable. A series of acts passed between 1944 and 1948 reorganized health and welfare services and abolished the 1834 Poor Law Amendment Act, which had instituted a poor law which had remained intact until 1929.[40] With the rise of the welfare state, medical benefits—no longer termed 'medical relief'—were available to all without loss of status. The motivating idea of eugenics that paupers formed a biological or racial group—bearers of hereditary taint and feeble-mindedness—ill fitted this post-war climate of national co-operation and optimism. The pauper class as an administrative and biological category disappeared, the outcasts were brought back into the society, and the threat of social revenge which

[35] Ibid., 167.

[36] Thomson, *The Problem of Mental Deficiency*, 299.

[37] Mazumdar, *Eugenics, Human Genetics and Human Failings: The Eugenics Society, its Sources and Critics in Britain* (London: Routledge, 1992), 149–77.

[38] L. Hogben, 'Modern Heredity and Social Science', *Socialist Review*, 16 (1919), 147–56, cited in Mackenzie, *Statistics in Britain*, 46.

[39] J. B. S. Haldane, *Heredity and Politics* (New York: Norton, 1938), quoted in Mazumdar, *Eugenics, Human Genetics and Human Failings*, 183. See Hansard, vol. 255, cols. 1251–6 for Haldane on the class biases of sterilization. The *Eugenics Review* complained that Haldane had harmed the eugenic cause by attributing to the 'true eugenists' of the society the extreme views of racism and compulsory sterilization: 'Notes of the Quarter', *Eugenics Review*, 20 (1938), 6.

[40] D. Porter, *Public Health*, 114. In the 1940s the discipline of social medicine sought, in an increasingly left-wing strategy of social reform, to bring back an emphasis on the environment in studying man in disease. See Porter, 'Social Medicine and the New Society: Medicine and Scientific Humanism in mid-Twentieth Century Britain', *Journal of Historical Sociology*, (1996), 9.

the middle class feared from the poorest sections of the population declined.[41]

After a period of abeyance during the two world wars and the egalitarian years that followed, biological determinism came back in the 1960s; favoured, once more, by economic, political, and social conditions. Two key publications were William Hamilton's *The Genetical Evolution of Social Behaviour* (1962), and George Williams's *Adaptation and Natural Selection* (1966). Interest in human heredity resurfaced as interest in human genetics and in 1963 the title of the Chair in Eugenics at University College London changed to the Chair in Human Genetics, and genetic determinism was expounded in Richard Dawkins's theory of *The Selfish Gene* (1976), which extended the notion of a relentlessly deterministic world deep into microbiology. In 1989, the British Eugenics Society changed its name to the Galton Institute, and shifted the main focus of explorations of heredity and social groups within Britain onto racial groups in developing countries. In the closing decades of the twentieth century, E. O. Wilson, founder of sociobiology, and evolutionary psychologists (notably Steven Pinker) reductively applied Darwinian ideas to all aspects of human consciousness and behaviour: in 1975 Wilson demanded that human society be run on the basis of a 'genetically accurate and hence a completely fair code of ethics'.[42] By contrast, Richard Lewontin's genetics stresses the significance of environment, arguing that 'context and interaction are of the essence',[43] and Stephen Rose and Stephen Jay Gould stress the complex nature of life, substituting variety and diversity for biological determinism. Gould writes 'we grasp at the straw of progress (a desiccated ideological twig) because we are still not ready for the Darwinian revolution.'[44] Daniel Dennett has allowed a space for collaboration in nature—an idea alive at the end of the nineteenth century, but, like Dawkins, insists on the gene's relentless drive to reproduce itself, emphasizing evolution as a process consisting of

[41] For an excellent discussion of the post-war decline of eugenics, see Mazumdar, *Eugenics, Human Genetics and Human Failings*, ch. 5, 'Human Genetics and the Eugenics Problematic'. On emergent theories of social mobility at this time, see Anthony Giddens, *The Class Structure of Advanced Societies* (London: Hutchinson, 1981), 53–68; and T. B. Bottomore, *Sociology as Social Criticism* (London: Allen, 1975), 19–28.

[42] Edward O. Wilson, *Sociobiology: The New Synthesis* (Cambridge, Mass.: Harvard University Press, 1975), 575. More recently, Wilson has moved towards a new interest in variability: see *Naturalist* (Washington, DC: Island Press/Shearwater Books, 1994) and *Consilience: The Unity of Knowledge* (New York: Alfred A. Knopf, 1998).

[43] Richard Lewontin, *The Genetic Basis of Evolutionary Change* (New York, London: Columbia University Press, 1974), 318.

[44] Stephen Jay Gould, *Life's Grandeur: The Spread of Excellence from Plato to Darwin* (London: Jonathan Cape, 1996), 29.

'nothing but a set of individually mindless steps succeeding each other without the help of any intelligent supervision'.[45]

Since Watson and Crick's discovery of the structure of DNA, in 1953, three new biotechnologies have developed.[46] The first to appear, in the early 1970s, is known as 'genetic engineering': genes—functional stretches of DNA—are transferred between organisms without the intervention of sex. The second, cloning by nuclear transfer, resulted ultimately in Dolly the sheep, cloned from an adult mammary gland cell in 1996. There were numerous, unpublicized, unsuccessful attempts, with resultant deformed foetuses, before this success resulted. The third, and most recent, biotechnology is genomics, the sequencing of all the DNA, and identifying of all the genes, in an organism's genome. The Human Genome Project, launched in October 1990, is the largest government-funded international scientific project ever. It aims to map and sequence 'the book of life'—all the genes in the human body—and, by 2003, to have identified the approximately 30,000 genes in human DNA and determined the sequences of the 3 billion chemical base pairs that make up human DNA. A working draft of the entire human genome sequence was announced in June 2000, with analyses published in February 2001.[47] The 1988 Office of Technology Assessment Report stated its aim as to identify 'the eugenics of normalcy' in order that genetic information could be used 'to ensure that ... each individual has at least a modicum of normal genes.'[48] In 2000 *The Times* reported:

[45] Daniel C. Dennett, *Darwin's Dangerous Idea: Evolution and the Meanings of Life* (New York: Simon Schuster, 1995), 511.

[46] See Colin Tudge, 'Problems of Genetic Engineering', in Robert A. Peel and John Timson (eds.), *A Century of Mendelism* (London: The Galton Institute, 2001), 45–63.

[47] See the Human Genome Special Issue of *Science*, 291 (16 February 2001), and Daniel Kevles and Leroy Hood (eds.), *The Code of Codes: Scientific and Social Issues in the Human Genome Project* (Cambridge, Mass.: Harvard University Press, 1992), 3–36.

[48] Evelyn Fox Keller, 'Nature, Nurture, and the Human Genome Project', in Kevles and Hood (eds.), *The Code of Codes*, 291–9. For recent studies on the Genome Project, see Philip R. Sloan (ed.), *Controlling Our Destinies: The Human Genome Project from Historical, Philosophical, Social, and Ethical Perspectives* (Notre Dame, Ind.: University of Notre Dame Press; 2000); Raymond A. Zilinskas and Peter J. Balint (eds.), *The Human Genome Project and Minority Communities: Ethical, Social and Political Dilemmas* (Westport, Conn.: Praeger Publishers, 2000); see also Tom Wilkie, *Perilous Knowledge: The Human Genome Project and Its Implications* (Berkeley, Calif.: University of California Press, 1993); Timothy Murphy and Marc A. Lappe (eds.), *Justice and the Human Genome Project* (Berkeley Calif.: University of California Press, 1994). In 2002 the interdisciplinary Economic and Social Research Council-funded Exeter Centre for Genomics in Society (EGenIS), led by the philosopher of science John Dupré, with associate directors the sociologist Barry Barnes and the biologist Steve Hughes, began research on the impact of scientific and technological developments in genomics on society.

Eugenics was not an evil interlude of the previous century; it is the defining feature of the new century . . . Genetically modifying human behaviour is not an assault on free will . . . Medicine could be to this century what metal-bashing was to the last: our premier industry. Central to this will be eugenics. Adequately controlled, it can provide wonderful, life-enhancing possibilities for humankind.[49]

In *Eugenics: A Reassessment* (2001), the psychologist Richard Lynn urges a new eugenics of human biotechnology and predicts how eugenic policies are likely to affect national configurations, geopolitics, and the balance of power in the twenty-first century. Like his Victorian predecessors, he uses the language of social equality to advance eugenics, concluding that the twenty-first century will be recognized as the time when humans took control of their genetic destiny, a conquest which will be regarded 'as one of the greatest advances in history'. Lynn argues that if the new eugenics of medical technology is only used by the affluent, then societies will become more class divided, with IQ, work ethic, motivation, and self-discipline—qualities which he considers to be genetic—rising among the affluent, and, conversely, a 'genetic underclass' of 'unskilled workers and unemployables' developing. Eugenics, the love of the late nineteenth century, has become, for Lynn, 'the truth that dare not speak its name'.[50]

While biological determinism has failed to achieve determining political influence,[51] the balance in the nature-nurture controversy has shifted to nature, and eugenic ideas are again in vogue, this time under the human genetics umbrella, and linked, again, to the idea of progress.[52] Nonetheless, Galton's idea of improving the human race

[49] *The Times* (3 July 2000), 18.

[50] *Eugenics: A Reassessment* (London: Praeger, 2001). See also Richard Lynn and Tatu Vanhanen, *IQ and the Wealth of Nations* (London: Praeger, 2002).

[51] On the rise of biological determinism, and its failure to achieve definitive political influence, see Dorothy Porter, 'Biological Determinism, Evolutionary Fundamentalism and the Rise of the Genoist Society', *Critical Quarterly*, 42 (2000), 67–84.

[52] See Mazumdar, 'Epilogue', *Eugenics, Human Genetics and Human Failings*, esp. 264. See Commission of the European Communities, *Predictive Medicine: Human Genome Analysis* (1989–1991) and, for resistances and reservations, Congress of the United States, Office of Technology assessment (OTA), *Mapping Our Genes. The Genome Projects: How Big, How Fast?* (Baltimore, Md: Johns Hopkins University Press, 1988); David Dickson, 'Genome Project Gets Rough Ride in Europe', *Science*, 243 (2 Feb. 1989), 599; Benedikt Härlin, 'Predictive Medicine: Human Genome Analysis (1989–1991): Report Drawn Up on Behalf of the Committee on Commission to the Council (COM/88/424–C2–119/88) for a decision adopting a specific research programme in the field of health', European Communities, European Parliament, *Session Documents Series* A, Documents A2–0370/88 SYN 146. See also See Kevles, *In the Name of Eugenics*, 257.

through rational reproduction had its greatest appeal in the late nineteenth century, as social and sexual ideas were in ferment, and the possibility of a new role for women arose. In the century that followed, the idea of women intervening rationally in the romance plot was eclipsed as the vision of controlling human heredity passed from the hands of New Women to the laboratories of genetic scientists.

Select Bibliography

UNPUBLISHED SOURCES

Farrall, Lindsay A. 'The Origin and Growth of the British Eugenics Movement', Ph.D. dissertation, University of Indiana, 1970.

Galton Papers, University College London.

Letters of Frances Elizabeth McFall, National Library of Scotland.

Letters of Sarah Grand [Frances Elizabeth McFall], Bath County Library.

Pearson Papers, University College London.

Ritt, Lawrence, 'The Victorian Conscience in Action: The National Association for the Promotion of Social Science, 1857–1886' Ph.D. dissertation, Columbia University, 1959.

Stetz, Margaret Diane, ' "George Egerton", Woman and Writer of the Eighteen-Nineties', Ph.D. dissertation, Harvard University, 1982.

Woodward, Calvin S. 'The Charity Organization Society and the Rise of the Welfare State', Ph.D. thesis, University of Cambridge, 1961.

TEXTS PUBLISHED BEFORE 1945

Allan, J. McGrigor, 'On the Real Differences in the Minds of Men and Women', *Anthropological Review*, 7 (1869), 195–216.

Allen, Grant, *Physiological Aesthetics* (London: Henry S. King & Co., 1877).

—— 'Plain Words on the Woman Question', *Fortnightly Review*, 52 (1889), 443–58.

—— *Falling in Love, with other Essays on More Exact Branches of Science* (London: Smith, Elder, & Co., 1889).

—— 'The Girl of the Future', *Universal Review*, 7 (1890), 49–64.

—— *The Woman Who Did* (1895; Oxford: Oxford University Press, 1995).

Anon., 'Woman in her Psychological Relations', *Journal of Psychological Medicine and Mental Pathology*, 4 (1851), 18–50.

Booth, Charles, *Charles Booth's London: A Portrait of the Poor at the Turn of the Century, Drawn from Life and Labour of the People in London*, ed. by Richard M. Elman and Albert Fried, 17 vols. (1902; London: Hutchinson, 1969).

Booth, William, *In Darkest England and The Way Out* (London: International Headquarters of the Salvation Army, 1890).

Buchan, William, *Advice to Mothers on the Subject of their own Health and on the Means of Promoting the Health, Strength and Beauty of their Offspring* (1803; Boston: J. Bumstead, 1809).

Bosanquet, Helen Dendy, *Social Work in London 1869–1912: A History of the Charity Organisation Society* (London: J. Murray, 1914).

Butler, Josephine, *Social Purity: An Address* (London: Social Purity Alliance, 1879).

Caird, Mona, *The Daughters of Danaus* (London: Bliss, Sands & Foster, 1894).

—— *The Morality of Marriage, and other Essays on the Status and Destiny of Woman* (London: George Redway, 1897); *The Morality of Marriage* is reprinted in Ann Heilmann, *The Late Victorian Marriage Question: A Collection of Key New Woman Texts*, (London and New York: Routledge (with Thoemmes Press), 1998), vol. 1.

—— 'A Defence of the So-called "Wild Women" ', *Nineteenth Century*, 31 (1892), 811–29; *The Morality of Marriage.*

—— 'A Moral Renaissance', in *The Morality of Marriage.*

—— 'Children of the Future', in *The Morality of Marriage.*

—— 'Early History of the Family', in *The Morality of Marriage.*

—— 'Ideal Marriage', Independent Section, *Westminster Review*, 130 (1888), 617–36 reprinted as 'The Future of the Home', in *The Morality of Marriage.*

—— 'Marriage Before and After the Reformation', Independent Section, *Westminster Review* 130 (1888), 186–201; *The Morality of Marriage.*

—— 'Married Life, Present and Future', in *The Morality of Marriage.*

—— 'Phases of Human Development' (Part I) *Westminster Review*, 141 (1894), 37–51; (Part II), 162–79; *The Morality of Marriage.*

—— 'The End of the Patriarchal System', in *The Morality of Marriage.*

—— 'The Evolution of Compassion', *Westminster Review*, 145 (1896), 635–43; *The Morality of Marriage.*

—— 'The Lot of Woman under the Rule of Man', in *The Morality of Marriage.*

—— 'The Pioneer of Civilization?', in *The Morality of Marriage.*

—— *The Pathway of the Gods* (London: Skeffington & Son, 1898).

—— 'Personal Rights: A Personal Address Delivered to the Forth-first Annual Meeting of the Personal Rights Association on 6th June 1913 by Mrs Mona Caird' (London: The Personal Rights Association, 1913).

—— *The Stones of Sacrifice* (London: Simpkin, Marshall, Hamilton, Kent & Co. Ltd, 1915).

—— 'The Greater Community', *Fortnightly Review*, 54 (1918), 742–55.

—— *The Great Wave* (London: Wishart, 1931).

Chant, L. Ormiston, 'Chastity in Men and Women: A Woman's Answer to a Woman in Regard to the Equality of the Moral Law', (pamphlet London: Dyer Brothers, 1885).

Chapman, Elizabeth Rachel, *Marriage Questions in Modern Fiction, and Other Essays on Kindred Subjects* (London and New York: John Lane, 1897).

Chesterton, G. K., *Eugenics and Other Evils: An Argument Against the Scientifically Organized Society*, ed. by Michael W. Perry (1922; Seattle: Inkling, 2000).

Clapperton, Jane Hume, *Scientific Meliorism and the Evolution of Happiness* (London: Kegan Paul, Trench & Co., 1885).

—— *Margaret Dunmore; or, A Socialist Home* (London: Swan Sonnenschein, Lowrey & Co., 1888).

—— *A Vision of the Future, Based on The Application of Ethical Principles* (London: Swan Sonnenschein & Co. Limited, 1904).

Clarke, Edward H., *Sex in Education; or, A Fair Chance for Girls* (Boston, Mass., 1874).

Corelli, Marie, Flora Annie Steel, Lady Jeune, and Susan, Countess of Malmesbury, *The Modern Marriage Market* (London: Hutchinson & Co. 1897).

Creighton, Louise, 'The Appeal Against Female Suffrage: A Rejoinder' [to Fawcett and Dilke in July], *Nineteenth Century*, 26 (1889), 347–54.

Darwin, Charles, *The Origin of Species; or, the Preservation of Favoured Races in the Struggle for Life* (1859; Oxford: Oxford University Press, 1996).

—— *The Descent of Man, and Selection in Relation to Sex*, 2 vols. (1871; Princeton University Press, Chichester, 1981).

Dowie, Ménie Muriel, *Gallia* (1895; J. M. Dent, 1995).

Egerton, George, *Keynotes and Discords*, ed. by Martha Vicinus (1893 and 1894; London: Virago, 1983).

—— *Symphonies* (London and New York: John Lane, 1897).

—— *The Wheel of God* (London: Grant Richards, 1898).

—— *Rosa Amorosa, The Love Letters of a Woman* (London: Grant Richards, 1901).

—— *A Leaf from the Yellow Book: The Correspondence of George Egerton*, ed. by Terence de Vere White (London: The Richards Press, 1958).

Ellis, Henry Havelock, 'Eugenics and St Valentine', *Nineteenth Century*, 59 (1906), 779–87.

—— *More Essays of Love and Virtue* (London: Constable and Co., 1931).

Galton, Francis, 'Hereditary Talent and Character', *Macmillan's Magazine*, 12 (1865), 157–66, 318–27.

—— 'Hereditary Improvement', *Fraser's Magazine*, 7 (1873), 116–30.

—— *Inquiries into Human Faculty and its Development* (London: Macmillan, 1883).

—— *Hereditary Genius: An Inquiry into its Laws and Consequences* (1869; 2nd edn., London: Watts & Co., 1892).

—— 'Photographic Chronicles from Childhood to Age', *Fortnightly Review*, 37 (1882), 26–31.

—— 'The Anthropometric Laboratory', *Fortnightly Review*, 37 (1882), 332–8.

Graham, Thomas John, *On the Management and Disorders of Infancy and Childhood* (London: Simpkin, Marshall and Co., 1853).

Grand, Sarah [Frances Elizabeth McFall], *Two Dear Little Feet* (London: Jarrold and Sons, 1873).

—— *Ideala, A Study from Life* (1888; 2nd edn., London: Richard Bentley and Son, 1899).

—— *A Domestic Experiment* (Edinburgh and London: William Blackwood and Sons, 1891).

—— *The Heavenly Twins* (London: Heinemann, 1893; Michigan: Ann Arbor Paperbacks, 1992).

—— *Our Manifold Nature* (London: Heinemann, 1894).

—— 'What to Aim At', in Andrew Reid (ed.), *The New Party* (London: Hodder Bros, 1894), 355–61.

—— 'The New Aspect of the Woman Question', *North American Review*, 158 (1894), 271–6.

—— 'The Modern Girl', *North American Review* 158 (1894), 706–14.

—— 'The Man of the Moment', *North American Review*, 158 (1894), 620–7.

—— *The Beth Book, Being a Study from the Life of Elizabeth Caldwell Maclure, A Woman of Genius* (1897; Bristol: Thoemmes Press, 1994).

—— *The Modern Man and Maid* (London: Horace Marshall & Son, 1898).

—— 'The Modern Young Man', *Temple Magazine*, 2 (1898), 883–6.

—— 'On the Choice of a Wife', *Young Man*, 12 (1898), 325–7.

—— 'On the Choice of a Husband', *Young Woman*, 7 (1898–9), 1–9.

—— 'Marriage Questions in Fiction', *Fortnightly Review*, 63 (Jan–June 1898), 378–9.

—— *Adnam's Orchard: A Prologue* (London: Heinemann, 1912).

—— 'The Case of the Modern Married Woman,' *Pall Mall Gazette* (February 1913), 203–8.

—— *The Winged Victory* (London: Heinemann, 1916).

—— Foreword, *The Heavenly Twins* (1893; London: Heinemann, 1923).

Greg, William Rathbone, 'Why Are Women Redundant?', *National Review*, 14 (1862), 434–60.

—— 'On the Failure of "Natural Selection" in the Case of Man', *Fraser's Magazine*, 78 (1868), 352–62.

Hopkins, Ellice, 'On the Early Training of Girls and Boys: An Appeal to Working Women Especially Intended for Mothers' Meetings', pamphlet (London: Hatchards, 1882).

—— 'Buried Seed', pamphlet (London: Wells Gardner, Darton & Co., 1883).

—— 'True Manliness', pamphlet (London: Wells Gardner, Darton & Co., 1883).

—— 'Man and Woman'; or, 'The Christian Ideal', pamphlet (London, Hatchards, 1883).

—— 'The British Zulu', pamphlet (London: Hatchards, 1883).

—— 'The Man with the Drawn Sword', pamphlet (London: Wells Gardner, Darton & Co., 1883).

—— 'The Purity Movement: A Pamphlet of the White Cross Series', pamphlet (for men only) (1885).

Hopkins, Ellice, 'Chastity of Men and Women', pamphlet (London: Dyer Brothers, 1885).

—— 'The Present Moral Crisis', pamphlet (London: Hatchards, 1886).

—— *The Power of Womanhood; or, Mothers and Sons: A Book for Parents and Those in loco parentis* (London: Wells Gardner, Darton & Co. 1899).

—— 'The Moral Effects of Charity; or, Character and Almsgiving' (London Society for Promoting Christian Knowledge, 1900).

Huxley, T. H., *Evolution and Ethics*, ed. by James Paradis and George C. Williams (1893; Princeton: Princeton University Press, 1989).

Kenealy, Arabella, 'A New View of the Surplus Women', *Westminster Review*, 136 (1891), 465–75.

Kropotkin, Peter, *Mutual Aid: A Factor of Evolution* (1902; London: Freedom Press, 1998).

Lankester, E. R., *Degeneration: A Chapter in Darwinism* (London: Macmillan, 1880).

Maudsley, Henry, 'Sex in Mind and Education', *Fortnightly Review*, 21 (1874), 466–83.

Meakin, Annette, *Women in Transition* (London: Methuen, 1907).

Nordau, Max, *Degeneration* (1892), trans. from the 2nd German edn., (Heinemann 1895; Lincoln and London: University of Nebraska Press, 1968).

—— 'The Matrimonial Lie', in *Conventional Lies of our Civilization* (London: William Heinemann, 1895).

Pearson, Karl, *The Ethic of Freethought* (London: T. Fisher Unwin, 1888).

—— 'Woman and Labour', *Fortnightly Review*, 61 (1894), 561–577, repr. in *The Chances of Death*, 2 vols. (London: Edward Arnold, 1897).

—— *The Life, Letters, and Labours of Francis Galton*, 4 vols. (Cambridge: Cambridge University Press, 1914–30).

Pankhurst, Christabel, *Plain Facts About a Great Evil (The Great Scourge and How to End it)* (London: Women's Social and Political Union, 1913).

Quilter, Harry (ed.), *Is Marriage A Failure?* (London: Swan Sonnenschein & Co., 1888).

Richardson, Benjamin Ward, 'Woman's Work in Creation', *Longman's*, 8 (1886), 604–19.

Romanes, George J., 'Mental Differences Between Men and Women', *Nineteenth Century*, 21 (1887), 654–72.

Saleeby, Caleb William, *Parenthood and Race Culture: An Outline of Eugenics* (London: Cassell and Company Ltd, 1909).

—— *Woman and Womanhood: A Search for Principles* (London: William Heinemann, 1912).

Scharlieb, Mary, *Womanhood and Race Regeneration* (London: Cassell & Co. Ltd., 1912).

Spencer, Herbert, *Social Statics; or, the Conditions Essential to Human Happiness Specified, and the First of Them Developed* (London: Chapman, 1851).

—— *Education: Intellectual, Moral, and Physical* (London: Williams & Norgate, 1861).

Smiles, Samuel, *Self-Help* (1859; London: Institute of Economic Affairs, 1996).

Sperry, Lyman B., *Confidential Talks with Young Women* (Edinburgh and London: Oliphant, Anderson & Ferrier, 1894).

—— *Confidential Talks with Husband and Wife, A Book of Information and Advice for the Married and the Marriageable* (Edinburgh and London: Oliphant, Anderson & Ferrier, 1900).

Stead, W. T., 'Book of the Month: The Novel of the Modern Woman', *Review of Reviews*, 10 (1894), 64–74.

—— 'Maiden Tribute of Modern Babylon', *Pall Mall Gazette* (6 July 1885).

Stopes, Marie, *Wise Parenthood: A Practical Sequel to Married Love* (1918; London: Putnam, 1931).

Strahan, S. A. K., *Marriage and Disease, A Study of Heredity and the More Important Family Degenerations* (London: Kegan Paul, Trench, Trübner, & Co. Ltd, 1892).

Swiney, Frances, *The Awakening of Women; or, Woman's Part in Evolution* (London: William Reeves, 1899).

—— *The Bar of Isis* (London: Open Road Publishing Company, 1907).

Talbot, Eugene S., *Degeneracy, its Causes, Signs and Results* (London: Walter Scott Ltd, 1898).

Weismann, August, *Essays upon Heredity and Kindred Biological Problems* (Oxford: Clarendon Press, 1889).

—— *The Germ-Plasm: A Theory of Heredity* (London: Scott, 1893).

Wells, H. G., *Anticipations of the Reaction of Mechanical and Scientific Progress upon Human Life and Thought* (1900; Dover, 1999).

White, Arnold, 'The Nomad Poor of London', *Contemporary Review*, 47 (1885), 714–27.

—— *Problems of A Great City* (London: Remington, 1886).

—— 'The Multiplication of the Unfit', *Humanitarian*, 8 (1896), 170–9.

—— *Efficiency and Empire* (London: 1901; Brighton: Harvester Press, 1973).

TEXTS PUBLISHED AFTER 1945

Ardis, Ann L., *New Women, New Novels: Feminism and Early Modernism* (New Brunswick: Rutgers University Press, 1990).

Beer, Gillian, *Darwin's Plots: Evolutionary Narrative in Darwin, George Eliot and Nineteenth-Century Fiction* (1983; Cambridge: Cambridge University Press, 2000).

Bland, Lucy, *Banishing the Beast, English Feminism & Sexual Morality (1885-1914)* (Harmondsworth: Penguin, 1995).

Bock, Gisela, and Pat Thane (eds.), *Maternity and Gender Policies: Women and the Rise of the European Welfare States 1880s–1950s* (London: Routledge, 1991).

Bowler, Peter, *Evolution: The History of an Idea* (1983; Berkeley and Los Angeles: University of California Press, 1989).

Bourne Taylor, Jenny, and Sally Shuttleworth (eds.), *Embodied Selves: An Anthology of Psychological Texts, 1830–1890* (Oxford: Oxford University Press, 1998).

Bradfield, Thomas, 'A Dominant Note of some Recent Fiction', *Westminister Review*, 142 (1894).

Brake, Laurel, 'Writing Women's History: The Sex Debates of 1889', in Ann Heilmann and Margaret Beetham (eds.), *New Woman Hybridities: Femininity, Feminism, and International Consumer Culture* (London: Routledge, 2004).

Brown, Ian, 'Who were the Eugenicists? A Study of the Formation of an Early Twentieth-century Pressure Group', *History of Education*, 17 (1988), 295–307.

Cannadine, David, *Ornamentalism: How the British Saw their Empire* (Harmondsworth; Penguin, 2001).

Childs, Donald J., *Modernism and Eugenics: Woolf, Eliot, Yeats and The Culture of Degeneration* (Cambridge: Cambridge University Press, 2001).

Cunningham, Gail, *The New Woman and the Victorian Novel* (London: Macmillan, 1978).

Davin, Anna, 'Imperialism and Motherhood', *History Workshop*, 5 (1978), 9–65.

Desmond, Adrian, and James Moore, *Darwin* (Harmondsworth, Penguin, 1992).

Digby, Anne and John Stewart (eds.), *Gender, Health and Welfare* (London: Routledge, 1996).

Fishman, William J., *East End 1888* (1988; London: Hanbury, 2001).

Gardiner, Juliet (ed.), *The New Woman: Women's Voices 1880–1918* (London: Collins & Brown, 1993).

Gilman, Sander, *Health and Illness: Images of Difference* (London: Reaktion Books Ltd, 1995).

Greenslade, William, *Degeneration, Culture and the Novel 1880–1940* (Cambridge: Cambridge University Press, 1994).

Harman, Barbara Leah, and Susan Meyer (eds.), *The New Nineteenth Century: Feminist Readings of Underread Victorian Fiction* (New York, London: Garland, 1996).

Heilmann, Ann, 'Mona Caird (1854–1932): Wild Woman, New Woman, and Early Radical Feminist Critic of Marriage and Motherhood', *Women's History Review*, 5 (1996), 67–95.

—— *The Late-Victorian Marriage Question: A Collection of Key New Woman Texts*, 5 vols. (London: Routledge with Thoemmes Press, 1998).

—— *New Woman Fiction: Women Writing First-Wave Feminism* (Basingstoke: Palgrave, 2000).

—— and Margaret Beetham (eds.), *New Woman Hybridities: Femininity, Feminism, and International Consumer Culture* (London: Routledge, 2003).

Himmelfarb, Gertrude, *The Idea of Poverty: England in the Early Industrial Age* (New York: Vintage, 1985).

Hollis, Patricia, *Ladies Elect: Women in English Local Government, 1865–1914* (Oxford: Clarendon Press, 1987).

Ingram, Angela and Daphne Patai, *Rediscovering Forgotten Radicals: British Women Writers, 1889–1939* (Chapel Hill: University of North Carolina Press, 1993).

Jones, Greta, *Social Darwinism and English Thought: The Interaction between Biological and Social Theory* (Brighton: Harvester, 1980).

—— *Social Hygiene in Twentieth-Century Britain* (London: Croom Helm, 1986).

—— 'Women and Eugenics in Britain: The Case of Mary Scharlieb, Elizabeth Sloan Chesser, and Stella Brown', *Annals of Science*, 52 (1995), 481–502.

Ledger, Sally and Scott McCracken (eds.), *Cultural Politics at the Fin de Siècle* (Cambridge: Cambridge University Press, 1995).

Ledger, Sally, *The New Woman: Fiction and Feminism at the Fin de Siècle* (Manchester: Manchester University Press, 1997).

Lewis, Jane, *Politics of Motherhood* (London: Croom Helm, 1980).

—— (ed.), *Before the Vote was Won: Arguments for and Against Women's Suffrage 1864–1896* (London: Routledge, 1987).

Kersley, Gillian, *Darling Madame: Sarah Grand and Devoted Friend* (London: Virago, 1983).

Kevles, Daniel, *In the Name of Eugenics: Genetics and the Uses of Human Heredity* (1985; Cambridge, Mass.: Harvard University Press, 1995).

Koven, Seth, and Sonya Michel, *Mothers of a New World, Maternalist Politics and the Origins of Welfare States* (London and New York: Routledge, 1993).

Langland, Elizabeth, *Nobody's Angels: Middle-Class Women and Domestic Ideology in Victorian Culture* (Ithaca and London: Cornell University Press, 1995).

Laqueur, Thomas, *Making Sex: Body and Gender from the Greeks to Freud* (Cambridge, Mass. and London: Harvard University Press, 1990).

Leckie, Barbara, *Culture and Adultery: The Novel, the Newspaper and the Law, 1857–1914* (Philadelphia: Philadelphia University Press, 1999).

Levine, George (ed.), *One Culture: Essays in Science and Literature* (Madison, Wis.: University of Wisconsin Press, 1987).

—— *Darwin and the Novelists: Patterns of Science in Victorian Fiction* (Cambridge, Mass.: Harvard University Press, 1988).

—— (ed.), *Realism and Representation: Essays on the Problem of Realism in Relation to Science, Literature, and Culture* (Madison, Wis.: University of Wisconsin Press, 1993).

Lewis, Jane, *Women and Social Action in Victorian and Edwardian England* (Stanford: Stanford University Press, 1991).

MacKenzie, Donald, *Statistics in Britain 1865–1930: The Social Construction of Scientific Knowledge* (Edinburgh: Edinburgh University Press, 1981).

MacNicol, John, 'Eugenics and the Campaign for Voluntary Sterilization Between the Wars', *Social History of Medicine*, 2 (1989), 147–69.

Mangum, Teresa, *Married, Middlebrow, and Militant: Sarah Grand and the New Woman Novel* (Michigan: University of Michigan Press, 1999).

Marks, Patricia, *Bicycles, Bangs, and Bloomers: The New Woman in the Popular Press* (Kentucky: University Press of Kentucky, 1990).

Mason, Michael, *The Making of Victorian Sexual Attitudes* (Oxford: Oxford University Press, 1994).

—— *The Making of Victorian Sexuality* (Oxford: Oxford University Press, 1995).

Mazumdar, Pauline, *Eugenics, Human Genetics and Human Failings: The Eugenics Society, its Sources and Critics in Britain* (London: Routledge, 1992).

Meller, Helen, *Patrick Geddes, Social Evolutionist and City Planner* (London and New York: Routledge, 1990).

Miller, Jane Eldridge, *Rebel Women: Feminism, Modernism and the Edwardian Novel* (London: Virago, 1994).

Morton, Peter, *The Vital Science: Beyond the Literary Imagination 1860–1900* (London: George Allen & Unwin, 1984).

Moscucci, Ornella, *The Science of Woman, Gynaecology and Gender in England 1800–1929* (Cambridge: Cambridge University Press, 1990).

Murphy, Patricia, *Time is of the Essence: Temporality, Gender and the New Woman* (State University of New York Press, 2001).

Nelson, Claudia and Ann Sumner Holmes (eds.), *Maternal Instincts: Visions of Motherhood and Sexuality in Britain, 1875–1925* (Basingstoke: Macmillan, 1998).

Neville-Rolfe, Sybil, *Why Marry?* (London: Faber and Faber, 1935).

—— *Social Biology and Welfare, together with a Handbook-appendix on Social Problems Edited by Ethel Grant* (London: George Allen & Unwin ltd, 1949).

—— *Sex in Social Life* (London: Allen & Unwin, 1949).

Parrinder, Patrick, 'Eugenics and Utopia: Sexual Selection from Galton to Morris', *Utopian Studies* 8 (1997), 1–14.

Paul, Diane, *Controlling Human Heredity: 1865 to the Present* (Atlantic Highlands, NJ: Humanities Press International, 1995).

Peel, Robert A. (ed.), *Essays in the History of Eugenics*, Proceedings of Conference Organized by the Galton Institute (London: The Galton Institute, 1997).

—— (ed.), *Maries Stopes, Eugenics and Birth Control* (London: The Galton Institute, 1997).

Pick, Daniel, *Faces of Degeneration: A European Disorder, c.1848–c.1918* (Cambridge: Cambridge University Press, 1993).

Poovey, Mary, *Uneven Developments: The Ideological Work of Gender in Mid-Victorian England* (London: Virago, 1989).

Porter, Dorothy, ' "Enemies of the Race": Biologism, Environmentalism, and Public Health in Edwardian England', *Victorian Studies*, 34 (1991), 159–78.

—— *Health, Civilization and the State: A History of Public Health from Ancient to Modern Times* (London: Routledge, 1998).

Porter, Roy and Dorothy Porter, *In Sickness and In Health: The British Experience*, 1650–1850 (London: Fourth Estate, 1988).

Pugh, Martin, *The March of the Women. A Revisionist Analysis of the Campaign for Women's Suffrage, 1866–1914* (Oxford: Oxford University Press, 2000).

Pykett, Lyn, *The 'Improper' Feminine: The Women's Sensation Novel and the New Woman Writing* (London and New York: Routledge, 1992).

—— *The Sensation Novel from* The Woman in White *to* The Moonstone (Plymouth: Northcote House, 1994).

Richardson, Angelique and Chris Willis (eds.), *The New Woman in Fiction and in Fact: Fin de Siècle Feminisms* (Basingstoke: Palgrave, 2001).

Ritvo, Harriet, *The Platypus and the Mermaid and Other Figments of the Classifying Imagination* (Cambridge, Massa.: Harvard University Press, 1997).

Rose, Steven, *Lifelines: Biology, Freedom, Determinism* (Harmondsworth: Penguin, 1998).

—— R. C. Lewontin and Leon J. Kamin, *Not in Our Genes. Biology, Ideology and Human Nature* (London: Pantheon Books, 1984).

Rowold, Katharina (ed.), *Gender and Science: Nineteenth-Century Debates on the Female Mind and Body* (Bristol: Thoemmes Press, 1996).

Rubenstein, David, *Before the Suffragettes: Women's Emancipation in the 1890s* (Brighton: Harvester, 1986).

Russett, Cynthia Eagle, *Sexual Science: The Victorian Construction of Womanhood* (1989; Cambridge, Mass. and London: Harvard University Press, 1991).

Schiebinger, Londa, *Nature's Body, Sexual Politics and the Making of Modern Science.*

—— *The Mind has No Sex? Women and the Origins of Modern Science* (Cambridge, Mass. and London: Harvard University Press, 1989).

Searle, Geoffrey, 'Eugenics and Class', in Charles Webster (ed.), *Biology, Medicine and Society 1840–1940* (Cambridge: Cambridge University Press, 1981), 217–42.

—— *Eugenics and Politics in Britain, 1900–1914* (Leyden: Noordhoff, 1976).

—— 'Eugenics and Politics in Britain in the 1930s', *Annals of Science*, 36 (1979), 159–69.

Shires, Linda M. (ed.), *Rewriting the Victorians: Theory, History and the Politics of Gender* (London: Routledge, 1992).

Shuttleworth, Sally, ' "Preaching to the Nerves": Psychological Disorder in Sensation Fiction', in Marina Benjamin (ed.), *A Question of Identity* (Rutgers University Press, 1997).

—— 'Demonic Mothers: Ideologies of Bourgeois Motherhood in the Mid-Victorian era', in Linda M. Shires (ed.), *Rewriting the Victorians: Theory, History and the Politics of Gender* (London: Routledge, 1992), 31–51.

Sloan, Phillip R. (ed.), *Controlling Our Destinies: The Human Genome Project from Historical, Philosophical, Social, and Ethical Perspectives* (Notre Dame, Ind. University of Notre Dame Press, 2000).

Small, Helen, *Love's Madness, Medicine, the Novel and Female Insanity, 1800–1865* (Oxford: Clarendon Press, 1996).

Smart, Carol (ed.), *Regulating Womanhood: Historical Essays on Marriage, Motherhood and Sexuality* (London: Routledge, 1992).

Soloway, Richard Allen, *Birth Control and the Population Question in England, 1877–1930* (Chapel Hill: North Carolina University Press, 1982).

—— *Demography and Degeneration: Eugenics and the Declining Birthrate in Twentieth-Century Britain* (Chapel Hill: North Carolina University Press, 1990).

Stedman Jones, Gareth, *Outcast London: A Study in the Relationship Between Classes in Victorian Society* (1971; Harmondsworth: Penguin, 1992).

Stepan, Nancy Leys, *The Idea of Race in Science: Great Britain 1800–1960* (London: Macmillan, 1982).

Vicinus, Martha (ed.), *A Widening Sphere: Changing Roles of Victorian Women* (London: Methuen, 1977).

Walkowitz, Judith R., *Prostitution and Victorian Society: Women, Class, and the State* (Cambridge: Cambridge University Press, 1980).

—— *City of Dreadful Delight: Narratives of Sexual Danger in Late-Victorian London* (London: Virago, 1992).

Wohl, Anthony S., *The Eternal Slum: Housing and Social Policy in Victorian London* (London : E. Arnold, 1977).

—— *Endangered Lives: Public Health in Victorian Britain* (London: Methuen, 1984).

Worsnop, Judith, 'A Re-evaluation of "the Problem of Surplus Women" in 19th-century England: The case of the 1851 Census', *Women's Studies International Forum*, 13 (1990), 21–31.

Young, Robert M., *Darwin's Metaphor: Nature's Place in Victorian Culture* (Cambridge: Cambridge University Press, 1985).

Index